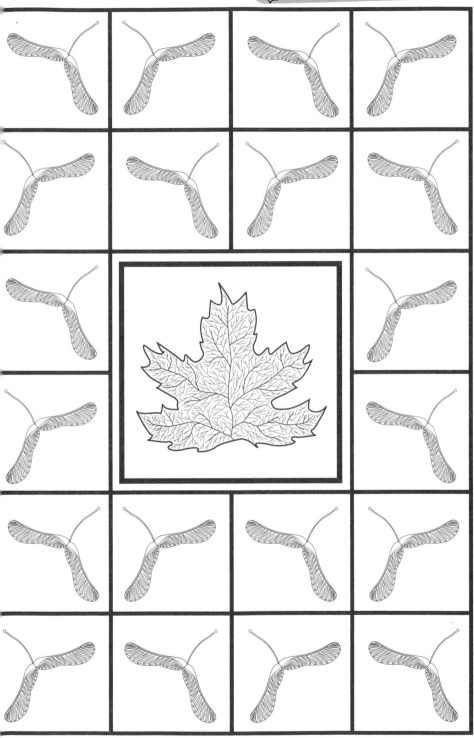

THE DIARY

OF

MRS. JOHN GRAVES SIMCOE

WIFE OF THE

FIRST LIEUTENANT-GOVERNOR OF THE PROVINCE OF UPPER CANADA, 1792-6

WITH NOTES AND A BIOGRAPHY

BY

J. ROSS ROBERTSON

AND TWO HUNDRED AND THIRTY-SEVEN ILLUSTRATIONS, INCLUDING NINETY REPRODUCTIONS OF INTERESTING SKETCHES MADE BY MRS. SIMCOE

PROSPERO

TORONTO
2001

The Diary of
Mrs. John Graves Simcoe
Wife of the Lieutenant-Governor of
the Province of Upper Canada, 1972-6

This edition first published by
Prospero Books in 2001
from the 1911 William Briggs edition

Prospero Canadian Collection edition © Prospero Books, 2001

National Library of Canada Cataloguing in Publication Data

Simcoe, Elizabeth, 1766-1850
The diary of Mrs. John Graves Simcoe,
wife of the first Lieutenant-Governor
of the province of Upper Canada 1792-6

(Prospero Canadian collection)
Facsim. reprint.
Originally published: Toronto:W. Briggs, 1911.
ISBN 1-55267-183-6

1. Simcoe, Elizabeth, 1766-1850 - Diaries.
2. Simcoe, John Graves, 1752-1806.
3. Onrario - Social life and customs - 18th century.
4. Ontario - Politics and government - 1791-1841.*
5. Wives - Ontario - Diaries.
6. Lieutenant governors - Ontario - Biography.
I. Robertson, J. Ross (John Ross). II. Title. III. Series.
FC3071.1.S54A3 2001   971.3'02'092   C2001-930669-5
F1058.S568A3 2001

Prospero Books
90 Ronson Drive, Toronto, Ontario, Canada
M9W 1C1

Printed on acid free paper
Printed in Canada by Webcom Inc.

ever most attachedly yrs

E Somes

(*From a Crayon Drawing at Wolford, Devon.*)

*Your most obedient and
most faithful Servant
J.G. Simcoe*

(From a Miniature at Wolford, Devon.)

AN ACKNOWLEDGMENT

The writer gratefully acknowledges his debt to the many persons in Canada and elsewhere who have shown a kindly and personal interest in the collection of data and of illustrations for this volume. It would not have been possible to present so much in the line of information and of illustrations in the volume without the aid of these friends.

Many portraits connected with the early history of Canada, and much of the information, have been generously supplied by His Excellency the Governor-General, Earl Grey; Mrs. John Kennaway Simcoe, of Wolford, Devon; Dr. Arthur Doughty, Archivist of the Dominion of Canada; Mr. L. P. Sylvain, Assistant Librarian of the Library of Parliament, Ottawa; Mr. Avern Pardoe, Librarian of the Legislative Assembly, Toronto; Dr. G. H. Locke, Chief Librarian of the Public Library, Toronto; Mr. T. O'Leary, Curator of the Chateau de Ramezay, Montreal; and Miss Janet Carnochan, President of the Niagara Historical Society.

Grateful acknowledgment for many portraits connected with the earlier history of Canada, and much of the information presented, is extended to Messrs. J. Ashbridge, J. S. Carstairs, J. E. Featherstonhaugh, Æmilius Jarvis, E. M. Playter, S. H. Townsend, J. S. Cartwright, K.C., A. Claude Macdonell, M.P., A. McLean Macdonell, K.C., Walter Read, K.C., H. Crawford Scadding, M.D., Col. George Shaw, C. C. James (Deputy Minister of Agriculture, Ontario), Mrs. Stephen Heward and Mrs. Robert Sullivan, of Toronto; Messrs. J. S. Brierley, Hertel La Rocque, H. Ryland Low, J. W. Molson, W. H. Whyte, Sir Edward Gordon Johnson, Bart., W. D. Lighthall, K.C., David Ross McCord, K.C., Miss Gertrude Coffin and Mrs. Henry J. Low, of Montreal; Dr. H. J. Morgan, and Mr. Errol Bouchette, F.R.S.C., of Ottawa; Philippe B. Casgrain, K.C., and Mr. L. Lemieux, of Quebec; Messrs. J. G. Elliott, Clark Hamilton, Abraham Shaw and Mrs. J. Maule Machar, of Kingston; Messrs. Charles E. Britton and Charles Macdonald, of Gananoque; His Honor Judge Herbert S. Macdonald, of Brockville; Messrs. W. E. McKeough and Sydney Stephenson, of Chatham; Messrs. William Johnson McKee and Francis Cleary, of Windsor; Prof. A. Macmechan and Rev. C. W. Vernon, of Halifax; F. J. French, K.C., and Mr. Edward Jessup, of Prescott; Andrew F. McCallum, C.E., Hamilton; Mrs. George Macbeth, London; Miss Mary Servos, of Niagara-on-the-Lake; Messrs. James H. Coyne, St. Thomas; James B. Sheehan, Dunnville; K. G. Thomson, Norwood; A. F. Hunter, Barrie; C. H. Hale, Orillia; William Forbes, Grimsby; W. R. Hickey, Bothwell; A. Courtney Kingstone, St. Catharines; A. C. Casselman, North Bay; Robert C. Givins, Chicago; Peter A. Porter, Niagara Falls, N.Y.; Basil Hamilton, Wilmer, B.C.; A. H. Askin, Walkerville; C. M. Burton, Detroit; J. A. Macdonell, K.C., Alexandria; A. E. Holland, St. Eleanor's, P.E.I.; A. E. C. Holland, Wallace Bridge, N.S.; Mrs. E. Vosburgh, niece of the late Reverend Prebendary Sadler, of Honiton, Devon; Miss H. E. Macaulay, Exmouth, Eng.; Hector Sinclair Fraser, Inverness; Mrs. Arklay Fergusson, Ethiebeaton, Scotland; Mr. A. M. Broadley, Bridport, Eng.; Mr. B. O. Pearce, Portland, Dorset, Eng.; Prof. Rushton Fairclough, Stanford University, and Mr. Thos. H. Gwillim, San Francisco, California; Ian Robert James Murray Grant, of Glenmoriston, Inverness-shire, Scotland; Mme. Falret de Tuite, Pau, France; the British Museum and College of Arms, London, Eng.; Miss Maude Givins, Toronto.

PREFACE

THE early history of Upper Canada has been usually sought for in constitutional documents and State papers. The social life of the period is recorded principally in the few private letters which have survived a century. To this scanty fund of information it is to be hoped that the diary of Mrs. John Graves Simcoe, the wife of the first Governor, will make an interesting addition.

This record is the simple recital of her daily life in the pioneer days when Niagara was the centre of military, civil and social life in the new province, and York, the future capital, could scarcely count a score of habitable dwellings outside the primitive barracks that the Governor had erected within the few acres of ground where still stands the Fort—the Old Fort—as it is familiarly called in these modern days. Yes, when Navy Hall, on the banks of the Niagara River, was the first Government house of the province and an attractive home, full of welcome for visitors, official and unofficial.

The original manuscript of the diary, of which this volume embodies the only copy, has been carefully transcribed by the kind permission of Mrs. Simcoe, of Wolford, the Simcoe estate, near the old town of Honiton in Devon, so well known to womankind for its manufacture of exquisite lace. Mrs. Simcoe is the present lady of the manor, and widow of the late Captain John Kennaway Simcoe, R.N., Justice of the Peace for the County of Devon. He was the only son of the late Rev. Henry Addington Simcoe (1800-1868) of Penheale in Cornwall, who was the third son of General Simcoe. Captain Simcoe died at Wolford in March, 1891.

As a general rule entries were made in this record day by day and the writings mailed every week to Mrs. Hunt, a lady who had undertaken the charge of Mrs. Simcoe's four daughters, Eliza, Charlotte, Henrietta, and Caroline, all under seven years of age, who remained at Wolford. Sophia, born in 1789, and Francis Gwillim, born in 1791, accompanied the Governor and his wife to Canada.

The diary was commenced on the 17th September, 1791, nine days prior to Mrs. Simcoe's departure from Weymouth for Quebec, on the "Triton," man-of-war. The last entries are on the 16th October, 1796, when Governor Simcoe and his wife again arrived in London.

My annotations, instead of being arranged and placed in the conventional form as footnotes, are incorporated with the text of the diary following the entries to which they belong. The notes are so voluminous that, if given at the foot of each page, they would be pages in advance of the text. The reader will, therefore, have the advantage of reading first the text and then the note which accompanies it. The few brief notes that appear in parenthesis throughout the actual text are principally from memoranda made by Mrs. Simcoe in connection with the small maps that form part of the diary.

The illustrations, except where otherwise stated, are reproductions of water-colors, pen sketches and pencil drawings made by Mrs. Simcoe on her outward-bound voyage, and during her residence in Canada and after her return in 1796 to her old home in Devon.

The originals of these drawings are nearly all at Wolford. But thirty-two, in sepia, are in a portfolio in the Royal Library in the British Museum. This library was given by George II. to the Museum, and with the gift the Royal privilege of receiving gratuitously a copy of every book copyrighted in the British dominions passed to the Museum. After his return to England, Governor Simcoe presented these drawings to His Majesty King George III. Some of them are copies of sketches made by Lieutenant Robert Pilkington (afterwards Major-General), one of the staff, while on various excursions with the Governor. The inscription on the title page of the portfolio which contains these pictures reads: "Thirty-two views in Upper Canada by Mrs. Simcoe, presented to His Majesty by Governor Simcoe, with a sketch of Upper Canada, drawn on bark." These have been carefully reproduced. Other water-colors of the collection which have so faded that they could not be satisfactorily reproduced have been redrawn, while the original pen-and-ink sketches and pencil drawings are in facsimile.

Notwithstanding its excellence, the value of the art work of Mrs. Simcoe lies not so much in its merit as an exemplification of good color and pencil work, but in the fact that it gives to present readers of Canadian history faithful pictures of places and scenes in Upper and Lower Canada from 1791-6, which we would have lost absolutely had it not been for the gifted hand of the wife of the first Governor.

Were it not for her work, we would not have views of Toronto Harbor at the end of the eighteenth century. We would not be able to contrast the quiet of the harbor and its surroundings in 1793, when it was the home of the aborigine and the haunt of the wild fowl, with the commercial activities of to-day. We would not have a picture of the Mohawk Village on the Grand River near Brantford, which, with the exception of the Mohawk Church, has passed away; nor of the early days of the Niagara and Kingston settlements that were then and are now important places in the history of the Province of Upper Canada.

Her sketches of places on the route from Quebec to York, in and about Niagara, and her copies of Lieutenant Pilkington's sketches in the Georgian Bay district, must also add much to the interest of the reader. One of Mrs. Simcoe's best efforts is a large water-color of the Falls of Niagara, made during her many visits to this favored spot. It adorns the walls of Wolford.

PREFACE

To the diary I have appended the journal of John Bailey, who for over thirty-seven years was in the service of the Simcoe family at Wolford. He entered the Simcoe household in the autumn of 1802, when a lad twelve years of age, and after the death of General Simcoe in 1806 he continued in the service of Mrs. Simcoe for about two years. He then went to sea for a short time, but once more wore the Simcoe livery from 1818 to 1850, when his mistress died.

In her travels in different parts of England and Wales never once did she neglect to have Bailey look after all arrangements for her comfort, and act when desired as her coachman. His opinions, his reverence for Mrs. Simcoe, his devotion to the family, mark him as a man of more than ordinary intelligence. It is most refreshing to read his narrative.

The writing of the biography of Mrs. Simcoe entailed much research. Every facility was courteously afforded me by Mrs. John Kennaway Simcoe. I can never sufficiently thank her for her unwearying efforts to help me in my quest concerning not only the life of Mrs. Simcoe, but also that of General Simcoe, whose biography will appear in another volume.

Nothing has ever been published concerning the esteemed and talented wife of the first Governor of Upper Canada. In presenting this record of her life my hope is that it not only may be read with pleasure, but also find a place on the bookshelf of all who take interest in the pioneer days of the province that started its pace in the making of history one hundred and twenty years ago.

J. Ross Robertson

Toronto, August, 1911.

CONTENTS

xiii

CONTENTS

xiv

CONTENTS

CHAPTER XIII.

BUILDING OF CASTLE FRANK ON RIVER DON.

CHAPTER XIV.

A WINTER AT YORK.

CHAPTER XV.

MRS. SIMCOE VISITS QUEBEC.

CHAPTER XVI.

RETURN TO UPPER CANADA.

CHAPTER XVII.

VISIT OF DUKE DE LA ROCHEFOUCAULD.

CONTENTS

CONTENTS

CHAPTER XXIII.
MRS. SIMCOE AND HER CHILDREN.

CONTENTS

CHAPTER XXX.

THE VILLAGE OF DUNKESWELL.

CHAPTER XXXI.

INCIDENT AND COMMENT.

CHAPTER XXXII.

MANY JOURNEYS WITH MRS. SIMCOE.

CHAPTER XXXIII.

TRIBUTE BY BAILEY.

ILLUSTRATIONS

ILLUSTRATIONS

ILLUSTRATIONS

ILLUSTRATIONS

ILLUSTRATIONS

ILLUSTRATIONS

ILLUSTRATIONS

ILLUSTRATIONS

ILLUSTRATIONS

ILLUSTRATIONS

ILLUSTRATIONS

DIARY OF MRS. SIMCOE

CHAPTER I.

MRS. SIMCOE—HER ANCESTORS.

The personal character of Mrs. John Graves Simcoe, the wife of the first Governor of Upper Canada, may be written in a few brief sentences. The records that have been handed down to us from her own pen and from the pen of others who were contemporary with her, all testify to her worth as woman, wife and mother. Mrs. Simcoe had not all the advantages that in natural course come to a daughter in girlhood days. She never saw her father, and in

"OLD COURT," NEAR ROSS, HEREFORDSHIRE.
(From a Drawing in the J. Ross Robertson collection.)

the first twenty-four hours of her life she lost her mother. Bereft of those she would have loved, it fell to other than the gentle hands of father and mother to care for her as she grew to girlhood.

Elizabeth Posthuma Gwillim was born in 1766 at Whitchurch, in Herefordshire, at the mansion known as "Old Court" near the town of Ross, the home of her mother, Elizabeth Spinckes, widow of Lieutenant-Colonel Thomas Gwillim. Her father died seven months before she was born, while her mother died a few hours after giving birth to this daughter—her only child. She was named Elizabeth after her mother and Posthuma to commemorate the circumstances of her birth. Her father was an officer in the army, attaining the rank of colonel a few years before his death. He served in Canada and was one of the three Majors of Brigade of General Wolfe at Quebec in 1759, and died in 1766 while his regiment was stationed at Gibraltar. The marble bust of General Wolfe, now in the saloon at Wolford, was presented to Colonel Gwillim by the General, and a

plaster bust of Colonel Gwillim from which the picture is taken is in the drawing-room of the old mansion. On the death of her mother and father the infant Elizabeth inherited " Old Court" and all that it contained. Mrs. Simcoe's mother was a daughter and co-heir of Elmes Spinckes, Esq., of Aldwinkle in North Northamptonshire, who died there in 1762. She succeeded to the fortune left by her mother and grandmother, both of whom were heiresses in their own right.

COLONEL GWILLIM.

"The old Church of Whitchurch on the Wye" was erected some hundreds of years ago, and was the church which the Gwillim family attended from the time of its erection. The registers show baptisms in connection with the family as early as 1754 and burials from 1766. The family tomb of the Gwillims is in the churchyard. In after years Mrs. Simcoe often visited Whitchurch and made sketches of spots so well known to her mother. Amongst them was the old church.

The Gwillims came of noble lineage. Among the Archives at Wolford is an elaborate pedigree of the family, which is a very ancient one, the genealogy being traceable in a straight line from the early kings of North and South Wales. To this family belonged the celebrated Herald Gwillim, Rouge Croix Pursuivant-at-arms, 1618.

Several pedigrees of the family have been drawn from time to time at the different visitations or investigations by a high heraldic officer whose duty is to examine into the pedigrees and inter-marriages of a family or the families of a district, with the view of ascertaining whether the arms borne by any person or persons living in that district are incorrect or unwarrantably assumed. Of the later ones entered at the College of Arms, one was drawn in 1569, another in 1683, and another was drawn for the subject of this biography by Francis Townsend, Windsor Herald, in 1806. It is a most elaborate document, being eighteen feet in length and forty-eight inches wide, and contains about four hundred quarterings of arms in colors, the work of a skilled artist, and forty-four feet of illuminated border. The penwork in which the names are written gives the document rank as an example of the best in heraldic art, and is said to have cost £300.

2

THE FAMILY OF GWILLIM

The Gwillims on the paternal side were originally from Brecon-shire, having been Lords of Brecon before the Conquest. At a somewhat later date their ancestral home was at Brayne Court, Herefordshire, where they were domiciled before the fifteenth century and again early in the sixteenth century at Fawley Court, Langstone Court and Whitchurch Court, and later at the Hunt House, Clodock, all in the county of Hereford. They married into many notable families and possessed at different periods vast landed estates, principally in the counties of Brecon, Hereford and Monmouth.

THE OLD CHURCH OF WHITCHURCH, 1792.

(From a Drawing by Mrs. Simcoe in the J. Ross Robertson collection.)

During the troublous times of the Conquest, and for some centuries after, the Gwillims were actively engaged in warfare, sometimes holding their commissions from the Welsh princes and sometimes from the English kings. At the Wigga, Rowleston, Hereford-shire, there are papers relating to farms that had been given to Gwillims more than eight hundred years ago for their services in the army.

The history of the family entwines with the well-known and historical Herbert family, of which the Gwillims are a branch, both paternally and maternally. William, eldest son of Howel-ap-Thomas, Lord of Perthhir, was the first of the family to adopt a

3

surname, in conformity with the English law, and the first patronymic of Ap-Howel became corrupted with Powell. Gwillim Dhu (William Herbert), Earl of Pembroke (beheaded at Banbury in 1469), was commanded by the King, Edward IV., to take the surname of "Herbert" in memory of his illustrious ancestor Henry Fitz Herbert, Chamberlain to King Henry I. The Gwillims seem to have adopted "Gwillim" as a surname about the same time, one Robert Gwillim, son of Gwillim ap Thomas and Margaret, daughter and heir of Sir James Abrahall, Knt. of Ingestone, County Hereford, being according to Francis Townsend, Windsor Herald in 1806, the first to do so. Prior to the edict of Edward IV. it had always been "the Welsh custom to change the surname at every descent." Hence the Welsh were always most careful to preserve authentic evidence of their family records.

The writings on this interesting document have been summarized from its beginning. It will be noted that the name of Gwillim first appears about the time of Edward IV. This summary shows an unbroken line back to William I., of England, commonly called the Conqueror, and also to the ancient kings of North and South Wales.

The arms granted to the Gwillim family are here given:—

Argent a lion rampant Ermines, collared Or. Crest—A dexter arm embowed in armour proper grasping a broken sword argent.

The introductory paragraph or preamble as written by the Windsor Herald reads:—

GWILLIM.

ARMS OF GWILLIM.

"The Genealogy of the ancient family of Gwillim deduced to Mrs. Elizabeth P. Simcoe, wife of Lieut.-General John Graves Simcoe. Tracing her descent paternally from the ancient British Lords of Brecon—from Henry Fitz Herbert, who was Chamberlain to King Henry the First and from King William the Conqueror; and paternally and maternally through Sir Giles de Brewes—or De Braisosa, Lord of Buckingham in the time of King Edward the First, from William de Braisosa, one of the Conqueror's companions—whose posterity were Lords of Brembre, Brecon, and Gower and from the ancient Earls of Clare, Gloucester, Pembroke, Hereford and Derby and other of the most noble and illustrious families of England and Wales, compiled from public records and other authentic evidences by me, Francis Townsend, Windsor Herald, MDCCCVI."

Then follows the line of descent:—

Gundreda, daughter of William the Conqueror, married William, Earl of Warren and Surrey. She died in 1085 and was followed

4

in 1088 by her husband, who, the records show, was buried in Lewis Priory.

The line is continued through Maynarch, Lord of Brecon, through whom also is traced the descent from the Welsh kings, he being the fourteenth in descent from Kariadoe Vrachfras and the daughter and heir of Pelinor, King of North Wales.

Maynarch married Ellen, daughter of Eynon ap Selif, Lord of Cwmmwd, and their second son was Blethyn ap Maynarch, Lord of Brecon, who married Elinor, daughter of Twdwr Mawr, King of South Wales, 1077 to 1091, and sister of Prince Rhys.

In 1090 A.D., Blethyn was slain by Bernard Newmarch, who became Lord of Brecon. Blethyn's second son, Gwrgan ap Blethyn, appears in the records as Lord of Llangorse.

Gwrgan ap Blethyn married Gwenllian, daughter and sole heir of Philip Gwys, Lord of Wilton. Their second son, Traharne ap Gwrgan, was the next Lord of Llangorse and married Joan, daughter of Sir Aaron ap Bledry, Kn't.

Howel ap Traharne succeeded his father and married Gwenllian, daughter and heir of Griffith ap Eynon of Senighenith in County Glamorgan. During his lifetime he waged prolonged but unsuccessful wars against the Lord of Brecon in an attempt to win back the ancient seat of his family.

At his death, Howell was succeeded by his son, Rees ap Howell, also known as Henry III., of Aberllfni, who married Katherine, daughter of Griffith Gwyre.

The line then comes through a cadet branch of the family, descended from Eynon Says ap Rees ap Howell, third son of Rees ap Howell, who succeeded to the family estate of Lywell, County of Brecon. The family burying-place was at Crych-Einon. The family arms are given as "Argent, 3 cocks gules."

Eynon Says ap Rees ap Howell married Joan, daughter and heir of Howell ap Meredith ap Cradock ap Justin, her mother being Ann, daughter of Gwillim of Llewellyn-Lagar ap Ivor ap Einon. Their son was named Howell ap Eynon.

Howell ap Eynon married Llelles Lettice, daughter and sole heir of Cadwallader ap Gruff ap Sitsile, Lord of Gwent, and had for heir Howell Vychan ap Howell, who took for his arms "a fess between two arming swords."

Howell Vychan married Ellen, daughter and heir of Llewellyn ap Howell-hen.

Their third son, Llewellyn ap Howell Vychan, married Malltion, daughter and co-heir of Jevan ap Rees ap Jevan. The family arms were "A lion rampant, sable armed, or."

Thomas ap Lln ap Howell, eighth son of Llewellyn and Malltion, succeeded to the family arms, which are given during his generation as "Argent, a lion rampant, sable armed, or." He married Margaret, daughter and co-heir of Philip ap Adam of Llanvair, Gelgedyn.

5

The name Gwillim, which afterwards became the family name, first appears as the given name of the son of Thomas ap Lln and Margaret—Gwillim ap Thomas, who is the next in line and who married Margaret, daughter and heir of Sir John Abrahall, Knight of Ingestone, Co. Hereford.

Robert, son of Gwillim ap Thomas and Margaret, took his father's name as a surname and was known as Robert Gwillim of Treken-

THE GWILLIM TOMB AT WHITCHURCH.
(From a Drawing in the J. Ross Robertson collection.)

keved. All the information given as to his wife is that she was the "Daughter of Egerton."

Thomas Gwillim succeeded his father Robert and is known in the records as Thomas Gwillim of Llangonoke. His wife was the "Daughter of Milbourne," and their sons were: (1) John Gwillim of Trerise, who died unmarried in 1600, and (2) William Gwillim, of Trekenkeved.

William Gwillim married Margery, daughter of Thomas Vaughan of Trevervyn, and the line to Mrs. Simcoe is continued through his third son, Thomas Gwillim, of Whitchurch.

Thomas Gwillim married Barbara, daughter and co-heir of Walter Powell of Whitchurch, who was descended in a direct line from Robert Corbet, to whom King Henry I. gave the town of Alcester ("In Com. Warn."). Corbet's daughter, Lucy, married Henry Fitz Herbert, the famous Chamberlain of King Henry I., and it was from this marriage that the family sprang of which Barbara Powell was a descendant.

Thomas Gwillim was succeeded in 1634 by his son Rudhall Gwillim, of Whitchurch, who married Jane, daughter of Edmund Fox, of Leighton Court ("aforesaid"). They had two sons: (1) Thomas, who died unmarried, and (2) Richard Gwillim.

Richard Gwillim of Whitchurch, who succeeded to the estate in 1683 at the age of 54, married Margaret, daughter of Charles Price, of Llanfoist in the County of Monmouth.

Then their son, Thomas Gwillim of Whitchurch Court, married Sophia, daughter of Selwyn of Matson, County of Gloucester.

Thomas and Sophia had two sons, Selwyn who died unmarried, and Thomas Gwillim who succeeded his father and married Elizabeth, daughter and co-heir of Elmes Stuart of Cotterstock, High Sheriff of the County of Northampton.

The children of Thomas Gwillim and Elizabeth Stuart were Jasper and Elmes, who died without issue, Henrietta Maria and Sophia, two daughters who died unmarried and were buried at Whitchurch, and Thomas Gwillim who succeeded to the estate.

This Thomas Gwillim of Whitchurch Court was a lieutenant-colonel in the Army and died in 1766 and was buried in Gibraltar. His wife was Elizabeth, daughter and co-heir of Elmes Spinckes, who died at Aldwinkle, Sept. 22nd, 1762, and is buried there.

Thomas and Elizabeth were cousins on the maternal side. Mrs. Gwillim died in 1766. The only child of this marriage was Elizabeth Posthuma, so called because she was born subsequent to the death of her father. She married John Graves Simcoe of Wolford on December 30th, 1782, and died at Wolford, January 17th, 1850.

The Simcoes were related to the Creed family of Northampton-shire, through the Gwillims. The connection is shown as follows:—

Sir Edward Montague, Knt., created Earl of Sandwich, July 12th, 1661, and from present Earl, 1806.

Nicholas Stuart of Pattishull, aforesaid, J. P. for County, living 1682, aged 57, married Susanna, daughter of Anthony Elmes and at length co-heir, living 1681.

Sir Thomas Elmes, Knt. (bro. of Susanna) of Lilford, High Sheriff of said County, 1670, died without issue.

DIARY OF MRS. SIMCOE

Sir Sydney Montague, Knt. Master of the Requests (living 1618) married Paulina, daughter of John Pepys of Cottenham, Co. of Cambridge.

Elizabeth, daughter of Sir Sydney Montague, Knt., married Sir Gilbert Pickering of Tichmarsh, County of Northampton, Bart. of Nova Scotia.

John Creed of Oundle, County Northampton, Gent., married Elizabeth, daughter of Sir Gilbert Pickering, Bart. of Nova Scotia.

Elizabeth, daughter of John Creed, Esquire, born 1672, married 1692, died 1742, buried at Whitchurch—married Elmes Stuart of Cotterstock, County Northampton, High Sheriff of said County, Ano. 12, Wm. III., aged 26 years, 1682, living 1710.

Anne, daughter and co-heir, died unmarried and was buried at Whitchurch.

Jemima, daughter and co-heir of Elmes Stuart of Cotterstock, aforesaid, Esq., died at Aldwinkle, 26th May, 1763; married Elmes Spinckes, Esq., Lord of the Manor of Warrington, County Northampton, died at Kidwarke. The issue of the marriage was a daughter who married Thomas Gwillim, the father of Mrs. John Graves Simcoe.

This closes the summary.

Thomas Gwillim, as before stated, died at Gibraltar in 1766, seven

COLONEL GWILLIM.

months before the birth of his daughter, and his widow died a few hours after the birth.

The child thus born was named Elizabeth Posthuma. She married Lieutenant-Colonel John Graves Simcoe, who was born in 1752 at Cotterstock in Northamptonshire, the ceremony being performed in SS. Mary and Giles, the Church of Buckerall parish in Devon in 1782. Colonel Simcoe, afterwards a general and the first Lieutenant-Governor of Upper Canada, died in 1806 in Exeter. Mrs. Simcoe, his widow, died in 1850. Both husband and wife are buried in the east end of the private chapel erected by the General on the estate of Wolford. General Simcoe was the only surviving son of Captain John Simcoe, R.N., of Cotterstock, who married Catherine Stamford on 8th August, 1747. The marriage took place in Bath Abbey. At the time Captain Simcoe was in command of the "Prince Edward." Afterwards he was promoted to H.M.S. "Pembroke" and died of pneumonia while his ship was off the island of Anticosti in the St. Lawrence River, on 15th May, 1759, four months before the capitulation of Quebec.

The following is an extract from the Registers of the Abbey Church of SS. Peter and Paul, Bath, regarding the marriage of Captain Simcoe:—

"1747, August 8th,—John Simcoe, Esqr., commander of His Majesties ship Prince Edward and Catherine Stamford, spinster, of Walcott, were married by License."

8

Part of the city of Bath is now in the parish of Walcott, and although search has been made in the registers of the parish church, which date from 1694, no trace can be found of the name of Stamford.

After the death of Mrs. Gwillim, the daughter was most tenderly cared for by her aunt, Mrs. Graves, a sister of her mother and wife of Samuel Graves of Hembury Fort, three miles from Wolford in Devon, who was Admiral of the White in 1717. There is a monument in Buckerall parish church to the memory of Admiral Graves.

To the west of Honiton one looks over a space of comparatively flat country, to the northwest overshadowed by St. Cyres Hill, and further north is the bold height of Dumpdon. On the top of this hill are the remains of an oval camp, and a few miles away the better known camp called Hembury Fort. The Fort stands very high and looks south to the sea beyond the vale of the river Otter,

THE RESIDENCE KNOWN AS HEMBURY FORT.

(From a Drawing in the J. Ross Robertson collection.)

and west to Haldon and the fringes of Dartmoor over Exeter. Three ramparts surround the fort, which covers a large space of ground. It is oval in shape, divided into two parts by an earthwork and enclosed by a triple "vallum" or line of palisades. Several Roman coins and an iron "lar" in the form of a small female figure three inches high, representing a goddess who presided over the fortunes of the home, have been found there. Past Honiton ran the great Roman road of the Fosseway to Totnes, and according to some authorities, on into Cornwall. It is thought that the Romans, in making these famous roads, usually followed the line of the oldest British ways.

Of Elizabeth Gwillim's very early youth little is known. Her aunt was most affectionate in disposition, a tender, kind and lovable woman, who in a thoroughly Christian spirit accepted the responsibilities of watching over her sister's child. This much may be gathered from the Graves' correspondence.

The years were not slow in passing with Miss Gwillim. As a child she evinced a natural ability that surprised her governesses. She gathered knowledge as eagerly as she gathered the wild flowers by the roadside, of which she was so passionately fond.

MRS. SIMCOE IN WELSH DRESS.
(From a Miniature at Wolford.)

She loved to ramble through the woods, where she could reproduce bits of landscapes that are still so charming all around Hembury Fort. Her delight as a girl was to be skilled in pencil, pen, and water-color work; and be it said that some of her water-colors that hang to-day on the walls at Wolford bear excellent evidence of

10

her artistic skill. It was readily admitted by all who met her at Hembury Fort that Mrs. Graves had in her niece Elizabeth an accomplished relative.

As a linguist Miss Gwillim was an apt pupil. She spoke German and French fluently and ventured occasionally to converse in Spanish when opportunity offered. To a letter from Miss Burgess, a friend at Tracey, near Honiton, Devonshire, she replied with one in Spanish.

She was fond of gaiety and outdoor life. To whirl in the dance, to cross country with the hounds, seemed second nature to her, while to tramp through the woods and along the rural roads with her young friends was one of the ordinary enjoyments of her life. Though she had an excellent ear for music, she never sang or played on any instrument.

BROCADE SKIRT WORN BY MRS. SIMCOE.

(From the Original at Wolford.)

She was below the average height, about five feet, not more, and this is indicated by a satin skirt, thirty-seven inches in length, which she wore in her married life when she was twenty-five years of age, just before leaving for Upper Canada. The waist is missing, but the skirt has been preserved at Wolford. The garment was known as Mrs. Simcoe's "presentation dress," and was worn by her at the opening of the first Legislature of Upper Canada at Niagara on the 17th September, 1792.

It was in the spring of 1782 that Colonel Simcoe first met Miss Gwillim; and as the story of her life is so interwoven with that of her husband, it is fitting that the reader should have some knowledge of the family of Simcoe; for the first Governor of Upper Canada was a man of marked ability, whose name is to-day a household word in the great province, the government of which he inaugurated under many difficulties.

CHAPTER II.

ANCESTORS OF JOHN GRAVES SIMCOE.

It was only in the summer of nineteen hundred and six that the writer finally after years of research determined that the Simcoe family was of Cheshire origin. There are no records in the papers at Wolford in Devon which give any trace of the birthplace or even the names of the ancestors of the first Governor of Upper Canada. Indeed, it was only after a continuous personal quest involving a careful examination of a score of parish and other records in villages, towns and cities of Northumberland, Yorkshire, Northamptonshire, Devonshire, Cheshire, and even north to the borderland of Berwickshire, that the writer was able to place his hand on documents that proved beyond doubt that the ancestors of John Graves Simcoe were born and bred in Bunbury, a village and large parish in West Cheshire about three miles from Tarporley and a mile and a half southeast of Beeston Castle. This old stronghold occupies a romantic and impregnable site on the summit of a huge and lofty isolated rock. It was built in 1220 by the fourth Earl of Chester and dismantled after surrender to the Parliamentary forces in the year 1646. The parish records date from the year 1559. Mrs. Simcoe visited the old ruin on one occasion but no date is given in the memoranda. It was probably about 1800-1.

The first trace of the name of Simcoe was found by the writer in the "Cantabrigiensis Graduati" of the University of Cambridge, published in the year 1800. At page 381 of this work under the letter "S" is the record "Simcoe, Gul., Christ, A. B., 1675 " and "Simcoe, John, Christ, A. B. 1716." The late Dr. John Peile, the master of Christ's College, 1887-1910, informed me that "this William Simcoe of 1675 was the son of a William Simcoe, born at a place not given, in Cheshire, was at school in Bunbury, and was admitted a sizar under Mr. Lovett at Christ's College, 5th April, 1672, aged 19." The parish records show that he was born in the parish of Bunbury. At Cambridge University and Trinity College, Dublin, a sizar was an undergraduate of limited means, and was allowed free commons and some other gratuities. Formerly menial duties were imposed upon a sizar.

A memorandum on a half sheet of note paper in the papers at Wolford states that ʻCaptain John Simcoe, R.N., father of General Simcoe, was born at Leamside farmhouse, some miles from the city of Durham; but other than this memorandum, though a close examination has been made of the property registers of Durham University, at one time owners of the farm, there is no entry to be

CAPTAIN JOHN SIMCOE, R.N.

found containing the name of Simcoe. It should be stated that the University records in this regard are not extant before 1752.

There are some hundreds of entries of births, marriages, and deaths of persons named Simcoe in the parish books of Bunbury and the adjacent parish of Acton, the earliest dating back to 1759, but there are so many entries with Christian names alike that it is impossible to fix upon the ancestor of William Simcoe who entered Christ's College, in 1675. The opinion prevails at Bunbury that "William Simcoe," a churchwarden who died in 1664, was his father.

GATE OF BEESTON CASTLE—CHESHIRE.

(From an old Drawing in the J. Ross Robertson collection.)

The same difficulty arises in determining the parentage of Captain John Simcoe, R.N., born in 1714 and father of John Graves Simcoe. Hodgson in his history of the parish of Long Horsley in Northumberland states that Captain John Simcoe was a son of the Rev. William Simcoe, vicar of that parish, who died in June, 1714. If this statement be true the vicar died in the year his son was born.

There are no letters or documents in the papers at Wolford to help in a verification of Hodgson's statement. Suffice it to say that Captain Simcoe was a distinguished naval officer. Of his early life nothing is known. His after life shows that he was a man of exemplary habits and character, highly educated, and had made a

13

special study of seamanship and naval tactics. He was thoroughly earnest in his work, eager in the obtaining of knowledge and with a mind most retentive, made the best use of leisure hours in perfecting himself so as to eventually reach the top round of the ladder in the profession he had chosen. He had an extensive knowledge of the classics and in mathematics he excelled. He was a voracious reader and his cabin was the home of a small library consisting not only of works on military and naval tactics but of the best authors in general literature. Through the influence of his father he entered the Royal Navy as a midshipman in 1730. The name of the ship is not on record.

In 1737 he was promoted to a lieutenancy and in 1743 at twenty-nine years of age he obtained a captain's commission. In 1747 he was in command of H.M. Ship "Prince Edward." His ability was recognized in many ways by the Admiralty, and his advice was often sought in considering questions of grave import. He was one of the members of the court-martial on the trial of Admiral Byng (1756-7).

About four years before the capitulation of Quebec he drew up a plan, and wrote an able paper suggesting the manner in which not only the ancient city could be captured, but how Canada could be possessed by the British Crown. He addressed this document to Lord Barrington, who was Secretary of War 1755-61; and the latter after giving the paper a careful reading complimented Captain Simcoe on its excellence, and said that when the time came to act, his suggestions would have due consideration.

Another paper entitled "Maxims of Conduct," or, as it is also called, "Rules for Your Conduct," was written in 1752 by Capt. Simcoe for the guidance of young officers in the naval and military service, and for the edification of his sons. It is an admirable paper, unexcelled in style and diction, as worthy of perusal in these modern days as when it was penned a hundred and fifty-nine years ago.

After his marriage with Catherine Stamford Captain John Simcoe decided that he would make his home in Cotterstock, a village about a mile from the old town of Oundle in Northamptonshire. Four children, all sons, were issue of this marriage, Paulet William, John, John Graves, and Percy William. The first and second sons died in infancy, and the fourth was drowned in 1764 at Sandy Point above the head of the river Exe near Exeter.

On August 22nd, 1747, Captain John Simcoe was granted by the Garter and Clarenceux Kings of Arms, the arms and crest here given, namely:—Azure, a fesse wavy ermine, between two stars of twelve points in chief and a cannon barwise in base or, and for his crest, out of a naval cross or a demi sea lion proper holding in his fore fin a mariner's cross staff erect or and on his shoulder a rose gules seeded proper. In October, 1747, application was made by Captain Simcoe for an alteration in his arms. The extract from the official document, dated 4th November, 1747, regarding the granting of this alteration, reads:—"The crest depicted on the other side granted to John

Simcoe of Chelsea, in the County of Middlesex, Esq., and his descendants is hereby altered from out of a naval crown or a demi sea lion proper holding in his fore fin a mariner's cross staff erect or and on his shoulder a rose gules seeded proper, to out of a naval crown or a demi sea lion proper, holding in his fore fin a dagger erect argent, the pomel and hilt gold and on his shoulder a rose gules barbed and seeded proper as the same is in the margin hereof more plainly depicted."

ARMS OF JOHN SIMCOE.

Captain Simcoe joined H. M. Ship "Pembroke," 60 guns, in 1757, as commander, with Mr. James Cook as master, and in 1759 sailed for Canada with the fleet under Admiral Saunders. Mr. Cook was afterwards the celebrated navigator who in 1768 circumnavigated the globe in the "Endeavor"; and in later years he declared that he was under many obligations to Captain Simcoe, for from him he had received a great part of his training in "navigation and seamanship." Captain Simcoe, however, was never to reap the reward of his years of study in naval work, for on Tuesday, May 15th, 1759, while the "Pembroke" was nearing the island of Anticosti he died of pneumonia and was buried at sea at six o'clock on the evening of the 17th.

Mrs. Simcoe, on receiving the sad news of the death of her husband on the "Pembroke," decided to leave Cotterstock, where she had spent many happy years, and remove to Exeter. She had friends in Devon, several of whom resided in Exeter, and she felt that the advantages for the education of her children would be much greater in a city, possessing better schools than Oundle. She accordingly rented a dwelling in the Cathedral City and determined that her life's aim should be the care and education of her boys.

CAPT. JAMES COOK.

But her cup of sorrow was not yet full. The death by drowning of her fourth son, Percy, saddened Mrs. Simcoe's heart for years; however, with an affection that was intensified by her affliction, she devoted her life to her surviving

15

son and to a certain extent outlived the last great sorrow that fell to her lot.

The future Governor of Upper Canada was an apt pupil. He received his primary education at the Free Grammar School in Exeter and in 1766, in his fourteenth year, he was sent to Eton. On 4th February, 1769, while in his sixteenth year, he entered Merton College, Oxford, and matriculated. There is no record of his graduation. It is said that owing to ill-health he was compelled to withdraw from college at the end of his first year. He accordingly returned to his mother's home in Exeter and with the assistance of a tutor he devoted the years 1770-1 to the acquiring of general knowledge and especially to the subject of military tactics, for he had the promise of an ensign's commission from friends of his mother in the War Office.

In 1771 at the age of nineteen he entered the army as an ensign in the 35th Regiment of Foot. He sailed on the outbreak of the war of the American Revolution for New England and joined his regiment in June at Boston a few days after the historic battle of Bunker Hill, or rather Breed's Hill; for that is where the battle took place on the 17th of June, 1775.

His anxiety to be of service to the Crown was shown by his offer to raise a corps of negroes for service in New England; but notwithstanding the strong influence of Admiral Graves, his godfather, who was in command of the fleet, his offer was declined by General Gage, who was in command of the forces. While his regiment was stationed in Boston he acted as adjutant, but there is no record of his appointment. At the evacuation of Boston in March, 1776, he embarked with General Howe's army for Halifax.

During his stay in Halifax he purchased a captaincy in the grenadier company of the 40th Regiment, and when New York was

threatened with attack he sailed with the forces early in June for Staten Island and disembarked with the army on 3rd July, 1776. He took an active part in the military operations in Long Island and the Jerseys during the summer and won commendation for his services.

While at winter quarters at Brunswick in 1776 he went to New York to see Sir William Howe and ask for the command of the Queen's Rangers, which was then vacant. But driven by stress of weather out of its course, the boat in which he sailed was delayed and he arrived at headquarters some hours too late, for the position had been filled. In the summer of 1777, still bent on an independent command, he wrote to General Grant, under whom he had served, requesting his influence in the securing of a command similar to that of the Queen's Rangers; but there were no vacancies, and once more he was disappointed. The Queen's Rangers were at

SIR WILLIAM HOWE.

that time commanded by Major Weymess. Shortly afterwards, on the 11th September, was fought the battle of the Brandywine. Simcoe led his company of the 40th Regiment and received a wound, from which he never fully recovered, although he was able to resume his duties.

At last his ambitions were realized, for on the 15th of October, 1777, Captain Simcoe was nominated major commander of the celebrated Provincial regiment known as the Queen's Rangers, which became under him one of the most efficient and gallant corps that took part in the War of the Revolution. It was at this time encamped with the army in the vicinity of Germantown, near Philadelphia.

In June, 1778, he received from Sir Henry Clinton the local rank of lieutenant-colonel of the Rangers. In an action in 1779 he had a narrow escape for his life and was taken prisoner. He obtained his release on the 31st of December, 1779, and returned to his regiment. His Majesty on the 19th of December, 1781, was pleased to confer upon him the rank of a lieutenant-colonel in the army, the duties of which he had fulfilled from the year 1778. His regiment was amongst the troops which were included in the surrender by General Cornwallis at Gloucester Point on the 19th of October, 1781.

The story of his part in the campaign as colonel of the Queen's Rangers, as told in his journal, will be found in another volume. His journal is one of the most interesting books of its kind. It was published in Exeter at the close of the war, and was received most favorably by the press and highly commended by the leading military writers of England. Simcoe returned to England in December, 1781, at the close of the war, married Miss Gwillim in 1782, and from 1783-7 he resided in the Cathedral City.

In 1784, the estate of Wolford, four miles from Honiton, in the parish of Dunkeswell, Devon, was purchased by Mrs. Simcoe. Although there was an old farmhouse on the property, a new residence was built; the estate was considerably improved during the years 1786-7, and in 1788 Colonel Simcoe and his family left Exeter and took up their residence at Wolford. He held the rank of colonel in the army from the 18th of November, 1790, and in the same year he was elected to Parliament for the borough of St. Maw's in Cornwall. His political career, however, was of short duration, for in 1791 he received his commission as Lieutenant-Governor of the new province of Upper Canada and sailed from Weymouth for Quebec on the 26th of September in the ship "Triton," 21 guns, accompanied by his wife and two of his children and Lieutenant Talbot.

In a despatch to the Secretary of State, Lord Dorchester had previously recommended Sir John Johnson as first Lieutenant-Governor of Upper Canada. Sir John Johnson had rendered valuable services, and in the matter of claim was entitled to consideration. On the other hand, his appointment was undesirable, not only on account of his large property holdings in the new province, and consequent local interests, but also from the fact that the policy of the British Government did not allow the appointment of residents of colonies in the government of the same.

The "Triton" arrived in Quebec on the•11th of November. Lord Dorchester, the Governor-General, was on leave of absence in England and Major-General Alured Clarke, who by the way was a Devonian, was acting as administrator. Simcoe had been entrusted with the commission of and instructions to the Governor-General which were to be issued on the division of the province into Upper and Lower Canada, together with the commission of Sir John Johnson, Bart., as Superintendent-General of Indian affairs, and the commission of Major-General Alured Clarke as Lieutenant-Governor of the.new Province of Lower Canada. All these documents were duly delivered on the day following his arrival.

Simcoe presented also a personal letter from the King to H.R.H. Prince Edward, Duke of Kent, the father of Queen Victoria, in which His Majesty commended the newly appointed Governor to his son, who was in command of the 7th Fusiliers, stationed at Quebec. It should be stated that Governor Simcoe was offered by the War Office before his departure for Canada the rank of Brigadier-General; but he declined the promotion because he foresaw that unless His Royal Highness should be promoted at the same time, his acceptance would place him above the King's son.

Moreover, Governor Simcoe understood that such promotion was not desired by Prince Edward, and from general belief it was also not his Majesty's intention to confer it. Governor Simcoe had always a dislike to nominal rank. His local Provincial rank in America was senior to that of Major-General Alured Clarke, for early in 1778 Simcoe had been gazetted a lieutenant-colonel, though of course ranking as the youngest of the service.

The Governor in a letter to Mr. Dundas on the 6th September, 1791, said: "I by no means wish to command or to wound the feelings of a senior officer, much less to interfere with the just pretensions of the son of my Sovereign."

The official proclamation and the text of the Act dividing the old province of Canada into two provinces was issued on 18th November, 1791, a week after the Governor's arrival in Quebec, and was published in the Quebec *Gazette* of December 1st, 1791. The natal day of the new provinces was fixed for the 26th of December.

General Alured Clarke was duly sworn in as Lieutenant-Governor of the Province of Lower Canada, but being administrator in the absence of the Governor-General he occupied a different position from that of Governor Simcoe. When the proclamation was issued for the division of the province, Lieutenant-Governor Clarke had full powers as regards his own government, but he had no authority to deal in any way with the affairs of the civil government of the Province of Upper Canada. But, at the same time, acting as administrator,

18

he could exercise all the prerogatives and powers of the Governor-in-Chief in either province.

The Act of 1791 making further provision for the government of the province of Quebec is familiarly known as the Act for dividing the province of Quebec into the provinces of Upper and Lower Canada. But Mr. Avern Pardoe in his excellent paper on "The First Chapter of Upper Canada History" (Ontario Historical Society Transactions, Vol. VII.) points out, the creation of the new provinces was an Act of the King under his royal prerogative. The Crown divided Quebec by proclamation and Parliament's duty and privilege in the matter was to provide a constitution for them.

The statute quoted enacts that these provinces which the King has created shall have a Legislative Council and Assembly and that these shall be assembled by the Governor or Lieutenant-Governor. But there is nothing in the Act authorizing the appointment of a Governor or Lieutenant-Governor. That is another prerogative of the Crown—in these days exercised on advice but hardly so in the days of George III. Nor does the Act contain any information as to the extent of the powers conferred upon the Governor or the Lieutenant-Governor of the Province. That is yet another prerogative of the Crown. The powers of the Governor and Lieutenant-Governor are those conferred upon them by their commissions and instructions.

Lieutenant-Governor Simcoe seems to have been from the first at a loss to know his exact relations to the Governor-General, Lord Dorchester. The commission of and instructions to Lord Dorchester as Governor-in-Chief and Captain-General over the provinces of Upper and Lower Canada issued on the division of the province, were brought out by Simcoe as before said, and Simcoe's own instructions directed him to read Dorchester's instructions and conduct himself accordingly.

The power of the Governor-General was almost unlimited. The whole duty of the Lieutenant-Governor was to follow out the instructions of the Governor-in-Chief. There were no instructions issued to Governor Simcoe other than his commission and the injunction to regard Dorchester's instructions, neither is there record of any instructions having been addressed to Simcoe. His commission, which was simply a few hundred words appointing him as Lieutenant-Governor, contained nothing that would throw light on the extent of the powers the Lieutenant-Governor should exercise.

Simcoe felt that in accepting office he should in the main have been free to administer the affairs of the province as one endowed with authority, and that he should not be hampered with edicts and instructions from Quebec, but should have the right to communicate direct with the home authorities. As a matter of fact he did so communicate.

In the Simcoe correspondence there is a letter from Sir George Yonge in connection with the military force, giving an "extract from the instructions given to the civil Governor."

These instructions show that, where no specific orders have been given by the Commander-in-Chief or by the General commanding the district, the civil Governor-in-Council may give orders for the marching of troops and other military services; but such order must be repeated to the Commander-in-Chief, and that the Civil Governor must not interfere with the detail of the military regimental duty. The complexity of the situation and the delay in getting his government formed was galling to Simcoe. He foresaw that he would be virtually cribbed, cabined, and confined in Quebec for the winter, and that he was absolutely powerless to make any immediate move in the direction of occupying his seat of government.

Meanwhile he occupied his time with various matters that concerned the new province. Many months before his departure from England, indeed before the Canada Act of May, 1791, was passed, he had considered the policy he would pursue in conducting his new government; for, of course, he knew at that time his appointment was assured.

One of Simcoe's first suggestions was the raising of a military force for service within the limits of the province. This suggestion was assented to in August of 1791, the corps being known as the Queen's Rangers. Another was that he should be permitted to visit Philadelphia, where the United States Congress was sitting, to discuss and mediate on the Indian question. But this suggestion was not acted upon.

Even in regard to the administration of justice in Upper Canada the Governor's hands were tied; for, as there was no majority of his Council in Canada, the oaths could not be administered. He, therefore, had no power to issue a proclamation. This was after the division of the provinces was proclaimed. Major-General Alured Clarke could act for Lower Canada, but Governor Simcoe, until he had taken the oath, had no legal power. This difficulty might have affected the organization of courts in Upper Canada, but when Judge Powell was appointed to hold court in Kingston in December, the difficulty was overcome by him, as, on the advice of Chief Justice Smith, he did not raise the question of authority to hold court in the new province.

Simcoe now occupied a singular position. By virtue of his commission he was the Governor of the new province of Upper Canada, but, notwithstanding, had no military command; and as regards his own military rank, he could not avail himself of his colonelcy until the corps—the Queen's Rangers, of which he was Commander— or part of it, was actually on service under him. This restriction was specifically set forth to Governor Simcoe in a letter from Sir George Yonge, the Secretary of State, on September 21st, 1791. Simcoe knew that the Rangers would not arrive until the summer of 1792 and keenly resented the inevitable delay in the recognition of his rank.

Furthermore, his civil powers as Lieutenant-Governor were not operative until a meeting of the Executive Council had been convened and the oaths of office administered. Four members of this body had been nominated by the authorities in London, namely, William Osgoode, William Robertson, Alexander Grant and Peter Russell. Mr. Grant was the only member who had arrived in Canada. Thus, in the absence of a majority of his Council, the Governor had practically to mark time and await their arrival.

Simcoe saw clearly the situation and at once applied to England for permission to nominate James Baby, of Detroit, as one of the three Councillors required and asked permission to appoint two more so that the seven members required by the act would meet and initiate the business of organizing the government of the new province. In June, however, Osgoode and Russell arrived, and with Baby made a quorum. The appointment followed of John Munro, of Matilda, in January, 1792, and later of Richard Cartwright, jr., of Kingston, Robert Hamilton, of Niagara and Richard Duncan, of Rapid du Plat. The Council was now complete. William Robertson, however, never came to Canada but

HON. JAMES BABY.

resigned, his place being filled in June, 1793, by the appointment of Aeneas Shaw.

All this delay was vexatious to Simcoe. True, he and his wife were the recipients of unbounded hospitality from the military, civil, and social leaders of the old capital, but the Governor was a man of active habit and eager to journey to his new province.

At the end of May and in the second week of June two divisions of the Queen's Rangers arrived at Quebec, and some weeks later reached the new province.

Governor Simcoe had paid a short visit to Montreal in December, 1791, but did not go further west. On the 8th June, 1792, with his family and Lieutenants Grey and Talbot he left Quebec for Kingston in bateaux, arriving in Montreal on the 17th, leaving there on the 27th and reaching Kingston on the 1st of July. On the 8th of July the Governor repaired to the Protestant church, and there the oaths were administered by Chief Justice Osgoode. The Honorable James Baby and the Honorable Peter Russell, together with the magistrates and principal inhabitants of the town, were present; and the ceremonial must have been, so far as the primitive environment permitted, of a very impressive character. A note containing the minutes of the Executive Council in connection with this event is given in its proper place in Mrs. Simcoe's diary for July, 1792.

From Kingston, Governor Simcoe, with his family and suite, sailed on the Government schooner "Onondaga" for Niagara, where they arrived on the 26th July, 1792. Navy Hall was undergoing alterations. These were not completed, so by the Governor's orders three marquees were pitched on the hill above the Hall. In these the Governor's family and suite were housed pending the completion of the alterations. Navy Hall had been originally built by Governor Haldimand for the use of the naval officers on the lakes. During Simcoe's time some additions were made. One of these was a council chamber, and it was used as a ball-room where Mrs. Simcoe entertained. Simcoe's work in the way of organizing the Provincial Government and carrying on the affairs of the Province, will be told in another volume.

Simcoe was energetic in his administration and was inspired by a determination to do his best for the people he was called upon to govern. The first Legislature was called on 17th September, 1792, at Navy Hall, Niagara, and was prorogued on the 15th of October. There has always been some doubt as to the building and the place where the first Legislature met. Some assert that the meeting was held in a tent pitched on the common above Fort George. This ground was marked by an old oak tree known as the "Parliament Oak." A picture of this tree in decay is in the Museum, Niagara-on-the-Lake. Another writer asserts that the Legislature met in Freemasons' Hall, Niagara. The records of the Upper Canada *Gazette*, however, dispose of all doubts, for in the issue of that paper of 18th April, 1793, the words "Government House, Navy Hall" are used, and on 3rd July, 1794, the same words are used, while on the 10th of August, 1794, Governor Simcoe calls the members to appear at "our Government House, Navy Hall." On the 14th of August, 1794, the latter expression is again used.

During Simcoe's term from 1792-6 five sessions of the Legislature were held at Niagara, in one of the four buildings known as Navy Hall, for there was no accommodation for the Legislature at York. The buildings at York were not ready for occupation till 1797, the year following Simcoe's departure. Rochefoucauld in his "Tour Through Upper Canada," 1795, writes that "during our residence at Navy Hall the session of the Legislature of Upper Canada was opened." He does not indicate any building other than "Navy Hall" and says the Governor "dressed in silk entered the hall with his hat on his head, attended by his adjutant and two secretaries."

Eight acts were considered and passed. The ancient laws of the Province of Quebec were abolished, the laws of England were to prevail, and all forms of law and equity were to be in conformity with the British rules of evidence. Trial by jury was established and provision made for the recovery of small debts. Jails and court houses were to be erected in the four Districts, the Eastern, the Middle, the Home and the Western. A marriage bill was introduced with the view of legalizing all irregular marriages, for at this period no marriage ceremony was legal unless performed by a clergyman of the Church of England. It was, therefore, necessary that all past marriages should be legalized and a law provided for the future validation of all such unions.

NAVY HALL, NIAGARA, 1792.

(From a Drawing by Mrs. Simcoe.)

But this act was withdrawn and another act was drawn during the recess, submitted to the authorities in England, and was then passed by the Legislative Assembly and assented to by the Governor. Shortly after the prorogation of the first Assembly the publication of the *Upper Canada Gazette or American Oracle,* the official journal of the province, was commenced.

In February, 1793, General Simcoe visited the western parts of the Province, accompanied by Major Littlehales, Captain Fitzgerald, Lieutenant Smith of the 5th Regiment, and Lieutenants Talbot, Grey and Givins. They proceeded west to the Mohawk village on the Grand River, then to the Moravian Settlement of the Delaware Indians, and returned by way of the present site of London, Ont., which at a later date Simcoe suggested as a proper place for the capital of the province.

On the 2nd May, 1793, he visited the site of Toronto for the first time and decided to call the new town York "in consideration and compliment of the Duke of York's victories in Flanders." But it was not until the 26th August, 1793, that the official notification of the name was published.

In 1793, Simcoe directed also the making of a roadway to the western part of the province, the present Dundas Street, and named it after the Right Hon. Henry Dundas, Secretary of State for the Colonies. In May, 1794, he paid his second visit to the site of his new capital (now Toronto), and ordered Mr. Alexander Aitken, a Government surveyor, to make a plan of the town. He also selected the site for a fort at the west end of the town so as to command the mouth of the harbor. This fortification was destroyed in 1813, but rebuilt in 1816, and is now (1911) being restored by the corporation of Toronto under agreement with the Dominion Government.

It must be remembered that Lord Dorchester, the Governor-General, was on leave of absence and did not return to Canada until September of 1793. From the date of Lord Dorchester's return down to the date of Simcoe's departure from Canada, there was constant friction between the Governor-General and the Lieutenant-Governor of Upper Canada. Indeed, it looked as if Dorchester had determined to make Simcoe's position as uncomfortable as possible. Simcoe had not forgotten the "unjust, humiliating and disgraceful order," as he termed it, issued by Guy Carleton in 1783, concerning a charge made against the Queen's Rangers as being guilty of "plundering and marauding" on Long Island Sound during the War of the Revolution, a charge, by the way, that was without foundation. The official correspondence shows that Dorchester seized every opportunity to clog the wheels of Simcoe's Government. As an example of this unfriendliness Dorchester compelled Simcoe to change the system of contracting for supplies and he ordered the change in a manner that was most mortifying.

Then again, Simcoe was strongly against the proposal of Dorchester to erect a fort in the Indian territory on the Maumee River.

Dorchester insisted that the fort should be established and his order was carried out by Simcoe. He did not agree with Simcoe on the choice of London as the capital of Upper Canada; and when Simcoe objected to Dorchester's policy of removing the best part of the troops from Upper Canada and taking them to Quebec, the Governor-General wrote to Simcoe saying that he would act on his own judgment irrespective of the opinion expressed by Simcoe. The official correspondence of the time teems with passages at arms between Dorchester, Simcoe, and the Duke of Portland.

Simcoe, of course, had carried on official correspondence during his term with the authorities at London. Dorchester naturally thought that Simcoe should use the Governor-in-Chief as the medium of communication. Indeed, Dorchester complained that he had not been treated as the Governor-in-Chief should be; and that the authorities in London, that is, the Duke of Portland, had no right to receive official communications from the Lieutenant-Governor, who was subordinate to the Governor-in-Chief.

The poles could not be further apart than Simcoe and Dorchester in their views as to the powers and prerogatives of the Governor and Lieutenant-Governor, respectively. Dorchester would have made the new province a military colony with forts for the protection of the settlers. On the other hand Simcoe's aim was to bring in colonists—even American colonists—and make Upper Canada a great agricultural province.

Simcoe often said that the day would come when every acre of land from the Ottawa to the Detroit River would so respond to the call of the husbandmen that the sickle would never be idle and the people never be in want.

The Duke of Portland tried to throw oil on the troubled waters, but without avail. Dorchester felt that Simcoe was his inferior officer, for he writes that Simcoe "seemed to think that he had an independent command." Simcoe held fast to the idea that, outside of actual military operations, he was supreme in his own province. The neglect to furnish Simcoe with individual instructions defining exactly his powers and duties seems to have been the cause of all the trouble.

This continued friction and unrest between the Governor and Lieutenant-Governor in Upper Canada led to the resignation by both of their respective commands in the usual form of "leave of absence." Dorchester sailed for England on the 9th July and Simcoe said farewell to Upper Canada on the 21st July, 1796. On the 10th September, with his wife and children he sailed from Quebec in H. M. Ship "Pearl," which anchored in the Downs on the 13th of October. On disembarking, the General and his family proceeded to Dover, Canterbury and Dartford, and on Monday, the 17th, reached Wolford.

In 1796 the British Government wanted an officer to take charge of the forces in San Domingo. General Simcoe, who had been gazetted Major-General on the 2nd of October, 1794, was offered the position. He called upon the Duke of Portland, who told him that he could retain his position of Lieutenant-Governor of Upper Canada or go as Commander-in-Chief of the forces in San Domingo, to succeed Sir Ralph Abercrombie.

Simcoe accepted the new position and on the 3rd of December, 1796, he was appointed Civil Governor and Commander-in-Chief of the British forces in San Domingo in place of Sir Adam Williamson, who had established the British protectorate over the island.

Simcoe was much disappointed. In a letter written to H. R. H. the Duke of Kent on 24th November, 1801, referring to his San Domingo appointment, Simcoe writes: "His Grace (the Duke of Portland) expressly told me that I was to be Commander-in-Chief. In this I was disappointed. Sir R. Abercrombie retained that office, but with the injunction communicated to him by a letter from Mr. Dundas, the Secretary of State, not to exercise any authority in San Domingo," and Simcoe further adds, "I believe such an injunction to be illegal, I am sure it was unmilitary." In this letter Simcoe also pointed out that his "services in Canada had been slighted" in that as Lieutenant-Governor he had a fair claim to the command of the Royal Americans in preference to General Hunter. The letter further shows that he was promised the position of Governor-General of Canada and also a peerage.

In 1797 General Simcoe proceeded to his new post with instructions to aid the French in restoring, if possible, order to the island. While the General did excellent work in his command, he became wearied with the kind of warfare in which he was engaged, and after eight months in the island he returned to England, either to procure a force adequate for the work or to abandon the cause. His place was filled by his second in command, Brigadier-General Sir Thomas Maitland, appointed 18th April, 1797. In 1798, owing to the fear that Napoleon would seek a landing on British soil, General Simcoe was appointed to the command of Plymouth and the Western District, and in February, 1801, he was gazetted as "Lieutenant-General in the Army."

In 1806 the General was appointed Commander-in-Chief of the British forces in India, to succeed Lord Lake, and he at once began to make arrangements for departure to his far-distant command. Mrs. Simcoe and one of her daughters had gone to London and were busily engaged in making purchases such as would be required in their new home, when an entire change of plan came from the authorities in London by special messenger to Exeter, the headquarters of the Western District.

The order was in effect that the British Government had information that led to the belief that an invasion of Portugal was contemplated by Napoleon. The orders were peremptory. The fleet under Earl St. Vincent was cruising off Brest, whence it was ordered to the Tagus, while Lord Rosslyn and Lieutenant-General Simcoe were directed to join Earl St. Vincent at Lisbon.

DIARY OF MRS. SIMCOE

General Simcoe had been in poor health, but by exercising the greatest care he was able without undue exertion to cover the large amount of work assigned to him in the command of the Western District. He was so confident of his physical strength that he did not hesitate to accept the India command when it was offered to him.

Indeed it was anticipated that after the negotiations in Lisbon he would return to England and then proceed to India. But it was not to be. He sickened on the voyage to Lisbon and was compelled to return to England. There was some delay owing to the non-arrival of the man-of-war which was ordered to convey him to England. But on the 28th of September, 1806, he sailed on H. M. S. "Illustrious" and on the 21st of October he landed at Topsham and the next day was carefully driven to Exeter and taken to the house of his friend, Archdeacon Moore, whose dwelling was in the Cathedral Close. He was too ill to make the journey to Wolford, and on the following Sunday, the 26th, the General passed away.

The remains of the General were embalmed and kept in Exeter until the 4th of November in order that the funeral arrangements might be perfected. His funeral was an imposing one and every mark of respect was paid by the citizens and by the military authorities. The burial took place at Wolford, fourteen miles from Exeter, and the old Roman road over which the cortege passed was lined by the volunteer militia of Devon. At the third mile of the journey a squadron of dragoons were drawn up and escorted the remains to Wolford. The regulars stationed at Exeter were unable to take part owing to the fact that there was a Parliamentary election in progress and during such an event the military were not allowed in the constituency. Reaching Wolford at six o'clock in the evening, the burial was by torchlight in the presence of his widow and family and the leading men of the county. The remains were interred at the east end of the private chapel, which had been erected by the General.

CHAPTER III.

COURTSHIP AND MARRIAGE.

Lieutenant-Colonel Simcoe after his return in 1781 from the American campaign, spent some days in London with the authorities of the War Office. During that summer he journeyed to Exeter and resolved that Devon, the county in which he had so many friends and connections, should be his permanent home.

There is no correspondence in the manuscripts at Wolford to show whether his mother, to whom he was devoted, was alive at the

BUCKERALL PARISH CHURCH, DEVON.
(From a Drawing in the J. Ross Robertson collection.)

time of his return. Nor is there any record of her death to be found in the registers of the Cathedral or of any of the churches of Exeter, although diligent search for entries has been made by the writer. The impression amongst the Devon connections of the family—all by marriage—is that Mrs. Simcoe died in Exeter shortly before the return of her son from the United States.

After his return the Colonel was not in the best of health. The strenuous activities of military life in the American campaign had told severely on his physique. He had not fully recovered from the effects of a wound he had received at the Battle of Brandywine; and, therefore, a quiet life and perfect rest were prescribed by his physician. He loved the balmy air of Devon and enjoyed short visits to the country houses of friends, who delighted to welcome him; for he had a happy and amiable disposition, and was an entertaining conversationalist.

BUCKERALL CHURCH—INTERIOR.

(From a Drawing in the J. Ross Robertson collection.)

But there was one country home where his presence gave more than ordinary pleasure. It was Hembury Fort, some miles from Honiton. Here on the site of this old Roman encampment resided two old friends of his father, A d m i r a l and Mrs. Graves. The Admiral was his godfather, and out of respect and deep regard for that officer, Captain S i m c o e, R.N., had given his son " Graves " as one of his Christian names. Mrs. Graves was a sister-in-law of C o l o n e l Gwillim of " Old Court " in Herefordshire.

On the first of these visits, in the spring of 1782, Colonel Simcoe met Miss Gwillim. It is said to have been a case of love at first sight. She was then sixteen, petite, fair to see, bright and entertaining, and attractive in manner. The Colonel, now in his thirtieth year, renewed his visits; and in this case the course of true love ran absolutely smooth, for the engagement followed, but no date for the wedding was fixed.

Mrs. Graves naturally thought that sixteen was rather an early age for her niece to assume the responsibilities of married life, but whatever objections she offered were evidently overcome, for Samuel Graves and Margaret Graves were witnesses to Simcoe's marriage at Buckerall Parish Church, on the 30th of December, 1782, which was solemnized by the Rev. Thomas Rosskilly, Curate of the Parish.

The marriage certificate reads:—

"No. 60—Lieutenant-Colonel John Graves Simcoe of this Parish and Miss Elizabeth Posthuma Gwillim of this Parish were married in this church by License this 30th Day of December in the Year One Thousand Seven Hundred and Eighty-two by me, Thos. Rosskilly, Curate. This Marriage was solemnized between Us, John Graves Simcoe, Elizabeth Posthuma Gwillim, in the Presence of Saml. Graves, Margaret Graves."

MARRIAGE OF COLONEL SIMCOE

Where the honeymoon was spent does not appear in the Wolford MSS., but the Colonel and his wife after marriage resided in Exeter. The Colonel felt that Devonshire was really his native county. He had practically lived in it for twenty-three years from 1759, when his mother and his brother Percy left Cotterstock, after the death of his father. With this idea in his mind he determined to settle down in some congenial spot, of which there are so many in Devon, the most charming of all the English counties.

His wife felt as he did, and her fortune made it possible to realize this desire. Accordingly in 1784 Wolford and the surrounding estate were bought by Mrs. Simcoe from the heirs of Peter Geneste. But it was not until 1788 that they made Wolford their permanent residence, after improvements in the house had been made.

THE SIMCOE MARRIAGE CERTIFICATE.
(From Register of Buckerall Parish Church.)

Shortly after the marriage, the College of Arms, on application, authorized the arms here depicted to be borne by Colonel and Mrs. Simcoe, viz., Dexter, Simcoe—Azure a fesse wavy Ermine between two stars of twelve points in chief and a cannon barwise in base or, Sinister, Gwillim—Argent, a Lion rampant, Ermines, collared Or. Crest, Simcoe:—Out of a naval crown Or a demi Sea Lion proper holding in his fore fin a dagger erect Argent the pomel and hilt gold and on his shoulder a Rose Gules barbed and seeded proper as hereon depicted.

Mrs. Simcoe was entitled to a large number of quarterings and at a subsequent date some of these were added to the arms borne by the Colonel and his wife. An explanation of the later arms is:—The arms in the first and fourth quarters are those of Simcoe. The arms

31

in the second and third quarters have not been identified by the College of Arms, London, England, and there is nothing in the College to show that Colonel Simcoe was entitled to make use of this quartering. With regard to the smaller shield—the first quarter is an incorrect representation of the Gwillim arms. The second, consisting of four lions and crosses, represent the Spinckes arms. The third quarter contains the arms of Stuart—Or a fesse chequy argent and azure, a bordure, ermine; and the arms in the fourth quarter of the smaller shield are those of Elmes—Ermine two bars sable each charged with five elm leaves or.

SIMCOE-GWILLIM ARMS, 1787.

SIMCOE-GWILLIM ARMS, 1792.

From 1783-7 the Colonel and his wife lived at St. Stephen's in Exeter, and in January, 1784, Eliza, their first child, was born. Then in August, 1785, at St. David's in Exeter, Charlotte, the second child, arrived, and in April of 1787, the third child, Henrietta, another daughter. The first child born at Wolford was Caroline in November of 1788, followed by Sophia, another daughter, in October of 1789. The sixth child, the first boy, Francis Gwillim, was born in June, 1791, some months before the departure of the Colonel and his wife for Canada.

The Exeter *Flying Post* of Thursday, June 9, 1791, announces the birth as follows:—"Monday, the Lady of Colonel Simcoe was safely delivered of a son and heir, at their seat, at Wolford Lodge, near Honiton."

The Colonel devoted his entire time for the first few years to re-organizing and improving his estate. Wolford, which was a small but well-built house, was remodelled. A new dwelling was built in front of the old-time farmhouse. Every convenience for those days was introduced; roadways were laid out through different parts of the estate, which covered about 5,000 acres; and under the direction of Colonel Simcoe and his active and well-informed manager, Mr. John Scadding, many valuable improvements were made. Mr. Scadding was the father of the late Rev. Henry Scadding, D.D., grand-uncle of Dr. H. Crawford Scadding, of Toronto.

All this delighted Mrs. Simcoe. She had a direct interest in the work of improvement, and it was at her suggestion that many of the acres, thickly wooded to-day, were planted and improved.

Mrs. Simcoe, as has been said, was of a vivacious disposition. She was fond of gaiety. Wolford in 1789 became the centre of attraction in that part of the county. The house had ample accommodation for visitors, and never a week passed without all its guest-chambers being filled.

Mrs. Simcoe had inherited all the Gwillim wealth and it was liberally spent, not only in improving the estate but in making life enjoyable in the manor house. She had a great admiration for her husband and was especially pleased when in 1790 he entered Parliament as the representative of St. Maw's in Cornwall.

WOLFORD, NEAR HONITON, DEVON.
(From a Drawing in the J. Ross Robertson collection.)

But a change in their lives came when the British Government decided in the summer of 1791 that it would require Colonel Simcoe's services immediately as the first Lieutenant-Governor of the new Province of Upper Canada. All plans for the coming winter were summarily disposed of, for arrangements had to be promptly made for the journey to Canada. Mrs. Simcoe and the Colonel went to London, the former to arrange for her outfit, the latter to interview the authorities at the War Office and receive his final instructions.

Then came the question of the children—which of the six could be taken to Canada. Eliza was seven years of age, Charlotte six, Henrietta four, Caroline three, Sophia two, and Francis Gwillim was only three months old. Mrs. Simcoe would have liked to take all her little ones with her, but that was impossible.

Fortunately, however, there were two old friends, Mrs. and Miss Hunt, in whom the Colonel and his wife had the greatest confidence and in whose care at Wolford they determined to leave the four eldest, Eliza, Charlotte, Henrietta and Caroline, taking Sophia and Francis to Canada. Mrs. Simcoe returned from London in the beginning of September and most energetically directed the packing and looked forward with pleasure to the days to be spent in the new world.

The story of Mrs. Simcoe's life from the day she with her husband left Wolford and sailed in H. M. S. "Triton" from Weymouth, cannot be told better than it is written in her diary. Some incidents of her life in Canada not given in the diary will be found in subsequent chapters.

When in 1759, her father, Captain Gwillim, ascended with General Wolfe the rugged path that led to the heights of Abraham, little did he think that thirty-two years later his daughter would give to future generations of Canadians pictures of places in the new land that he and his companions were winning for the Empire. But the daring and resolute soldier of Wolfe transmitted to his daughter not only the courageous qualities that had been necessary to win this new land for Britain, but also the foresight and the genius by which she has preserved by pen and pencil the spirit both of the natural scenery and the social life of the New Britain that was being planted.

CHAPTER IV.

FAREWELL TO WOLFORD.

The air at Wolford was filled with loving farewells as Colonel Simcoe, his wife, his children and attendants left one of the happiest of England's homes to face the perils of an Atlantic voyage. For a week before their departure the county people had called to say good-bye, and wish the new Governor and his wife a safe voyage to their colonial home in the western continent.

Wolford had during the few years of residence by the Simcoes been the most hospitable of all the country houses in that part of

NORTH VIEW OF WEYMOUTH IN 1788.
(From a Drawing in the Broadley collection.)

Devon. Its guest chambers were never without an occupant, and the reception days of Mrs. Simcoe had a welcome and a charm for the large circle of friends who had the pleasure of being entertained there.

Colonel Simcoe's name was a household word, not only in county families, but in military circles in Devon and Cornwall, and as a Devon chronicle writer says, "more distinguished men than ever dined under one roof in Devon were often found at Colonel Simcoe's table."

The afternoon of Thursday, 17th September, 1791, was fixed for the journey to Weymouth, from which port they were to sail. The luggage—and there was plenty of it—had been sent forward on Wednesday. On Saturday morning, the 17th, the party arrived at

DIARY OF MRS. SIMCOE

Weymouth and in a few hours were comfortably settled in lodgings which faced the esplanade and the bay.

Weymouth is a well known port in Dorset, on the English Channel south of Dorchester, on a bay at the mouth of the river Wey. The river separates the two quarters of the town. Old Weymouth is on the south side and Melcombe Regis faces the bay on the north. The sands are extensive and there is a magnificent esplanade. George III. after his serious illness in 1788 found the place an excellent health resort and visited it nearly every year between 1788-1805. He resided at Gloucester House, built by the Duke of Gloucester and bought by the King. Owing to the King's visits the town soon attained considerable social prominence.

Colonel and Mrs. Simcoe thoroughly enjoyed the days spent in Weymouth before sailing in the "Triton" frigate which lay anchored in the bay awaiting the embarkation of its distinguished passengers. The first entry in Mrs. Simcoe's diary was made on the day of her arrival in Weymouth.

Weymouth, Saturday, 17th Sept., 1791—We arr'ved at Weymouth. I walked with Lady Collier on the Esplanade in the evening.

NOTE.—Lady Collier was Elizabeth Fryer, second wife of Sir George Collier, whom he married in 1781. He was Senior Naval Officer, Halifax, July, 1776-9, and in 1780 commanded the "Canada."

Sunday 18th—Went to church with Lady Collier and to the Rooms in the evening. The King looked very well.

NOTE.—Robert Huish (1777-1850) in his "King George III." writes:

"The time of His Majesty was chiefly occupied at Weymouth in receiving the formal address of the corporation or the visits of the nobility and gentry of the vicinity, and partly on horseback, rambling over the hills and downs or walking on the esplanade amidst respectful joyous groups of his loyal subjects. The Sabbath day was always passed in the offices of religion, the royal family walking to church without parade or ceremony, the service of the day always ending with 'God Save the King.'"

GEORGE III.

Mr. A. M. Broadley, of Bridport, Eng., informs me that the "Weymouth Rooms" patronized by the Royal Family were those known as "Stacey's," formerly part of the Royal Hotel, which can be clearly seen in the earlier pictures and engravings of Weymouth (1789-91) of which he possesses a large collection. The "Royal" spoken of by Dr. Wolcot in his satire "Weymouth Amusements" (1795), was pulled down several years ago and has been replaced by a modern building.

36

GAVEL-KIND IN PORTLAND ISLE

Mon. 19th—I went to Portland Island, a rock peninsula of Dorsetshire, connected with the mainland, with Lady de la Pole, wife of Sir John de la Pole, and went round the Island in a cart, the conveyance generally used on those rough roads. The sea views are very fine. There is an uncommon aperture in the land in one spot, where we looked down as if into a vast well and saw the waves dashing below. We drove by the lighthouse. There are some buildings in ruins covered with ivy which have a very picturesque appearance. We stopped to take some refreshment after the drive at one of the largest villages in the island, where we tasted Portland mutton. The inhabitants of the island have laws and regulations peculiar to themselves. For instance, there is an official of the island called a Reeve. He collects rent and has a staff called the Reeve Staff, a very long stick on which payments are recorded in notches cut on the face of the stick. In buying and selling land the buyer and the seller go to the church, and sign a register before witnesses. They call it a Church Gift. It's very simple—no writings or parchment used, no lawyers consulted. We crossed a very narrow passage to the island, but it is sometimes very rough.

NOTE.—The Isle of Portland, really a peninsula, though generally called an island, is in Dorset, south of Weymouth, projecting into the English Channel and terminating in the Bill of Portland. It is four and a half miles long and about two miles wide and nine in circumference. It is connected with the mainland at Abbotsbury by the shifting Chesil Beach, a narrow ridge of gravel and shingle ten and a half miles long. This peninsula is practically a great bed of stone, first used in the reign of James I. The stone is quarried in blocks of three to fourteen tons each. St. Paul's Cathedral and other great structures were built of stone from these quarries. Portland is a "liberty" of itself, and the custom of "gavel-kind" prevails, which is an old land tenure in England still in vogue in Kent, by which land descends to all the sons in equal shares.

In Portland service of lawyers is not necessary in connection with the sale and purchase of land. The ordinary method of conveyance is almost unknown in Portland. This is done by what is called a Church Gift, a form used for the purchase from time immemorial. The buyer and seller go to the church and in the church is a register. The Church Gift is signed in presence of two witnesses who must be " Tenants " of the Manor. The deed is called a Church Gift instead of a common law conveyance.

One of the officials of the Island of Portland is called the Reeve. His duty for his year of office is to collect the Chief or Quit rent. He holds the office for one year only and never for a second term. A new Reeve is appointed annually by the Court Leet, which is held twice a year, in May and November. A woman or a man may hold the office. Men and women have had equal rights in Portland, long before any Married Woman's Property Act was passed by Parliament giving women their rights. This has been the case in Portland from time immemorial and women make wills and hold offices and buy and sell property quite apart from their husbands.

The duty of the Reeve for his year of office is to collect the Quit

Rent or Chief Rent which is due to the Lord
of the Manor, who in this Manor is the King
or Queen, this being a Royal Manor. The
Quit Rent is an annual payment at the rate
of three pence per acre to the Lord of the
Manor by landowners in the Island for their
private lands as distinct from Crown Lands
and Common or Parish lands. Every such
landowner is called a "tenant" of the
Manor, but the private lands are treated as
freehold notwithstanding this annual payment to the Chief. On the death of a tenant
there becomes due to the Chief a payment
of 2/6 which is paid out of the lands owned
at his death. There are three kinds of
land, viz.: The Crown lands, Private lands
and Commonable or Parish lands, the latter
belonging to the King and the tenants, and
in which the tenants have equal rights with
the King.

The Reeve Staff or Stick is the record of
the payment of this Quit Rent and is of
Saxon origin. It is a stick from ten to
twelve feet long and one and a half inches
square. Payments are represented by
notches cut across the face of the stick. A
deep notch cut across the whole side of the
face represents one shilling. A notch half
way across represents sixpence, a lighter and
not so deep a notch across the whole face
represents a penny. A notch the same depth
as the last named half way across the stick
represents a halfpenny, and a quarter across,
one farthing. No one pays less than a
farthing, but it is easy to see that an acre
may be so divided as to make many owners
who would pay one farthing each. This was
the custom before books for keeping accounts
were in vogue. It is done every year, but in
these modern days books are kept as well.
Each Reeve prepares a new Staff and retains
it as his own—as the stick he used during
his term of office.

The Chief or Quit rent is paid on private lands only. The total amount has stood
at £14 14s. 3d. from time immemorial and
although by the sub-division of land the

A REEVE STAFF

Reeve collects more, only this sum is paid over to the Chief. No
question is asked and so the extra amount goes into the pocket of the

SOCIAL FUNCTIONS AT WEYMOUTH

Reeve. The payment proper to the Reeve is £1 per year. Formerly he had no money payment, but had the use of a piece of land for the year. This piece of land is called the " Reeve Plot."

VIEW OF WEYMOUTH, LOOKING WEST, 1791.

Showing (A) Gloucester Lodge, (B) Stacey's Hotel Rooms.

(From a Water-color in the Broadley collection.)

The picture of a Reeve Staff is from a drawing kindly made for me by Mr. B. O. Pearce, an Ex-Reeve, prominent in business circles in Portland. He also furnished the information in this note concerning the peculiar customs of Portland and the use of the Reeve Staff.

BARON GRENVILLE.

Mon. 19th—I dined with Lady de la Pole at Stacey's Hotel on the Esplanade, and went in the evening to see the play of "As You Like It," which was very well performed. Col. Simcoe dined with Lord Grenville.

NOTE.—This conclusively proves Mr. Broadley's contention as to Stacey's Rooms existing in 1791. They were quite close to Gloucester Lodge. Lady de la Pole was the wife of the sixth Baronet.

George William Wyndham—Baron Grenville (1759-1834), Home Secretary, 1789-90 and Secretary of State for Foreign Affairs 1791-1801 in Pitt's administration.

Tues. 20th—I was tired with writing, and did not go to the ball.

Wed 21st—The Chancellor, Edward, Lord Thurlow, is gone into Flintshire.

DIARY OF MRS. SIMCOE

The sealers, those officials who prepare documents for sealing in the Lord Chancellor's department, are following with Gov. Simcoe's commission, but not having yet overtaken him, we are detained here and complaining of losing a fine east wind. We give two and a half guineas a week for a very small lodging. I could not go to Lullworth Cove to-day lest the Commission should arrive, in which case we are to sail immediately.

NOTE.—Thurlow, Edward, first Baron Thurlow (1731-1806), Lord Chancellor, 1778, prepared a celebrated report on the Quebec Bill which was quoted at length in Christie's History. He intrigued with George, Prince of Wales, against Pitt, and was obliged to resign in 1792. His political principles were merely a high view of royal prerogative and an aversion to change. It was of him that Macaulay said, "I wonder if any man ever was as wise as Thurlow looks."

Lullworth Cove is a beautiful inlet in the English Channel, almost landlocked, deep and narrow with lofty cliffs, and very fine scenery. It is a few miles from Weymouth, and is usually visited

BARON THURLOW. by excursionists.

Thur. 22nd—Intelligence is received that the Chancellor is gone to Cumberland.

Fri. 23rd—I was pleased with a camera obscura I saw fixed in the top of a room. I bought a wooden pentograph, an instrument for the mechanical copying of engravings, diagrams and plans. The Misses Rolle, members of Lord Rolle's family (a Devonshire nobleman) are here and very civil to me. I went five miles with Lady Poulett and her children in her Sociable (a carriage of the period), and dined with her.

NOTE.—Henry Rolle was created Baron Rolle of Stevastone in January, 1747, and died without issue in 1759. His nephew John Rolle eventually succeeded to the Stevastone property. He was M.P. for Devonshire, 1780-4, 1790, and was a staunch adherent of Pitt. In 1796 he was created Baron Rolle of Stevastone. He died without issue in April, 1842. The "Misses Rolle" were Isabella Harriot Charlotte, born 1754, and Florence, born 1762.

Fri. 23rd—In the evening we walked on the esplanade. The Royal family came and spoke to Lady P., and the Princess Royal carried Lady Mary Poulett, daughter of the Earl, a heavy child three years old, the whole length of the esplanade.

NOTE.—Princess Charlotte Augusta Matilda, born 29th September, 1766, eldest daughter of George III., (1738-1820) married in 1797, her

PRINCESS OF WURTEMBURG.

cousin Frederick William Charles, Duke of Wurtemburg, who subsequently became King of Wurtemburg. He formed an alliance with

40

MRS. SIMCOE MEETS KING GEORGE.

Napoleon in 1805, his army fighting for Napoleon for several years, but eventually joining the allies in 1813.

Lady Mary Poulett was the second daughter of John, the fourth Earl Poulett, by Sophia his wife, daughter and heir of Admiral Sir George Pocock, K.B. Lady Mary in 1821 became the second wife of Lord Charles Henry Somerset.

Sat. 24th—I walked on the sands with Coll. Simcoe before breakfast. We met the King. He asked me whether I left my children at school, how I should like being at sea, &c. I was not well and dined at home. Sir de la Pole sent me landrails. My French cook dressed them without taking out the inside, and I found a shell as large as a nut in one of them. I thought they lived by suction. How could this be?

LADY POULETT.

NOTE.—The Landrail or Corncrake, a migratory bird, leaves England before the winter, and repairs to other countries in search of food. It appears in England the latter end of April.

Sun. 25th—I was at the Rooms to-night, and met Capt. Sydney Smith. He wore a handsome star given him by the King of Sweden, in whose service he distinguished himself. He is thought to be like Charles the Twelfth of Sweden. His countenance reminded me of pictures of some great men in Elizabeth's reign—a marked countenance, expressing the reverse of a trifling character.

The whole of this day it blew so heavy a gale that the "Triton," the ship on which we are to sail for Canada, was obliged to go out to sea, it being dangerous to remain at anchor. From Lady de la Pole's windows in this hotel, where I dine, the waves looked tremendous. The scene was grand, but, as the Queen (Charlotte) observed this evening, was "mixed with too much horror to be pleasing."

NOTE.—Sir William Sydney Smith (1764-1840) a naval officer who entered the Navy in 1777, became captain in 1782, knighted

in 1792. He was captured off Havre by the French in 1796, imprisoned in Paris for two years, escaped in 1798, and in 1799 undertook the defence of St. Jean d'Acre. In March, 1799, he captured the French vessels and held the town until the siege was raised. He died in 1840.

Sun. 25th—I dined yesterday, 24th, at Sir G. Collier's, with Capt. Murray. of the "Triton," who appears a very gentlemanly man, and his hav-

SIR GEORGE MURRAY.

SIR SYDNEY SMITH

ing the reputation of being an excellent officer is a great consolation to us who are about to sail in so late a season for a northern climate. Sir J. Jervoise is the only man who tells Coll. Simcoe that he is certain of making his passage at this time of the year. Others think it is too late,

DIARY OF MRS. SIMCOE

but he is a man of knowledge in nautical affairs, and, therefore, his opinion is to be trusted to.

The King asked Capt. Murray about his stock of provisions for the voyage, and hoped he had prepared for making my passage as comfortable as possible to me.

NOTE.—Sir George Murray, 1759-1819, Vice-Admiral, of a younger branch of the Elibank family. His actual services in the Navy probably began about 1772 when he joined the "Panther" on the Newfoundland station. He was afterwards in the "Romney," the flagship of Rear Admiral John Montague, on the same station. In 1792 he was appointed to the "Triton" frigate, and afterwards to the "Nymphe." In 1807, he was appointed commander-in-chief of the naval operations against Buenos Ayres. On 25th October, 1809, he was promoted to be a Vice-Admiral, was nominated a K.C.B. on 2nd January, 1815, and died suddenly at Chichester on 28th February, 1819.

EARL ST. VINCENT.

John Jervoise (Jervis), Earl St. Vincent, the first Viscount, was born at Meaford, Staffordshire, 17th January, 1734. He entered the navy in his tenth year, led the advanced squadron in charge of transport past Quebec, was entrusted by Wolfe with his last message to his betrothed, 1759, and was a personal friend of Captain John Simcoe, R. N., father of Governor Simcoe. He became admiral of the blue and commander of the naval forces in the Mediterranean in 1795, and in consequence of his victory over the Spanish fleet off Cape St. Vincent in February, 1797, was raised to the peerage. In 1821 he became admiral of the fleet.

CHAPTER V.

THE GOVERNOR AND SUITE EMBARK.

Mrs. Simcoe's description of the trip from Weymouth to the New World forms an interesting commentary upon the ocean travel of a century ago. Long was the voyage and great was the discomfort even upon the "Triton," which compared most favorably with the usual sailing craft of the day. With wind as the only motive power, the man-of-war which bore the Simcoe party towards the West took forty-six days upon a voyage which the fleet liner of to-day would make in less than five. And the gain in comfort has been no less marked.

However, Mrs. Simcoe was possessed of an industry which prevented her long passage from being irksome. Much of the time she spent in reading and writing. Every incident of importance found its way into her record. The vessel's speed and weather conditions were, of course, sedulously jotted down by the diarist; there is mention of the rare passing vessels; while the description of the routine life upon an eighteenth century warship has a peculiar interest to the luxury-loving traveller of to-day.

When land was sighted, the Captain's chart was always consulted and every point of land that had a name found a place in her daily writings. She certainly had a traveller's mind, with powers of observation that added to her voyage pleasure both for herself and for the friends to whom she wrote.

Mon. 26th Sept.—Wind east, blowing fresh, fine and clear. It became calm this morning, and at one o'clock p.m. we embarked on board His Majesty's frigate "Triton," 28 guns, Captain Murray. Capt. Stevenson accompanied us, and Lt. Grey, a son of Sir Charles Grey's, for whom Coll. Simcoe requested a passage, who is going to join the Fusiliers or the 7th Regt. at Quebec, the regiment of which Prince Edward is Colonel.

SIR CHARLES GREY.

I became giddy as soon as I entered the ship and went to my cabin, an apartment just large enough to swing a cot, which I immediately got into. On leaving Weymouth and in going through a surf called the Portland Race, one of the port hole windows was stove in, and the gentlemen at dinner were quite wet.

NOTE.—Sir Charles Grey, first Earl Grey, 1729-1807, a General in the Army, was conspicuous for his services to the King in the American Revolution. He was created Earl Grey and Viscount Howick in 1806. Earl Grey, the present Governor-General of Canada, is the fourth bearer of the title, and is directly descended from Sir Charles Grey. Lieutenant Thomas Grey, who sailed with

DIARY OF MRS. SIMCOE

Governor Simcoe, was fifth son of Sir Charles Grey, was lieutenant-colonel of the 12th Regiment of Foot, which embarked for the East Indies, 8th June, and anchored in Table Bay, 19th September, 1796. The regiment was in bad health while in Table Bay, so Grey was probably left behind when it sailed on the following 10th of November. He retired by sale of his commission, 1st December, 1796, and died at the Cape of Good Hope, 17th January, 1797, unmarried.

Tues. 27th—East, fresh and fine. Went before the wind at 9 knots an hour.

Wed. 28th—East, fresh and fine. Went upon deck. Our hours are early. We breakfast at 8; dine at 2, and never take any supper.

Sunday, Oct. 2nd—Calm.

Mon. 3rd—Rough.

Tues. 4th—I got the better of my sickness yesterday, but there blew so strong a gale of wind that I was obliged to remain in my cot or in a corner behind the stove in the great cabin, to secure myself from falling. It was by persevering to go on deck and by eating salt beef, covered with mustard, that I soon became well. As my health amends my spirits rise, and I am rather diverted at the difficulties we meet with at dinner, when, in spite of all care, the dishes are often tossed to every corner of the room. The ship not having sufficient ballast makes her roll so unreasonably. I think I have great merit in beginning to write to you this early, in spite of rough weather. The children (Francis and Sophia) are well, but never appear to be safe except when in their cots, for the nurses are much indisposed and have very indifferent sea legs. I am learning to walk on deck, but cannot yet do it without leaning on the arm of a gentleman. Capt. Murray, who has been in France, plays at reverse, the French card game, with us. Sophia's amusement is seeing the poultry on deck, where a little midshipman carries her every day. The wind has for several days driven us to the southward of our course. It begins to blow hard again, so I must retire to my cot.

Wed. 5th—Calm. Went five knots an hour.

Thur. 6th—Went six knots an hour.

Fri. 7th—We saw porpoises.

Sat. 8th—Calm and fine. It is expected we shall see the Azores or Western Isles to-morrow night.

Sun. 9th—Hot and fine. We rose from dinner at three o'clock to see a ship pass. She was the " Minerva," of London, from New York to Malaga, a Spanish port on the Mediterranean. I admired the sight as she sailed close to us. She did not give any intelligence. At 10 p.m. an island was seen.

Mon. 10th—Fine, very hot. The heat was so excessive I could not sleep, and rose at 6 o'clock to look at the island, which was Corvo, the most northerly of the Azores. The mist presently dispersing, we saw Flores, the westernmost island of the Azores, where, in 1591, Sir Richard Grenville, in a small man-of-war, held the "Revenge," held at bay fifteen Spanish warships till his own was but a wreck. The atmosphere far from clear. Corvo is extremely high land, lat. 39, Corvo S.S.E., 3 leagues.

Coll. Simcoe has been reading " L'Histoire Generale de la Nouvelle France," by Francois Xavier Charlevoix, the French Jesuit traveller, who twice visited Canada and sailed down the Mississippi to New Orleans, and who says that Corvo was discovered by a Portuguese, who found it uninhabited, but saw an equestrian statue on a pedestal, of what metal made he knew not; but there was an inscription on it which was not legible. The right hand of the finger pointed to the west.

The Western Isles are inhabited by Portuguese, who are fond of buying black clothes whenever ships call there, which they frequently do to

44

take in water, and which we should have done had not the lateness of the season in which we quitted England made it necessary not to lose an hour on the passage, as we are doubtful of reaching Quebec before the St. Lawrence is filled with ice.

I should have liked to have gone on shore here, as the climate is said to be delightful and the islands abounding in grapes, oranges, melons, chestnuts, etc. No boats came to us with fruits, and they rarely fish beyond their harbour on account of the heavy squalls to which the coast is subject, which endangers their being blown out to sea. From the description of the islands I would like to make a voyage here instead of going to Tunbridge Wells (in England) or other watering places, where people frequently tire or weary themselves. The scheme would be more enlarged, and I believe much more amusing. Being at sea in good weather is delightful, and there is no occasion to execute such a voyage in the equinoxial season.

Tues. 11th—Wind light, very hot and contrary. A ship on her larboard tack was seen last night; we, being on the starboard, did not speak with her. I rose this morning at three o'clock and looked at the constellation of Orion and its stars in great brightness. The heat is excessively oppressive, though we have the windows open all night.

Wed. 12th—I copied some prints of ships Capt. Murray lent me. An American vessel was seen.

Thurs. 13th—Fine. A sail passed this morning, supposed to be an English 44 guns. At noon a Portuguese vessel was seen.

Fri. 14th—Very hard gale this morning. The sea ran mountains high. I sat on deck and saw the men reefing the sails. Their situation appeared tremendous. Mr. Benge, the Purser, gave Coll. Simcoe an account of his having been twice wrecked on the 14th October, which made him rather distrust his safety on this anniversary. He was on the "Deal Castle" when she and seventeen ships were lost on the Spanish main. She was carried by a violent gale of wind over a high rock, and struck on the sands. At two in the morning her bottom stove in, but she did not sink till after daylight, when all the men except seventeen got on shore on rafts. The account of such perils during such weather was not very amusing to us.

NOTE.—On the 10th of October, 1780, a dreadful hurricane commenced on the island of Barbadoes, and continued without intermission for forty-eight hours. Ships were driven from their anchors, the capital of the island was destroyed, and the inhabitants were compelled to take refuge in cellars. Many were killed by falling buildings, and on the following day there was not a house in the island that had escaped damage, many of them were levelled to the ground, and the loss of life amounted to thousands. Many of the ships moored at St. Lucia were driven out to sea. The "Andromeda," 28 guns, and the "Deal Castle," 24 guns, were lost on the coast of Martinique, while the "Thunderer," among other vessels, was never heard of again, and the exact place of their loss was never ascertained.

Sat. 15th—Wind N.W.. cold, hard gale. This hard gale did not cool the cabins, which had been so extremely heated; I was, therefore, glad to be on deck to get rid of the headache, notwithstanding the weather was so rough that I was obliged to hold fast by a cannon. The waves, rising like mountains, have the grandest and most terrific appearance, and when the ship dashes with violence into the sea, much as a chaise in the act of overturning, it is surprising that she rights again. I viewed this tempestuous scene with astonishment.

DIARY OF MRS. SIMCOE

Sun. 16th—A very stiff gale. Fine weather makes me very happy, but when it blows hard this abode is certainly horrid beyond the imagination of those who have not experienced it. The noises on board a ship, till one becomes accustomed to them, almost deprive one of one's senses; in bad weather they are doubled; every place wet and dirty, besides being bruised by sudden motions of the ship and half drowned by leaks in the cabin. The gale has to-day been stiff and contrary. Two days since we expected to have been ere this catching cod on the banks of Newfoundland, and now we are far off. Those who are of a sanguine temper think we may get to New York; others foresee that we shall be driven to Barbadoes, where we must pass the winter, and in May sail for Antigua to refit.

Coll. Simcoe is the only person who supposes it possible to reach Quebec. It will be so late before we come into the River St. Lawrence that the pilots will probably have quitted the Isle of Bic, an island in the river near Rimouski, below Quebec, and the master of the "Triton" cannot carry her up without a pilot. In this case we must return to the Gulph, and the season being too severe to keep in a northern latitude, we must steer for Barbadoes, and there shall meet with millions of those black beetles I so much detest, those *verdaderos ninos d'eponomon*—lizards, centipedes and scorpions besides: *Desdichada de mi que tengo de ayer?* (I miserable, what have I of yesterday?)

After being amused during the day by a description of those vile reptiles, the evening proved so rough and dismal that everybody sat melancholy and unoccupied. I learnt a hymn in the *Spectator*, happening to open the book where there was one applicable to our present situation. I then sat myself down to copy pictures of ships, and by perseverance and determined opposition to unfavourable circumstances I finished six pretty correctly. My cot striking against the side of the cabin most uncomfortably, Coll. Simcoe thought of the method used by the ancients to lessen the force of battering rams by hanging up feather beds to receive them. This device made the cot slide up and down very easily.

NOTE.—Addison's *Spectator*—the first number of this periodical was published in March, 1711, and the last on the 20th December, 1714. The *Spectator* newspaper was not published till 1828.

Mon. 17th—We saw porpoises.

Tues. 18th—A pleasant morning. At 12 a sudden gale of wind arose, and while I was engaged in a game of Piquet, the French card game much played in England, with Capt. Murray, a lee lurch threw me to the side of the cabin against the fender. I was vexed at the accident, though not hurt, having piqued myself on having been so expert as always to have avoided falling.

Wed. 19th—A brig seen. A shag (or green cormorant) with a red bill was seen. Wind variable.

Thurs. 20th—Wind moderate. We are 130 leagues from Newfoundland. This distance we have kept these last five days. I began to draw a map of the Genesee River, New York State—falls into Lake Ontario.

NOTE.—Mrs. Simcoe was very fond of drawing maps. One of her maps of Upper Canada, about four feet square, is preserved at Wolford. It is very accurately drawn.

Fri. 21st—Very hard gale. A tempestuous night. It rained upon my bed, but a thick greatcoat covered me, and I slept well. This ship is a good sea boat, but so leaky in her upper works that the floor of my cabin is scarcely ever dry, and the baize with which it is covered retains the wet. Therefore, I always wear clogs. Some shrouds were lost in this gale of wind.

MRS. SIMCOE'S LOVE OF BIRD LIFE

Sat. 22nd—N.E. hard gale.

Sun. 23rd—Wind N.E. Whales seen near the ship, and many birds, which are signs of being in soundings, though none can be obtained. As the sun has not been seen for some days no observation can be taken, and the compass is so bad a one that it traverses to all points in a gale of wind, so that the Master knows not where we are, or, in bad weather, what course we are going.

Mon. 24th—Wind N.E. Cold and clear. Number of gulls and shearwaters and Mother Carey's chickens flying about. They are a brown

A SNOWBIRD.
(From a Drawing by Mrs. Simcoe.)

bird with white spots, pretty and rather larger than a sparrow, a storm petrel, a little bird which frequents this part of the Atlantic. The shearwater is a bird measuring 15 inches in length, 31 inches in breadth. It has a black and yellow bill, white under wings and body, back and tail black, found on waters all over the world. Mother Carey is Mater Cara. The birds are called "Sailors'" friend; their appearance portends bad weather. To kill them is unlucky. Each bird is supposed, so legend says, to contain a soul of a dead sailor. At 12 o'clock we were in 75 fathoms of water. Cod, haddock and halibut were caught. A very cold night and rained into my cot.

Tues. 25th—N.W. wind excessive. No soundings since 12 last night. It is extraordinary to be out of them so soon. It is hoped we shall keep clear of Sable Island, 30 leagues east of Nova Scotia, which is frequently enveloped in fog, and, therefore, very dangerous. No trees grow on it, but there is plenty of wood from the frequent wrecks that are driven on its shores. It abounds with rats, snipe, and so forth.

Wed. 26th—Wind N.W. So extremely cold that I could not stay on deck without a fleecy, hosiery greatcoat on; a bird like a linnet and a

A CROSSBILL.
(From a Drawing by Mrs. Simcoe)

crossbill alighted on the rigging. It was out of the reach of land. I hoped to have kept it in my cabin, but it soon died. This bird is about the size of a lark and 7 inches in length. It has a peculiar bill, the upper and under mandibles curve in opposite directions and cross each other at the points. Its eyes are hazel, and its general colour reddish mixed green, but these birds are sometimes rose colour or yellowish green.

Thurs. 27th—Wind moderate. A beautiful owl, olive colour, with white spots and black about his face, was caught to-day. He was not larger than a thrush and not wild; also a bird the size of a lark.

Fri. 28th—Wind N.E. A fine morning, and we fortunately made the Isle of Sable, thirteen leagues N., only 8½ fathoms water, before 12 o'clock, when a very thick fog came on.

NOTE.—Sable Island is a small island off Nova Scotia, first sighted by Cabot in 1497, situated in the Atlantic Ocean, lying 110 miles southeast of Cape Canso, lat. 43° 58′ N., long. 59° 46′ W. It is

DIARY OF MRS. SIMCOE

deep, low and sandy, about 25 miles in length and surrounded by shoals and sandbanks, and known as "the ocean graveyard." In 1791 it was forty miles long; in 1890 it had been reduced to 25 miles. Cape Sable Island is the southwesternmost extremity of Nova Scotia and is frequently confused with Sable Island.

28th, p.m.—If it blow hard until to-morrow we hope to go through the Gut or Strait of Canso, a beautiful passage between Nova Scotia and Cape Breton from the Atlantic Ocean into Northumberland Strait, between high, rocky shores, and the shortest way to the Gulf of St. Lawrence. I am now reconciled to being at sea. I am well enough to work, write or draw; and sailing at the rate of 10 miles an hour without fatigue or trouble (which in this good weather is the case) is very pleasant. I should like to embark in summer, see various coasts, look into the harbours, and pass two or three months in this way. For example, come to Spanish River, on the Cape Breton Coast, where we hope shortly to be, and I am told is a pretty place, and I hope to visit Mrs. McCormick, wife of Lieut.-Col. McCormick, governor of the island of Cape Breton, to-morrow.

NOTE.—Spanish River is known to-day as Sydney Harbour.

Sat. 29th—Wind N.W. The wind against our going through the Gut of Canso. At 8 to-day we saw the coast of Nova Scotia. At 12 observed White Island, east of Liscomb Harbour. We saw American schooners. The white sails appeared very pretty to us who had been so long without seeing any objects, and the breakers along the coast, contrasted with some dark shores, had a good effect. We saw the Gut of Canso at a distance. At 4 we saw at the south end of Cape Breton, Richmond Island, so called in some charts, in others Isle Madame. We were very near it. It is a bold, perpendicular, dark red rock, shaded almost to black, and covered with pine, which looks richer than oak, and the conic shape when in maps looks well. Some large blasted pine, quite white, had a wild, fine effect. At the end of this island are rocks under water, which form fine breakers, dashing up a great height and sinking beneath the blue tide. A little distance from Richmond lies Green Island, a small, low, smooth, olive-coloured slip of land south of Isle Madame. Behind Richmond island is Arichat Harbour, on the west coast of Isle Madame, off the southern coast of Cape Breton, from whence we saw a schooner coming. Within half an hour she came up with us, but could not pilot us into Arichat harbour, or we should have anchored safely there and waited for an E. wind to carry us thro' the Gut of Canso, the passage between Nova Scotia and Cape Breton Island.

Coll. Simcoe quotes "there is a tide in the affairs of men," and says our losing the opportunity of going thro' the Gut of Canso makes him, for the first time, doubtful of reaching Quebec. He is particularly disappointed at not seeing this passage, as his father, Capt. John Simcoe, R.N., of the "Pembroke," proposed to the Admiralty to carry large ships through it, and would have gained much time by so doing. This advantage was lost, as his proposal was objected to by the officers, who were afraid to risk the passage. We are now beating about, not making much way or venturing to make more sail than will carry us 5 knots an hour during this night, lest we get among the numerous breakers hereabouts.

Sun. 30th—Wind W., clear and cold. Passed Louisbourg at seven this morning. Coll. Simcoe was very sorry he had not seen that harbour, so often mentioned in his father's papers. At ten we passed the Isle de Scatari, Lat. 46, long. 59, 45 W., off Cape Breton (near the entrance to Miré Bay). Then saw Cape Breton. At eleven made Flint Island and Cape Percé (north of Miré Bay). We passed Spanish River at 6 in the evening. I did not see it. Gov. McCormick lives there, and has a brig in which he goes to England.

48

OFF CAPE BRETON COAST

NOTE.—Flint Island is east of Cape Breton between North and South Head at the entrance of Cow Bay.

Governor Macormick, of Cape Breton, was appointed to that office October 11th, 1787, as successor to Des Barres, and in September of the following year, entertained at Sydney, the capital, Prince William Henry (afterwards William IV.), who had arrived there in his yacht the "Andromeda." Governor Macormick resigned on 27th May, 1795. He was a personal friend of Governor Simcoe and was frequently at Wolford.

Mon. 31st—Wind N.E. Snow. At eleven we passed Niganiche (Niganish) Island, off the east coast of Cape Breton, near Middle Head. At 12 Cape Nord, the N.E. extremity of the island of Cape Breton, which is

ISLAND OF ENTRY, 1791.

(From a Drawing by Mrs. Simcoe.)

broken into rifts and chasms, a very bold coast. There was a good deal of snow on the trees, and as it was still falling, together with fog, I saw but little. It had a wild appearance. Lat. 47, long. 42½. This place abounds with ducks.

NOTE.—In Bayfield's Admiralty charts Inganish Island is situated north of Middle Head, between North Bay and South Bay, lat. 46° 50′ on east coast of Cape Breton. It is sometimes spelled "Ingonish."

Tues. November 1st—Wind N.W. Cold. We saw the Magdalen Islands about the centre of the Gulf of St. Lawrence. They are uninhabited, and in summer frequented by sea cows. There is good duck shooting on them, and codfish near them, for which purpose an American schooner is now at anchor off one of them. At 12 saw Amherst Island, the south island of the Magdalen group, and afterwards to the north and east the Isle Entry, another of the group.

Wed. 2nd—Wind N.W., very cold. I saw Amherst Island in another point of view; also Deadman's Isle, which appears in shape like a ram.

4   49

DIARY OF MRS. SIMCOE

NOTE.—Deadman's Island is a small island to the west of the Magdalen group. In a French map of 1755 by Vangoudy, the island is given as "Isle de Corps Mort."

THE "LIBERTY."
(From a drawing by Mrs. Simcoe.)

Wed. 2nd—We met the "Liberty," of Whitby, bound to Portsmouth from Miscou (Misco) Harbour, in Miscou Island, at the entrance to the Bay of Chaleur, laden with plank. The "Liberty" informed us that the "Alligator," with Lord Dorchester on board, had put into Halifax the 7th of September, having sprung her bowsprit, and the "Penelope" was nearly being lost at the same time. Capt. Murray sent a boat on board the "Liberty," with letters for England. During the time we lay to, several codfish were caught. I like the chowder made of them very much. Coll. Simcoe has the gout in his hand.

NOTE.—Guy Carleton, who was created first Baron Dorchester in 1786, served in America from 1758 to 1762, and from 1766 to 1770, was acting Governor of Quebec. Upon his return to England in 1770, he advocated the passing of the Quebec Act and in 1775 returned as Governor of that province. For five months he successfully defended Quebec against the Americans, and in October of the same year, 1776, defeated them on Lake Champlain. In 1782-3 he was Commander-in-Chief in America. As Governor he resided in Quebec from 1786 to 1791, and as Governor-General from 1793 to July, 1796, when he returned to England.

LORD DORCHESTER.

Fri. 4th—Wind N.E. Dreadful gale and snowstorm; several men frost bit during the last night, which was the worst weather we have had. The ship pitched her forecastle under water continually. In the morning the Isle Bonaventure, just north-east and opposite the Percé Rock, on the Gaspé coast, was seen, but the wind being contrary they tacked all day and lost ground. We were under single reef courses the whole day. Coppers, or kettles from the ship's galley, are kept boiling night and day to thaw the tackle and ropes, which are continually freezing. The sailors have no clothing more than they would have on a West India voyage, and suffer severely. Had we been 8 leagues more to the northward, this wind would have served to carry us up the St. Lawrence River.

Sat. 5th—Wind N.W., moderate. N.W. during the day, but at night the wind came S.W., and we ran our course at the rate of 8 knots an hour. Isle Bonaventure was seen again.

Sun. 6th—Wind N.W. Passed Cap des Rosiers north of Cap Gaspé, in fine weather, but at 12 o'clock a most heavy gale of wind came on, which lasted till 12 at night, the highest sea and the roughest weather we have had. Two reefs in the foresail. Tacked all day and lost much ground. If this weather continues many hours we cannot weather it, but must be blown out of the river and go to New York, if we can, more probably to be blown to the West Indies, the men being so disabled by the frost and so many on the sick list that there are not enough to work the ship against adverse winds. The dinner overset, the tea things broke, but I eat broth without spilling it.

Mon. 7th—Wind moderate. Saw Anticosti Island. It's a large island in the estuary of the St. Lawrence.

Tues. 8th—Wind moderate, N.W., hard frost and clear. We saw part of the coast called in the chart Les Vallees, two rivers in Gaspé County falling into the Gulf of St. Lawrence. Tacked all day and made some way.

NOTE.—Called "Great and Little Valley" in chart of Gulf of St. Lawrence published by Robert Sayer, London, 1st August, 1785.

Wed. 9th—N.E. Clear and moderate. Saw Mons. Camille and Riviére Matane.

NOTE.—Mount Camille, in Rimouski County, is one of the highest mountains in Quebec, being about four thousand feet in height. River Matane, also in Rimouski County, rises in the Shickshock Mountains and falls into the Gulf of St. Lawrence.

ISLAND OF ANTICOSTI.

(From a Drawing by Mrs. Simcoe.)

I walked two hours on the deck this afternoon, and saw a fine sunset behind Bique (Bic), a village in Rimouski County, near Rimouski. When we came within sight of Bique, Capt. Murray fired a gun for a pilot, and one very soon after the signal came on board. He had arrived from Isle aux Coudres (or Hazel Island, 17 leagues N.E. of Quebec) this day to attend a dance at Bique, which latter place he had quitted a week before, not expecting any ships from England at so late a season. To-morrow he would have returned to Coudres, and we must have left the river for want of a pilot. Our arrival this day was, therefore, most fortunate. I copied some of Des Barres' charts this morning. The wind was so fair that all the sails were set, even the sky scrapers, and the ship went so steadily that I did not feel any motion.

NOTE.—Bic, or Sainte Cecile de Bic, is a post-village of Rimouski County, about a hundred and eight miles below Quebec City and nine miles west of Rimouski. There is an island opposite this village three miles in length and three-quarters of a mile in breadth called Bic or L'Islet au Massacre. According to tradition two hundred

Micmac Indians were murdered here by the Iroquois about two hundred years ago. The place is also called Bicque and Bique.

DES BARRES.

Joseph Frederic Wallet des Barres was born in 1722. He was the descendant of the Protestant branch of a noble French family who emigrated to England after the revocation of the Edict of Nantes. In 1756 he embarked, as lieutenant, in the 60th Regiment of Foot for America. From 1784-1787, Des Barres was Lieutenant-Governor of the Isle of Cape Breton, and in 1785 founded Sydney. He ranked in the army as Colonel (Brevet) from 1st January, 1798, and retired in 1803. A large part of the Maritime Provinces were surveyed by Des Barres and many of the best maps of the period were made by him. He was Captain Cook's teacher in navigation. His death took place in Halifax, N.S., in October, 1824, at the age of 102.

Thurs. 10th—N.E. Rain and mild. We saw three ships on their way to England anchored off the Brandy Pots Islands, N.E. of Hare Islands. Passed Hare Island and the Kamouraska Islands. I feel the air much heavier since we have been so near land. We expect to be at Quebec in

BRANDY POTS ISLANDS, 1791.
(From a Drawing by Mrs. Simcoe.)

the night. The Island of Orleans (N.E. of Quebec) reaches from nearly opposite Cape Tourmenté to within a league and a half of Quebec. It is seven leagues in length and three in width. As Baron Jean de la Hontan writes in his "Voyages dans l'Amerique Septentrionale" (published in 1704), "north of the Isle of Orleans the river divides into two branches;" the ships sail through the south, the north channel being foul with shoals and rocks.

CHAPTER VI.

THE GOVERNOR AND HIS FAMILY IN QUEBEC.

Governor Simcoe, although he had brought his commission as Lieutenant-Governor of Upper Canada with him, was compelled, owing to circumstances related in a previous chapter, to remain at Quebec until June of 1792, before proceeding to the Upper Province and to Kingston, where he would take the oaths of office. There were many matters of importance to be arranged before he entered upon the active duties of his position.

The Act of the Imperial Parliament dividing the old province of Quebec into the two provinces of Upper and Lower Canada was passed in May, 1791. The commission of Governor Simcoe is dated 12th September, 1791, and the proclamation in accordance with the Act was issued at Quebec on November 18th, 1791. In June, 1792, he proceeded to Upper Canada, arriving at Kingston in July, where he took the oaths of office in presence of his Executive Council.

Fri. 11th—I expressed so much concern to quit the ship that Capt. Murray said he was almost afraid to dine on shore, lest I should order the ship under weigh to sail on a further voyage. The "Triton" anchored at Quebec at one this morning. At 7 I looked out of the cabin window and saw the town covered with snow, and it rained the whole day. Coll. Simcoe and Capt. Murray dined with General Alured Clarke, the Lt.-Governor, administrator, to meet H.R.H. Prince Edward.

NOTE.—Sir Charles Alured Clarke had a long and distinguished military career. When fourteen he entered the army as an ensign. Seventy-three years later, on the accession of William IV., he was made a field marshal. He died in September, 1832. Sir Alured was Governor of Jamaica from 1782-90, when he was transferred to the staff at Quebec. He was sworn in as Lieutenant-Governor of the Province of Quebec, 8th of October, 1790. He received his commission as Lieutenant-Governor of Lower Canada, September 12th, 1791, and remained in office until January 21st, 1796. During the two years' absence of Lord Dorchester, he acted as administrator of the province. Subsequently he

SIR ALURED CLARKE.

became Governor-General of India and later Commander-in-Chief of the forces there.

Edward Augustus was the fourth son of George III. and the father of Queen Victoria. He was not liked by his parent and spent most of his time in military service abroad. For a while he was in command of the 7th Royal Fusiliers at Gibraltar and at once showed

himself a thorough martinet, and became so unpopular with his
men that he was sent to Canada in 1791. Three years later he
served in Martinique and St. Lucia, but on the close of operations

returned to Canada. In 1799 several promotions
came his way. He was made Duke of Kent, and
Commander-in-Chief of the forces in British
North America. In 1802 he was appointed Gov-
ernor of Gibraltar. In July, 1818, he married
Victoria May Louisa, widow of Enrich Charles,
Prince of Leiningen. Eighteen months later he
died.

The 7th Regiment or Royal Fusiliers was
formed in 1685. In 1773 they proceeded to
Canada and were stationed at Quebec, Montreal
and St. John's. When Quebec was besieged by
Montgomery and Arnold, the garrison, of which
sixty men of the Fusiliers formed part, defended

PRINCE EDWARD.

the place with firmness and intrepidity. The regiment fought during the War of the Revolution. They returned to England in 1783,
on conclusion of the treaty of peace. In May, 1791, the regiment
was again in Canada under the command of Prince Edward, who
in 1799 was created Duke of Kent. In 1801 the Duke was removed to the First or Royal Regiment, and was succeeded in the
colonelcy by Lieutenant-Governor Sir Alured Clarke, from the 5th
Foot, who had commanded the Fusiliers during a great part of the
American war. In 1810, the regiment, which was stationed in the
West Indies, returned to England.

Fri. 11th—I was not disposed to leave the ship to enter so dismal
looking a town as Quebec appeared through the mist, sleet and rain, but
at 6 o'clock Lt. Talbot went ashore with me, and General Clarke's covered
carriole, a small chaise on runners instead of wheels, was ready to carry
me to the Inn in the Upper Town, to which we ascended an immensely
steep hill through streets ill built. The snow was not deep enough to
enable the carriole to run smoothly, so that I was terribly shaken, and
formed a very unpleasant idea of the town which I had come to, and the
dismal appearance of the old-fashioned inn I arrived at, which, I could
suppose, resembled my idea of a Flemish house, was not prepossessing.
My rooms were all on the first floor and a large kitchen adjoining the
sitting room. I did not suffer from cold, for it was heated by poils or
stoves, which were so well supplied with wood that I found it sometimes
necessary to open the finettes, or sliding panes of glass in the windows.
I met with fine partridges and excellent apples called Roseaux, pink
throughout, and they had a flavour of strawberries—a very early apple,
and they do not keep.

Sun. 13th—Capt. Murray sailed for Halifax. I sent letters to England
by a merchant vessel. I was amused by seeing dogs of all sizes drawing
traineaux or sleds with wood. Mastiffs draw loads of provisions, and very
small dogs carrioles, with children in them.

Fri. 18th—I walked with Coll. Simcoe to Cape Diamond and saw the
citadel, which is fortified by many works, and from whence there is a very
grand view of the town, shipping and distant mountains as far as Cap
Tourmenté, near the mouth of the river. The inhabited country near
Quebec is embellished by the villages of Montmorency at the Falls, Charles-

bourg, Lorette, St. Foix (Ste. Foy), all within a few miles of Quebec. It seemed very perilous walking over acres of ice, but cloth shoes or worsted stockings over shoes prevent slipping.

Sat. 19th—I went to the house we have hired in St. John Street, which is a very moderate one, but the only one at present to be let. There is a poil or stove in one parlour, and a fireplace in the other.

Mon. 21st—I went to a subscription concert. Prince Edward's band of the 7th Fusiliers played, and some of the officers of the Fusiliers. The music was thought excellent. The band costs the Prince eight hundred a year.

Sat. 26th.—A Mr. Hazeel, who is lately come from the River la Tranche (the Thames in Middlesex, U.C.), dined with us, and confirms the favourable opinion we have entertained of the country on its banks. We supped at Major Watson's. Mrs. Watson appeared pleasing. Mrs. Caldwell, wife of Coll. Caldwell, was there.

NOTE.—There was a Major Watson on the staff at Quebec in 1791. He belonged to the 3rd Foot Guards. He became Major-General, 20th December, 1793.

THE RECOLLET CHURCH—INTERIOR VIEW.

Sun. 27th—I went to church. The service is performed in a room occasionally used as a Council Chamber. Prince Edward always goes to church, and his band plays during the service. On the death of the two Jesuits the Recollet Church will devolve to the English, and as these men are very old, the English Government do not think it necessary to build a church for the use of Protestants; indeed, the French allow us to use the Recollet Church between the hours of their service, but as they will not admit of fires in it, the Council Chamber is generally used as a church in the winter.

NOTE.—The Recollet Church in 1791 was situated on the site of the present English Cathedral. The Convent gardens occupied the site of the present Court House. The picture is from a drawing showing the interior of the church restored after the Siege of Quebec.

DIARY OF MRS. SIMCOE

Mon. 28th—I went to a concert, and afterwards to a dance at the Fusiliers' Barracks.

NOTE.—The Fusiliers' Barracks were on the site of the present City Hall, Quebec.

Tues. 29th—I supped at Major Stewart's, of the Royal Regiment of Artillery, and met Mrs. P. V. (full name not in MSS.), the most unpleasing woman I have seen in this place. She is just arrived from London.

NOTE.—Major John Stewart became Lieutenant-Colonel of the regiment in 1793.

Wed. 30th—St. Andrew's Day. Coll. Simcoe dined with Dr. Mabane at Woodfield, near Quebec. He was an army surgeon, came into the Council at Quebec, amassed money, and lived what is called most hospitably, far beyond his fortune.

NOTE.—Judge Adam Mabane was a member of the first Executive Council of Quebec (1775). He at one time resided at Woodfield,

JUDGE MABANE.

formerly "Samos," which is situated three miles from Quebec. It was an elegant mansion and richly laid out estate. In 1646, the Company of New France owned the estate surrounding Woodfield. After various owners it passed in 1731 into the hands of Monseigneur Dosquet, Bishop of Samos, who built the dwelling house. He was consecrated Bishop of Samos in 1726, and evidently gave the name of the diocese to the house. 1733 he was made Bishop of Quebec, having been for three years coadjutor to Monseigneur Duplessis-Mornay. In 1763, the land on which the house stood was conceded by the Quebec Seminary to Thomas Ainslie, who renamed the dwelling "Woodfield," and in 1769, Judge Adam Mabane acquired it.

He died in 1792, and his sister Miss Isabella Mabane bought it in 1794, holding it until 1805, when it was purchased by the late Honorable Matthew Bell, who in 1816 sold it to Mr. William Sheppard.

The original house was built on the brow of the hill overlooking the St. Lawrence. It was of stone, one storey high, peaked roof, after the style of architecture which prevailed in those days, something the same as that of the manor house at Beauport. Judge Mabane made many alterations, adding a second storey and two pavilion wings connected with the house by corridors. In 1775-6, it was used as an hospital for American soldiers. In December, 1842, the house was destroyed by fire and a new residence built by Mr. Sheppard. In 1847 Woodfield was sold to Mr. Thomas Gibb, who exchanged it with his brother, Mr. James Gibb. In 1879, the estate was sold as a site for a rural cemetery.

The information concerning Samos is from an excellent paper written by P. B. Casgrain, K.C., Clerk of Circuit Court, Quebec, and presented to the Royal Society of Canada in 1906.

VISITS SURVEYOR-GENERAL HOLLAND

Thurs. 1st Dec.—A fine, clear day. I walked near three miles to Major Holland's, Surveyor-General, where I saw some fine prints of Italy and Mount Vesuvius.

Observing that the stoves are generally heated to an excessive degree, I was told that in this house they were always moderate. I looked at the Fahrenheit's thermometer in the room, and it was 74°. They said that it had been 86° at Chief Justice Smith's a few evenings ago.

THE RESIDENCE KNOWN AS SAMOS.
(From a Drawing in possession of P. B. Casgrain, Quebec.)

NOTE.—Major Samuel Holland was born in England in 1717, receiving his military education there and in Holland. At an early age he entered the Army as Lieutenant of Artillery and served some time on the Continent. In 1756 he was promoted to a captaincy and in the following year was appointed aide-de-camp to General Wolfe. He took part in the expedition against Louisbourg and was engineer-in-chief with Wolfe and Saunders at Quebec. According to some critics he stood near Wolfe when that officer fell. In 1763 Holland was appointed Surveyor-General of Quebec and Director of Surveys in British North America, and also a member of the Council, Quebec. Many of the manuscript plans in the Dominion Archives are signed by him. During his stay in Quebec, Prince Edward paid Holland many visits at his old mansion on the Ste. Foye Road. He married Marie Josephte Rolet, by whom he had eight children, the eldest, Colonel John F. Holland, being the first British subject born on Prince Edward Island. The only living grandson of the Surveyor-General is Augustus E. C. Holland (son of Frederic Braham Holland), of Wallace Bridge, N.S. A. E. Holland, of St. Eleanor's, P.E.I., is a great-grandson through his father, Samuel Holland, Jr., while Miss Marion

SURV.-GEN. HOLLAND.

Holland, of Melbourne, Que., and Mrs. Alton Rowland, of Windsor Mills, Que., daughters of the late H. A. P. Holland, are also great-grandchildren of the Surveyor-General.

From hence I went in an open carriole (which is a sort of phæton body on a sledge or runners, shod with iron instead of wheels) to Woodfield, to call on Dr. Mabane's sister. It is three miles from Quebec, a beautiful situation among woods, on the steep and high banks of the St. Lawrence, and within a mile from Wolfe's Cove, the spot where Wolfe landed. From hence I went to "Sans Bruit," a house of Coll. Caldwell, let to a Mr. Philip Tosey, a Church of England clergyman, who emigrated from Sussex. He is military chaplain, and is also engaged in clearing 7,000 acres of land, and of his skill in farming Mr. Young, the agriculturist, has written so largely. I walked from hence to Quebec, two miles. It is fatiguing to walk on snow when not perfectly frozen, and my half boots were heavy with icicles.

CANADIAN CARRIOLE.
(From a Drawing by Mrs. Simcoe)

NOTE.—"Sans Bruit," on the Ste. Foy Road, was bought by Colonel Murray, a nephew of General Murray, and named "Sans Bruit," which means "without noise." It appears that on one occasion the Colonel wrote to a merchant in the Lower Town asking him to send him a list of articles, and at the foot of the letter he wrote "Sans Bruit, 1 June." The merchant, thinking that this was simply a caution to him to deliver the goods without noise, arrived at the house at night and as secretly as possible. The Colonel heard the disturbance at the door, and discovered that the merchant was doing his best to call attention to his presence with the least noise possible. Explanations were given, but the merchant still thought that *"Sans Bruit"* was simply a word of caution, and could not possibly be the name of a residence.

Rev. Philip Tosey was appointed rector of the parish of Quebec in 1786. He was the second authorized Protestant minister in the city and was also Ecclesiastical Commissary for the Eastern District.

GOVERNOR SIMCOE LEAVES FOR MONTREAL

Fri. 2nd—We dined at Belmont, four miles from Quebec, Coll. Caldwell's, a very indifferent house in appearance, but comfortable within. I nearly fainted with the heat this evening, and was told that Fahrenheit thermometer in this drawing-room had one evening been at 100. I eat part of a metiffe, a bird between a wild goose (the outarde) and a tame one. It was much better than the tame goose. I found it so cold coming home after supper in a covered carriole that I wore one of the fencing masks lined with fur which Capt. Stevenson gave me.

NOTE.—The estate of Belmont, on the north side of the Ste. Foy Road, near Quebec, originally belonged to the Jesuit Fathers. After passing through different hands it came into the possession of Honourable Colonel Henry Caldwell, who was Assistant Quartermaster-General under Wolfe, in 1759. He settled in Quebec after the conquest, held the Provincial rank of lieutenant-colonel and was appointed to the Legislative Council in 1792. In 1794 he became Receiver-General of the Province. Colonel Caldwell built the mansion, which was burned in 1798 and rebuilt in 1800. He died there in 1810.

BELMONT, NEAR QUEBEC.
(From a Drawing by Mrs. Simcoe.)

During the years that followed the property was owned by different parties until the late manager of the Beauport Asylum bought it, and it is now a private sanitarium, known as the "Belmont Retreat."

Sat. 3rd—Coll. Simcoe set out for Montreal, accompanied by Capt. Stevenson. They wore large beaver coats, and the carriole was filled with buffalo skins. I copied some views of Italy that Major Holland lent me.

NOTE.—I find mention of Captain Stevenson in a letter of General Simcoe, dated 6th September, 1791. Simcoe refers to Captain Stevenson in these words: "I have recommended him to the office of Deputy Quarter-Master General, to relinquish the idea of not joining his regiment till the spring, and to accompany me to Quebec, not thinking it fitting in respect to the commission with which I am honoured that if I should be blown off the St. Lawrence into an American port that I should arrive there unattended, and in case of personal accident that those whom I value more than life would be without a protector."

Sun. 4th—Mrs. Tosey, wife of the military chaplain, carried me to church in a carriole like a narrow coach, which, from its length, was much

OFFICERS' CARRIOLE.
(From a Drawing by Mrs. Simcoe.)

easier than those usually used, but too heavy for one horse to draw with ease, therefore seldom used.

Mon. 5th—A thaw to-day; the air raw and cold, and the roads full of cahots—a word used in Quebec for the holes and pits made on the snow

RUINS OF INTENDANT'S PALACE, QUEBEC, 1791.
(From an Engraving in the Dominion Archives, Ottawa.)

roads—makes driving very jolty; but it did not deter Prince Edward and a party from driving 8 miles to the village of Lorette. It is the custom here to make parties to dine in the country at a distance of ten miles. They often carry a cold dinner, and return to a dance in the evening, and this in the severe weather, which seems as much relished by the English as the Canadians. Their partners must be very agreeable, or they could never have liked these parties. I drank tea with Mrs. Watson, wife of Major Watson.

A slight shock of an earthquake was felt in Saint Louis Street this evening. Quebec is divided into Upper and Lower town. The latter is inhabited by the merchants for the convenience of the harbour and quays. They have spacious houses three stories high, built of dark stone, but the streets are narrow and gloomy. In the suburbs of St. Foy are ruins of the Intendant's Palace, which was a very large building. The upper town is more airy and pleasant, though the houses in general are less.

NOTE.—Ste. Foy—this form of spelling has been used by the Abbé Scott, who found it in the original documents. When Talon filled the office of Intendant, he had a brewery built at the Palais, which was finished in 1671. This industry, quite a new one in the

THE FORT AND CHATEAU ST. LOUIS, QUEBEC.
(From an Engraving in the Dominion Archives, Ottawa.)

country, did not prove as profitable as expected. Thereupon the Intendant made the building his residence, and the Superior Council held its sittings there. The Council, when first established, held its sittings in a house called the "Palais" at the corner of the Place d'Armes and St. Louis Street, on the very spot, in fact, where the present Court House stands. Talon's brewery was destroyed by fire in the night of the 5th January, 1713. On its ruins was erected the splendid building of the Intendant's Palace, of which Kalm and Charlevoix speak in terms of admiration. It was almost entirely demolished during the siege of 1759. At the present day a large brewery stands on the ruins of the Intendant's Palace, and thus the site is restored to its former use.

Mon. 5th—The Chateau, the residence of the Governor, just above the lower town, contains some very good rooms built by Sir Frederick Haldimand. The situation is very high, and commands a most noble prospect down the river. The old chateau is in a ruinous state, but it is used for public offices, and convenient for the Governor as being so near his own residence that there is only a courtyard between them.

NOTE.—Champlain in 1620 built the first Fort St. Louis. In the year 1646, a contract was passed between the Company of New France and the contractors for more extensive works of defence in Quebec. In the following year the foundation of the first Chateau was laid. The Chateau was built within the boundary of the Fort, and the distinction between Chateau and Fort has not always been preserved. Many imagine that the famous Chateau St. Louis was

THE OLD CHATEAU
STONE.

but one structure, whilst in reality it was composed at one time of three, viz.: Fort St. Louis, Chateau St. Louis and Haldimand Castle. The Chateau overhung the cliffs, as may be seen by the view in "Hawkins" and other works, and in fact it occupied the site of the present terrace. In 1784, while levelling the yard at the Chateau, workmen dug up a large stone with a Maltese cross on it, bearing date 1647. In later years there was some controversy as to whether the date on the stone was 1646 or 1647, but it was finally decided to be the latter, and that the old relic was intended to commemorate a double event, viz:— the years in which the Fort St. Louis Bastion was begun and finished, 1646 and 1647. The stone was first placed in the cheek of the gate of the new building, Haldimand Castle, at the rear, about on the site of the present Chateau, and subsequently was placed over the entrance to the hotel known as the Chateau Frontenac. The Chateau St. Louis was rebuilt in 1694-8 and another storey added in 1811. It was destroyed by fire in 1834. Sir Frederick Haldimand lived there from 1777 to 1784.

Wed. 7th—Gen'l. Clarke's servant threw himself from the Chateau into the Lower Town, some hundred feet, without breaking a bone or being killed. I received a letter from Coll. Simcoe, who travelled in the carriole to Three Rivers, 100 miles, where he found the river open, and was obliged to cross it in a boat and proceed the remaining 100 miles to Montreal in a calèche, a carriage like a gig, with a seat in front for the driver. He reached Pt. aux Trembles, on the island of Montreal and within three leagues of Montreal, the second day from Quebec.

Sun. 11th—I dined at Coll. Caldwell's, and soon after I returned home Coll. Simcoe arrived from Montreal, which place he left yesterday. He brought with him Mr. Talbot, of the 24th Regt., a relation of Lady Buckingham, who was aide-de-camp to the Marquis while he was Lieutenant of Ireland, and at whose request Coll. Simcoe takes Mr. Talbot into his family.

NOTE.—Thomas Talbot, son of Richard Talbot and Margaret, afterwards (1831) Baroness Talbot, was born at Malahide, near Dublin, on 19th July, 1771. In May, 1783, when little more than eleven years of age, he received a commission in the army, as ensign in the 66th Regiment of Foot. In September of the same year he became a

HALDIMAND CASTLE, QUEBEC, RESIDENCE OF SIR FREDERICK HALDIMAND.
(From a Water-color by H. Bunnell, 1887.)

lieutenant, his retirement on half pay, from 1784 to 1787, immediately following. The Lord Lieutenant of Ireland at that time was the Marquis of Buckingham, a relative of Talbot's, and he, with Arthur Wellesley, afterwards Duke of Wellington, acted as aides to the Marquis. In 1790, Wellesley became a member of the Irish Parliament, and Talbot joined the 24th Regiment at Quebec. Soon after Governor Simcoe's arrival in Canada, Talbot became his private and confidential secretary, remaining a member of the Governor's family until 1794. In June of that year he returned to England, having been summoned to join his regiment. In 1796 he was appointed Lieutenant-Colonel of the 5th Foot, which had been stationed at Niagara during the period he had been on Simcoe's staff, and three years later commanded the second bat-

COLONEL TALBOT.

talion of the regiment in Holland. Talbot returned to Canada in 1801, seeking a place to establish a settlement. Through an oversight he did not accomplish his purpose and again went to England, where he was assisted in his efforts by General Simcoe. In

COLONEL TALBOT'S RESIDENCE, PORT TALBOT.
(From a Sketch sent to England in 1806, and copied by Mrs. Simcoe.)

1803, Colonel Talbot took up permanent residence in Upper Canada, receiving a grant of 5,000 acres in the Township of Dunwich. He founded what is known as the Talbot Settlement, which in 1831 was estimated at 40,000 souls. During his residence in Canada, Colonel Talbot occasionally visited England, and it was on his last visit, in 1851, that he met the companion of his early youth, Arthur Wellesley, then Duke of Wellington. It is a coincidence that they died within a few months of each other, the "Iron Duke" passing away on 14th September, 1852, and the "Founder of the Talbot Settlement" on 6th February, 1853.

The house was situated on the cliff at the top of a green slope rising to the west from the mouth of the Talbot Creek, in Dunwich. The place has always been called Port Talbot although there is neither port nor village in the vicinity. The site of Colonel Talbot's home is now occupied by a residence built by Colonel (afterwards Lord) Airey about 1849, left of the wing shown in the picture on the brow of the hill, nearest the creek.

Thurs. 15th—We walked to the provision store, a road by the riverside below Cape Diamond, always sheltered and well beaten.

Sun. 18th—We dined at Belmont.

Mon. 19th—Dined and supped at Madame Bâby's, wife of Monsr. (Hon.) François Bâby, a member of the Legislative Council. I ate part of the moufle of the orignale, or elk. They are sometimes shot by the Indians, and much esteemed. It was a very rich dish, with an excellent sauce. I am told the lip of the ox is sometimes sold for it. A pie made of *crête de coys* (a pie garnished with cocks' combs) is also a very favourite dish among the Canadians, and easily procured, as quantities of poultry are killed in the beginning of the winter and kept hung up in a frozen state. The poultry eat dry, but when preserved in barrels of snow, as is the custom at New York, they retain the juices much better.

Tues. 20th—We supped at Mr. Thomas Ainslie's, the Collector of Customs here.

Wed. 21st—We dined with Mr. Jenkins Williams, the Clerk of the Legislative Council. The supper was very elegant. Mrs. Williams is a very genteel woman, and paints beautifully and dresses very well. She has not been here above two years, having been educated in London.

MGR. HUBERT.

NOTE.—Jenkins Williams was Judge Jenkins Williams of the District of Quebec in 1797. He succeeded Judge Mabane as Judge of the Court of Common Pleas in 1792.

Thurs. 22nd—I had an order from Mgr. François Hubert, the Catholic Bishop of Quebec, for admittance to the Convent des Ursulines, where I went to-day with Madame Bâby. The Superieure (La Mère Saint Louis Gonzague) is a very pleasing, conversible woman of good address. Her face and manner reminded me of Mrs. Gwillim (Mrs. Simcoe in this writing refers to a relative of her own, not her mother, who died at her birth). The nuns appeared cheerful, pleased to see visitors, and disposed to converse and ask questions. Their dress is black with a white hood, and some of them looked very pretty in it. They carry cleanliness and neatness to the greatest pitch of perfection in every part of the convent, and are industrious in managing a large garden. They educate children at this convent, taking both pensionnaires and day boarders. They make many decorations for their altars and church, and gild picture frames. They showed a fine piece of embroidery worked by an English nun, since dead. Some of them make boxes and pin cushions of birch bark, worked with dyed hair of the orignale or elk. It is so short that it must be put through the needle for every stitch, which makes it tedious. All sorts of cakes and sweetmeats are made here, and all the desserts in Quebec are furnished by the nuns. They dry apples in a very peculiar manner. They are like dried apricots. All these things are of use to maintain them, their finances being very moderate.

Another convent is called the Hotel Dieu, for the reception of the sick, whether French or English. It is attended by the medical men on the staff, who speak highly of the attention payed by the nuns to the sick people. The General Hospital is a convent a mile out of the town, where sick and insane people are received.

NOTE.—Mgr. Jean François Hubert was born in Quebec on the 23rd February, and became Bishop of Quebec on 12th June, 1788. He died at the General Hospital, Quebec, on 17th October, 1797, Mother St. Louis de Gonzague, who was several times Superior of the Ursulines Convent, died on the 23rd March, 1802.

CONVENT OF THE URSULINES, QUEBEC, 1791.
(From a Drawing by Richard Short.)

NOTE.—The General Hospital of Quebec occupied the site of the Convent of the Recollets on the banks of the River St. Charles. It was first occupied as an hospital on 30th October, 1692. In 1740 and 1859, additions were made, and considerable repairs in 1850. There do not appear to have been many editions of pictures since 1743. The present hospital is on the same site as it was in 1791.

Fri. 23—The great church or cathedral stands in the centre of the town, and appears to be filled with people at all hours of the day. It is a handsome building. Near to it is the seminary, where boys are educated, and some of the Catholic clergy reside there. The Jesuits' or Recollet

Church is a handsome building, ornamented with some pictures, but no fine paintings. Two models of ships are suspended in it, placed there in commemoration of the arrival of some of the settlers from France. The only two Jesuits living have spacious apartments near the church, and a good library and large gardens. I went to a subscription ball this evening. There were three rooms well lighted, and the company well dressed.

NOTE.—The Cathedral stands on the same ground as in 1791. The first parish church at Quebec was destroyed by fire in 1640 and the new structure, which afterwards became the Cathedral, was not commenced till September, 1644, under the name of Notre Dame de la Paix. It was opened in 1650. During the siege of Quebec in 1759 nearly all the wooden portion of the church was destroyed, but it was

THE GENERAL HOSPITAL, QUEBEC.
(From an old Drawing in the Dominion Archives, Ottawa.)

restored between 1769 and 1771. In 1843 considerable changes were made at the east end, but the building is practically the same in the interior as it was in 1791.

Sat. 24th—Dr. T. M. Nooth says a great light was observed last night in the air in a direction N.E. beyond St. Paul's Bay, which is 30 leagues below Quebec, opposite Isle aux Coudres, in the St Lawrence. He supposed an eruption had taken place from a volcano, which is believed from the reports of Indians to be in those parts, and a fresh eruption might have taken place there, occasioned by an earthquake which was severely felt a few days since near St. Paul's Bay. However, there is much of conjecture in the supposition about the existence of this volcano.

NOTE.—The Quebec *Gazette,* of the 22nd December, 1791, contains a letter from St. Paul's Bay written on December 11th, giving an account of a violent earthquake that occurred on the 6th at Bay St. Paul and relating the fact that there were thirty shocks in one day. On the 17th, about five o'clock in the evening "a globe of fire appearing to the eye of the size of a 48-pound cannon ball was observed in the sky coming from the southwest striking towards the northeast, disappearing in its perpendicular descent above St. Paul's Bay, after bursting with an explosion." This strange "great light" which Dr. Nooth observed on the evening of the 23rd may have been a repetition of "the globe of fire" on the 15th.

Sun. 25th—Christmas Day. I went with Madame Báby at 5 in the morning to the Cathedral Church, to see the illuminations of the altar, which to those who have not seen the highly-decorated Roman Catholic churches in Europe is worth seeing. The singing and chanting was solemn. I was wrapped up very much, and wore a kind of cloth lined with eiderdown, a very comfortable head-dress; but the cold was intense, for the Roman Catholics will not admit of fires in their churches, lest the pictures should be spoiled. I saw no fine pictures.

Mon. 26th—This day the division of the Province of Quebec into Upper and Lower Canada, and the new constitution given to the former, was announced by proclamation. There were dinners at the hotels and illuminations at night to commemorate this event.

NOTE. — This proclamation was issued at Quebec on the 18th of November, 1791, and decreed that the division of the two provinces should take effect on 26th December, 1791.

Wed. 28th—I was at a very pleasant ball at the Chateau, and danced with Prince Edward.

THE CATHEDRAL, QUEBEC, AS RESTORED.

(From Routhier's "Quebec.")

Thurs. 29th—We drove to Woodfield, and admired the beautiful scenery around it.

Sat. 31st—We drove to Belmont. We saw two Indians from the village of Lorette who had mocassins to sell, a kind of leather shoe made of untanned deer skins, which I was glad to buy for the children on account of their softness. These Lorette Indians were originally Hurons, converted, but reluctantly, by the Jesuits. They speak French, and are so intermixed with that people that they scarcely appear to differ but in dress. They wear shirts, leggings and blankets, and the men wear fur or cloth caps.

I walked this evening at nine o'clock to Fort Louis Gate, one of the old gates of the city.

NOTE.—The Indians at Lorette, about eight miles from Quebec, were of the Huron tribe. After the Indian massacres of 1648-9, parties of the tribe sought refuge in different places, one section seeking refuge on the Island of Orleans. They were afterwards located in Quebec, and upon Marquis de Tracy effecting a truce in 1665 with the Iroquois, the enemies of the Hurons, the latter left the

ST. LOUIS GATE, 1791.
(From a Drawing in the Dominion Archives, Ottawa.)

city. After several flittings they finally, in 1697, settled at Lorette, where some hundred descendants of the once warlike race live to-day.

Mrs. Simcoe had reference to St. Louis Gate, the entrance to Quebec from the west. The Fort St. Louis stood on the edge of the cliff, and the entrance to the remains of the Fort in 1792 was through the Chateau Haldimand.

DRESS OF THE HABITANTS

Sat. 31st—The moon shone bright, and, however intense the cold is here, it is so extremely still at night that it is less felt than in England, where a less degree of cold is attended with wind. There is little wind here, except with a snowstorm of fine snow. The French call it poudre or powdered snow, and to travel with that blowing in one's face is very dis-agreeable. The Canadians wear scanty, thick woollen coats, and sometimes leather ones, with hoods to them, over a bonnet rouge, a red bonnet. The habi-tants call it a capitshaw, and their coats are tied round with a coloured worsted sash. They have always a pipe in their mouths. The French women wear long, thin linen cloaks, sometimes hoods lined with eiderdown, but often walk in the street with only a muslin cap.

Mons Gravé de la Rive.

There was an anniversary dinner to-day, attended by those gentlemen who particularly distinguished themselves in the defence of the town when attacked by Montgomery on 31st Dec., 1775. Coll. Caldwell was among the most active persons on this occasion.

This day five years since (31st Dec., 1786) the air became in a few hours so dark that it was neces-sary to light candles. At three o'clock black clouds were continually rolling onwards from the southwest. The darkness continued the whole of the next day, when a person could not be discerned on the opposite side of the street. It was supposed to be occasioned by the eruption of a volcano. Père Gravé, Superieur, Seminaire, believes the report of Indians, who assert that they have seen a burning mountain to the north-east of St. Paul's Bay.

Accounts received from Montreal of the defeat of 2,000 of the people of the United States, about twenty miles from the Miami Fort, by 1,400 Indians. They had barricaded their camp with flour barrels, etc. The Indians attacked them, beat them, and took six pieces of cannon, all their provisions, new clothing, etc., killed 1,200 men, Coll. Butler and other officers, among whom, it was supposed, St. Clair fell. The troops retreated and were pursued by 400 Indians, who probably would have destroyed them all if they had not stopped to plunder.

Colonel Butler.

NOTE.—Mons. François Gravé de la Rive during the interval between 1768 and 1802, was several times Superior of the Quebec Seminary. He was born in France and came to Canada in 1754, and for many years was Vicar of the Diocese of Quebec. He died, aged 71, in the Hotel Dieu, Quebec, on 4th February, 1802, and was buried in the Seminary Chapel.

John Butler was born in New London, Conn., in 1725, his father, an Irish officer, having come to the North American Colonies with his regi-ment about 1711. Butler's first service was as a captain in the Indian Department in the expe-dition against Crown Point under Sir William Johnson, where he greatly distinguished himself. He also served under Abercrombie at Ticonderoga and with Bradstreet at the capture of Fort Frontenac. He accompanied Johnson against Fort Niagara as second in command of the Indians and after General Prideaux's death he followed him in the command. He afterwards served

GEN. ST. CLAIR.

throughout the Revolutionary War in command of the famous corps of "Rangers" bearing his name. This corps was disbanded June, 1784. Butler, after the war, was appointed Deputy-Superintendent of the Indians. He died near Niagara in 1796, and was buried in the private burying ground of the family.

General St. Clair was an American General of considerable reputation. He commanded at Ticonderoga in 1777 and had to evacuate the fort on Burgoyne's attack in July. He was Governor of the Ohio territory in 1789-1802. The fight at Miami between the Indians and the United States troops occurred on the 3rd November, 1791. He was defeated in an ambuscade by Indians near Fort Recovery in Ohio. After defeat he resigned his command and was succeeded by General Wayne, who was appointed to conduct the cperations with a newly recruited force. (See Archives, Q. 57, p. 178.)

CHAPTER VII.

MRS. SIMCOE SPENDS AN ENJOYABLE WINTER.

From the day of her arrival in Quebec, Mrs. Simcoe's time had been fully occupied. It was one round of unalloyed pleasure. Everyone in military and social circles seemed determined that there should be nothing lacking to make her winter's sojourn enjoyable. The deeds of hospitality were exemplified in the fullest sense of the term and ofttimes after the return of the Governor and his wife to England, the memories of the pleasant months spent in the "Ancient City" during the winter and spring of 1791-2 were the subject of conversation at Wolford. The Simcoes made many friends in Quebec. Mrs. Simcoe was a most lovable woman, highly educated, well informed, bright, cheerful, and always ready to join in the social festivities that were a great feature in Quebec a century ago. Her husband during this period won the lasting friendship of Prince Edward. They seemed by instinct to be drawn to each other. Between them a personal correspondence continued up to the time of the General's death. The intimacy, begun in Quebec, was cemented in the years that followed. It was a generous friendship, and Prince Edward, then and after he became Duke of Kent, never forgot to write from time to time a friendly line to Simcoe.

BISHOP PLESSIS.

But, with all the social appointments, Mrs. Simcoe found time to keep up her diary, and her first record in 1792 was of a sermon she had heard in the old Cathedral of Quebec.

Fri. 6th Jan., 1792—Le Jour des Rois—the Epiphany visit of the Wise Men to Christ. I went with Madame Báby to the Cathedral, and heard Monsr. du Plessis, the Bishop's Chaplain, preach a most excellent sermon on the subject of the Kings of the East seeking Jesus Christ. His action was animated and his sermon impressive. The Bishop himself was present. He wore a white muslin dress and a rich mantle embroidered with gold; blue silk gloves, worked with gold; his mittens pink and silver, blue and gold. He changed them two or three times during the service, which had a theatrical, poor and unfit appearance.

NOTE.—Joseph Octave Plessis was born at Montreal in March, 1762. He was ordained priest at Quebec on 11th March, 1786, and from time to time was employed as professor of humanity at the College of St. Raphael, also as Secretary to the Bishop of Quebec and curate of the capital. In September, 1797, he was created coadjutor to Bishop Denault, and obtained the royal acceptance

73

DIARY OF MRS. SIMCOE

through General Prescott. He succeeded Mgr. Denault and took
possession of his seat on 17th January, 1806. He left for England
and Rome in 1819, and in consideration of services rendered to
England during the French Revolution and during the War of
1812, he met with a kind and hearty reception from Lord Bathurst.
He died at the General Hospital, Quebec, on 4th December, 1825.
Bishop Plessis was the greatest man who ever occupied the Roman
Catholic episcopal seat at Quebec since François de Laval Montmorency.

St. Joseph Street, in the suburb of St. Roch, Quebec, was named
after Bishop Plessis, and it is interesting to note that the church in
St. Roch's was built by him on land donated by Mr. John Mure,
a Presbyterian. The church was dedicated to St. Joseph.

Sat. 7th—Fahrenheit's thermometer 23 degrees below. I rub silk
gowns with flannel to see the beautiful streams of fire which are emitted
with a crackling noise during the cold weather.

Tues. 10th—I bought an eiderdown quilt which cost £4 16s.

NOTE.—It is generally admitted that money has doubled in value
since 1791, so £4 16s. would now be worth £9 12s. or $36.85. Lambert
says in his Travels (1806-8) that the dollar or Spanish piastre
was worth five shillings in Canadian currency, and that to bring
sterling money into Canadian currency, one-ninth must be added.

Thurs. 12th—I drove out in a covered carriole.
Wed. 18th—A ball at the Chateau. This being Queen Charlotte's birth-
night, there were near 300 people. The ladies were well dressed.

Sat. 21st—Miss Johnson dined with me, and we went to a dance in
the evening at the Fusiliers' mess room—very agreeable. The thermometer is 24 degrees below. In the New York paper I read of "a leaf
imported from Botany Bay, which when dried goes off by the application
of a match with an explosion like gunpowder, and the air is agreeably
perfumed."

NOTE.—Miss Johnson was Ann, eldest daughter of Sir John
Johnson. She married, in 1797, Colonel Edward Macdonell, Deputy
Quartermaster General.

Tues. 24th—I gave a dance and supper to a dozen of the 7th Fusiliers
and as many young dancing ladies. My rooms being small obliged me to
invite so few, and only those who danced.

Sun. 29th—Drove in a covered carriole towards the Isle of Orleans, an
island in the St. Lawrence seven miles below Quebec. The ice was so
rough and snow uneven that I was almost seasick.

Mon. 30th—I went in an open carriole to see the Falls of Montmorency, six miles from Quebec. The river roars over a rocky bed among
woods before it reaches the precipice, over which it falls 280 feet. The
rocky sides are covered on the summit with wood. Sir Frederick Haldimand built a summer house projecting over the water, supported by
beams. We descended to it by steps cut in the rock, and from it we had
a fine view of the Fall. Sir Frederick Haldimand built a good house near
the bank of the river and commanding a fine prospect. Prince Edward
hired it last year, but as he went to Quebec every day, found the stony
roads prejudicial to his horses' feet.

74

MONTMORENCY HOUSE AT THE FALLS

NOTE.—Sir Frederick Haldimand (1718-1791), lieutenant-general, colonel commandant of the 60th Foot, was a Swiss by birth. In 1756 he was lieutenant-colonel of the Royal Americans, afterwards the 60th Foot and now the King's Royal Rifle Corps, then being recruited in America under command of the Earl of Loudoun. On the 27th of June, 1778, he was appointed to succeed Sir Guy Carleton, afterwards the first Lord Dorchester, as Governor and Commander-in-Chief in Canada, which post he held until 1784, when he returned to England. As an administrator in Canada he is accused, says Lee in the National Biography, of being harsh and arbitrary and more than one action for false imprisonment was successfully maintained against him on his return to England. Haldimand's commissions, 1758-85, including the entire records that accumulated during his public career, are in the British Museum and copies are in the Archives Department in Ottawa. He built the residence known as Haldimand House, Quebec.

SIR F. HALDIMAND.

Of the summer house, the Baroness Riedesel says in her diary: "When we first went to see that sublime scene (Montmorency Falls) I happened to say to the General that it must be delightful to have a little dwelling opposite to it. Three weeks later (in the summer of 1782) we accompanied him thither a second time and after having climbed up a steep ascent and the detached rocks, which were connected by small bridges and reminded me of some descriptions of Chinese gardens, we at last reached the top, where the General begged my hand to show me into a small house, which was as it were suspended on the cataract . . . . . The foundations of the house consisted of eight strong beams laid athwart beneath which the cataract hurried down with tremendous velocity."

"The good house" Mrs. Simcoe refers to was Montmorency House, which is not to be confused with Chateau Haldimand, the addition built in 1784 to the Castle of St. Louis. With Montmorency House Prince William Henry fell in love when in Canada; from 1791 to 1794 Prince Edward made it his home in the summer time; and now the Haldimand House—Kent Lodge—is a summer hotel, the home of many a tourist, who comes to be thrilled by the rushing waters of the Montmorency.

In the Supplement to the Quebec *Gazette,* 22nd December, 1792, is the following notice. "For sale, the elegant villa of the late Sir Frederick Haldimand, K.B., delightfully situated near the Falls of Montmorency, with the farm house, Quebec, 1st December, 1791."

Tues. 31st—A very pleasant dance at the Chateau this evening.
Tues. Feb. 7th—At two o'clock the kitchen chimney was on fire. It was soon extinguished, as the people here are expert in using fire engines. The houses being covered with shingles (wood in the shape of tiles), fires

spread rapidly if not immediately put out. Prince Edward, General Clarke, etc., dined with Coll. Simcoe, and this accident retarded the dinner, so I went to bed before the dinner.

Wed. 8th—Supped at Mrs. Smith's, wife of the Chief Justice.

NOTE.—Chief Justice William Smith, born at New York, 1728, educated at Yale, was appointed a member of His Majesty's Council in 1769. After the evacuation of New York he withdrew to England with Sir Guy Carleton, who was at that time commander-in-chief. Mr. Smith remained in England until 1786 when he was appointed first Chief Justice of Canada and continued to hold the office until his death seven years later. His second son, Honorable William Smith, wrote our first Canadian history in English.

CHIEF JUSTICE SMITH.

Thurs. 9th—Coll. and Mrs. Caldwell and Major and Mrs. Watson dined with us. We went to the Assembly, where an account was brought of our house being burnt down. Coll. Simcoe went home and found it only the chimney on fire. I was not told of it, though an officious man afterwards assured me he would have informed me had he known it.

Sat. 11th—We supped at Madame Báby's, but not till 12 o'clock, it being a fast day. Then there was a good dinner.

Sun. 12th—Walked by the sea.

THE PROVISION STORE, QUEBEC.
(From a Drawing by Mrs. Simcoe.)

Mon. 13th—We walked to the provision store before breakfast; dined at Belmont. The thermometer 3 degrees below.

Tues. 14th—Supper at Major Stewart's (of the Royal Regiment of Artillery). The Prince was there. During the winter large masses of ice float down the river, and the people who come to market from the opposite shore pass in canoes, which they quit when they come to one of these large bodies of ice, and carry their canoes across the ice on their shoulders and launch them again in the water, and this is repeated several times before they reach Quebec, where they sell a fat turkey for 15d. and provisions, all kinds, in proportion. The mode of crossing the river appears so difficult and dangerous that it seems hardly credible till it has been seen. This evening it was announced that " le pont est pris " (the bridge has formed), that is, there is now a complete body of ice filling up the river, and canoes will be no longer used, as carrioles will drive across, which is very useful to the peasants and very pleasant to those who drive for amusement, and this year the weather, having been calm and the wind with the tide when it froze, the ice is very smooth. It is seven years since a bridge was formed.

Wed. 15th—Coll. Simcoe and I were going to walk on the ice bridge. As there was a narrow space containing water between the land and the ice, a plank was laid across, which Coll. Simcoe had passed, and stepping back to give me his hand, he slipped into the water, but luckily caught hold of the plank which supported him until the Canadians who were near and on my screaming out " Au secours " (help) assisted him out. Had the plank given way he must have gone under the ice, and it would have been impossible to have got out. We walked to Monsr. Baby's, and I ran home to order dry clothes to be brought there.

Fri. 17th—I went to the ball at the Chateau. There was also a dance at the barracks to-night.

Sat. 18th—One of the casmettes (or bombproof chambers) near Fort Louis Gate has been fitted up for a theatre. Some Canadian gentlemen represented the French play of " Le Medecin malgre lui " (Moliére) and " La Comtesse D'Escarbagnas " (Moliére). I was surprised those people, unused to see theatrical representations, could perform as well as they did, and I was much amused. The Fusiliers are going to act plays, and as Coll. Simcoe does not like to see officers so employed he does not intend to go to the theatre again. I went across the river to Point Levy yesterday. The ice was excellent, and the sun excessively hot. We walked as far as the church. The firs looked beautiful among the snow this bright day. We met the Prince in a carriole. I gathered bunches of berries from a low shrub Dr. Nooth called a clither. People cut holes in the ice and catch fish through them. Poisson d'or (gold fish) pickerall are the most esteemed fish.

NOTE.—Superintendent-General T. M. Nooth was on the staff of the Quebec Hospital.

Sun. 19th—Dined at Monsr. Báby. Met Madame Tonacour and Monsr. and Madame De Salaberry, etc.

NOTE.—Colonel, the Honorable François Báby, Adjutant-General of Militia of Lower Canada, was born in Montreal, 4th December, 1733. He HON. FRANÇOIS BÁBY. was a member of the Executive and Legislative Councils and deputy of the French-Canadians to the Court of Great Britain in 1773. He married in 1786, Delle Marie-Anne Tarieu de Lanaudière. He took an active part, together with his brother-in-law, Charles Tarieu de Lanaudière, then A.D.C. to Lord Dorchester, in the events of the time. His death occurred at Quebec in October, 1820.

DIARY OF MRS. SIMCOE

Monsieur Ignace-Michel L. A. de Salaberry, whose father settled in Canada in 1735, was born at the Manor House, Beauport, Que.,

MONS. DE SALABERRY.

5th July, 1752, and was educated in France. He married Catherine François de Hertel. Monsieur de Salaberry was a friend of the Duke of Kent. Colonel Charles de Salaberry, hero of the Battle of Chateauguay, which took place on 26th October, 1813, was the son of Monsieur and Madame de Salaberry. She died at Beauport on 28th January, 1824, her husband's death taking place on 22nd March, 1825.

MME. DE SALABERRY.

Mon. 20th—The heads of the French clergy dined with Coll. Simcoe —the Bishop, Monsr. Gravé the Vicar-General, Père Barré, etc. Père Barré quite an Irishman and too jocose for his station.

FATHER DE BEREY.

NOTE.—From his wit and repartee, Mrs. Simcoe evidently thought Father P. Felix de Berey, (pronounced Barry) an Irishman. He was, however, born in Montreal on 10th June, 1720, and elevated to the priesthood in 1743. His father was a military officer, and Father de Berey was a military almoner, wounded on the battlefield in ministering the last Sacraments. He was the last Provincial of the Recollets in Canada. De Berey gave dinners to the Governors, even to the Duke of Kent, and proposed a toast in his honor. He was invited to the officers' mess and his witty remarks and brilliant conversation were greatly appreciated there. He died 18th May, 1800.

Tues. 21st—Madame Báby, Mons. and Madame de Salaberry, etc., dined with us and stayed till two in the morning. Ther. 26 degrees below.

Sat. 25th—Walked to the provision store. The scene on the river is now a very gay one. Numbers are skating; carrioles driven furiously, as the Canadians usually do; and wooden huts are built on the snow, where cakes and liquor are sold, and they have stoves in their huts.

Thurs. March 1st—Walked to Pt. Levy.

MONS. DE SALABERRY.

Fri. 2nd—I gave a dance to forty people. The Prince was present. We have left the house we had in St. John Street, and taken one the back rooms of which look into the Ursuline gardens. By removing a wooden partition upstairs we have made a room, 45 feet long, with a tea room

SNOW SHOEING A MODE OF TRAVEL

and a card room adjoining, which makes a good apartment for a dance, with a supper room below. The Fusiliers are the best dancers, well dressed, and the best-looking figures in a ballroom that I ever saw. They are all musical and like dancing, and bestow as much money, as other regiments usually spend in wine, in giving balls and concerts, which makes them very popular in this place, where dancing is so favourite an amusement that no age seems to exclude people from partaking of it; and, indeed, I find giving dances much the easiest mode of entertaining company, as well as the most pleasant to them. Mr. Talbot (Lieut. Talbot) manages all the etiquette of our house, and is *au fait* in all those points which give weight in matters of no moment.

Sun. 4th—Capt. Shaw, of the Queen's Rangers, and four other gentlemen arrived from Frederickstown, in New Brunswick, which is 370 miles from hence. They walked on snow shoes 240 miles in 19 days, came up the river St. John, and crossed many small lakes. Their mode of travelling was to set out at daybreak, walk till twelve, when they stood ten minutes (not longer, because of the cold) to eat. They then resumed walking till half-past four, when they chose a spot, where there was good firewood, to encamp. Half the party (which consisted of 12) began felling wood; the rest dug away the snow till they had made a pit many feet in circumference, in which the fire was to be made. They cut cedar and pine branches, laid a blanket on them, and wrapping themselves in another, found it sufficiently warm, with their feet close to a large fire, which was kept up all night. Capt. McGill, who set out with them, cut his knee in felling wood, and was forced to stay at the Madawaska Settlement (now Edmundston, N.B.).

One of the attendants, a Frenchman, used to the mode of travelling, carried 60 lbs. weight and outwalked them all. They steered by the sun, a river, and a pocket compass. Captain Shaw is a very sensible, pleasant Scotchman, a Highlander. His family are to come from New Brunswick to Upper Canada next summer.

Capt. Shaw gave me a description of the moose deer, which they call here "Orignale," and of which we eat the moufle. Their legs are so long and their bodies so heavy that they step to the bottom of the snow, but they are so strong that they notwithstanding trot 10 miles an hour and travel through the most unbeaten country, subsisting on the moss of the trees and young boughs. They travel in droves, the strongest going first, and when they come to a good place for browsing stay till they have taken all the tender, and then seek another station. They may be tamed, but if several are not kept together, in the spring they will probably return to the woods. The moose deer is frequently met with in New Brunswick, and the caribou, which is so light an animal as scarcely to break the snow. I have seen a caribou at Mr. Finlay's. It was like an English fawn.

COLONEL SHAW.

NOTE.—Captain Æneas Shaw was a captain in the Queen's Rangers and served in the American War. He settled in York (Toronto) in 1793 and lived in a dwelling some hundred feet northwest of the present site of Trinity College on Queen Street. He became Lieutenant-Colonel in 1799. He attained the rank of Major-General, and was a member from June, 1793, of the Executive Council of Upper Canada. General Shaw died 15th February, 1815, and was buried in St. James' Churchyard, on the west side of the cathedral. His grandson is Colonel George

Shaw, formerly of the Post Office Department, and in his time an active member of the militia.

Captain John McGill was an officer of the Queen's Rangers under Lieutenant-Colonel Simcoe in the War of the Revolution. He settled in Upper Canada and was Commissioner of the Stores in 1793, Inspector-General of Accounts in 1805, and Receiver-General in 1818. He owned the site on Queen Street where the Metropolitan Church now stands, and built a commodious cottage upon it. This residence was known as "McGill Cottage," and in 1813, when the Americans visited York the women and children of the town were sent for safety to McGill Cottage, which was occupied by Captain McGill and his wife, who was a sister of the Honorable George Crookshank. A sister of Captain McGill married a McCutcheon, their sons being Peter and James McCutcheon. The elder son, Peter, was the inheritor of the bulk of the property in Upper Canada of Honorable Peter McGill, and it was a condition of his will that Mr. McCutcheon should assume the name "McGill." The Honorable Mr. McGill was from Dumfriesshire, Scotland, and came to Canada in 1809. He was President of the Bank of Montreal from June, 1834, until June, 1860, and died in September of that year.

The Honorable James McGill, founder of McGill College in Montreal, was not related to the foregoing family. He was born in Glasgow in 1744, and died in Montreal in 1813.

Bishop Strachan, of Toronto, also married a McGill, a daughter of Dr. Wood, of Cornwall, and widow of Dr. Andrew McGill of Montreal, but she was not connected with the families of either John, Peter or James McGill.

Many references to the McGill families in Canada in different publications conflict, owing

HON. JAS. McGILL.

to the fact that there was similarity of Christian names in all the families, hence the detail of relationship given.

Tues. 6th—We dined and supped at the Hon. Hugh Finlay's, the Deputy Postmaster-General of Canada under P.G.M. of Great Britain.

NOTE.—The Honorable Hugh Finlay was Deputy Postmaster-General for Canada from 1774 to 1800. He had served from 1750-1774 under Benjamin Franklin, first English Deputy Postmaster-General for the British-American Provinces.

Wed. 7th—Drove in an open carriole to Coll. Caldwell's. I gave a dance to thirty people this evening. I was this week in a covered carriole, ariving towards the Isle of Orleans, but part of the river having frozen, the ice was in so rough a state that I was quite seasick in the carriage. As we passed the furrows of ice, the learge heaps, collected in some places many feet high, formed an extraordinary sight.

Fri. 9th—Chief Justice Smith dined here. The Fusiliers acted "The Wonder" to-night.

Tues. 13th—Supped at Mr. Isaac Ogden's, Judge of the Admiralty.

MRS. SIMCOE'S ROUND OF PLEASURE

NOTE.—Honorable Justice Isaac Ogden of Quebec and Montreal, Court of King's Bench district of Montreal, appointed by Guy Carleton. He was born in New Jersey in 1740. In 1785, he was Judge of the Admiralty Court, Quebec, and later returned to Montreal. He resigned in 1818 and died in London, Eng., in 1824.

Wed. 14th—Supped at Mr. Coffin's.

HON. ISAAC OGDEN.

NOTE.—Thomas Ashton Coffin was a member of the celebrated family who had their descent from Tristram Coffin of Alwington, south of the boundary between Somerset and Devon in England, who settled in 1643 in New England at Salisbury and then went to Nantucket, at that time a dependency of New York. Thomas Ashton Coffin was private secretary of Sir Guy Carleton (Baron Dorchester in 1786) by whose side he sat in the last boat which left Castle Garden on the evacuation of New York in 1783. When Dorchester became Governor-General of Canada in 1786, Coffin accompanied him and by his influence was appointed Secretary and Controller of Accounts in Lower Canada. He died in England in 1810. Miss G. L. Coffin of Montreal is a connection of Thomas Coffin.

Thurs. 15th—Went to a musical party and a dance at the barracks, which was very pleasant. The Fusiliers all dance as well as Count Schernischoff or any famous Russian.

Another mail arrived, and no letter from you, my dear friend (Mrs. Hunt, who, with her daughter, Miss Hunt, took charge of Mrs. Simcoe's children at Wolford during the absence of the parents in Canada). How is it that you I esteem so wise should not have had observation enough to have found out by the newspapers that packets go to New York and Halifax every month, and are immediately forwarded from thence here? Do you not remember Lake Champlain and Lake George, Hudson's River, Skeneborough, on a creek of that name, Albany and all that route from New York to Quebec, which you have so often drawn, and which is passed constantly and in a rapid manner when the lakes are frozen? This town is now supplied with fresh cod in a frozen state from Boston, distant 500 miles, and it is sold at 6d. per lb. We have had some excellent venison from the township of Matilda (Iroquois, in Dundas County). I daresay you remember that name on the map, above 400 miles from hence. I find our maps to be little better than sketches, little of the country having been surveyed. The surveyors draw slowly, and, I am told, when they want to suit their maps to the paper, do not scruple cutting off a few miles of the river or adding to it.

Coll. Simcoe has had a letter from Capt. Murray, of the "Triton," from Halifax, which place he compares to Capua, in southern Italy. Coll. Simcoe makes the same complaint of Quebec, where he finds few men of learning or information, literary society not being necessary to the amusement of ladies. I am very well off amongst the women, and really find this a delightful place. The morning Coll. Simcoe and I spend together in reading, walking, etc. In the evening I go to balls, concerts, suppers, and, when I am with French families, *je fais la conversation d'une façon à peu près parisienne* (I speak as readily as a Parisian)—as Monsr. Báby is pleased to say—and to have everybody I see assiduous to please me, and to have nothing to do but to follow my own fancy, is a satisfactory mode of living, not always attainable on your side of the Atlantic. How happy I am.

I quite enjoy the thoughts of the long journey we have before us and the perpetual change of scene it will afford, but the people here think it as arduous and adventurous an undertaking as it was looked upon to be by my friends in England. It is surprising that those who are so much nearer to a country should esteem it as impracticable as those who are so many thousand miles distant.

Capt. Murray was all but lost in going to St. John, and from thence to Halifax. The day after he left Quebec the river was so full of ice his sailing would have been impossible. No ships ever left Quebec as late as the "Triton." The merchantmen sail on the 10th of October. Capt. Shaw also advises me not to believe the formidable accounts I have heard of rattlesnakes, of which he has seen numbers in Carolina. He affirms they never bite but when trod upon or attacked, and the wound they make is cured by well-known herbs, as horehound and juice from the plantain plant.

Sun. 18th—We walked from seven till nine this morning on the Heights of Abram, the plain on which Genl. Wolfe was killed. It is said he was shot from behind a fence by a French priest who is still living. The troops daily practice walking on these plains in snowshoes. The racket is made of deer or elk skins. The frame is of light wood an inch thick, 2½ feet long, 14 inches broad. We found it dry at this early hour on the track the troops had beaten.

NOTE.—During the engagement of the 13th September, 1759, Wolfe received three wounds. The first was probably from the Indians on  the right, the second from the French-Canadians who were advancing in the centre; and the third seems to have been from the Indians or Canadians in the bushes on Wolfe's right, sheltered in the only bit of short brushwood on the top of the cliff. The statement that Wolfe was shot by a French priest behind a fence is absurd, because there were no fences on the Plains, nor any kind of shelter beyond the bushes before mentioned, on the cliff. It has also been said, and the statement often repeated by newspapers, that Wolfe was shot by one of his own men in revenge for some punishment which Wolfe had inflicted for disobedience. This is also improbable, because Wolfe, at the time of his fatal wound, was at the head of his army in advance of Bragg's Regiment. As he received the wound in front, it must have proceeded from the enemy.

GENERAL WOLFE.

Mon. 19th—We dined at Mr. William's, the Clerk of the Council. Went in the evening to the concert, and returned to supper, an elegant supper in the Council Room, after which there was music.

Thurs. 22nd—Walked to "Sans Bruit." Capt. (Benjamin) Fisher, of the Royal Engineers, lent me his portfolio, in which there were some beautiful views taken in the Island of St. Domingo; I almost regretted not to have been in the West Indies. We supped at Mr. Ainslie's, the Collector of Customs, to-night.

Sat. 31st—We walked to Coll. Caldwell's before breakfast, and returned as far as "Sans Bruit" in a carriole and dined there. The most unpleasant time of the year is now commencing. The snow melting prevents the use of carrioles, and there is still too much to use calèches. During the month of April the people are, from this circumstance, little able to go from their houses; besides easterly winds, which bring rain, prevail very much.

Tues. April 3rd—We walked to Belmont before breakfast, and found the road dry, but in the middle of the day the snow was so melted by the excessive heat of the sun that we stayed there until eight o'clock and then walked home, the snow being then perfectly frozen again.

Wed. 4th—Mr. Fisher, of the Engineers, showed me some beautiful views he took of Windsor Castle for Prince Edward. His oil painting did not please me.

By the River, Quebec, 1792.
(From a Drawing by Mrs. Simcoe.)

Note.—This is evidently a rapid sketch of part of the river at Quebec, 1792. The building on the right is the Chateau St. Louis, and on the left is shown a powder magazine near the King's bastion.

Sun. 8th—We walked a mile before breakfast about Cape Diamond. After church we repaired to the lines with Mr. Talbot, who showed us an unfrequented terrace where Sir F. Haldimand began to make a walk on the side of this noble cliff, which is crowned by fortified works. The terrace commands the St. Lawrence as far as Cape Tourmenté, eleven leagues below Quebec, rocky and precipitous, and the Isle of Orleans to the east.

The shipping and the Lower Town are immediately below and towards the *Heights of Abraham* the blue distant hills of Vermont are seen, and the spray from the fall of the Chaudière River rising in Lake Megantic and joining the St. Lawrence about seven miles from Quebec. The rocks and brushwood that adorn the precipitous side of the hill form a fine foreground to this grand scene, with which we were so delighted that we came to view it again in the evening, and did not return home till it was dark, or rather starlight.

Note.—The commander of Quebec is styled "Commander of the Fortress of Quebec and of the Town Lines," which means the walls which encircle the city. The "lines" referred to in this passage would be some part of the grounds immediately within the walls.

83

DIARY OF MRS. SIMCOE

Fri. 13th—Walked towards Wolfe's Cove and upon Cape Diamond. Dined with Mrs. Winslow, wife of the Acting Paymaster-General.

NOTE.—The Winslows, one of the best known families on the American Continent, settled as U. E. Loyalists in Eastern Canada.

Joshua Winslow, who is given in the Quebec Directory of 1791 as residing at 12 St. John Street, was Paymaster-General of the British Forces in North America. His great-great-grandfather, John Winslow, born at Droitwich, England, in 1597, came to America in 1621, settled at Plymouth, Mass., and was a merchant and shipowner. He married in 1624, Mary, daughter of James Chilton, who came out in the "Mayflower." Joshua Winslow married Anna Green. They had a daughter Anna who while at school in Boston wrote an interesting diary. Joshua Winslow died in Quebec in 1801. Edward Winslow, a brother of John Winslow, was Governor of Plymouth for some years.

CASCADE NEAR WOLFE'S COVE, 1792.
(From a Drawing by Mrs. Simcoe.)

Fri. 20th—The Prince dined with us, Gen'l. Clarke, Mrs. Murray and St. Ours; a very cold evening indeed. As the cold weather and the short days leave us people cease to be sociable, and no kind of gaiety is continued but a few dinner parties. I have been so unaccustomed to pass evenings alone this winter that I do not like relinquishing balls, concerts, suppers and cards.

NOTE.—Honorable Paul Roch de St. Ours (sometimes Rocque) was born in 1747. He was Colonel commanding of the Assomption Division of the Militia in Lower Canada. In 1787, he was a member of the Legislative Council. His death took place in 1814.

PAUL ROCH DE
ST. OURS.

Sun. 29th—We walked twice this day to Cape Diamond. In the morning we saw a merchant vessel sail to England, the "Recovery," in which I sent letters by Mrs. Tosey, the Sussex clergyman's wife, to you and other friends. Walking on Cape Diamond after a rainy day, I saw amongst the distant hills to the north a cloud rise in a conic form in a light sky until it united with black clouds above. We thought it might be a waterspout. Last week the thermometer fell

84

ARRIVAL OF CHIEF JUSTICE OSGOODE

30 degrees in three hours and 54 in eleven hours. A beautiful moth was sent to me. It remained all day in a torpid state, and flew away at night.

Mr. Fisher, of the Royal Engineers, exchanges duty with Mr. Wolfe, in order to go to Niagara to take views of the Falls. I saw mosquitoes this evening while walking on the ramparts. They are like gnats. Last week I walked to Powell Place and Woodfield. The woods are beautiful, and we went near to Sillery, that pretty vale Emily Montague describes; indeed, her account of Quebec appears to me very near the truth.

A boat going to the Isle of Orleans was overset a few days ago. Fourteen passengers were drowned. Accidents often happen on this river by carrying too much sail. When the wind is against the tide it is very dangerous. The currents are excessively strong.

NOTE.—Powell Place was owned by Sir Henry Watson Powell, who resided there from 1780-95. It was renamed Spencer Wood by the Honorable Michael Henry Percival, a relative of the Honorable Spencer Percival, the Chancellor of the Exchequer, who was assassinated in England in 1812. The situation was most picturesque, about two miles from the city walls, on the south side of the St. Louis Road. It is now the residence of the Lieutenant-Governor of Quebec. The land occupied is about one-half of the estate as it was when known as Powell Place.

The "History of Emily Montague," by Mrs. Frances Brooke (Frances Moore) 1724-89, published in 1769, was a series of letters addressed from Sillery by Emily Montague, the heroine, to her friend, Arabella Fermor, to military admirers, and to some British noblemen, friends of her father. The work, which is dedicated to Guy Carleton, afterwards Lord Dorchester, is the earliest novel written in Canada. Mrs. Brooke was the wife of Rev. John Brooke, D.D., Rector of Colney, Norfolk, and Chaplain to the garrison at Quebec in 1764-8. It is said that the "handsome Colonel Rivers" who won the heart of Emily Montague was none other than Colonel Henry Caldwell. In all probability he was a friend of the novelist.

Sat. 2nd June—Mr. Osgoode, the Chief Justice of Upper Canada; Mr. Peter Russell, the Receiver-General; and Mr. White, the Attorney-General, arrived from England. Mr. Russell has his sister with him.

Miss Rolle sent me a doll in the Duchess of York's Court dress. My clothes for the 4th of June not being arrived, I made myself a turban like the doll's.

CHIEF JUSTICE
OSGOODE.

NOTE.—At the early age of fifteen William Osgoode entered Christ College as a commoner. He studied law, became M.A. in 1777, and was called to the bar of Lincoln's Inn. He was appointed first Chief Justice of Upper Canada in 1792, his active judicial duties commencing in August of that year. He was a Legislative Councillor of the Province, appointed to the Council in July, 1792, and in the following September was appointed Speaker. In consequence of his charge to a grand jury that slavery ought not to exist in the colony of Canada, the Legislature of Upper Canada passed in July, 1793, an Act entitled "An Act to prevent the further introduction of slaves, and to limit the terms of contracts for service within this Province." In 1794 Osgoode became Chief Justice of Lower Canada, retaining the office until 1801, when he resigned and returned to England. He died in 1824, aged seventy.

The Honorable Peter Russell was in 1792 appointed Receiver-General of Upper Canada by Governor Simcoe. As President of the Council he succeeded the Governor in 1796, retaining the position until 1799. In accordance with Simcoe's instructions the second Parliament of the Province met at York on 1st June, 1797, and several acts were passed during Russell's administration. His plan was to follow in the footsteps of Governor Simcoe, with whose policy he was familiar. He died at his home, Russell Abbey, Toronto, in 1808.

John White was Attorney-General of Upper Canada, and was killed in a duel, 3rd January, 1800.

HON. PETER RUSSELL.

Mon. June 4th—A splendid ball at the Chateau, but the heat was so great that I was very near fainting after having danced Money Musk and the Jupon rouge.

Tues. 5th—This afternoon we drove to Montmorency, about eight miles from Quebec, and drank tea there. I walked a little way up the river, which dashes over a very rocky bed among the woods, which, being now in leaf, made the accompaniment of the falls much finer than when I was last there.

NEAR THE FALLS OF MONTMORENCY, QUEBEC, 1792.

(*From a Drawing by Mrs. Simcoe.*)

CHAPTER VIII.

JOURNEY TO UPPER CANADA.

The pleasant sojourn of seven months at Quebec was "a new chapter in my life," said the Governor's wife in a letter to an English friend. The kindness, the hospitality, the respect and the courtesy which had been paid to them by those of the official circles in the ancient city gave untold pleasure to the newcomers. The Governor was popular because he was a man not only of extensive military experience but also of wide general knowledge, a gifted and interesting conversationist, and, withal affable and courteous to all with whom he came in contact. His wife made friends rapidly, and as became the wife of one occupying a distinguished position, she maintained a dignity and gentleness of manner that some say "was born with the Gwillims," while at the same time she had an attractiveness that was always remembered by the many friends she met.

On the 8th of June, 1792, Governor Simcoe, with his wife and party, set out towards his post in the Western province. Mrs. Simcoe often declared that she required a deal of courage to entrust herself and her children to the Canadian bateaux, which were the only possible means of transportation.

Fri. 8th June—At six this morning we left Quebec, walked through Fort Louis Gate, and descended the hill to the river, where we embarked in a large batteau (bateau) with an awning, accompanied by Lts. Grey and Talbot. Another batteau carried the children, and a third the servants and baggage. In three hours we reached Pt. aux Trembles (En Bas), on the north shore of the river, seven leagues above Quebec, landing a mile below the Maison de Poste. A small tent being pitched, we breakfasted, and afterwards went to see the church, which is a neat one and contains a picture of St. Cecilia, given by Gen'l. Murray, which is highly esteemed. We took an early dinner, of which an eel, caught here, formed a part, and as we had just finished our repast al fresco, the Bishop of Caps, who resides in this village, came to wait on Coll. Simcoe. He is a man more esteemed for his learning than religion; being once accused of having Voltaire's works in his library, he replied: "Les meilleurs médecins tiennent les poisons en leur boutique" (The best doctors keep poisons in their dispensary). He apologized for not inviting us to his house, as it was repairing.

We waited until near six for the tide, when we embarked, and passed some beautiful high banks covered with wood. At Jacques Cartier, on the north shore of the river, eight leagues above Quebec, between Three Rivers and Quebec, are mills on a river which flows into the St. Lawrence from between two very high hills much enriched by wood. It is an exceedingly strong pass and a picturesque scene.

The evening was delightfully calm. My admiration of the setting sun on the unruffled surface of this wide river was interrupted by meeting a boat, which brought English letters forwarded from Montreal, and the satisfaction of reading some of yours (letters from Mrs. Hunt at Wolford) engaged my attention as long as it was light enough to read.

It was ten o'clock when we arrived at Cap Santé, on the north shore. The man who kept the Maison de Poste was so ill that we could not be admitted there, so we walked towards a cottage where the habitants were going to bed, but with all possible French *politesse* the woman removed her furniture and children, and presently accommodated us with two empty rooms, with a thousand compliments and regrets that "des gens comme nous" (strangers) should be so ill lodged. The apartment was indifferent enough, but as we travel with a *boydet*, which is a folding camp chair as large as a mattress, the "Triton's" cot, blankets, and a mosquito net tent to hang over the bed, we soon furnished a room comfortable enough for people whom a long day's voyage had given sufficient inclination to sleep. The gentlemen slept in a batteau. It was too late to get our provisions from the boat, and we supped on the bread, eggs and milk the cottage afforded.

NOTE.—Cap Santé is on the west bank of the mouth of the River Jacques Cartier. It was here that the French encamped and threw up works after the capitulation of Quebec. John Montressor's map of 1760 shows the fort on the bank of the river. In his diary he says that when serving under that 'mad Murray' he disguised himself (being then a captain of engineers) as a drummer boy of marines and went to Jacques Cartier with a flag of truce, by which means he was able to examine the works and direct operations against them a few days later on.

Sat. 9th—We rose at six this morning, and walked on the hill which rises abruptly behind this house. It is a fine turf, with large trees scattered over it, and has a very park-like appearance. To the east the view is finely terminated by the church, which is covered with tin, as is usual in this country. It is surprising to me that it does not rust. It proves the habitual dryness of the air. The effects of tin roofs and steeples are very brilliant. Beyond Cap Santé the tide ceases. We embarked at nine and passed the rapids of Richelieu, after which the steeple of the church of Deschambault, 12 leagues above Quebec, embosomed in wood, becomes a fine spot. Coll. Simcoe wished to examine the ground at Deschambault with reference to it as a military position. I went on shore there with him while the gentlemen proceeded to the boat. I waited at the Maison de Poste (for I was indisposed) while Coll. Simcoe walked to the point, and in about an hour we set out in a calèche—a small carriage, buggy, on two wheels, with a hood, goes very fast, and is very light in weight, used in the Province of Quebec amongst the habitants—and drove nine miles through a beautiful woody country, over very rough roads, to Grondines, a village 16 leagues above Quebec, on the north shore, where we dined and slept at the house of Madame Hamelin, the seigneuresse of this village, whom we saw in the evening sitting in the churchyard, amid a large audience of peasants, reading and commenting on some handbills dispersed by a Quebec merchant (Mr. McCord), a candidate to represent this county (Hampshire) at the next election.

NOTE.—Hampshire was one of the original divisions of the Province of Quebec in its first Parliament. In the next electoral changes in 1829, the name Portneuf was applied to the county.

EN ROUTE TO UPPER CANADA

John McCord was a leading merchant in Quebec, one of the pioneers, son of John McCord, a leader of the English party after the cession of Canada. John McCord, Jr., appears to have thought of being a candidate for Hampshire in 1792, but apparently changed his mind, for his name is not given in the Parliamentary lists. His brother, Judge Thomas McCord, was, however, elected in 1810 for Montreal West, and for Bedford in 1817, which then comprised a vast tract. The McCord family was one of the most prominent in Quebec.

JOHN McCORD, JR.

David Ross McCord, K.C., of Temple Grove, Montreal, is a great-grandson of John McCord, Sr., and grandson of Judge Thomas McCord. John McCord, Jr., of whom Mrs. Simcoe writes, was his great-uncle.

The ruins of the old church and parsonage at Grondines may still be seen on the beach, about half a mile from the newer church of 1841.

Sat. 9th—The tone and *air decidé* of the reader, the attention of the audience and the Flemish appearance of their figures would have afforded an excellent picture. The Canadian women are better educated than the men, who take care of their horses and attend little to anything else, leaving the management of their affairs to the women.

I saw here a kind of mespilus, or medlar tree, which bore fruit almost pear shaped. They called it "*Poire sauvage*," and a fruit "*superbe*." "Magnifique" and "superbe" are words the Canadians apply on all occasions. Nothing could less call for such an epithet than the present fruit. A pretty wild plant, somewhat like buckwheat, called "*herbe à la puce*," is said to blister the hands and faces of those who touch it, though it is not equally poisonous to all persons. Here I met with an ugly insect of the beetle kind, called "*frappé d'abord*," which fetches blood wherever it strikes.

Sun. 10th—We left Grondines at 8. The current becoming very strong, the men were obliged to *tirer à la cordelle*, or drag the boat by ropes on a narrow beach under high, woody banks. We picked up pieces of chalk or clay, which drew like crayon, but the strokes were not so easily effaced. I saw millions of yellow and black butterflies, called New York swallow-tails, on the sand. We dined in the boat and passed St. Pierre les Becquets, a village (in Nicolet County) 22 leagues above Quebec, and its church on a very bold projecting point nearly opposite to Batiscan (in Champlain County). We disembarked this evening at Cap de la Magdelaine, the most dirty, disagreeable receptacle for mosquitoes I ever saw, the inhabitants even catching wood pigeons in a *most disagreeable manner*.

I take no sketch of a place I never wish to recollect. Mr. Talbot gave a shilling to liberate some wood pigeons I must otherwise have seen and heard fluttering most disagreeably. I was much obliged to him for this polite attention.

NOTE.—Batiscan is in Champlain County, 81 miles above Quebec, on the north shore of the St. Lawrence, near Three Rivers, which is 95 miles northeast of Montreal.

Mon. 11th—We rose at four and embarked, and went a league to Trois Rivières, in the County of St. Maurice, a town which takes its name from

DIARY OF MRS. SIMCOE

three rivers—St. Maurice, Richelieu and St. Lawrence—which spring from one source and, after having flowed some miles separately, unite and fall into the St. Lawrence half a mile below the town. There is a small convent here, and they work remarkably well on bark. We paid a great price for a bad breakfast at an inn kept by an Englishman, for we were not so lucky as to go to the French Maison de Poste, where we should have fared better and paid less. Three leagues from hence we reached Point du Lac, in St. Maurice County, at the entrance of Lake St. Pierre (St. Peter), which is about 15 leagues long. Three leagues farther we stopped to dine in the boat near Machiche, in a small cove, where the heat was intense and the mosquitoes numerous. From hence we passed extremely flat shores and confined scenery. The gentlemen were impatient of the heat, and perpetually wearying the conductor of the batteau with questions as to 'how far we were from Cap de Loup, complaining of the inconvenience of the trajet, meaning journey or voyage. At length he would say nothing except "*Mais pourtant il ne fait pas froid*" (It is nothing compared to the cold), which, indeed, we were all very sensible of. Went on shore early this evening at Rivière du Loup. (This village and river is the same in name as Rivière du Loup, in Kamouraska and Temiscouata Counties.) The village has a pretty bridge, and lies in a flat, cultivated country. We were but ill accommodated here, and nothing amusing occurred but Mr. Talbot's ineffectual efforts to paddle a canoe across the river. The difficulties he met with in this first attempt, and the handkerchief tied round his head, *à la Canadien*, diverted me much.

Mr. (Lieut.) Grey cut his finger, and applied the turpentine from the cones of the balm of Gilead fir, a remedy for wounds greatly esteemed. Collins the nurse girl's slow manner, characteristic of the Western States, diverted us. Being desired to make haste, she replied, "Must I not put the sugar in the children's breakfast?" in the true American tone.

NOTE.—Machiche is a village on the river of the same name in St. Maurice County, Quebec. The spelling Machiche is the common abbreviation of Yamachiche, from the Algonquin, meaning a muddy stream or river.

Tues. 12th—We embarked at four, and soon after we left Lake St. Pierre, stopped at Sorel (on right bank of River Richelieu, at mouth of Lake St. Peter), and took some refreshment at Mr. Doughty's, a clergyman whose wife is from New York, and the house was the cleanest and the neatest I have seen.

NOTE.—The Rev. John Doughty was chaplain in the King's Royal Regiment in the war of 1775. He was formerly a minister of the gospel at Schenectady on the south side of the Mohawk River in the State of New York. In 1781 he went to England; but returned to Canada and officiated as a missionary at Sorel.

The situation of Sorel is so flat that nothing relieves the prospect but the masts of a few small ships building here. We dined in the boat, and the heat was excessive, but the evening calm and so very pleasant as almost to persuade me it is worth while to cross the Atlantic for the pleasure of voyaging on this delightful lake-like river, the setting sun reflecting the deepest shades from the shores and throwing rich tints on the water. This repose is finely accompanied by the songs of the batteau men, which accord in time to the regular stroke of the oars and have the best effect imaginable. No wonder Spenser, Ariosto, etc., dwelt on the delight of sailing in a boat on lakes, and make it the approach to islands of delight. After a day of fatigue, where strong currents require peculiar exertion, they sing incessantly and give a more regular stroke with the oars when accompanied by the tunes. This practice has been learned from Grand

92

INCIDENTS ON THE JOURNEY

Voyageurs, or Canadians who are hired by the North-West Company to take canoes to the Grand Portage beyond Lake Superior. Now and then an Indian halloo breaks the often-repeated notes, and enlivens the sound. We admired one of their songs, *"Trois filles d'un Prince"* (Three Daughters of a Prince), so much that we desired it to be often repeated.

NOTE.—Edmund Spencer, a celebrated English poet, 1552-1599. Ariosto Ludovico, 1474-1533, a celebrated Italian poet, author of "Orlando Furioso."

Our attention was engaged by hearing firing from the shore. The batteau men said, *"Comme il faut à Mon'sr le Gouverneur"* (It is a welcome to Monsieur, the Governor), but who paid this respect we did not find out.

We reached the Maison de Poste at Dautray (Dautré) on north shore, just out of Lake St. Peter, west, before sunset, pitched the little tent, and admired rich tints and deep reflections from the opposite shore. We met with tolerably good rooms here. Mr. Littlehales, Coll. Simcoe's Military Secretary, overtook us here, and brought with him letters from you (Mrs. Hunt) which made me very happy. He travelled post from Quebec, where he arrived in the last vessel.

NOTE.—Major E. B. Littlehales, who was Military Secretary to Governor Simcoe during the period of his residence in Canada, was

an excellent official of the Crown as well as of Governor Simcoe, in preparing plans and obtaining information respecting the newly settled country, the affairs of which his chief was called upon to administer. He was also an author of some repute, being the writer of the " Journal of an Exploring Excursion from Niagara to Detroit," first given to the public in 1834, though the expedition took place in 1793.

Major Littlehales, who returned to England on the recall of Governor Simcoe, was shortly afterwards promoted to the rank of lieutenant-colonel, and in 1801 became Under-Secretary of the Military Department in Ireland, which position he held until 1820. In 1802 Lieutenant-Colonel

SIR E. B. BAKER.

Littlehales was created a Baronet, and by Royal License in 1817 assumed the surname of Baker in lieu of that of Littlehales, on inheriting the property of Ranston in Dorsetshire, thus being for the rest of his life Sir Edward Baker Baker. His grandson, Sir Randolph Littlehales Baker, M.P. for North Dorset and residing at Blandford, Dorset, England, is the present baronet.

Wed. 13th—We set out at four in the morning. In the afternoon we saw the Blue Mountains of Chambly, a village in Chambly County, on the Richelieu River, five leagues from Montreal, and Beloeil Mountain, a considerable elevation in the County of Rouville, seven leagues from Montreal, both of which we noticed with pleasure, not having before seen any distant view during our voyage.

We passed Varennes (in Verchères County), a large village and handsome church on the shore, six leagues below Montreal. That of Cap Santé, twelve leagues above Quebec, was built in imitation of it. At eight

DIARY OF MRS. SIMCOE

we reached Pointe aux Trembles (En haut), on the island of Montreal, and ten leagues from Dautray. Here we went on shore, intending to go by land the remaining three leagues to Montreal. We found Capt. Stevenson

CHAMBLY, ON THE ST. LAWRENCE, 1792.
(From a Drawing by Mrs. Simcoe.)

just arrived in Mr. Frobisher's phaeton, sent for me, as a hired calèche is a wretched conveyance on the excessive rough roads around Montreal. Notwithstanding the merits of the phaeton and the river, I every moment

VARENNES, ON THE ST. LAWRENCE, 1792.
(From a Drawing by Mrs. Simcoe.)

expected to have been thrown out by the violent jerks in passing over the ruts in this bad road.

At eleven o'clock we arrived at Montreal, and after a little delay, occasioned by the lateness of the hour, we got into Government House,

JOSEPH FROBISHER.

and I was delighted with the size and loftiness of the rooms, which are so much better than any I have been in at Quebec. On the road we passed a group of Indians sitting around a fire near the river, which in this dark night afforded a good subject for a picture.

NOTE.—Joseph Frobisher was one of those who in the winter of 1783-4, with Simon McTavish, formed what has been known in Canadian history as the "North-West Company." He was the first to proceed to the great unknown West, and went as far as the Churchill River. Up to 1774, all the Indians of that vast region were accustomed to carry their furs to the Hudson's Bay. Mr. Frobisher meeting several bands of Indians on the way thither induced them to trade with him. He remained two years in the country, enduring great hardships, but established a firm trade with the red men. He returned in 1776, and during these two years, so plentiful were the

94

furs and on such advantageous terms were they bought that when he arrived in Montreal he had secured what at that time was considered a competency. His brother Benjamin, who died in 1787, travelled even further west and was the first white man who ever reached "Isle à la Croix."

In 1798, Joseph retired from commercial life. He had come from England, and with James McGill was a vestryman of what was then called the "Protestant Congregation of Montreal." This afterwards became Christ Church, erected in Notre Dame Street, and burned down. It is now the English Cathedral on St. Catherine Street. He and John Richardson represented the East Ward of Montreal in the first Parliament of the Province of Lower Canada in 1792-6. His son represented St. Laurent District in 1804.

GOVERNMENT HOUSE—CHATEAU DE RAMEZAY, MONTREAL.
(From "Hochelaga Depicta.")

Sun. 17th—The joy I felt in finding myself in spacious apartments was checked the next day by finding the heat more insufferable than I had ever felt. The thermometer continued at 96 for two days, and the heat was not ill-described by a sentinel who exclaimed, "There is but a sheet of brown paper between this place and hell." In the town are abundance of merchants' storehouses, the doors and windows of which are iron, and many of the houses, as well as churches, are covered with tin. By these circumstances, I believe, the heat is increased. The Government House is built on arches, under which are very large offices, which might be made very comfortable summer apartments.

NOTE.—The Government House referred to was the building now known as the Chateau de Ramezay. The earliest view of the Government House, Montreal, is found in "Hochelaga Depicta," published in 1839, but it is not very accurate. The elaborate railing and coping of the wall shown do not date back so far.

It was the residence of Claude de Ramezay, Governor of Montreal, from its erection in 1705 until his death in 1724, and although

Madame de Ramezay made several attempts to get the Government to purchase it for a Governor's residence, she never succeeded. So in 1745 the heirs sold it to "La Compagnie des Indes," which company made it the headquarters of the fur trade in Canada, and so it continued until the conquest. The company's further trade in Canada having been interdicted, it sold "India House" to William Grant, who in 1774 leased it, and four years later sold it to the Government. Governor Haldimand often resided in it, and no doubt others too, but there is not much documentary history relating to it from its purchase in 1778 until about 1820, when sundry items began to appear in the estimates for the repairs and the upkeep of the Government House at Montreal. Later Mrs. Monk, widow of a petty officer

MONKLANDS, A FORMER GOVERNMENT HOUSE, MONTREAL.
(From "Montreal After 250 Years.")

in one of the regiments of the line who had been keeper of stores at St. Johns, was appointed housekeeper to the Government House. She was the mother of the celebrated Maria Monk.

On the complaint of Lord Aylmer, Governor-General, in 1831, that the Government House was in bad repair, and so destitute of furniture that it necessitated great expense in moving his furniture to and from Montreal every time he visited the place, a bill was passed authorizing the expenditure of £300 to £400 in furnishing the Government House and a large sum to put it in repair. A commission was appointed to supervise this expenditure and plans and specifications were made for elaborate repairs which included the addition of another storey, but the amount required so exceeded the vote that little was done and the amount appeared as an unexpended balance on the estimates for several years afterwards.

THE TOWN OF MONTREAL

In 1837, the house was made the headquarters of the special council which was appointed during the rebellion and sat there until 1841. The Governor, then of necessity a regular resident in the city, occupied a rented house on the opposite corner. In 1845, when the seat of government of the united provinces was moved from Kingston to Montreal, the building was set apart for departmental offices and Monklands acquired for the Government House. It was then that some of the changes that characterize the Chateau de Ramezay of to-day were made. In 1894 the Chateau was sold by the Provincial Government and purchased by the Corporation of the City of Montreal, and in 1895 the Numismatic and Antiquarian Society obtained the building for the purpose of founding an Historical Portrait Gallery and Museum.

Monklands was built by the Monk family and was situated at Côte St. Antoine on the side of the mountain. The house is now called the Ville Marie Convent and is the boarding school of the Nuns of the Congregation. On each side the nuns have had large additions made but the house still remains just as it was when Government House. In the fire which destroyed the Convent some years ago, the original building escaped.

Mon. 18th—I was so oppressed by the heat that it diminished the pleasure of driving on the mountain of Montreal. A mile from the town it rises in the midst of a plain, like the Wrekin, one of the highest points in Shropshire. The view from it is remarkably fine, commanding a vast extent of river diversified by islands. The towns of Longueuil, on the right bank of the river, and L'Assomption, etc., are opposite, and the distance terminated by the Blue Hills of Chambly.

The town of Montreal is large, and the spires of the churches, covered with tin, give a brilliancy to the scene and look like mosques. The country around is much cultivated, and orchards cover nearly all the top of the mountain. Capt. Stevenson carried us two miles beyond the fine prospect towards La Chine (Lachine), which is three leagues above Montreal, I think merely to show how bad the road was, and we returned about nine o'clock to Mr. Frobisher's villa on the side of the mountain, and drank tea there.

In going from hence to Montreal we saw the air filled with fire flies, which, as the night was dark, appeared beautiful, like falling stars. I dined at Mr. Frobisher's house in the town, where the chairs were the same as I have seen sold in London for four guineas each.

NOTE.—Mr. Frobisher's villa, or country house, which Mrs. Simcoe speaks of as being on the side of the mountain, was named Beaver Hall and was situated on the ridge of the Beaver Hall Hill, near the present position of Belmont Street, Montreal. It was on the line of the latter street and across the line of the present street called after it, Beaver Hall, which latter was on the site of Frobisher's avenue leading to the house. It blocked the present Beaver Hall (street).

Tues. 19th—I dined with La Baronne de Longueuil at a pretty house she and Mr. Grant have built on the north shore of her island of St. Helen's, opposite the east end of Montreal. Though the distance is so short, the current is so strong that the passage is rather alarming. The island is four miles in circumference, and the views from many points very pretty. Montreal and Longueuil are good objects to view from it. La Baronne has the only hothouse I have seen in Canada. Ice houses are very general here, but seldom used for the purpose of furnishing ice for a dessert. They use the ice to cool liquors and butter, and the ice houses are used for larders to keep meat.

NOTE.—The third Baron de Longueuil, Charles Jacques Le Moyne, died while on active military service in 1755. His infant daughter, Marie Charles Joseph, born some months later, inherited the title as fourth Baroness. Her mother (Marie Fleury d'Eschambault, of a noble French family), known as the Dowager Baroness, married a second time, in 1770, Honorable William Grant, Receiver-General, while the daughter became the wife in 1781 of Captain David Alexander Grant, nephew of the Receiver-General.

DOWAGER BARONESS
DE LONGUEUIL.

Shortly after her marriage with Honorable William Grant the Dowager Baroness built a residence on the picturesque family property on St. Helen's Island. It was here Mrs. Simcoe was entertained during her first visit to Montreal, and where in all probability she met the younger people.

It is stated that the fourth Baroness in her own right, a much loved person in the family and respected in Montreal society of her day, did not assume rank until the death of her mother in 1818. In her marriage contract, however, she is styled "Mademoiselle Marie Charles Joseph

HON. WM. GRANT.

Lemoine de Longueuil, Baroness de Longueuil et Dame de Beloeil, fille majeure usante et jouissante de ses droits," which shows clearly that she assumed title on attaining her majority. The contract further states that she was sole inheritor of the name, arms and estate of the third Baron.

There is no portrait of the fourth Baroness in existence, except the one as an old lady, here given, while her mother's picture is from an oil painting made comparatively early in life.

Mrs. M. Arklay Fergusson of Ethiebeaton, Scotland, Mrs. Fairclough, wife of Prof. Rushton Fairclough, Stanford University, Cal., and Mrs. J. Maule Machar, Kingston, Ont., are, on their mother's side, great-great-granddaughters of the third Baron de Longueuil, while Madame F. Falret de Tuite, Reginald, Baron de Longueuil, John Grant de Longueuil and Mademoiselles de Longueuil, Pau, France, bear the same relation through their

FOURTH BARONESS
DE LONGUEUIL.

father. Mrs. Machar's husband was the only son of the late Rev. Dr. Machar, at one time principal of Queen's University, Kingston, and only brother of Agnes Maule Machar, the well-known Canadian authoress. The nephew of the present Baron is heir to the title and property.

Fri. 22nd—We went from Montreal to La Chine (Lachine), ten miles of very rough road, in Mr. Frobisher's carriage. The river from Montreal to La Chine is so shallow and full of rocks, and currents so strong that the boats always go up unloaded, the baggage being sent in waggons. Sir John Johnson, the agent for Indian Affairs, has a neat-looking house in this village.

We slept at a very indifferent house, to which, as it bore the name of an inn, we did not bring our beds or provisions, and were the worse off as to lodging. I disliked the dirty appearance of the bed, and slept on a blanket upon the table. Opposite this place and on the other side of the river is Caughnawaga, a village of Indians who are Catholics (in Laprairie County, on south shore of the St. Lawrence). They have a neat church there.

Sat. 23rd—We embarked at six. Soon afterwards left Pointe Claire and Isle Perrot (15 miles from Montreal, an island in the River St. Lawrence, S.W. of the island of Montreal, between the Lake of the Two Mountains and Lake St. Louis) to the north, and saw the junction of the Ottawa or Grand River, which divided Upper and Lower Canada with the St. Lawrence, the former pouring its dirty coloured water into the transparent stream of the St. Lawrence at the St. Anne's rapids, above the island of Montreal.

NOTE.—Besides the Ottawa or Grand River here mentioned, there is another Grand River (known also as the Ouse) in Ontario, which empties into Lake Erie.

We soon arrived at the Cascades, the commencement of the rapids above La Chine. The term "rapid" is meant to describe shallow water, strong currents and a rocky bottom, which causes the whole surface of the water to appear foaming and white, like breakers at sea. The batteau men kept as close to shore as possible, and by dint of exertion and labour they pole and tow the boat up against the current. We went on shore at the Cascades, and walked a mile through a wood and saw the boats pass some tremendous rapids near this place, where Gen'l. Amherst lost eighty men during the last war by coming down without conductors in the boats. Saw a swordfish in a little stream near the mill. After our re-embarking we came to a very strong current at Point au Diable (a prominent headland four miles west of the Cedars village).

The gentlemen walked to lighten the boat. I was tired by the heat, and laying my head on a trunk in the boat, I slept till the rapid was past. Two leagues from hence we met with one more formidable, so that the baggage in the boats was moved into waggons, and we went in a calèche as far as the Cedars, a village ten leagues above Montreal, where there is a tolerable inn, at which we slept. M. de Longueuil has a seigneurie near this place. These properties, estates or grants of land were given to the old French families who had settled in the Province of Quebec, by Louis XIV. Seigneur was the title for the Lord of the Manor.

Sun. 24th—Seven miles from Les Cedres is Coteau du Lac (or St. Ignace, a village in Soulanges County, 37 miles south-west of Montreal), where we passed through locks. A few troops are stationed in a house here. Opposite to it is an island called Prison Island. It was so called from some rebels having been confined on it during the last war, some of whom escaped by swimming across the rapids by which it is surrounded.

NOTE.—This island is at the mouth of Lake St. Francis, an expansion of the St. Lawrence, midway between the west part of Grand Isle and the estuary of the River de L'Isle.

A few miles beyond this entered Lake St. Francis, and saw a part of the blue ridge of the endless mountains. Four leagues from Coteau de Lac is Pointe au Bodet, the centre of Lake St. Francis and the commencement of Upper Canada.

NOTE.—Pointe au Bodet is on the north shore of Lake St. Francis, in the Seigneury of Monsieur de Longueuil, and a little east of the cove in which is the boundary line between the Provinces of Quebec and Ontario.

We arrived here about sunset, and at a small inn on the Point found the principal inhabitants of the Township of Glengarry (Highlanders in their national dress). They came to meet the Governor, who landed to speak to them. They preceded us in their boat, a piper with them, towards Glengarry House, Mr. McDonell's, where the gentlemen went, but the wooden awning of our boat being blown off by a violent and sudden squall arising, we were glad to make towards the shore as fast as possible at Pointe Mouille on Lake Francis, west of Pointe au Bodet, and thought ourselves lucky that the boat had not been overset. We met with a miserable, wretched, dirty room at a Highlander's, the only house within some miles.

NOTE.—Colonel John Macdonell was a captain in Butler's Rangers (his father having first settled in America at the breaking out of the Revolutionary War). In 1792 he was elected member for Glengarry and was afterwards Speaker of the first House of Assembly of Upper Canada. He was lieutenant-colonel commanding the 2nd Royal Canadian Volunteers, recruited in 1796 and disbanded after the Peace of Amiens. He married Helen, daughter of Henry Yates, at one time Governor of the State of New York. Colonel Macdonell built one of the first stone houses in Ontario at a point on the St. Lawrence below Cornwall and west of Pointe au Bodet. The house was burned down in 1813 but the ruins still remain and the point is known as Glengarry Point or Stonehouse Point.

Colonel John Macdonell of Glengarry has been frequently confused with Colonel John Macdonell who was killed at Queenston Heights in 1812. The latter, however, was a nephew of the first Speaker, and J. A. Macdonell, K.C., of Alexandria, Ont., is a great-grandnephew of Colonel John Macdonell, the First Speaker, and a grandnephew of Colonel John Macdonell, the Attorney-General who was also A.D.C. to General Brock. He was killed with that officer at Queenston, and buried under the monument erected on the Heights. A. McLean Macdonell, K.C., Toronto, is also a great-grandnephew of the first Speaker of the Legislature of this Province, while A. Claude Macdonell, K.C., M.P., is a near kinsman.

Mon. 25th—We breakfasted with Mr. McDonell, four leagues from Pointe Mouille; his new house (Glengarry) he has not finished, and resides in that which he first erected on his ground. A Catholic priest, his cousin, was there, who has lived five years among the Iroquois Indians at St. Regis (near Cornwall). They have a church, and he performs

POINTE AU BODET, 1792.
(From a Drawing by Mrs. Simcoe.)

divine service in the Iroquois, of which he is a perfect master, and he says their attention to the church service is very great, and the women sing psalms remarkably well. After breakfast we proceeded a league to Coll. Gray's, from whence the Governor went to the Isle of St. Regis, to visit the Indians at their village, where they received him with dancing in a fierce style, as if they wished to inspire the spectators with terror and respect for their ferocious appearance. We slept at Coll. Gray's, at Gray's Creek, four miles below Cornwall.

NOTE.—The Catholic priest to whom Mrs. Simcoe refers was the Rev. Roderick Macdonell, well known as "Mr. Roderick," a cousin of Colonel John Macdonell. He was educated at the Scots College, Valladolid, and was first priest in Glengarry, being stationed at St. Regis on the south shore of the St. Lawrence, a short distance below Cornwall. This was always an Indian settlement.

James Gray, known as Colonel Gray, was born in Scotland and served in the British Army for 26 years. In 1763 he was captain in the 42nd or Black Watch Regiment, and was afterwards major of the 1st Battalion of the King's Royal Regiment of New York. He settled at what is known as Gray's Creek, near Cornwall. He died on 11th May, 1796. Colonel Gray's son, Robert Isaac Dey Gray, was the first Solicitor-General for Upper Canada. His name was second on the list of charter members of the Law Society of Upper Canada, 1797. In 1804, he was lost in the "Speedy" on Lake Ontario on his way to Presqu' Isle, where an Indian was to be tried for murder.

Tues. 26th—Capt. Munro came here and brought a horse of Mr. Duncan's for me to ride. As it would be very tedious to go up the Long Sault in the boat, we propose riding beyond that and another rapid called Galettes. We set off about ten o'clock. On our way we passed through Cornwall (22 leagues south-west of Montreal), a settlement four miles from Coll. Gray's. There are about fifteen houses and some neat gardens in them; and rode eleven miles to Mr. Macdonell's at the Long Sault, his farm being very near that Grand Rapid, which rapid continues a mile; the whole of the river foaming like white breakers, and the banks covered with thick woods, is a very fine sight.

NOTE.—Captain Munro was the Honorable John Munro of Matilda, a member of the first Legislative Council. Born in Scotland in 1731, he came to America in the 48th Regiment in 1756. As a magistrate he had come into fierce opposition before the Revolutionary War with Seth Warner and Ethan Allan in northern New York. He was captain in the King's Royal Regiment of New York and lost in consequence of the Rebellion a

HON. JOHN MUNRO.

large area of land near Fort Bennington, N. Y. In the Canada Archives, 1891, will be found a report by him (1784) on the lands of New Brunswick. By one daughter who married Colonel Eustache de Lotbiniere he was the ancestor of Sir Henry Joly and the Harwoods of Montreal; Major W. F. W. Carstairs of Strathcona, and

J. S. Carstairs of Toronto, are descendants of another member of his numerous family.

The Long Sault Rapids are in the St. Lawrence River, between Barnhart and Long Sault Island, twelve miles above Cornwall. They are about nine miles long.

Mrs. Macdonell sang Erse songs very pleasingly, and her children and servants speak no language but Erse, the language of the descendants of the Gaels or Celts in the Highlands of Scotland; Gaelic, belonging to Erse (Irish). I wish'd they had not thought it necessary respect to dine very late. There are wolves and bears in this part of the country. They sometimes carry off sheep, calves or pigs, but do not attack men.

Mr. Duncan's (Capt. Richard Duncan, late of 55th Regt.) horse carried me very well. It is certainly necessary to have a horse of the country to pass the bridges we everywhere met with, whether across the creeks (very small rivers) or swamps. The bridges are composed of trunks of trees unhewn, of unequal sizes, and laid loosely across pieces of timber placed lengthways. Rotten trees sometimes give way and a horse's leg slips through, and is in danger of being broken. The horse I am now riding had once a fall through an old bridge. He now goes very carefully. Coll. Gray tells me that the juice of horehound and plantain, a tropical plant yielding fruit extensively serviceable for food, cures the bite of a rattlesnake. A negro in Carolina obtained his freedom in the last war for the discovery. We had black bass for dinner. Great numbers are caught near the rapids. They are extremely good, nearly as large as carp, as firm as a dory and of very good taste, but we dined too late to be pleasant. I suppose it was meant for respect.

NOTE.—Honourable Richard Duncan, whose memory still survives in Dundas County as "Judge Duncan," and whose daughter's name is perpetuated in Mariatown, now really an outlying part of Morrisburg, came to America in 1755. He became a captain in Sir John Johnson's corps, and married a sister of Captain (afterwards Colonel) Thomas and Captain William Fraser. He was a member of the first Legislative Council.

When Mrs. Simcoe was on her way west to Niagara Mr. Duncan presented her with a horse named "Jack" which was taken to Navy Hall and used during her residence there.

Wed. 27th—We rode ten miles to a tolerable inn, where a dinner was prepared, but we were engaged to dine and sleep at Capt. John Munro's, who had served in the Revolutionary War, twelve miles beyond this place. The first eight we went in the boat, and the remaining four we rode.

An Irish Captain gave us a basket of wild strawberries, which were as large and as well flavoured as the best scarlet strawberries in gardens in England. We passed Capt. Duncan's house a mile before we came to the Rapid Plat, close to which is Capt. Munro's. His wife is a Dutch woman, and the house was excessively neat and clean, and one of his daughters very handsome. We went to see Mr. Munro's sawmill, where a tree was cut into 16 planks an inch thick in an hour.

NOTE.—In the list of Justices of the Peace appointed June 10th, 1793, are found the names of William and John Fraser, Richard Duncan, John Munro and James Gray.

The cutting of a log into sixteen planks twelve feet long and an inch thick, would in a saw mill to-day take three minutes.

CANADIAN WHEAT IN 1792

Thurs. 28th—We set out on horseback this morning; took some refreshments at Mr. T. Frasier's, six miles from the Long Sault, and then rode five miles to Mr. W. Frasier's, where we dined. His house is just beyond Les Galettes (Galoos or Gallops, off Pointe Gallop), the last rapid on this side of Lake Ontario.

NOTE.—Colonel Thomas Fraser, born in Scotland, was a son-in-law of Hon. John Munro. Before enlisting in McAlpine's Corps, in which he served as lieutenant, his record is given as "a farmer of property in the Province of New York, lost by the Rebellion." He served during the Revolutionary War, at the close of which he received a grant of land in Grenville. In 1796 he was chosen as a non-resident member for Dundas. Two of the leading military officers of Dundas, John Munro and Richard Duncan, being out of reach, the electors determined to select a representative military officer residing outside of their townships, and so Thomas Fraser was chosen.

Captain William Fraser, also a Loyalist, was a brother of Colonel Thomas Fraser.

Thurs. 28th—I observed on my way hither that the wheat appeared finer than any I have seen in England, and totally free from weeds. Mr. Frasier mentioned an instance of the fertility of the soil. One of his fields having produced a great quantity of wheat, and that what fell out in reaping had the next year produced a very fine crop, without the field having been plowed or sown. There are many Dutch and German farmers about here, whose houses and grounds have a neater and better appearance than those of any other people. This afternoon we proceeded in the boat to Monsr. Lorimer's, an agent for Indian Affairs, where we had good venison but indifferent lodging. Coll. Simcoe stopped on the way to look at Isle Royale.

NOTE.—Chevalier Lorimer was an interpreter of the Indian Department in 1797.

Isle Royale is between Gallop Island and River de la Vielle Galette, near Point Patterson.

Fri. 29th—We embarked early and met the 26th Regt. in a brigade of boats. We stopped to speak to Capt. Talbot, who is in Prince Edward's family. He had been to see the Falls of Niagara, and was returning with the 26th Regt.

NOTE.—Captain Talbot was one of Prince Edward's suite, when in Canada. He is previously mentioned by Mrs. Simcoe when staying in Quebec, as Prince Edward was then residing there, at Montmorency House, near the Falls. In August, 1790, the 26th proceeded to Niagara and in June, 1792, returned to St. John's. Captain Talbot was not an officer of the 26th, nor was he related to Mr. Talbot, private secretary of Colonel Simcoe. In the Quebec Directory of 1791, there appears "Captain Talbot, H.R.H's suite 4 Ann St."

Fri. 29th—We passed to-day some rocks beautifully variegated with yellow and grey tints. I believe clay was among it. We saw a number of fine hemlock spruce trees. They are an exceedingly handsome tree, like yew, but of a lighter foliage, though as dark a colour, and grow to a more immense height than the English people can suppose probable. We came to so miserable a house where we were to lodge to-night, within a league of Grenadier Island, that we preferred pitching a tent for ourselves, letting the children sleep in the boat, and left the house for the gentlemen. While the tent was pitching I fished and caught a small perch. Many people carry trolling lines, or lines which run out of a small fishing wheel or pulley lying out of the stern in their boat, and catch abundance of black bass and other fish all the way up the St. Lawrence. Capillaire or maidenhair fern and its species grows in great perfection throughout this country. Much surprised to find the blankets so wet in a tent, although the weather had been dry.

NOTE.—Grenadier Island, one of the Thousand Islands, is four-teen miles above Brockville, and is about five miles long.

Sat. 30th—After passing Grenadier Island we came to the Thousand Islands. The different sizes and shapes of these innumerable isles have a pretty appearance. Some of them are many miles in extent, many of them only large enough to contain four or five trees, pine or oak, growing on a grey rock, which looks very pretty, variegated by the different mosses with which the crevices are filled.

We passed the river Gananowui (Gananoque), and half a mile beyond it came to Carey's house, which was so dirty a house that we again pitched the tent, which, notwithstanding it rained incessantly the whole evening and the greatest part of the night, kept us quite dry, and I slept vastly well. I was surprised to find how wet the bed clothes were in the tent when I rose, and yet I caught no cold, though these nights were the first in which I slept in a tent. In spite of the rain Coll. Simcoe went to the mill on the Gananowui River near its mouth, where a harbour might be made for shipping. This river has communication a great way back with the river Rideau, and by some lakes to the Ottawa River. These and other advantages make this one of the most eligible situations for the establish-ment of a town, but Sir John Johnson obtained a grant of the land here-about, which prevents the probability of any such improvements being made by Government.

NOTE.—Judge McDonald, of Brockville, informs me that ac-cording to a statement said to have been made in 1854 by one Mrs. Charlotte Jameson, then the oldest inhabitant of Gananoque, Joel Stone was the first white person who ever resided on the peninsula on the west side of the Gananoque River. He was landed from a French bateau and left to his own resources. Fortun-ately a resident on a nearby island espied the handkerchief with which Stone was signalling for help and sent two Indians to rescue him. They took him over to the is-land where a Frenchman named Carey, an uncle of

CAREY'S HOUSE, GANANOQUE.
(From a drawing by Mrs. Simcoe.)

Mr. Jameson, lived alone in a hut. Eventually Mr. Stone and Carey removed to the mainland, and the latter kept a house of public enter-tainment. The place was only accessible by open boat, while no bread could be obtained except hard biscuits. For Mr. Stone and for

VIEW NEAR THE THOUSAND ISLANDS, 1792.

(From a Drawing by Mrs. Simcoe.)

travellers, they kept a kind called King's biscuit, while for the others they provided navy biscuit. They kept two cows and exchanged the milk with the bateau men for biscuit, and exchanged the latter again with the Indians for fish, venison, game and wild fruit. Carey had been formerly a waiter and knew how to cook and wait upon gentlemen, so that he and Stone were tolerably comfortable. One day when they were all absent, the building and Mr. Stone's effects were burned, and this was the means of breaking up their family arrangement, as Carey took a farm two miles above Gananoque at Jameson's or Sheriff's Point, and lived there with his sister, Mrs. Sheriff, and a little girl, afterwards Mrs. Jameson. The picture shown is of Carey's house at Gananoque.

VIEW NEAR GANANOQUE, 1792.
(From a Drawing by Mrs. Simcoe.)

Sun. July 1st—We rose very early this morning in order to take a view of the mill at Gananowui before we proceeded on our way to Kingston. The scenery about the mill was so pretty that I was well repaid for the trouble of going. Then we returned to our large boat and proceeded. After passing Grande Island and Isle Cauchois, we drew near to Kingston, which we were aware of before we saw the houses, as we discerned the white waves of Lake Ontario beyond, looking like a sea, for the wind blew extremely fresh.

NOTE.—Wolfe Island, three miles from Kingston, was called by the French Grande Island. General Simcoe in his proclamation, 1792, directed it to be called Wolfe Island. Howe Island, nine miles from Kingston, was called by the French Isle Cauchois, and was named by General Simcoe or his advisers, Howe Island, after Lord Howe.

Kingston is six leagues from Gananowui, and is a small town of about fifty wooden houses and merchants' storehouses. Only one house is built of stone. It belongs to a merchant. There is a small garrison here and a harbour of ships. They fired a salute on our arrival, and we went to the house appointed for the commanding officer, at some distance from the barracks. It is small but very airy, and so much cooler than the great house in Montreal that I was very well satisfied with the change. The Queen's Rangers are encamped a quarter of a mile beyond our house, and the bell tents have a pretty appearance. The situation of this place is entirely flat, and incapable of being rendered defensible. Therefore, were its situation more central, it would still be unfit for the seat of government.

CHAPTER IX.

SIMCOE TAKES OATH OF OFFICE.

Kingston in 1792 was the most important spot on the map of Canada, west of Montreal. It was not only the military but the commercial centre of the new province and occupied that position for many years. The Legislature of the Province of Canada after the Union Act of 1841 held three sessions there from 14th June, 1841, until 5th March, 1844, when the seat of government was removed and the settlements west on the lake secured in natural course the trade that from humble beginnings has to-day a volume ever increasing with the great tide of population.

Kingston is situated at the head of the St. Lawrence at the outlet of Lake Ontario. The harbor is an excellent one, and ships of any size can be accommodated in perfect safety. In 1672 the place was known as Cataraqui, and visited by De Courcelles, the Governor of New France. He was succeeded by Count Frontenac and the fort was built by him and named in his honor. This fort was held by the French until 1758, when it fell into the hands of the British under Colonel Bradstreet.

In 1783 a number of Loyalist emigrants under Captain Michael Grass settled in what is now the Township of Kingston. The surveys were made by Deputy Surveyor John Collins. The town plot was laid out in 1783. The first picture of Cataraqui showing what was left of Fort Frontenac, was made in 1783. It was styled "a southwest view of Cataraqui drawn by James Peachey, Ensign 60th Regiment. Taken by Louis Kotte."

About 1788 Kingston was selected by the British Government as a military and naval station—the principal one on Lake Ontario. Surveyor Collins in his report to Lord Dorchester did not favor the selection of Kingston as the best situation for vessels, "as it lies open to the lake and has not very good anchorage near the entrance, so that vessels are obliged to run a good way up for shelter from the most frequent winds." Collins, therefore, proposed Carleton Island, as it "afforded the best shelter." Lord Dorchester thought otherwise, and Haldimand Cove between Point Frederick and Point Henry, opposite Kingston, was selected as the site for the dockyard and storehouses.

In 1792, according to Mrs. Simcoe, the town contained about fifty houses. In 1795, the Duke de la Rochefoucauld-Liancourt visited Kingston and wrote that it had "about 129 or 130 houses."

Mrs. Simcoe made three pictures of the town, dated 1792, 1794 and 1796. The first is a sketch from the water-front, evidently made from a distance. The view in 1794 is also from the water-front, but shows distinctly the principal houses, including the steeple and belfry of the first church, known from 1820 as St. George's, while her latest picture was taken from a point between Fort Frederick and Main Street, Kingston, looking toward the northwest.

Mon. 2nd—We went across the bay this morning to see the shipyard. There are two gunboats lately built on a very bad construction. Coll. Simcoe calls them the "Bear" and the "Buffalo," as they are so unscientifically built, and intends they shall aid in carrying provisions to Niagara. The present establishment of vessels on this lake consists of the "Onondaga" and "Mississaga," named after the Indian tribes, top-sailed schooners of about 80 tons, and the "Caldwell," named after Coll. Caldwell, which is a sloop. They transport all the troops and provisions from hence for the garrison of Niagara, Forts Erie and Detroit. They land them at Niagara, from whence those for the higher ports are forwarded nine miles across a portage by land to Fort Chippawa, three miles above the Falls of Niagara, from whence they are embarked in boats and

---

KEY TO ILLUSTRATION ON OPPOSITE PAGE.

No. 1 represents a small house, but of the owner or occupant nothing is known. It is near the site of the old Recollet Church, which appears to have been removed or destroyed.

No. 2 represents the Commandant's house, which was on the line of Queen Street not far from Bagot Street.

No. 3 represents the barracks built by Count Frontenac inside the fort, the walls of which are designated by No. 4. The barracks appear to have been on the north-west side of the fort. The wall of the fort in the original picture is partly dark shaded and partly light. The light part represents the south-west side of the wall, the dark the south-east side.

No. 5 is a round tower built within the bastion at the corner of the fort. This was the south bastion. The tower was built of strong rubble masonry, and continued in existence until 1832, when it was razed to the ground. The site of the tower, indicated by the circular stone work, is distinctly visible to-day in the barrack square close to the ball alley.

No. 6 is a three-cornered building, which was built of stone in front of, and a protection to, the entrance to the fort, which was on the north-east side, facing Barriefield. One angle pointed towards Barriefield, and the building was constructed in this shape in order to divert the fire of guns which might be directed against the gate.

No. 7 represents a storehouse with a wharf in front of it, which formerly belonged to Mr. Forsythe.

No. 8, further east, represents the storehouse owned by the Honorable Richard Cartwright, with a wharf in front of it. The adjoining building also probably belonged to him. Beyond this storehouse the land runs to a point and then sweeps into the left, forming a bay, which has now been nearly all filled up, on which are the Montreal Transportation Company's shipyard, Anglin's mill and other works. The other houses are probably engineers' or officers' quarters, or houses occupied at the time by inhabitants.

NOTE.—This drawing or sketch was taken twenty-five years after the bombardment of the fort by Bradstreet (1758), and the walls bear traces in the picture of the bombardment. Bradstreet's batteries were placed one to the west of the house marked "1," another on the high ground behind the house marked "2," No. 1 being about the site of the present market-place, and the other on the high ground, on Queen Street, near the corner of Bagot Street.

It is claimed by some old inhabitants of Kingston that Forsythe's wharf was at the foot of Brock Street where Folger's Wharf now is.

3   4   5   6   7

CATARAQUI (KINGSTON), 1783.
(From a Drawing by Ensign James Peachey.)

2

1

8

carried 18 miles to Fort Erie, from whence vessels take them to Detroit, at the extremity of Lake Erie, which is about 250 miles in length.

Coll. Simcoe went on board the "Onondaga," and says we shall find tolerable accommodation in her when we go to Niagara, though he is much disposed to row round Lake Ontario in a boat, but everybody about us opposes the scheme as tedious and dangerous. Probably those who are of the party do not like the trouble of such a voyage, and I suppose Coll. Simcoe will go at last in a vessel rather than oppose these Sybarites of Italy, devoted to luxury and pleasure.

A DISTANT VIEW OF KINGSTON IN 1792.

(From a Drawing by Mrs. Simcoe.)

I gathered a very sweet and pretty white flower, the petals of the texture of orange flowers, five petals, ten chives, tipped with orange colour, the style pink, the leaves a light green, growing from the root, eight or ten flowers on short foot stalks on a long stalk, seed vessel round and small. Some ladies came to see me in the evening. I walked.

Tues. 3rd—There are Mississaga Indians here. They are an unwarlike, idle, drunken, dirty tribe. I observe how extremes meet. These uncivilized people saunter up and down the town all day with the apparent nonchalance, want of occupation and indifference that seems to possess the London beaux in Bond Street.

Sat. 7th—I walked this evening in a wood lately set on fire by some unextinguished fires being left by some persons who had encamped there, which in dry weather often communicates to the trees. Perhaps you have no idea of the pleasure of walking in a burning wood, but I found it so great that I think I shall have some woods set on fire for my evening walks. The smoke arising from it keeps the mosquitoes at a distance, and where the fire has caught the hollow trunk of a lofty tree the flame issuing from the top has a fine effect. In some trees where but a small flame appears it looks like stars as the evening grows dark, and the flare and smoke, interspread in different masses of dark woods, has a very picturesque appearance, a little like the poet Tasso's "enchanted wood."

Sun. 8th—The Governor went to church and took the oaths preparatory to acting as Governor.

NOTE.—The following is an extract from the Minutes of the first Executive Council of Upper Canada held on July 8th, 1792, from

115

the records of the Archives Department at Ottawa, with reference to Governor Simcoe taking the oaths.

"UPPER CANADA.

" Kingston, July 8th, 1792.

"His Excellency John Graves Simcoe, Esqr., Lieutenant-Governor of the Province of Upper Canada, Colonel commanding the forces in the said Province, etc., etc., etc., having appointed the Protestant Church, as a suitable place, for the reading and publishing of His Majesty's Commissions. He accordingly repaired thither attended by

The Honourable William Osgoode, Chief Justice,
The Honourable James Baby,
The Honourable Peter Russell,

together with the Magistrates, and principal inhabitants, when the said Commission appointing His Excellency, (GUY) LORD DORCHESTER Captain General and Governor-in-Chief, etc., etc., etc., of Upper and Lower Canada, and also the Commission appointing the said John Graves Simcoe, Lieutenant-Governor of the Province of Upper Canada were solemnly read and published.

"His Excellency then took the Oaths mentioned in an Act of Parliament passed in the first Year of His late Majesty King George, as altered and explained by an Act passed in the 6th year of the reign of his present Majesty, and also made, and subscribed the declaration mentioned in an Act of Parliament made in the Twenty-fifth year of the reign of Charles II., for preventing the dangers which may happen from Popish Recusants. The Oath for the due execution of his place and trust was administered to him by the Hon. W. Osgoode, Chief Justice, and he also took the Oath, required by an Act passed in the 7th and 8th years of the reign of King William III. to be taken by Governors of Plantations to do their utmost that the laws relating to the plantations be duely observed."

The Protestant church referred to was opened in 1792. The Synod authorities at Kingston state that the earliest minutes of the vestry extant, dated 1820, designate the church as St. George's. In 1827, the building was removed to make room for business houses, and the present St. George's Cathedral was erected on the corner of King and Johnson Streets. It was, however, called St. George's Church until 1862, when Kingston was made the seat of a diocese. The Cathedral was enlarged in 1892, the deep chancel and apse being added. In 1899 the building was destroyed by fire, only the walls remaining. It was rebuilt in 1900.

The *British Whig* office, 306-10 King Street, formerly called Church Street, now stands where the first church stood. Its front was where the rear wall back of the printing office rests. The Kingston *News* of some years ago gives an interesting account of the inception and erection of the church, which reads:

THE FIRST CHURCH IN KINGSTON.

"On April 15th, 1791, a meeting was held in Kingston (the record does not say where, but most probably in the house of Dr. Stuart), to consider the desirability of building a church and to procure the necessary means to do so. Besides the Rev. John Stuart, there were present at this meeting, Richard Cartwright, senior; Richard Cartwright, junior; James Richardson, Joseph Anderson and Archibald Thomson. It was decided to build a church and the contract was awarded to Archibald Thomson, who, by the way, was not a churchman, but a Presbyterian, though probably not a very strict one, as for the short period he remained in Kingston after the church was opened he was a pewholder therein. Archibald Thomson was of Scottish birth, having been born at Moudie Hill, Canobie, Dumfriesshire. About the middle of the last century, he and two of his brothers, Andrew and David, emigrated to the American colonies when they were very young men, probably just before the Revolutionary War. At its close they left the United States and settled in Upper Canada, Archibald, the one we are referring to, coming to Kingston. He was father of Hugh C. Thomson, an active business and newspaper man in Kingston from 1814 until his death in 1834. Early in 1793 Archibald Thomson, who was a U. E. Loyalist, left Kingston and removed to Markham, where he resided until his death. He is buried in St. Andrew's churchyard in Scarborough, some twelve miles from Toronto.

"Another meeting was held on October 25th, 1791, at which was present the Rev. J. Stuart, Messrs. Christopher Georgen, James Richardson, Wm. Atkinson and Archibald Thomson. Resolutions were unanimously passed as follows:

"First—That the money subscribed for the purpose of erecting a church should be immediately applied to that use.

"Second—In consequence of the foregoing resolutions, a carpenter is to be employed to erect a frame building of 40x32 feet in the clear. To weather board, shingle and floor it; also to ceil and sash it.

"As has been stated Archibald Thomson was the builder, and the total cost was less than $600. The church was opened in March, 1792. Among the first pewholders were Peter Smith, William Coffin, Allen McLean, John Baird, Robert Macaulay, Neil McLean, two pews; Honorable Richard Cartwright, who also had two pews. The rent of the pews was $4 a year, or one pound, Halifax currency. In 1795, Robert Macaulay and Peter Smith were the churchwardens. Nothing occurred to mar the harmony that existed among the congregation. That was before the days of surpliced choirs and choral services, and when it would have been an unheard-of innovation had the clergyman preached a sermon less than half an hour in duration. As regards the musical arrangements a hundred years since, at first there was a barrel organ, which some little time after was replaced by a manual. Whether the organist was accompanied by a bass viol and flute, history sayeth not, but it is more than likely such was the case.

117

DIARY OF MRS. SIMCOE

"On June 13th, 1795, a public meeting was held of the parishioners, when so much had the congregation increased that it was resolved to extend the church by putting in a gallery, and this was done."

The son of Hugh C. Thomson, editor of the Kingston *Herald,* was the late Rev. C. E. Thomson of St. Mark's Church, Toronto Junction, who in 1903 was the president of the U. E. Loyalists Association of Ontario. K. G. Thomson of Norwood, Ont., is a son of the late Rev. C. E. Thomson, and a great-grandson of Archibald Thomson.

Tues. 10th—The Council met. I walked this evening. Some Indians arrived from a distance. They fired a salute with muskets, which was returned with a cannon.

Wed. 11th—The Indians came to dance before the Governor, highly painted and in their war costume, with little clothing. They were near enough to the house for me to hear their singing, which sounded like a repetition in different dismal tones of he', he', he', and at intervals a savage whoop. They had a skin stretched on sticks imitating a drum, which they beat with sticks. Having drank more than usual, they continued singing the greatest part of the night. They never quarrel with white people unless insulted by them, but are very quarrelsome amongst themselves. Therefore, when the women see them drunk they take away their knives, and hide them until they become sober.

This evening I walked through a pretty part of the wood and gathered capillaire and a very pretty, small flower, five white petals of an exceeding firm texture, the purple short chives which support the anther of the flower proceeding from a purple rim that surrounds a very prominent green seed-vessel, on long foot stalks; from the top of the stalk the leaves spear shaped, sawed, polished, of the darkest green, and almost as firm as holly; numerous. It grows in very shady places, an evergreen. I was driven home by the bite of a mosquito through a leather glove. My arm inflamed so much that after supper I fainted with the pain while playing at chess with Capt. Littlehales.

Fri. 13th—Mrs. Macaulay, the garrison surgeon's wife, drank tea with me. She is a naval officer's daughter, and a very agreeable woman.

NOTE.—Dr. James Macaulay, born in Scotland in 1759, entered the army as surgeon to the 33rd Regiment, about 1785. He came to Canada with the Queen's Rangers and was stationed at Kingston and Niagara. Subsequently he received the appointment as deputy inspector-general of hospitals. In the army list, 1795, he is given as "Surgeon James M'Aulay, on garrison duty." Dr. Macaulay was twice married, first in 1790 to Elizabeth Tuck Hayter, and second in 1817 to Rachel Crookshank. He had issue by his first wife only, namely:—(Hon.) John Simcoe, Colonel of the Royal Engineers; (Sir) James Buchanan, first Chief Justice of Common Pleas, Upper Canada; George, a barrister-

DR. MACAULAY.   MRS. MACAULAY.

at-law; and Allan, a clergyman; Elizabeth, who married Judge Hagerman; Mary, who married John William Gamble, of Woodbridge; Ann, who married Dr. Peter Diehl, and Sarah Hayter, who became the wife of John S. Cartwright. Two sons of the last named are James S. Cartwright, K.C., Master in Chambers, Toronto, and John R. Cartwright, K.C., Deputy Attorney-General. Of the daughters of Honorable John Simcoe Macaulay, Sarah Sophia Bingham, Henrietta Emma and Mrs. Purcell (Elizabeth Mary) live in England.

When Toronto became the seat of government instead of Niagara, Dr. Macaulay settled in the former place with his family. Teraulay Street, Toronto, preserves the last syllable of Hayter and the two last syllables of Macaulay.

Sat. 14th—Mr. Scadding caught a beautiful green grass snake, which was harmless. After keeping it a day or two he let it go. The way of clearing land in this country is cutting down all the small wood, pile it and set it on fire. The heavier timber is cut through the bark five feet above the ground. This kills the tree, which in time the wind blows down. The stumps decay in the ground in the course of years, but appear very ugly for a long time, though the very large, leafless white trees have a singular and sometimes a picturesque effect among the living trees. The settler first builds a log hut covered with bark, and after two or three years raises a neat house by the side of it. This progress of industry is pleasant to observe.

Sun. 15th—I went to church twice. The clergyman, Mr. Stuart, is from the United States. He preached good sermons with an air of serious earnestness in the cause which made them very impressive.

NOTE.—Dr. John Stuart was born in Harrisburg, Pa., in 1740. He was originally a Presbyterian, but later sought for admission in the Church of England, was admitted to Holy Orders in 1770 and appointed as a missionary to the Indians at Fort Hunter on the Mohawk River for eight years. He translated part of the New Testament and Book of Common Prayer into the language of the Mohawks; came to St. Johns in the Province of Quebec in October, 1781; was appointed chaplain to the garrison at Kingston and arrived there in August, 1785, and was the first incumbent of the Protestant church in Kingston, which was erected in 1791. He died in Kingston on 15th August, 1811, and was succeeded as Archdeacon by Dr. John Strachan, afterwards first Bishop of Toronto. It is somewhat of a co-

REV. JOHN STUART.

incidence that Bishops Strachan and Bethune, like Archdeacon Stuart, were sons of parents who belonged to the Church of Scotland. Archdeacon Stuart's son, Rev. George O'Kill Stuart, was born at Fort Hunter in 1776; ordained in 1800 by the Bishop of Quebec, and in 1801 was sent as a missionary to York, where he became first rector of the Anglican church, now St. James Cathedral, Toronto. He was appointed rector at Kingston in 1812, was the Bishop of Quebec's

DIARY OF MRS. SIMCOE

"official" in Upper Canada and later Archdeacon of York, and was the first Dean of the See of Ontario. He died in 1862.

Mon. 16th—We sailed half a league this evening in a pretty boat of Mr. Clark's, attended by music, to Garden Island, opposite Kingston.

NOTE.—Garden Island is immediately west of Wolfe Island, whose western portion is opposite Kingston. In French maps it is called "Ile aux Forêts."

Wed. 18th—We sailed towards the mills.

NOTE.—The grist mills, "Kingston Mills," were in 1782-3 built by Mr. Robert Clarke for the Government, some five miles back from Kingston, at the site of the first lock of the Rideau Canal, where a waterfall furnishes the only water power in this vicinity.

Thurs. 19th—The Governor went to-day to see Carleton Island, nearly opposite the shore from Kingston, where there were extensive fortifications, now dismantled. The island was afterwards discovered to be within American territory. Returned at six with wild raspberries, which were exceedingly fine. Carleton Island abounds with them and strawberries and plums, while the air is esteemed so healthy that the people go there to get rid of the ague, a complaint which is very prevalent in this province. The flowering raspberry grows wild here, and bears a very insipid, flat fruit. Mr. Fisher, of the Engineers, is here on his way to Quebec from Niagara. He showed us some beautiful sketches he has taken of the Falls of Niagara.

NOTE.—Carleton Island lies near Wolfe Island, opposite Kingston, close to the south shore of the St. Lawrence.

Sat. 21st—There are no rides about Kingston, or any pleasant walks that we have met with. Sailing is, therefore, our only amusement. To-day we were prevented by rain from going to the mills on the Cataraqui. It is in the interest of the people here to have this place considered as the seat of Government. Therefore they all dissuade the Governor from going to Niagara, and represent the want of provisions, houses, etc., at that place, as well as the certainty of having the ague. However, he has determined to sail for Niagara to-morrow.

Mon. 23rd—At eight this morning we went on board the " Onondaga " —Commodore Beaton, the naval officer who has charge of the armed vessels on Lake Ontario. We sailed with a light wind. A calm soon succeeded, and we anchored seven miles from Kingston. The men who navigate the ships on this lake have little nautical knowledge, and never keep a log book. This afternoon we were near aground. The lake is beautifully transparent. We saw the bottom very plainly.

Tues. 24th—A wet day and a foul wind. I played at chess or at cards all the day. Our Devonshire steward was surprised to find in the ship's steward an acquaintance, Charles Trump, who had left Kentisbeare, the village six miles west from Wolford, 16 years ago.

Wed. 25th—A clear, cold day; made little way—a head wind. I saw the spray of the Falls of Niagara rising like a cloud. It is 40 miles distant.

CHAPTER X.

MRS. SIMCOE'S ARRIVAL AT NIAGARA.

Thursday, the twenty-sixth of July, 1792, was a day that created no little stir in the little hamlet at the mouth of the Niagara River, which was to become the home, at least for a few years, of the first Governor of Upper Canada.

Navy Hall had not any charms from an architectural standpoint. It was about as primitive in construction as the log cabin of the pioneers. Still, the group of four frame buildings that Mrs. Simcoe closely scanned as the "Onondaga" came up the river, had at least the merit of being well built in every detail.

The best picture extant of Navy Hall is that of 1792 made by Mrs. Simcoe, the original of which is now in the Royal Library in the British Museum. There is another view, a water-color, made by Mrs. Simcoe, 13th Setember, 1794, on board the sloop-of-war "Mississaga," while lying just outside the mouth of the Niagara River.

The group of buildings known as Navy Hall stood on the brink of the river, just below Fort George, the fortification commenced in 1796, whose guns commanded the old French fort on the opposite side of the river. The buildings were four in number, as shown in maps and drawings of 1792-6-9, and also on a map made by Surveyor-General Chewett in 1804. One building only is shown in the plans of 1817-19-35. There is only one map, dated 1851, on which it is not called Navy Hall. The old building shown in the picture was removed about 1862 from its original site to its present location. When the terminus of the Southern Railway, now the Michigan Central, was to be changed it was found that the tracks would go partly through the oak grove and this old building. In order to save the relic of olden time, permission was obtained from the Government to remove the building. It was then removed back into the enclosure of Fort George near the old Ferry House. In doing so the building was placed parallel with the river instead of an end slanting to it. An old lady, a Mrs. Quade, who was born at Niagara in 1804, and lived there till 1829, in visiting the town in later years said to her children as they passed the old building, "There is the old Parliament House," so that there seems to be no doubt that the building is one of the four buildings comprising Navy Hall in 1792-6.

The principal building, longer than the others, stood nearly at right angles to the river, while the remaining three were to the northwest and parallel to the river. These buildings were built for the use of the commanders of the sloops-of-war on Lake Ontario, not so much for residential purposes as for the housing of stores to supply the vessels when cruising on the western part of the lake. The principal supplies for these vessels were, however, kept at Kingston, the colonial naval centre in early days.

The site is fixed beyond doubt by the report of Captain Gother Mann of the Royal Engineers, who on 22nd September, 1789, after reporting as to the condition of Fort Niagara on what is now the American side of the river stated that "a survey of the heights also, on the opposite side of the river about Navy Hall, has been made with a view to ascertain the best system of fortifying the same so as to establish a permanent post there, and which might also counteract the designs of an enemy in his attack on the Fort of Niagara." Gother Mann further reported on 1st March, 1790, that "the ground above Navy Hall, if chosen for a principal post, will admit a wall of good capacity, but, as it will be retired from the river, there must be subordinate batteries on the banks thereof to command the passage;

ONLY REMAINING BUILDING OF NAVY HALL GROUP.
(From a Drawing [1887] in the J. Ross Robertson collection.)

it will be about sixteen hundred yards distant from the Fort at Niagara, which, though within the distance of annoying an enemy, could not prevent his carrying on operations against the Fort." The result of this recommendation was the erection of Fort George, the earthworks of which are still standing and have received but little care from the Dominion Government.

The buildings of Navy Hall did not favorably impress the Duke de la Rochefoucauld-Liancourt during his visit to Niagara in 1795. In his writings he refers to the Governor's residence, where he was a guest for some time, as a "small, miserable wooden house, which was formerly occupied by the commissaries." There seems to be no doubt that all the buildings comprising Navy Hall except one which is still standing, with alas, part of the roof fallen in, were burnt by the Americans in 1813.

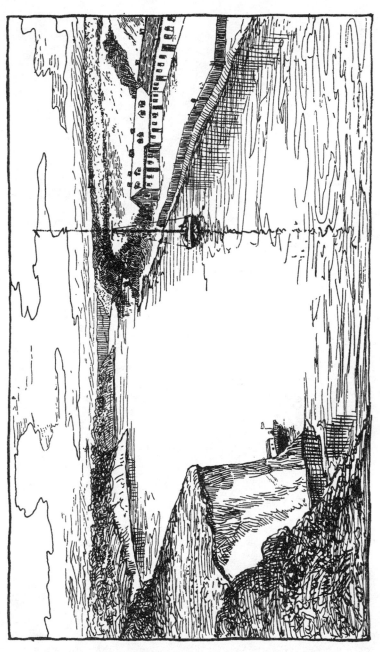

NAVY HALL, NIAGARA—FROM THE RIVER, 1792.

(From a Drawing by Mrs. Simcoe.)

FIRST VIEW OF NAVY HALL.

Thurs. 26th July—At nine this morning we anchored at Navy Hall, opposite the garrison of Niagara, which commands the mouth of the river. Navy Hall is a house built by the Naval Commanders on this lake for their reception when here. It is now undergoing a thorough repair for our occupation, but is still so unfinished that the Governor has ordered three marquees to be pitched for us on the hill above the house, which is very dry ground and rises beautifully, in parts covered with oak bushes.

A fine turf leads on to woods, through which runs a very good road leading to the Falls. The side of our hill is terminated by a very steep bank covered with wood, a hundred feet in height in some places, at the bottom of which runs the Niagara River. Our marquees command a beautiful view of the river and the garrison on the opposite side, which, from its being situated on the point, has a fine effect, and the poorness of the building is not remarked at this distance, from whence a fine picture might be made.

The Queen's Rangers are encamped within half a mile behind us. In clear weather the north shore of Lake Ontario may be discerned. The trees which abound here are oak, chestnut, ash, maple, hickory, black walnut.

NOTE.—Here Fort George stands. Below, the path slopes from Fort George to the river. The part "covered with oak bushes" is now (1911) called Paradise Grove. The last troops to occupy Fort George were the Royal Canadian Rifles, about 1856.

Sun. 29th—There is no church here, but a room has been built for a Freemasons' Lodge, where divine service is performed.

NOTE.—There has, for many years past, been a difference in opinion as to the exact site of the building in Niagara occupied by the Masonic Lodge in 1792-3. It is contended by some that on the northwest corner of King and Prideaux Streets, a tavern was built, and next to it the Freemasons' Hall. This is borne out by the fact that the Land Board of Niagara in 1791 gave permission to erect a tavern at the east corner of the town, near the river, and a Masonic Lodge next to it. On the other hand however, in the Crown Lands Department in a list of the lots of 1795, lot 33 is marked "The Lodge" and in another document lot 33 (northwest corner of King and Prideaux Streets) is marked "Freemasons' Lodge." The site of the present lodge is one block from the first lodge, and it might be that although the Land Board gave permission to build, the hall may not have been erected there. It is practically an unsolved mystery where the lodge met the first two years, but certain it is that in 1792 there was a Freemasons' Lodge, and both tradition and the two documents mentioned point to the north side of the lower end of King Street as the place of meeting.

Mon. 30th—At eight this morning we set off in calèches to go to the Falls, fourteen miles from hence. We stopped and breakfasted at Mr. Hamilton's, a merchant who lives two miles from here at the landing (Queenstown), where the cargoes going to Detroit are landed and sent by land eleven miles to Fort Chippawa.

We had a delightful drive through the woods on the bank of the river, which is exceedingly high the whole way. As we approached the landing I was struck with the similarity between these hills and the banks and those of the River Wye about Symond's Yat (the name of a rising ground or eminence overlooking the Wye), and the lime rock near Whitchurch, both in Herefordshire, which differs very little, except in the superior width and clearness of the Niagara River.

NOTE.—Honorable Robert Hamilton, son of Rev. John Hamilton, was the Deputy Provincial Grand Master of the First Provincial Grand Lodge of Freemasons, under Mr. William Jarvis. He was a merchant at Niagara, a member of the Land Board in 1791 at that place, a member of the first Executive Council of the civil government in 1792, and a man prominent in affairs in that part of Upper Canada. He was also the first judge of the district of Nassau. Lord Dorchester formed western Canada into four districts, of which one was Nassau, and it was located 'between the river Trent on the east and a line extending from Long Point north from the western boundary, which included the Niagara peninsula.

HON. ROBERT
HAMILTON.

In 1797, the lodges at Niagara elected Hamilton as Provincial Grand Master in the place of Mr. William Jarvis, although the records after that date give the name of the latter officer as continuing in the office to which he had been appointed. Mr. Simon McGillivray, however, in a letter which he wrote to the Grand Master of England, in 1822, states that after Mr. Jarvis removed to York "the lodges at Niagara held a meeting and elected the late Robert Hamilton Provincial Grand Master," but, he added, "Jarvis retained his warrant." It is possible that the lodges did this in 1797 and at a subsequent meeting in 1799-1800 re-elected Jarvis, for in a circular, dated 29th March, 1803, "R. W. Bro. William Jarvis, Esq., G. Master," is given.

During the American revolution, Mr. Hamilton, in partnership with Mr. (afterwards Hon.) Richard Cartwright, established a store on Carleton Island, near the military post which was known as Fort Haldimand, and carried on an extensive trade with the Indians. Soon after the close of the war Mr. Hamilton removed to Queenston, and was appointed one of the local judges, having Lieutenant-Colonel John Butler as his colleague on the bench.

Captain Patrick Campbell, who visited Niagara in December, 1790, says:

"Mr. Robert Hamilton, a gentleman of the first rank and property in the neighbourhood, and one of the Governor's Council, came also to wait on me and invite me to his house, an honour I readily embraced. He and Mrs. Hamilton were so very obliging as to go along with me in their oak sled to see the Grand Falls of Niagara."

Hamilton built a large stone residence at Queenston, a brewery and a warehouse. In 1792 he was appointed a member of the Legislative Council for the new Province of Upper Canada, an office he retained until his death. For some time he distinguished himself in connection with Mr. Cartwright, his old partner, also a member, by opposing Government measures, thereby incurring Lieutenant-Governor Simcoe's lively displeasure. In one of the Governor's despatches he denounces Hamilton as an " avowed republican," but when it was hinted that certain privileges would be taken away from them the opposition ceased. Governor Simcoe acknowledged that he had received much valuable information from Mr. Hamilton respecting the commerce of the country and particularly the Indian trade of the far West.

Mr. Hamilton married about 1786, Catherine (Askin) Robertson, widow of John Robertson. There were five children by this marriage; Robert, of Queenston; (Hon.) George, who in 1812 moved to Burlington Bay, where he became the founder of the city of Hamilton; James, of London; Alexander and Samuel. Hamilton took as his

RESIDENCE OF HONORABLE ROBERT HAMILTON ON THE
NIAGARA RIVER ROAD, 1792.
(From a Drawing by Mrs. Simcoe.)

second wife Mary (Herkimer) McLean, widow of Neil McLean, and had issue, Joseph, Peter Hunter and (Hon.) John, of Kingston, one of whose sons, Clark Hamilton, was formerly collector of the port of Kingston; while another was the late Judge J. M. Hamilton, County Judge of Halton.

Mon. 30th—Mr. Hamilton has a very good stone house, the back rooms overlooking on the river. A gallery, the length of the house, is a delightful covered walk, both below and above, in all weather. After an excellent breakfast we ascended an exceedingly steep road to the top of the mountain, which commands a fine view of the country as far as the garrison of Niagara and across the lake. From hence the road is entirely flat to the Falls, of which I did not hear the sound until within a mile of

DIARY OF MRS. SIMCOE

them. They are heard at Navy Hall before the rain when the wind is easterly, though the Falls are to the S.W. of Niagara. The fall is said to be but 170 feet in height. The river previously rushes in the most rapid manner on a declivity for three miles, and those rapids are a fine sight. The fall itself is the grandest sight imaginable from the immense width of waters and the circular form of the grand fall, to the left of which is an island, between it and the Montmorency Fall, so called from being near the size of the fall of that name near Quebec. A few rocks separate this from Fort Schlosser Fall, on the American side of the river, which, passing over a straight ledge of rock, has not the beauty of the circular form or its green colour, the whole centre of the circular fall being of the brightest green, and below it is frequently seen a rainbow.

NOTE.—By the interposition of two islands the river Niagara is separated into three falls, that of the Great Horseshoe on the west or British side, and those of Fort Schlosser and Montmorency on the eastern or American side. The three falls, with the islands, describe a crescent.

Mon. 30th—I descended an exceedingly steep hill to get to the Table Rock, from whence the view of the Falls is tremendously fine. Men sometimes descend the rocks below this projecting point, but it is attended with great difficulty and perhaps little picturesque advantage. The prodigious spray which arises from the foam at the bottom of the fall adds grandeur to the scene, which is wonderfully fine, and after the eye becomes more familiar with the objects I think the pleasure will be greater in dwelling upon them. After taking some refreshment on Table Rock, we went three miles to Chippawa Fort, admiring the rapids all the way. The Chippawa River, which falls here into the St. Lawrence, is a dull, muddy river running through a flat, swampy country.

NOTE.—The St. Lawrence River may be said to rise at the source of the St. Louis, which flows into Lake Superior. It receives different names in different parts of its course. Between Lake Superior and Huron it is called the St. Mary; between Lake Huron and Erie, the St. Clair and Detroit; between Lake Ontario and Erie, the Niagara; and between Lake Ontario and the ocean it takes the name of St. Lawrence. The part of the river below Kingston is called sometimes "The Lake of the Thousand Islands."

People cross from Chippawa to Fort Schlosser, but great caution is necessary, the current is so extremely strong, and if they did not make exactly the mouth of the Chippawa the force of the water below it would inevitably carry them down the Falls without redress. Eight soldiers, who were intoxicated, met with this accident in crossing the river some years since. Their bodies were taken up entire some distance below the Falls. An Indian was asleep in his canoe near Fort Schlosser. The canoe was tied to a tree; some person cut the rope; he did not wake until the canoe had got into the strong current. He found all his endeavours to paddle ineffectual, and was seen to lay himself down, resigning himself to his fate, and was soon carried down the Fall.

In the evening we returned to Mr. Hamilton's and slept there. I suffered exquisite pain all the day from a mosquito bite, which the extreme heat increased, and at night my sleeve was obliged to be cut open. I did not see any rattlesnakes, though many ladies are afraid to go to the Table Rock, as it is said there are many of these snakes near it. There are crayfish in very small pools of water. Mr. McDonnell said that pounded crayfish applied to the wound was a cure for the bite of a rattlesnake.

Tues. 31st—Returned to dine in our marquee. Information is received from Prince Edward that he will be here the 20th of August, which will

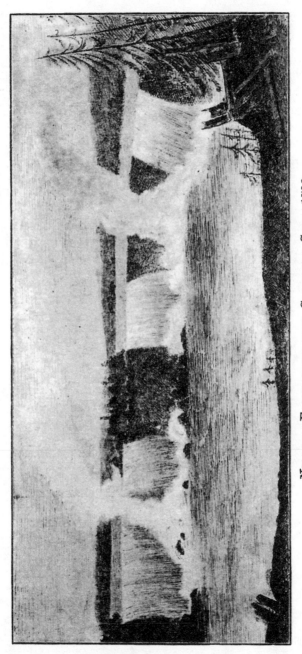

NIAGARA FALLS FROM THE CANADIAN SIDE, 1792.

(From a Water-color by Mrs. Simcoe.)

FORMING NEW FRIENDSHIPS

prevent our going to Detroit immediately, as the Governor had intended. Here are numbers of winged grasshoppers. They are hard, scaly and ugly as rhinoceros, and the colour of dead leaves. The high grounds above Navy Hall are so covered with them that the whole field appears in motion.

Wed. Aug. 1st—We dined with Major and Mrs. Smith (the Major was afterwards the Colonel of the regiment). He is in the 5th Regt., and commands the garrison. Lt. Smith, his son, is married to a beautiful Irish woman. A great many officers of the 5th are married. Though the buildings look so well from the other side, I found the quarters very indifferent.

Mrs. Smith has two tame racoons. They resemble a fox, are exceedingly fat animals, with bushy tails. It is remarkable that they have a joint in the nose. When they eat they use their fore feet, as monkeys do. I also saw a flying squirrel, which I did not admire. Its tail was like a rat's, and the eyes very large. I thought the ground squirrel much prettier. The black squirrel is large and quite black. It is as good to eat as a young rabbit.

NOTE.—Major John Smith, afterwards lieutenant-colonel of the Fifth Foot, was commandant of the fortress of Niagara, where he died in 1795. His son, Lieutenant Smith, was subsequently Sir D. W. Smith, Surveyor-General, Upper Canada. Mrs. Simcoe speaks of Lieutenant Smith being married "to a beautiful Irish woman," who was his first wife, Anne, daughter of John O'Reilly, Ballykilchrist, County Longford, Ireland. The 5th Regiment of Foot or Northumberland Fusiliers, of which Lieutenant-Colonel Smith was in command at Niagara from 1792 until his death, was formed in 1674, fought in Flanders and also in the war of the American Revolution. In 1774 the regiment landed in Boston; in 1778 was in various parts of the West Indies and returned to England in 1781. In 1787 the regiment embarked for Canada and in 1790 was quartered at Detroit, whence it was removed in June, 1792, to Niagara. It was here reviewed by H.R.H. the Duke of Kent and General Simcoe, who reported to the commander-in-chief that it was the "most fit for actual service." The regiment remained at Niagara till that fort was given up to the Americans in 1796, when it was ordered to Quebec. In 1797 it returned to England.

Fri. 3rd—The Governor set out this evening to sleep at the Landing (Queenstown), intending to go to-morrow to Fort Erie, thirty miles. Mr. Talbot (Gov. Simcoe's private secretary) drove me to the Landing, and we returned to supper at Navy Hall. We saw a fine bald eagle on the wing.

Sat. 4th—The Governor returned to dinner quite unexpectedly, having heard that the vessels he meant to have seen had sailed from Fort Erie to Detroit. Mrs. Macaulay drank tea with me. The weather is so exceedingly hot that I am quite oppressed by it, and unable to employ myself. I am sorry I have not a thermometer to ascertain the degree of heat. We have a very large bower, composed of oak boughs, in which we dine, it being greatly cooler than a tent. We like this place much better than Kingston. Mrs. Hamilton and her sister, Miss Askin, daughters of Coll. John Askin, a wealthy merchant of Detroit, dined with us. They are French women from Detroit.

NOTE.—John Askin, or Erskine, a kinsman of John Erskine, Earl of Mar, who headed the revolt in 1715 in favor of the Old Pre-

131

tender, emigrated to America about 1759 and was a merchant at Albany. About 1762-3, he with others, came with supplies to the relief of the British besieged by Pontiac at Detroit. In 1764, he went as King's Commissary to Michillimackinac and in 1780 returned to Detroit to engage in trade. In 1787 Askin was captain of militia for Detroit, in 1796 was lieutenant-colonel of militia for the Western District, and in 1801, was colonel in the same corps. He was also one of the magistrates of the District. On the evacuation of

Detroit by the British in 1796 he came to Canada. Colonel Askin married first a French lady whose name cannot be ascertained and by her had three children, John, Catherine (Robertson) who became the wife of Honorable Robert B. Hamilton, of Niagara, and Madeleine, who married Dr. Richardson, of the Queen's Rangers. The children by his second wife, Marie Archange Barthe, were Therese, who married Colonel Thomas Mc-Kee, son of Colonel Alexander McKee, Deputy Superintendent-General of Indian Affairs; Archange, married Colonel Meredith, of the Royal Artillery, afterwards commandant at Halifax;

COL. JOHN ASKIN.

Adelaide, married Colonel Elijah Brush, of the Michigan Militia; Charles, captain in Colonel Clark's Lincoln Militia, married Monique Jacobs; James, colonel of militia; Alexander, artillery driver, 1812-15; Eleanor, married Richard Pattison, of Sandwich, captain of militia. A. H. Askin, of "Strabane," near Walkerville, is a son of Charles; J. Wallace Askin, of Sandwich, is a grandson of James, while William Johnson McKee, of Windsor, is a great-grandson of Therese Askin.

Mon. 6th—The Queen's Rangers are encamped at the Landing, and are employed in building huts near the river to live in next winter. It is a very picturesque place. The Governor crossed the water from thence, and ascended a very steep road to see the remains of the French fort at Lewiston.

From thence there is a fine view towards the head of Lake Ontario, 50 miles distant. Near this fort are tumuli, or earth mounds, where bones have been dug up, and it is supposed to have been an Indian burying place. I received some shaddocks, a species of orange, from the West Indies, which I considered an excellent fruit.

NOTE.—The original corps known as "Rogers' Rangers" was raised in Connecticut and the vicinity of New York by Colonel Robert Rogers, under whom it served in the war with the French. Their strength was at one time 400, all Americans and all Loyalists. In 1776 Rogers was appointed Governor of Michillimackinac. He was succeeded in his command of the Rangers by Colonel French and afterwards Major Weymess, whom Major Simcoe succeeded. The latter reorganized the corps as the Queen's Rangers and it fought under him in the war of the American Revolution. It was disbanded in 1782. The Queen's Rangers of Niagara history were a

QUEENSTOWN, OR THE LOWER LANDING, 1792.

(From a Drawing by Mrs. Simcoe.)

A STORM AT NIAGARA

different body. They were raised in Canada from old soldiers of the regular regiments, strengthened by a detachment of ex-soldiers from English regiments, which was drafted and came out to Canada with William Jarvis, the first Provincial Secretary, in 1792. They were camped at Queenstown in 1792 and in August of 1793 the two divisions of the regiment were stationed at York, now Toronto. The British War Office ordered the disbandment of the regiment in 1802. There was a Masonic Lodge in this regiment, known as No. 3 on the Provincial Masonic Register. Provincial Secretary Jarvis, who was the Provincial Grand Master for Upper Canada, issued a warrant establishing this lodge in 1793. It ceased work in 1802 at the time the regiment was disbanded.

NIAGARA RIVER AT QUEENSTOWN, 1792.
(From a Drawing by Mrs. Simcoe.)

Fri. 17th—I desired to drive out last evening, though everybody foretold an approaching thunderstorm, which indeed came on with great violence when we were half way to the Landing. I feared that the lightning would make the horse run away, but he only started at every flash. The recollection that it was my own determination brought me into danger was very unpleasant. However, we got back safe and in time to save the marquees from being blown down. Mr. Grey's and Mr. Talbot's were overset, but the Governor preserved ours by having the cords held until the violence of the storm was over. The tents were so near the river that we were afraid they would be blown into it.

We were so cold and wet we were glad to drink tea. It was quite dark, and too windy to allow of our burning candles, and when the forked flashes of lightning enlightened the air I was able to drink tea. I wrapped myself up in two or three great-coats, and intended, if the tent was blown down, to take shelter under the great dinner table. The rain and wind did not cease for two hours, and we had no means of drying our clothes and were obliged to sleep in a wet tent. However, we have not caught cold.

135

DIARY OF MRS. SIMCOE

I received a very pretty set of Nankeen china from England to-day, and in an hour after it was unpacked the temporary kitchen (an arbour of oak boughs) took fire, and in the hurry of moving the china it was almost all broken. Luckily the weather was calm, or the tents might have taken fire. We are in daily expectation of the Prince. The canvas houses are not arrived or Navy Hall finished, and the dilemma has been whether to give him the marquees for his residence or the damp house. We have decided to take the latter ourselves, so here we came in a cold, blowing, dismal night.

I sat by myself in a miserable, unfinished, damp room, looking on the lake, where it blew quite a gale, the "Bear," a gunboat, tossing about terribly, and not a cheerful thought passing through my mind, when I had the happiness of receiving a letter from you, which raised my spirits, though for some hours after that pleasure I felt more dejected than at all other times, from the recollection of absence from my friends.

The "Bear," a Government sloop, is arrived from Irondiquet Bay and the Genesee River, both in New York State, and brought two families from Carolina to settle in this province. They have had a most terrible passage, being obliged to stay under the hatchway almost all the time.

Sat. 18th—We crossed the river; from a green bank had a very pretty view of Navy Hall.

Mon. 20th—Cold weather. We walked.

Tues. 21st—Very cold; we walked by the side of the lake, which is quite like a sea beach, only the marine smell is wanting.

Tues. Sept. 18th—Prince Edward came here the 21st of August. He went to the Fort at Niagara, and when a salute was fired the Governor was standing very near the cannon, and from that moment was seized with so violent a pain in his head that he was unable to see the Prince after that day, and kept his room for a fortnight. He had a gouty pain in his hand before, and it is supposed the shock of the cannon firing so immediately above him fixed the disorder in his head. He is now recovered, and has a pain in his foot, which perhaps would more effectually relieve his head if it were more violent.

Lord Garlies and Capt. Markham stayed here a week, but the Governor was not well enough to see them more than once.

NOTE.—Prince Edward, afterwards Duke of Kent, arrived at Navy Hall to visit General Simcoe, August 21, 1792. On the 23rd he went to Fort Niagara to review the troops, and on the 26th he sailed for Kingston.

VISCOUNT GARLIES.

George, Viscount Garlies, was the eldest son of the 7th Earl of Galloway. He was in command of the "Winchelsea" with Sir John Jervis' fleet in the West Indies and was mentioned for distinguished conduct. He became 8th Earl in November, 1806. He died 27th March, 1834, and was succeeded by his eldest son Randolph.

John Markham, second son of William, Archbishop of York, was in command of the "Blonde" with Jervis' West Indian fleet and was mentioned in despatches 21st April, 1794, for distinguished conduct in the attack on St. Pierre.

Wed. 19th—I send you May apple seeds. I think it is the prettiest plant I have seen; the leaves extremely large, of a bright green; the flower consists of five white petals of the texture of orange flowers, but three times larger; ten yellow chives round a large seed vessel, which

QUEEN'S RANGERS' HUTS AT QUEENSTOWN, WHERE THE REGIMENT WAS STATIONED IN 1792.

(From a Drawing by Mrs. Simcoe.)

becomes a fruit of the colour and near the size of a magnum bonum plum, the seeds resembling a melon. The flower is on a short foot stalk, one or two sitting between the leaves. They grow near the roots of old trees in good land. The fruit is ripe in August. Manitou means the "Evil Spirit" or "Devil" in the Iroquois language; Niche is "friend," and sago "How-do-you-do?" These are the Indian words I have learnt.

Sun. Nov. 4th—We have had a great many whitefish. They are caught here from October to April. In summer they go into deeper water. They are most exquisitely good. We all think them better than any other fresh or salt water fish; they are so rich that sauce is seldom eaten with them, but it is a richness that never tires, it is of so delicate a kind. They are usually boiled, or set before the fire in a pan with a few spoonfuls of water and an anchovy, which is a very good way of dressing them. The sturgeon are about six feet long. Those that are caught here are infinitely better than those which go to the sea; cooks who know how to dress parts of them, cutting away all that is oily and strong, make excellent dishes from sturgeon, such as mock turtle soup, veal cutlets, etc., and it is very good roasted with bread crumbs. The 5th Regt. have caught 100 sturgeon and 600 whitefish in a day in nets.

A great many settlers come daily from the United States, some even from the Carolinas, about 2,000 miles. Five or six hundred miles is no more considered by an American than moving to the next parish is by an Englishman. Capt. Duncan has sent me the horse I rode to Mr. Frazier's. Mr. Talbot went with Coll. Butler to distribute presents to the Indians at Buffalo Creek, near Buffalo. He bought a very pretty fawn skin of one of them for me, and I made it into a tippet. He also brought me a cake of dried hurtleberries made by the Indians, which was like Irwin's patent black currant lozenges, but tastes of smoke.

The Indians make very long speeches at their councils. One of them, named Cowkiller, spoke for five hours in a late debate between them and the people of the United States.

I have seen some translations of speeches, full of well-expressed, fine sentiments, marking their reliance on the Great Spirit. They appear to have great energy and simplicity in their speeches.

NOTE.—Buffalo Creek is south of Buffalo City, near New Amsterdam, and four miles above Fort Schlosser.

Cowkiller was a Seneca Chief, and a speaker at a council meeting February 7th, 1794, at Buffalo Creek.

Mon. Nov. 5th—The ships sail for Kingston this week, and remain there closed up by the ice in that harbour until April. The Governor will now have less to write, and, I hope, fewer headaches. The winter express indeed will afford an opportunity of sending some despatches. It arrives here from Quebec late in January, and after going to Detroit returns here; it was established for the use of the merchants, and travels on snowshoes, coming by way of Fort Oswego. Capt. Stevenson has gone to England, and Mr. Littlehales to Philadelphia, to see Mr. Hammond, the British Ambassador to the United States.

NOTE.—George Hammond was sent in 1791 by Lord Grenville, Secretary for Foreign Affairs, to Philadelphia to act as Minister plenipotentiary to the United States. Although only twenty-eight, Hammond was the first British minister accredited to the United States. Thomas Jefferson, the American Secretary of State, regarded his arrival as a "friendly movement." The conflicting claims of the two countries in giving effect to the Treaty of 1783 involved

DIARY OF MRS. SIMCOE

Jefferson and Hammond in very serious controversy. In 1795 Hammond left America to become Under-Secretary at the Foreign Office in London.

Tues. Nov. 6th—I have met with a beautiful blue flower near the river. The edges of the petal are finely sawed. The cardinal flower, which grows in the wettest and most shady places, is a beautiful colour. I am told the Indians use the roots medicinally.

I send you some seeds of the wild asparagus. It may be eaten when very young; afterwards it becomes poisonous. The milky cotton in the seed vessel is very pretty, and makes excellent pillows and beds. I hope you will grow enough to stuff a muff. I do not know how to describe the flower, it is so unlike anything I ever saw.

Mon. 26th—We have had very little snow, which is melted; the weather is again as the autumn, has continued very mild and pleasant. Mr. Bouchette has surveyed Toronto Harbour. It is 35 miles from hence across the lake.

NOTE.—Commodore Jean Bouchette was born at Quebec on the 5th July, 1736. He was the son of Marc Bouchette, who held a Government appointment under the French régime. The family is of Breton extraction, being, according to tradition, descended from Jean Bouchet, who wrote chronicles at the time of Joan of Arc. When Sir Guy Carleton was forced by the Americans to withdraw from Montreal in 1775, Bouchette took the Governor-General and two aides, all disguised as peasants, in an open boat to Quebec. A flotilla of eleven boats was captured by the enemy.

In 1783, Bouchette was placed in command on Lake Ontario and established the Naval Docks at Kingston. He held this position until his death in 1804. There appears to have been some difference of opinion between General Simcoe and Commodore Bouchette as to the respective merits of Toronto and Kingston as the naval base on Lake Ontario, the latter declaring that as the American base was at Sackett's Harbour, the British forces should be concentrated at Kingston. Bouchette married in 1772 Angelique Duhamel.

COL. JOSEPH BOUCHETTE.

Lieutenant-Colonel Joseph Bouchette, son of the Commodore, began his career in the provincial navy under his father. He made the first survey of the harbor of Toronto in May, 1793, received his appointment as second lieutenant in the following year, serving in the navy until 1796. In 1797, he commanded an armed row-galley which cruised between Montreal and Quebec. His reports seem to have led to the arrest of Colonel McLean, afterwards executed as a spy. He took a military course in 1800. In 1804, he was appointed Surveyor-General of Lower Canada, raised a regiment, Quebec Volunteers, in 1812, and in 1813 was appointed lieutenant-colonel and transferred to staff and intelligence service. In August, 1814, Bouchette left for England, and while there was nominated

Surveyor-General under the several articles of the Treaty of Ghent, for establishing the boundary between the United States and His Majesty's possessions in America. He published maps of Canada and two works—"Topography of Lower Canada," in one volume, 8vo, London, 1815; and "Topography of the British Dominions in North America," 3 volumes, 4to, London, 1831-2. He married Adelaide, daughter of Charles Chaboillez of the North-West Company, and had three sons, Joseph, Deputy-Surveyor-General; Frank, 68th Light Infantry, and Robert Shore Milnes, Commissioner of Customs until 1875. The surviving representatives of the family in Canada are Errol Bouchette, F.R.S.C., of Ottawa, a writer on economics and sociology, and Robert Shore Milnes Bouchette of Montreal.

Wed. 28th—Went to the Fort this morning. Mrs. Macaulay drank tea with me, and I had a party at whist in the evening. The partition was put in the canvas houses to-day, by which means I have a bedroom in it as well as a sitting-room. These rooms are very comfortable, about thirty feet long. The grates did not answer for burning, and I have had a stove placed instead, though as yet a fire has not been wanted. The weather is so mild that we have walked in the garden from eight till nine in the moonlight these last two evenings.

Mon. 3rd Dec.—The Governor went to the Landing, and I went to the Fort to see Capt. Darling's stuffed birds. The most beautiful of them he called a meadow lark, the size of a blackbird, the colours the richest yellow, shaded to orange intermixed with black; the Recollect, a light brown with a tuft on its head and the tips of the wings scarlet, like sealing wax; a blackbird with scarlet on the wings—they abound here in swamps; a scarlet bird called a King bird, the size of a small thrush; a bird like a canary bird, but the colours much brighter; a grand Duc Owl. Among the animals there was a skunk like a polecat, with black and white marks.

NOTE.—Henry Darling was ensign in the 5th Regiment in 1780. In April, 1783, he had rank as lieutenant in the army, and in the regiment the following September. He eventually became General. In September, 1793, he, with Lieutenant Pilkington of the Royal Engineers, Lieutenant Givins of the Queen's Rangers, and Mr. Alexander Aitkin, Deputy Provincial Surveyor, accompanied Governor Simcoe to Matchedash Bay.

Sun. 9th—Capt. Brant (Thayendanegea), Chief of the Six Nations Indians, dined here. He has a countenance expressive of art or cunning. He wore an English coat, with a handsome crimson silk blanket, lined with black and trimmed with gold fringe, and wore a fur cap; round his neck he had a string of plaited sweet hay. It is a kind of grass which never loses its pleasant scent. The Indians are very fond of it. Its smell is like the Tonquin or Asiatic Bean.

NOTE.—Joseph Brant's Indian name Thayendanegea denotes strength and is translated "Two sticks of wood bound together." He was born on the banks of the Ohio in 1742, where his parents were engaged in a hunting expedition. The home of the family was at Canajoharie Castle, the central of the three castles of the Mohawks in their native Mohawk valley. Brant's father, who was a fullblooded Mohawk of the Wolf tribe, died when the lad was quite young. The widow married a second time an Indian whose Christian name was Barnet, hence the contraction Brant. Joseph was educated

at "Moor Charity School" in Lebanon, Connecticut. He accompanied Sir William Johnson with the army during several expeditions against the French, and took part in many of the encounters between the revolutionists and the Indian tribes. His allegiance to Britain so provoked the Americans that the valley of the Mohawks, the original home of Brant's people, suffered more than any other part of the country during the war.

In 1776 he visited England and was presented to the Court. He proudly declined to kiss the King's hand, but remarked that he would gladly thus salute the Queen. While in England he was initiated into Freemasonry in "The Falcon Lodge" in Princess St., Leicester Fields, London, and presented by George III. with a Masonic apron.

THAYENDANEGEA.

After the war, he, with a greater part of the Mohawks, and a number of Indians from the other five tribes, withdrew to Canada, where the Six Nations subsequently received grants of land on the Bay of Quinte and the Grand River. Brant had a grant of land near Wellington Square, now Burlington, Ontario, where he built a dwelling long known as Brant House.

In 1785 through his efforts a wooden church was erected at the Mohawk village near Brantford, where was placed the first " churchgoing bell" that ever tolled in Upper Canada.

In 1791-2, when Governor Simcoe arrived as Lieutenant-Governor of Upper Canada, he was the bearer of a letter of introduction to Brant from the Duke of Northumberland, who had been adopted by the Mohawks under the Indian name "Thorighwegeri," or the Evergreen Brake. This name involves the very pretty conceit that a titled house never dies.

In the years 1791-2 Brant was energetically negotiating for peace between the Indian tribes and the United States. Governor Simcoe on his way to Detroit in 1793

BRANT HOUSE AT BURLINGTON, ONT.
(From a Drawing in the J. Ross Robertson collection.)

had a conference with him at the Council House in the Mohawk village on the Grand River. An important conference between the

GOVERNOR SIMCOE WALKS TO BURLINGTON BAY

United States Commissioners and the Indian chief was held at Navy Hall, Niagara, and a subsequent conference was held at Detroit. He died in Brant House on the 24th November, 1807, aged 64, and his remains were interred in a vault on the south side of the Mohawk Church on the Grand River.

It is noteworthy that Brant, although a chief by courtesy and ability, and always so called, was not such by descent.

Mon. 10th—The Governor set out to walk to Burlington Bay (now Hamilton, Ont.), at the head of Lake Ontario, about fifty miles from hence.

Sat. 15th—Mrs. Macaulay gave me an account of a subscription ball she was at, which is to be held in the town of Niagara every fortnight during the winter. There were fourteen couples, a great display of gauze, feathers and velvet, the room lighted by wax candles, and there was a supper as well as tea.

Sun. 16th—I sat up all night to read poems of Louis Velez de Guevara, the Spanish poet and dramatist (1570-1644), and the history of Prince Ctesiphon, and some pages of "Don Quixote"; went to bed in my clothes at six, rose at nine, dressed, breakfasted at ten.

Mon. 17th—The Governor returned at five to-day from his walk to Burlington Bay. The shores of the lake are, for a great distance, as high as the Falls of Niagara, and several small rivers, falling from that height, make picturesque scenes. He was delighted with the beauty of the country and industry of the inhabitants. He lodged every night in houses, where he was accommodated with a clean room and a good fire.

Sun. 23rd—I left Trojan, my hound, in my room while I went to dinner, and he tore to pieces my best map of Canada and the United States, which I had taken great pains to draw. I must paste it together again, but its appearance is spoiled. The Governor made some very pretty verses on the occasion.

Sat. 29th—Coll. Simcoe walked to the Landing and Fort Schlosser, opposite Chippawa. The weather is so mild we breakfasted with the door open into the garden.

NOTE.—Simcoe must have crossed the river at Queenston Landing and thence walked to Fort Schlosser on the American shore, about a mile and a half above the Falls, almost opposite Chippawa. It was built by Colonel Schlosser of the British Army in 1760 to replace the second Fort Little Niagara which had been burned by order of General Pouchot, who was in command of Fort Niagara in 1759 when the British besieged the greater fort. This second Fort Little Niagara was a short distance down stream from the site of Fort Schlosser. Both forts were at the upper end of the portage which ran from Lewiston to that point. Queenston and Lewiston were called the Lower Landings, and Chippawa and Schlosser the Upper Landings, on the Canadian and American shores respectively. In 1792, the first Fort Little Niagara (abandoned in 1751) was merely the remains of a blockhouse, and the second Fort Little Niagara but a memory. Fort Schlosser, an earthwork fort, was at that time garrisoned, though it was never a strong fort. The eleven blockhouses (shown on the map) built by Montresor in 1764, were in 1792 in a dilapidated condition, and when given up in 1796 at the end of the "hold over" period, were almost useless. There are now no remains of Fort Schlosser, which stood near the river bank. A

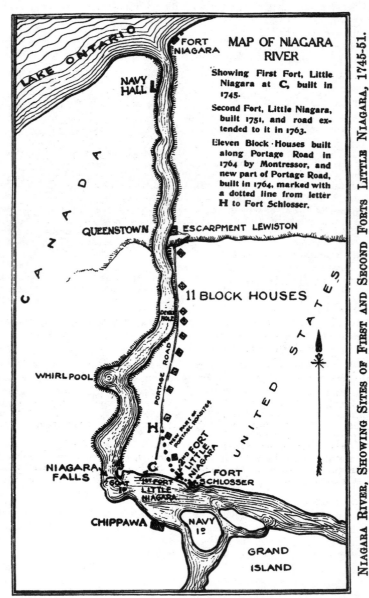

MAP OF NIAGARA
RIVER

Showing First Fort, Little Niagara at **C**, built in 1745.

Second Fort, Little Niagara, built 1751, and road extended to it in 1763.

Eleven Block·Houses built along Portage Road in 1764 by Montressor, and new part of Portage Road, built in 1764, marked with a dotted line from letter **H** to Fort Schlosser.

NIAGARA RIVER, SHOWING SITES OF FIRST AND SECOND FORTS LITTLE NIAGARA, 1745-51.

(From a Drawing by Peter A. Porter.)

stone chimney, however, which stood a short distance away, still exists. It was moved about a hundred feet from its original site and re-erected stone by stone in 1896. Mr. Peter A. Porter writes that it was, prior to its removal, the oldest remaining bit of perfect masonry on the frontier. It was attached to the barracks which the French built for Fort Little Niagara, and was later attached to the mess house which the British built in connection with Fort Schlosser. The frame of that mess house was prepared at Fort Niagara, at the mouth of the river, while the French were in possession there. It was intended for a Catholic church but the British took the frame to the site of the new fort, and put it up there. Judge Porter resided in the building from 1806 to 1809. It was burned in 1813. The sketch of the chimney was

REMAINS NEAR FORT SCHLOSSER.

made for Lossing by Colonel Peter A. Porter, of Niagara Falls, N.Y., who was killed in the American Civil War. He was the father of Mr. Peter A. Porter of Niagara Falls, N.Y., who has done much for the research of Niagara Falls history.

The map gives the relative position of the existing forts on the American and Canadian sides of the river in 1792 and the sites of first and second Forts Little Niagara.

Mon. 31st—A large party at dinner. Mrs. Hamilton, wife of Hon. Robert Hamilton, came to see me. We play at whist every evening. Coll. Simcoe is so occupied during the day with business that it is a relaxation. I have not lost one rubber since the 28th of November. We usually play four every evening.

Mr. Chief Justice Osgoode is now in his own house, which is so near that he always came in an evening to make up our party. Till within this fortnight he resided in our house, not having been able to meet with any that suited him, and Coll. Simcoe finds him a very agreeable companion.

CHAPTER XI.

JOURNEYS OF THE GOVERNOR.

Shortly after Major Littlehales' return from Philadelphia in January, 1793, Governor Simcoe set out for Detroit, walking with his party a greater part of the way. This midwinter trip, which to a certain extent was one of exploration, occupied about five weeks. Not only did the country west of Niagara impress the Governor favorably, but he was convinced that an admirable site for Canada's capital would be New London, on La Tranche (Thames) River, now London, Ontario.

Sun. 3rd Feb., 1793—Mr. Littlehales returned from Philadelphia. He gave the following journal of his travelling to New York: "Crossed the water at Queenstown (the Landing), ascended the mountain which is a part of the Alleghany. Six miles beyond the Landing passed the Tus-carora village, and forty miles farther the Tonawanda village, on the Niagara river, which runs into Tonawanda Creek, and is eleven miles S.E. of Niagara Falls. The Tonawanda Creek is navigable for batteau nearly to its source; from thence through a thick wood, full of swamps and creeks, twenty miles to Butter Milk Falls, so named from the richness of the land, to the Genesee River, 95 miles from Niagara; thence to Lake Cayuga ferry two miles, 150 miles from Niagara, to Onondaga Lake, two miles N.W. of Syracuse, 190 miles to Niagara." Mr. Littlehales travelled late; after passing Onondaga Lake lost himself in the woods, and was thirty hours without provisions. Whitestown, in Oneida County, N.Y., near Fort Stanwix, on the Mohawk River, 250 miles from Niagara, has 6,000 inhabitants. Seven years ago it was a desert. From Whitestown to Schenectady, 80 miles; fine meadows called German Flats, chiefly inhabited by Germans. Schenectady, N.Y., is a regular-built, considerable town, containing 3,000 Dutch. It is 300 miles from Niagara. New York is finely situated. Mr. Littlehales stayed there but two days, and pro-ceeded to Philadelphia, 600 miles from Niagara. He left it on the 5th of January, and on the 9th reached Northumberland, on the forks of the Susquehanna. Each town has a thousand inhabitants. Mr. Littlehales forded the Tioga seven times, crossed the Conestoga and Conhocton Rivers, then went 60 miles over extremely steep ridges of the Alleghany mountains to Williamsburgh, in the Genesee, and arrived at Niagara on the 20th, which by this route is but 400 miles from Philadelphia.

Note.—There are no entries in the diary from 31st December, 1792, until February 3rd, 1793. On the 16th of January, 1793, Katherine, the seventh child and sixth daughter of Mrs. Simcoe, was born at Niagara. This little one died in York and was buried in the Military Burying Ground west of the old Fort on the 17th April, 1794. There is no record in York of the birth or baptism of this child. There was no parish register in 1793; for the first church in York was not erected until 1802, when the parish was constituted. Religious services at that time were held in the barracks of the Fort. There is, however, a record in the parish book of Dunkeswell, which

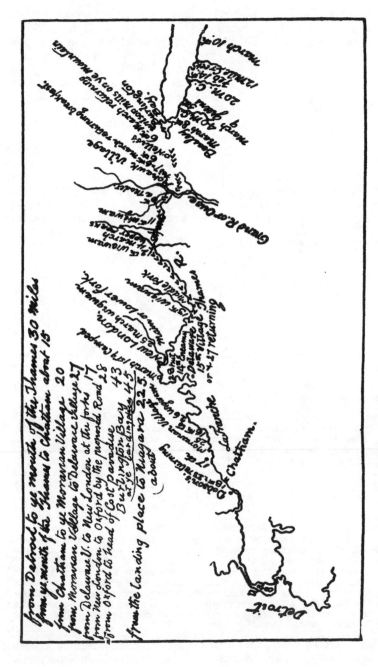

OUTLINE OF GOVERNOR SIMCOE'S ROUTE FROM NIAGARA TO DETROIT, 1793.

(From a Drawing by Lieutenant Pilkington, copied by Mrs. Simcoe.)

states that the daughter Katherine was born 16th January, 1793, at York and died at "two years of age" and was buried in York on the 17th of April, 1795. There is no doubt as to the birth date, but the burial date is an error. Katherine was only a year and three months old at the time of her death and burial, which took place at York on either the 17th or 18th of April, 1794, while Mrs. Simcoe was living there. It could not have occurred in April, 1795, for Mrs. Simcoe was then at Kingston.

It is odd that Mrs. Simcoe makes no reference in the diary to the birth of her daughter, but in a letter to Mrs. Hunt, dated February, 1793, she writes "I have the pleasure to inform you my little Katherine goes on well, eats, sleeps and grows fat, so I hope she will not feel the want of a wet nurse, which was what I could not procure for her. Will you do me the favor to join with Mrs. Montagu, in answering for the little stranger. I shall be happy further to cement our friendship by this mark of it. I have already had her privately baptized."

The Montagus and Gwillims were cousins. Mrs. Simcoe evidently wished both Mrs. Montagu and Mrs. Hunt to "answer" or act as godmothers for the little Katherine.

The record in the Dunkeswell Parish register is undoubtedly incorrect as regards the place of birth, age and date of burial of the child. It was probably inserted by Mrs. Hunt, who apparently forgot that Mrs. Simcoe was in Niagara at the time the child was born.

A small headstone of marble was sent from Honiton about 1795, before the Governor left Upper Canada, and placed at the head of the grave, but was removed by persons unknown, prior to 1850, for it was not standing at that date.

Mon. Feb. 4th—The Governor set off from hence in a sleigh, with six officers and twenty soldiers, for the Mohawk village on the Grand River (near Brantford), where Capt. Brant and twenty Indians are to join him and guide him by the La Tranche river to Detroit, no Europeans having gone that track, and the Indians are to carry provisions.

The Governor wore a fur cap, tippet and gloves and moccasins, but no great-coat. His servant carried two blankets and linen. The other gentlemen carried their blankets in a pack on their backs.

Fri. 8th—I draw maps, write, read and work so much that the days do not seem long, though I am alone. I am so persuaded that the journey will be of service to the Governor's health that I rejoice he has undertaken it. This evening I received some letters from England, brought from Montreal by Indians, who hung the packet so near their fire that the edges of the letters were burnt and the dates illegible. I received a letter from the Governor, who had proceeded forty miles and had a pleasant journey, but it now rains very much, which I fear will spoil the roads.

Tues. 12th—I heard of the Governor's safe arrival at the Mohawk village the third day after he left this place. He was much pleased with seeing their church and hearing their women sing psalms. The Indian women have remarkably sweet voices.

The following letter, found in the MSS. at Wolford, was written in February 1793, by Mrs. Simcoe to Mrs. Hunt. It is appropriate

The Council House.　　　　　The Mohawk Church.

THE MOHAWK VILLAGE, GRAND RIVER, 1793.

(*From a Drawing by Lieutenant Pilkington, copied by Mrs. Simcoe.*)

to insert it in the diary at this date, for what it contains might well have been written in the diary:

"Navy Hall, Feby., 1793. My Dear Mrs. Hunt:—Expecting an express soon from Quebec, I prepare my letters beforehand, that they may be ready. I have the pleasure to inform you my little Katherine goes on vastly well, eats, sleeps and grows fat, so I hope she will not feel the want of a wet nurse, which was what I could not procure for her. Will you do me the favour to join with Mrs. Montagu in answering for the little stranger. I shall be happy further to cement our friendship by this mark of it. I have already had her privately baptized. I long for the arrival of the express, as it is some time since I have heard from England. The accounts I have received from every correspondent of the great improvement of the little girls under your tuition is a very great happiness to me, the greatest that can be next to being an eye-witness of it. The whole winter has been like an exceeding fine, dry autumn in England; the climate is delightful and the country plentiful, and a pleasant society within a certain circle; in short, we have nothing to complain of but not seeing the children and the absence of some friends. Coll. Simcoe is gone to Detroit, on foot the greatest part of the way, a journey of about 400 miles, but as I am convinced the exercise and air will do his health and spirits great good I rejoice in his absence, though it will be a month or six weeks; he has five officers as companions, a dozen soldiers and twenty Indians with him as guides. As it is a service of no danger, and I think will afford him amusement, I am quite easy about it, and have so much writing, drawing, arranging papers and working to do that the days pass very quick; besides, I have now and then card parties here and at the Chief Justice's, for I am become a great whist player. Francis is the most engaging, pretty child you ever saw at his age; he is at present very handsome. Pray give my love to Miss Hunt; tell her there are as many feathers, flowers and gauze dresses at our balls (which are every fortnight) as at a Honiton assembly, and seldom less than eighteen couples. I have not attended them because I was, the greatest part of the winter, in daily expectation of being confined. I have taken the canvas house we brought from England for my own apartment; it makes two very comfortable and remarkably warm private rooms; it is boarded outside to prevent snow lying on it. The comfort I derived from these apartments was extremely great when I lay in, because, being in a manner separate from the rest of the house, it was so very quiet. The greatest inconvenience in this country is want of servants, which are not to be got. The worst of people do you a favour if they merely wash dishes for twenty shillings a month. The sergeant's wife I took with me I am happy to keep in my house, for she is a very steady person, remarkably fond of the children and attentive to them, and a good worker, and Joseph makes himself very useful.

"Mr. Scadding seems very well satisfied with his sixty pounds a year as clerk, and sometimes has the amusement of shooting; he looks as rosy as ever, though he leads so much more sedentary a life. Adieu, my dear Madam.—Believe me, very sincerely yours,

"E. P. SIMCOE.

"To Mrs. Hunt,
"Wolford Lodge,
"Honiton, Devonshire."

Sun. 17th—I heard that the Governor was well and within four days of Detroit. I went to dine with some ladies of the Queen's Rangers at the Landing, where the Rangers are quartered in huts. The Governor has had a hut built for himself, and we have hung up the tapestry in it which came from Stowe (the seat of the Marquis of Buckingham, England), which makes the room very comfortable. I slept here.

DIARY OF MRS. SIMCOE

Mon. 18th—Mrs. Hamilton drank tea with me. Mrs. McGill, wife of the commissary, Capt. John McGill, and Miss Crookshank, her sister, are pleasant women from New York. I gave a dance this evening. There were above ten couples.

NOTE.—The allusion to the two ladies as being from New York arose from the fact that they were sisters of the Honorable George Crookshank, whose wife was Miss Sarah Susannah Lambert of New York. The ladies had been visiting in the United States. Honorable George Crookshank, was Deputy Commissary-General during the War of 1812, and a member of the old Legislative Council of Upper Canada. His daughter, who resides on Peter Street, Toronto, is the widow of the late Mr. Stephen Heward. Miss (Rachel) Crookshank referred to by Mrs. Simcoe, afterwards became the second wife of Dr. James Macaulay,

MISS CROOKSHANK.

Tues. 19th—The bugle horns sound delightfully here; they echo among the rocks so finely. I called on Mrs. Hamilton on my way to Navy Hall, and brought Miss Butler, sister of Coll. Butler, home with me.

NOTE.—There is doubt as to the location of Butler's Barracks. In the opinion of Miss Janet Carnochan, President of the Niagara Historical Society, Butler's Barracks were on the hill north of Navy Hall, not where the present Butler's Barracks are. Buttons from the uniform of Butler's Rangers have been found on the hill north of Navy Hall.

Wed. 20th—I dined at the Chief Justice's (Osgoode), who had a large party to meet me. I played seven rubbers at whist.

Thur. 21st—I received a letter from the Governor, dated Upper Delaware village, on the La Tranche (now Delaware, Ont.). He had a pleasant journey, passed a fine open country, without swamps. The La Tranche, at 150 miles above its mouth, is as wide as the Thames is at Reading (capital of Berkshire, England).

Mon. 25th—I had company at dinner and cards in the evening.

Wed. 27th—The coldest day we have had this winter. The thermometer stood at 55 deg. at the Chief Justice's, though the stove was almost red hot.

Fri. Mar. 1st—A lady dined with me, and we played at whist in the evening with the Chief Justice.

Fri. 8th—Mr. McGill dined with us. A snowstorm the whole day, drifted by a high wind; the river so full of ice that it appeared immovable for some hours.

Sat. 9th—A fine, clear day; the river full of ice. Towards two o'clock it separated and floated down, and a boat came over from the garrison.

Sun. Mar. 10th—The Governor and Mr. D. W. Smith returned. It is exactly five weeks since he left this place. He is remarkably well, and not fatigued. He went a part of the way in sleighs, but walked the greater distance. The Journal does not contain many incidents. The map which accompanies it shows the various creeks they passed, or fallen trees, which require some care and dexterity to cross. His Excellency's leaving Detroit under a salute from all His Majesty's ships lying there is mentioned, as also that "His Excellency ordered prayers to be read in the

LOG HUTS OR BARRACKS AT QUEENSTOWN, 1793.
(*From a Drawing by Mrs. Simcoe.*)

woods on Sunday, and forty people attended. His Excellency and suite eat raccoons and porcupines, which were good, the latter like pork." The porcupine's quills stuck into Jack Sharp's neck (a Newfoundland dog), and they were very difficult to extract and made him ill for many days.

The Governor rose early on the march and walked till five o'clock. A party of the Indians went on an hour before, to cut down wood for a fire and make huts of trees, which they cover with bark so dexterously that no rain can penetrate, and this they do very expeditiously; when the Governor came to the spot the Indians had fixed upon the lodge for the night, the provisions were cooked; after supper the officers sung "God Save the King," and went to sleep with their feet close to an immense fire, which was kept up all night. The Governor found his expectations perfectly realized as to the goodness of the country on the banks of La Tranche, and is confirmed in his opinion that the fork of the river is the most proper site for the capital of the country, to be called New London (London, Ont.), on a fine, dry plain without underwood, but abounding in good oak trees. A spring of real petroleum was discovered on the march by its offensive smell.

NOTE.—The section of country referred to is near "Moravian Town," a little east of which settlement was a petroleum spring. The Moravian village is in the Moravian Reserve, Township of Orford in the County of Kent, on the direct route from Niagara or York (Toronto) to London and Detroit. It lies between Bothwell and Thamesville and is a few miles east of the Grand Trunk Railroad. There were no white settlers in the township till after 1817, but there was a settlement of Delaware Indians from about 1792, in a place called "New Fairfield," since better known as "Moravian Town," in the north of the township. Old Moraviantown was in the township of Zone, Kent County, but the present place known as Moraviantown is as stated, in Orford, across the river Thames, and opposite to old Moraviantown. It is five miles from the town of Bothwell and is about the same distance from Thamesville and Highgate.

The petroleum spring referred to by Mrs. Simcoe was, no doubt, a reality, as the crude oil or petroleum was obtained a century ago from the surface of the water of the river Thames in several places along the river in this neighborhood. Mr. W. R. Hickey of Bothwell, who so kindly furnished me with this information, states that settlers seventy years ago used to gather the petroleum from the surface of the water and sell it as a medicine. There were several of these springs or exudations within the range of three miles east of where old Moraviantown stood. When the first oil excitement in Bothwell, about 1865-6, was at its height, a refinery was in operation on the north bank of the river. The first well that started the oil boom in 1865 was drilled about five miles east of the site of old Moraviantown, just at the boundary line between the counties of Kent and Middlesex, near the location of the Longwoods Road, or London Road, as it used to be called.

The Delaware Indians were the principal remnant of the once flourishing congregation of the Moravians or United Brethren Church of the United States, who were compelled in 1792 to seek an asylum in Canada, where they were favorably received by the

provincial authorities and were permitted to settle on the River
la Tranche (Thames). By an Order-in-Council dated the 19th of
July, 1793, fifty thousand acres of land bordering on the river were
granted for their use. They built twenty-nine houses and huts and
a chapel wherein ministered the German missionary supported by the
Moravian Society. The population was a hundred and sixty-seven
Indians of the Delaware and Iroquois nations. By a second Order-
in-Council issued 26th February, 1795, a survey of the original grant
was made and the land appropriated to the trustees of the "Moravian
Society" to be reserved forever to the Society, in trust, for the sole use
of their Indian converts. The first settlement was made on the north
side of the river Thames.

The site of old Moraviantown is now occupied by cultivated farms,
and there are on the north side of the river a few graves, where the
early Indians had their burying-ground.

The ground is historic, for a battle was fought there on the 5th
of October, 1813, between the British and Indian forces under General Procter and the celebrated Indian chief, Tecumseh, and the
American army under General Harrison. Tecumseh was killed
after a desperate resistance, and the Indian village was burned by
the invaders.

Across the lot where the graves are is a small ravine leading
to the river, and old residents say that it was there or near there that
Tecumseh fell.

After the battle the Indians removed to the opposite side of the
river. In 1836 these Indians were induced to surrender a large
portion of their land, about six miles square, for an annuity of one
hundred and fifty pounds.

This second letter found in the MSS. at Wolford is also written
to Mrs. Hunt. It is a motherly letter showing a great regard for
Mrs. Hunt and deep affection for the children under her charge at
Wolford. It reads:

"Navy Hall, March 13th, 1793. My Dear Mrs. Hunt:—The contents
of your last letters, informing me of Mrs. Graves's quitting Wolford, was
not any great surprise to me, as I thought such an event not improbable.
Be assured, my dear Madam, that the confidence we repose in your care
and attention to our children makes us perfectly indifferent to any expense
that must necessarily be incurred by your keeping house for them. The
benefit they will receive from the good and religious principles you will
instil into their minds will be cheaply purchased, and pray do not be
uneasy at any trifling expense which you deem proper to be incurred.
Coll. Simcoe desired Mr. Flood to get a second-hand carriage for yours and
their accommodation. We are very anxious that they should stay at
Wolford. I should never be satisfied about their health were they at
Bath, as I have a great prepossession against that place for children. I hope
with a carriage (and be as liberal of fires as possible) that you and Miss
Hunt will reconcile yourselves to Wolford, as we should not be happy to
have the children removed. It is a great pleasure to me to have them
brought up so near Miss Burgess, that they may get the habitude, by
seeing her often, of acquiring a great regard for a friend to whom I am
so much attached, and I think it much better as you have determined it,

to be at Wolford than to encumber her house with so many children, though the offer was extremely kind of her.

"As for Mrs. Graves' desire of having Eliza on a visit, we cannot refuse it; but it is Coll. Simcoe's and my absolute desire that she does not stay above a month or six weeks in these annual visits, because we should be sorry the child's education should be stopped, or that she should be longer separated from her sisters, which reasons alone determined us to deprive ourselves of her company. Besides, I think the child has too great a tendency to weak lungs to make it at all proper for her to be longer there, was there no other reason. The other children, of course, Mrs. G. would not wish to be troubled with; if she did, the same system should prevail as with regard to Eliza.

"Pray give my love to Miss Hunt; tell her I should have answered her letter, but I send this by a pacquet as the quickest conveyance to you, and letters sent by pacquets cost such sums of money that I will not write to her till I send to Mr. Burgess. They are rather longer going through the Secretary of State's office, but without there is anything material to be speedily answered it is the best way to write, on account of the expense.

"Give my kindest love to the children. Tell them the same reason and being greatly pressed for time (as this is an unexpected opportunity) hinders my writing to them, and thanking Charlotte for her very pretty ruffles, which I value much, and Harriett for her letter. Tell Eliza there are no guava trees here. The country is not hot enough, but her father thanks her for her thinking of it. Let them know that their father is just returned from Detroit; looks remarkably well in health, and is grown really fatter, though he has performed a journey of six hundred miles in exactly five weeks, and walked a great part of the way. I will write them a further account by the first opportunity of sending to Mr. Burgess.

"I enter exactly into what Miss Hunt's and your feelings have been, because I have known and experienced enough of these kind of proceedings.

"I am sure Miss Hunt's instructions are much better than Mr. Pigot's few visits. In short, we are quite happy in every account I hear of your proceedings with respect to the children, and are only anxious that everything should go on comfortably to yourself and Miss Hunt. Mr. Flood will be of any assistance in his power. Believe me to be, my dear Mrs. Hunt, with great regard and confidence in your friendship,

"Very sincerely yours,

"E. SIMCOE.

"Coll. Simcoe desires his best compliments. Eliza or Charlotte have not sent me any drawing lately. I hope they continue to like drawing; she writes vastly even on one line. I wish I was as good an arithmetician as you have taught her to be. I think you were quite right to discharge a gardener that must be a useless expense. I am glad Melly is still with you; I hope she continues to merit your good opinion, for I always liked her much.

"To Mrs. Hunt,
    "Wolford Lodge, near Honiton,
        "Devonshire, England."

Wed. 13th—Coll. Simcoe has gout in his hand.
Sat. 16th—Coll. Simcoe so much better as to walk on the sands. The thermometer 72 in the shade. There are thousands of duck fly up the river daily. They are called cawines, a species of wild duck. They have a fishy taste and are never eaten; their down appears to me exactly the same as that of the eider duck. I lately dreamt of being fired at by small shot in passing through a wood, and have since had quite a horror of the sound of a musquet or anything military.

DIARY OF MRS. SIMCOE

I have been much amused by reading Watson (Richard Watson, Trinity College, Cambridge) on chemistry, in which there is an account of the making of an artificial volcano that I think would please you, an experiment of putting diamonds and rubies in separate vessels and exposing them to a violent fire—the diamonds were dissipated and the rubies unchanged in weight or colour.

Mon. April 1st—Rode to Queenstown, where we intend to reside a fortnight. Mr. Grey and Mr. Talbot are going to New York.

Tues. 2nd—Very warm weather.

Wed. 3rd—The weather extremely warm, but we find the log huts cool from the thickness of the timber with which they are built. We do not keep house here (Queenstown). As there are not offices belonging to our rooms we did not bring many servants, but dine at the mess. Immediately after I have dined I rise from the table, one of the officers attends me home, and the band plays on the parade before the house until six o'clock. The music adds cheerfulness to this retired spot, and we feel much indebted to the Marquis of Buckingham for the number of instruments he presented to the regiment. The bugles sound at five every morning, and Coll. Simcoe goes out with the troops and returns to breakfast at nine.

Fri. 5th—Fahrenheit ther. 78 deg. in the shade, 112 deg. in the sun to-day at Navy Hall. "Trojan" has been so ill, in consequence of a blow he received on his head since we left Navy Hall, that the servants supposed him to be mad and shot him, which we regret most excessively, not believing he could be mad, as he ran into the water a short time before he was killed. I gave a dance this evening. A soldier was pointed out to me by the name of Swambergh, a Swede who had distinguished himself in a battle where the King of Sweden was present; this incident and the admiration I know you feel for Swedes caused me to observe something peculiarly fine in his countenance, when, on further enquiry, it proved that the man shewn was not Swambergh, but a worthless thief—so much for my skill in physiognomy.

Sat. 6th—I rode a pleasant horse of Mr. Mayne's to Navy Hall; returned here in the evening, but not being expected, found a cold, wet room and spent an uncomfortable evening. St. Denis, of the 5th, caught yesterday, at Niagara, 500 whitefish and 40 sturgeon; this is common sturgeon, one nearly 6 ft. long.

Note.—Captain William Mayne belonged to the Queen's Rangers. He returned to England in 1797.

Sun. 7th—We dined with Mrs. Hamilton, wife of Mr. Robert Hamilton, and walked in the evening where I observed some trees on fire; the flames, in part concealed, appeared like stars, and had a beautiful effect.

Mon. 8th—A very warm day. I rode to the Falls; there are still heaps of ice below them, but it had not a brilliant or fine appearance, as I had expected to see.

Tues. 9th—Mrs. Richardson breakfasted with me. Very wet weather. We played at chess all the day.

Wed. 10th—Very cold and some snow. We drove to Navy Hall and slept there.

Thur. 11th—A very fine day. Went to Queenstown; walked by the river half a mile to a beautiful spot among the rocks. The rapid, clear water, with a bright tinge of green from the reflection of the high banks covered with trees, had a fine effect, and we determined that it would be a delightful spot to have a cold dinner at, and the music would sound well among the rocks.

Sat. 13th—Returned to dinner at Navy Hall. Jacob and Aron (Mohawks) came express from Detroit in eight days; they walked 56 miles this day.

AT THE WHIRLPOOL RAPIDS, NIAGARA, 1793.

(From a Drawing by Mrs. Simcoe.)

FIRST PAPER IN THE PROVINCE

Mon. 15th—I dined at the Fort, and caught cold by crossing the water this very cold day. In a newspaper from the States was the paragraph: "His Serene Highness of Upper Canada gives great encouragement to settlers."

The "Caldwell" sloop, an armed vessel of the Provincial Government, arrived at Kingston from home on the 6th April; the day before the harbour had been so full of ice that she could not have got in. An Indian who speaks English, being asked at what hour he arrived, pointed to the west and said, "when the clock was there." It reminded me of a line in Spencer, "The clock in Jones high house."

Thur. 18th—A newspaper is published here, called the "Upper Canada Gazette or American Oracle" (first issue April 18th, 1793). As yet it is filled with proclamations and advertisements. The only printer to be met with was a Frenchman named Louis Roy, and he cannot write good English. A surveyor went to the first forks of the La Tranche, and gives the most favourable account of the land.

NOTE.—Governor Simcoe's Proclamation of July 16th, 1792, which would fain have converted La Grande Rivière into "The Ouse," permanently transformed La Tranche into the Thames.

Fri. 19th—Capt. Æneas Shaw is arrived, with his wife and seven children, from Oswego, where he met his family and spent the winter with them. The south shore of Lake Ontario being uninhabited, from Oswego they brought with them an Indian to build huts and shoot partridges and ducks. They came the whole way in a boat. The only alarm they met with was from trees falling near their hut one night. The children had made fires for diversion too near large trees, without considering which way the wind might blow them down, and the hut was in danger from their fall.

Tues. 23rd—I thought of you (Mrs. Hunt) as by agreement. I rode to the whirlpool, a very grand scene half way between Queenstown and the Falls, where the current is so strong that eddies are formed in which hewn timber trees are carried down the Falls, from a saw mill, upright. Vast rocks surround this bend of the river, and they are covered with pine and hemlock spruce; some cascades among the rocks add to the wild appearance. These scenes have afforded me so much delight that I class these days with those in which I remember to have felt the greatest pleasure from fine objects, whether of art or nature, as at Blenheim (seat of the Duke of Marlborough), the "Valley of Rocks," near Lynmouth and Lynton, in North Devon. I met with some pretty flowers and a beautiful milliped. I gave a ball this evening. Some small tortoises, cut up and dressed like oysters in scollop shells, were very good at supper.

Wed. 24th—I rode to the whirlpool with Mr. Pilkington (Robert Pilkington, lieutenant in the Royal Engineers). As we came back it was almost dark, and the fires the Indians had made by the waterside for the purpose of spearing fish had a picturesque appearance among the rocks. The light attracts the fish, and the Indians are very expert in spearing them.

Fri. 26th—A very wet night. It rained into the huts, but I found one corner of the room dry, and there I placed my bed. Capt. Shaw has given me a tea-chest in bird's-eye maple. It is a beautiful wood, the colour of satinwood. The tea-chest was made at New Brunswick. Capt. Shaw mentioned many instances of persons settled in New Brunswick who, having marry'd women from the United States, were persuaded by them to quit the country, as they would not live without the apples and peaches they had been used to at New York. The Americans are particularly fond of fruit. The Indians bring us cranberries in spring and autumn which are as large as cherries and as good; the best grow under water.

11   161

They also supply us with chestnuts, which they roast in a manner that makes them particularly good.

Mon. 29th—Rode before breakfast. At Navy Hall, the "Onondaga" arrived from Kingston in 22 hours. There is a large stone house, built by the French, in the Fort at Niagara, and from thence it is said to take its name, as Niagara, in the Indian language, signifies "great house." Pray take notice we call it "Niágara."

NOTE.—This house is a large stone building which stands within the precincts of the American Fort, and was built by the French prior to 1750 by order of Governor Vaudreuil. The Fort and its defences were completed by General Pouchot, in 1759. The British afterwards added a storey with, in the opinion of Mr. Peter A.

"The Castle," Fort Niagara, N.Y.

(From a Sketch sent to England about 1830 and copied by Mrs. Simcoe.)

Porter, a timbered roof. During the War of 1812 the Americans are said to have torn it off, made a flat roof, with stone walls projecting a foot or so above it, and to have mounted a cannon on the roof. After the war they evidently restored the timbered roof, and the present cupola was put on in 1823. As it is not supposed the British ever used any brick at the Fort, the erection of the brick chimneys is fixed at a date subsequent to the War of 1812.

The origin of the name Niagara is disputed. Some say that the word is of Indian origin, meaning "thunder of water," and others derive it from Onghiara, the name of the old Indian village near the Falls.

Tues. May 2nd—Coll. Simcoe set off, accompanied by seven officers, to go to Toronto. He means to go round by the head of the lake in a batteau.

Wed. 3rd—I borrowed Sir Joshua Reynolds' "Discourses." They amuse me very much.

GOVERNOR'S FIRST VISIT TO TORONTO

NOTE.—Mrs. Simcoe refers to "Discourses Delivered to the Students of the Royal Academy" by Sir Joshua Reynolds, Knight, with introduction and notes by Roger Fry.

Fri. 5th—A very cold day.

Tues. 9th—I am feverish and ill. I caught cold by sitting late with the windows open after a very hot day, and the dew falls here most heavily.

Sat. 13th—Coll. Simcoe returned from Toronto, and speaks in praise of the harbour, and a fine spot near it covered with large oaks, which he intends to fix upon as a site for a town. I am going to send you some beautiful butterflies.

NOTE.—This was the Governor's first visit to the site of Toronto. The "fine spot" was on the bay front, east of the present George Street as far as Berkeley Street. The lower part of the present Berkeley Street, from the present King south to Palace (Front Street), was later called Parliament Street, as it led to the Legislative Buildings. Berkeley Street, north of King, was not opened until some years later.

According to the plan made by Aitkin in 1793, the original town of York was divided into ten blocks, five south and five north of King Street, the west boundary being George Street, the east Parliament (Berkeley), the north Duke Street, and south Palace (Front Street). Although the streets were not named in 1793, the plan shows the location of the present George, Frederick, Sherbourne (Caroline), Princes, Ontario, and Berkeley (the first "Parliament" Street) all running from the south to the north, and Palace (Front Street), King and Duke, all running from the west to the east.

The area covered by the Aitkin plan was not extensive. The number of feet from the south side of Palace (Front Street) at the east side of George Street to the north side of Duke Street was 740 feet. From the west side of George to the east side of Parliament the measurement was 1770. When the streets were laid out on this plan Front was known as King and in a later plan as Palace Street. The modern King was Duke Street, and the modern Duke, Duchess Street. These street names were intended as compliments to King George III., and the Duke and Duchess of York. George Street was named after the Prince of Wales, Frederick after the Duke of York himself, Caroline in honor of the niece of George III., who, in 1795, married her cousin the Prince of Wales, afterwards George IV. Princes Street commemorated collectively the male members of the Royal Family, the Dukes of Clarence, Kent, Cumberland, Sussex and Cambridge. It will be noted that the correct orthography of the present Princess Street is "Princes" Street.

CHAPTER XII.

AMERICAN COMMISSIONERS GUESTS AT NAVY HALL.

The life at Navy Hall was enlivened by many pleasant incidents during the years of its occupancy by Governor Simcoe and his wife. Prominent people from Britain touring the western continent who brought letters of introduction, always had a generous welcome and a pleasant time as long as they occupied the guest chambers of that primitive residence, the pioneer Government House. Americans in official positions who visited Niagara ofttimes expressed their gratification with the kindly reception accorded them by the Governor and his wife.

It is true that the Governor had, to a greater or less extent, his likes and dislikes, and sometimes was rather frank in expressing his opinions, but he never forgot the requirements of his official position. So that whatever the Governor's sentiments might be regarding the United States and its Government, all guests from the Republic were made to feel as much at home as if they were seated at their own fireside. Accordingly the best of treatment was accorded the American Commissioners who came to Niagara to discuss the Indian boundary question with Governor Simcoe and a deputation of fifty Indians headed by Brant. The negotiations at Navy Hall and subsequently at Miami came to naught, as the redskins insisted that the settlers on their side of the Ohio River should be evicted.

Sun. 14th—Three commissioners, who are appointed by the United States to treat with the Indians at Sandusky, Ohio, are arrived here, and intend to stay at our house until they receive further orders from Philadelphia. Mr. John Randolph, a political friend of President Jefferson, is a Virginian. Benjamin Lincoln and Coll. Timothy Pickering are both of Massachusetts, New England. Coll. Simcoe calls the latter my cousin; his ancestor left England in Charles 1st's reign, and this gentleman really bears great resemblance to the picture Mr. Gwillim (a relative of Mrs. Simcoe) has of Sir Gilbert Pickering.

GENERAL LINCOLN.

JOHN RANDOLPH.

If the proffered mediation of England with respect to this treaty of Sandusky had been accepted by the States, and Washington had gone thither, Gov. Simcoe would have gone to meet him. I am not sorry that the circumstance is avoided.

THE INDIAN BOUNDARY QUESTION

NOTE.—John Randolph of Roanoke, an American orator, was born in Virginia in 1773. He claimed to be a descendant of Pocahontas, the Indian princess. He studied for short periods at Princeton and Columbia College. In 1799 he was elected to Congress and re-elected many times. He gained a high reputation as a debater. He became estranged from Jefferson about 1806 and tried to defeat the election of Madison and opposed the War of 1812. He was defeated at the election in 1813, but was again elected in 1815. He was a man of genius and was distinguished for his ready wit, which, joined to his mastery of the weapons of sarcasm and invective, rendered him a formidable opponent in debate.

General Benjamin Lincoln was born in Massachusetts in 1733. He was originally a farmer. He was a member of the Provincial Congress assembled in 1775 at Cambridge and Watertown and one of the secretaries of that body, and also a member of the committee of correspondence appointed to communicate with the several towns in Massachusetts and with other colonies upon the circumstances of the time. In 1776 he was appointed a major-general of militia and joined the army of Washington in 1777. He was appointed to the chief command of the Southern department about September, 1778, and defended Charleston against Prevost in 1779. Later Lincoln was besieged by Sir Henry Clinton in that place and compelled to surrender. In October, 1781, he became Secretary of War and retired in 1784. He was elected Lieutenant-Governor of Massachusetts in 1787 by the Federalists. He died in 1810.

Timothy Pickering, an American statesman, was born in Massachusetts in July, 1745. He graduated at Harvard in 1763 and became Judge of the Common Pleas in 1775. He joined the army of Washington in 1776 and took part in the battles of Brandywine and Germantown in October, 1777. He was appointed Postmaster-General of the United States by Washington in 1791 and Secretary of War in 1794. From 1814-1817 he was a member of the national House of Representatives.

TIMOTHY PICKERING.

There are no entries in the diary between Sunday, May 14th, and June 14th, for between these dates Mrs. Simcoe was on a visit to Fort Niagara and apparently did not continue her diary during that period. But to revert to the Commissioners' stay at Navy Hall —the 4th of June was a gala day at Niagara, for the second session of the Legislature was in progress, and the day was the anniversary of the birth of His Majesty the King.

The *Upper Canada Gazette* in its issue for the second week in June (1793) says:—" On Tuesday last, the fourth of June, being an anniversary of His Majesty's birthday, His Excellency the Lieutenant-Governor held a levee at Navy Hall. At one the troops in garrison and at Queenstown fired three volleys. The field pieces above

Navy Hall under the direction of the Royal Artillery, and the guns at the garrison, fired a royal salute. In the evening His Excellency gave a ball and elegant supper in the Council Chamber, which was most numerously attended."

Of this ball and supper another notice is extant. The three distinguished Americans, General Lincoln, Colonel Pickering and Mr. Randolph, were amongst the guests at the ball and supper. General Lincoln in his private journal, since printed in the Massachusetts Historical Collections, Vol. V., 3rd Series, makes the following note of the entertainment:

June 4th—"The King's birthday. At eleven o'clock the governor had a levee at his house, at which the officers of government, the members of the legislature, the officers of the army, and a number of strangers attended. After some time the governor came in, preceded by two of his family. He walked up to the head of the hall and began a conversation with those standing in that part of the hall, and went around to the whole, and I believe spoke with every person present. This was soon over and we all retired. At one o'clock there was firing from the troops, the battery and from the ship in the harbor. In the evening there was quite a splendid ball, about twenty well-dressed and handsome ladies, and about three times that number of gentlemen present. They danced from seven o'clock till eleven, when supper was announced and served in very pretty taste. The music and dancing were good, and everything was conducted with propriety. What excited the best feelings of my heart was the ease and affection with which the ladies met each other, although there were a number present whose mothers sprang from the aborigines of the country. They appeared as well dressed as the company in general, and intermixed with them in a measure which evinced at once the dignity of their own minds, and the good sense of the others. These ladies possessed great ingenuity and industry, and have great merit; for the education they have acquired is owing principally to their own industry, as their father, Sir William Johnson, was dead and the mother retained the manners and dress of her tribe. Governor Simcoe is exceedingly attentive in these public assemblies, and makes it his study to reconcile the inhabitants, who have tasted the pleasure of society, to their present situation in an infant province. He intends the next winter to have concerts and assemblies very frequently. Hereby he at once evinces a regard to the happiness of the people and his knowledge of the world; for while the people are allured to become settlers in this country from the richness of the soil and the clemency of the seasons, it is important to make their situation as flattering as possible."

The American guests were evidently impressed with the function, and the tribute they paid to the beauty of the Canadian ladies who were present could not fail to please the Governor, who some time later had the pleasure of reading this extract from the private journal of the gallant General who had been his guest.

SIR WILLIAM JOHNSON, BART.

The compliments paid to the daughters of Sir William Johnson were well deserved. Their mother, with whom Sir William had contracted an Indian marriage, was Mary Brant, or, as she was familiarly known, "Miss Molly," sister of Chief Joseph Brant.

Sir William Johnson, Bart., was the eldest son of Christopher Johnson, of Warrentown, County Down, Ireland. His mother was Anne Warren, sister of the brothers Oliver and Peter Warren, whose names are identified with the naval glory of England. Sir William was born in 1715 and came to America in 1738. He settled

on the banks of the Mohawk. About 1740, he married Catherine Weisenberg and had one son, afterwards Sir John Johnson, and two daughters, Mary and Nancy. Mary married Colonel Guy Johnson, nephew of Sir William, and Nancy (Ann) married Colonel Daniel Claus.

In 1756 Sir William exerted himself to revive the waning friendship of the Mohawks towards the British

SIR WM. JOHNSON.   LADY JOHNSON.

as against the French. He succeeded, became their captain, and was called Warraghiyagey, signifying "Superintendent of Affairs." The Indian tribes then united with Johnson at their head. There is no trace of when he attained the rank of colonel, but it must have been about 1746. In a letter written in that year, Governor Clinton addresses him as "Colonel William Johnson at Albany." In November of 1747 he had command of the northern frontier of New York. His management of the Indian Department was most favorably recognized by the British Government.

In 1750 Colonel Johnson was appointed to a seat in His Majesty's Council for the Province of New York, in the room of Philip Livingstone, deceased. This was the first step towards the prominent and influential position he was destined to occupy in later years. In 1755, during the war against the French, he was made a major-general and was created a baronet in November of the same year. In July, 1759, General Prideaux, while besieging Fort Niagara, was killed by the bursting of a shell carelessly discharged by one of his own gunners, and Sir William Johnson took command. The fort was attacked, and after a terrific siege and the defeat of the French General D'Aubry, who was hastening to the relief of Niagara, General Pouchot surrendered and the flag of Britain was raised over its walls. General Prideaux was buried in the chapel of the fort. "I was the chief mourner," writes Sir William Johnson in his private diary. The jurisdiction of Sir Willam extended over all the tribes of the northern colonies. He died in July, 1774, and was succeeded by his son, Sir John, who had been knighted during his

father's lifetime. The third baronet was Sir Adam Gordon Johnson, the eldest surviving son of Sir John. Sir Adam Gordon dying without issue, Sir William George Johnson became fourth baronet, and he was succeeded by his nephew, the present holder of the title, Sir Edward Gordon Johnson, of Montreal.

Johnstown, in Fulton County, New York, originally (1798) named Caughnawaga, was founded by Sir William Johnson, who resided there during the later period of his life. Sir William erected in 1764 a fine mansion house about a mile from and on ground gently elevated

SIR JOHN JOHNSON. above the village of Johnstown. The hall itself is built of wood, but the buildings or wings on each side are of stone, pierced with loopholes for musketry. When Sir William occupied these buildings he had them surrounded by a stone breastwork. While in possession of the Johnson family this was a place of resort for the Sachems of the Six Nations, and all the Mohawks repaired thither to receive their presents from the British Government.

Sir William Johnson's sons-in-law were both interested in the Indians. In 1761 Colonel Guy Johnson was appointed one of the Deputy Superintendents of the Indian Department, and in 1774, shortly before his death, Sir William wrote the King asking that Colonel Guy be allowed to succeed him as Superintendent. The request was granted, Colonel Daniel Claus becoming his brother-in-law's Deputy. The commission held by Sir William came from the colony of New York and the other colonies which were leagued together against the Indians. After the Revolutionary War, however, this commission held by Colonel Guy as Sir William's successor was dropped, and Sir John Johnson became Superintendent of Indian Affairs in British North America.

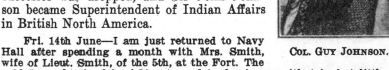

COL. GUY JOHNSON.

Fri. 14th June—I am just returned to Navy Hall after spending a month with Mrs. Smith, wife of Lieut. Smith, of the 5th, at the Fort. The cold I caught the 9th of May turned to dumb ague (that is, but little of the cold fit and a continual fever). With this indisposition I found myself extremely inconvenienced by the Commissioners' residence in our small house, and I accepted Mrs. Smith's friendly invitation to visit her, and her nursing and great attention to my health enabled me to recover as soon as I have done. Commodore Grant, who commands the vessels on Lake Erie, was staying at Major Smith's. The Queen's Rangers have left the huts at Queenstown, and are encamped on the mountain above.

IN CAMP NEAR QUEENSTOWN, 1793.

(From a Drawing by Mrs. Simcoe.)

It is a fine, dry, healthy spot, and the tents look extremely pretty among the large oaks which grow on the mountain.

NOTE.—Honorable Alexander Grant, born 1734, was second son of Patrick, seventh laird of Grant of Glenmoriston, Inverness-shire. He served in the Royal Navy as a midshipman, and was with Amherst in the Lake Champlain expedition in the Seven Years' War. Later he was placed in command of lake vessels from Niagara to Mackinaw, and was known as Commodore Grant. He was a member of the first Executive and Legislative Council, and Administrator of Upper Canada from 11th September, 1805, to 24th August, 1806, during the interval between Lieutenant-Governor Hunter and Lieutenant-Governor Gore. In 1774 he married Therese Barthe, by whom he had eleven children—one son, Colonel Grant of Brockville, and ten daughters. His fifth daughter, Archange, married Thomas Dickson of Queenston. His sixth daughter, Phyllis, married Alexander Duff,

HON. ALEX. GRANT.

of Amherstburg. His seventh daughter, Isabelle, married Captain Gilkinson of Brantford, with issue, seven sons including Archibald, County Court Judge, Picton, and Colonel Jasper of Brantford. Nancy, the eighth daughter, married George Jacob, of Kent County. The ninth daughter, Elizabeth, married James Woods of Sandwich, two of their sons being the late Joseph Woods, M.P. for Kent, and the late Judge R. S. Woods, of Chatham. Another daughter, Jean Cameron, married William Richardson of Brantford, and their daughter became the wife of the late Henry Racey of Brantford, proprietor of the Brantford *Expositor*. Grant's wife was a sister of the second wife of Colonel John Askin. The Commodore's death took place in May, 1813, at his residence at Grosse Point, called Grant Castle, on Lake St. Clair, which was noted for the courtesy of its host and his open-handed hospitality. Here Tecumseh and his warriors were frequent guests of the Commodore, who was a man of commanding presence, a good officer and a general favorite. There are many great-grandchildren and great-great-grandchildren. A mural tablet to the memory of Grant was erected by his grandson, the late Judge Woods of Chatham, in St. John's Church, Sandwich.

Sun. 23rd—Mr. Talbot went to Sandusky to deliver papers to Coll. McKee.

NOTE.—Colonel Alexander McKee, who was Indian Agent at Pittsburg before the Revolutionary War, was imprisoned at that place during the outbreak by the Revolutionists. He escaped, however, and later became Deputy Superintendent-General of Indian Affairs, the Superintendent-General being Sir John Johnson. Colonel McKee was a Justice of the Court of Common Pleas at Detroit. He died on 14th January, 1799. His son, Thomas Alexander McKee

DIARY OF MRS. SIMCOE

(known as Colonel Thomas or Colonel Alexander McKee), who married Therese Askin, daughter of Colonel John Askin, was one of the members for Kent in the Second Legislature of Upper Canada, 1796-1800, and one of the members for Essex in the third Legislature. It is a coincidence that in the Legislature of Ontario from 1894-1902, William Johnson McKee of Windsor, his great-grandson, and consequently great-great-grandson of Colonel Alexander McKee, represented the county of Essex.

Wed. 26th—The Indian Commissioners went to Fort Erie. Coll. Pickering gave me a receipt to make chowder of salmon, sea biscuit and pork; it is stewed for twenty minutes.

Thurs. 27th—We dined alone for the first time since we left Quebec. The Governor having no business to attend to, and the weather delightful, we crossed the water, and drank tea on a pretty green bank, from which there is a good view of Navy Hall, and we enjoyed this half-holiday amazingly.

Fri. 28th—We rode to Queenstown and slept there. The thermometer was 86 to-day.

Sat. 29th—Breakfasted in the camp and rode on to the Falls, seven miles; dined there, and went to Burch's Mills, two miles above the Falls. We returned to tea in the camp, but the heat was so excessive we were obliged to stop on the road and drink milk and water, and eat fruit at Mrs. Tice's, wife of Lieut. Tice, of the Indian Department, who lived at the Falls. The thermometer has been at 96 to-day. We slept in the hut, but I determined in future to sleep on the mountain. I saw a stuffed rattlesnake, which was killed near Queenstown in the act of swallowing a black squirrel. The snake measured five feet six inches long, and had seven rattles.

NOTE.—John Burch had a saw and grist mill near the Falls on lot 174, township No. 2, in the year 1786. In 1791 he was a member of the Land Board and in 1795 was Justice of the Peace. In Lundy's Lane Cemetery is an inscription "In Memory of John Burch, Esq., who departed this life March 7th, 1797, aged 55." His son, John Burch, Jr., was Grand Secretary of the Provincial Grand Lodge of Freemasons of Upper Canada at Niagara, 1817-1819.

Gilbert Tice came to Niagara in 1786, where he was a member of the Land Board in 1791. He is given as Captain Gilbert Tice in the list of United Empire Loyalists in the Indian Department, with a wife and four children. He was a veteran of the French War, and, under the patronage of Sir William Johnson, kept a large inn at Johnstown, N. Y., before the Loyalist migration.

Sun. 30th—Returned to Navy Hall in a boat the Commissioners left here, which is a very good one, with an awning and green curtain. The heat excessively great.

Tues. July 2nd—Jacob Lewis and Aaron Hill, the two Indians who carried mails from Detroit, came here. The latter was well dressed and looked very handsome. Lewis' wife was with him; a very pretty woman, the only handsome woman I have seen among the Indians. We treated them with cherries. The Indians are particularly fond of fruit. We have thirty large May Duke cherry trees behind the house, and three standard peach trees, which supplied us last autumn for tarts and desserts during six weeks, besides the numbers the young men eat. My share was trifling compared with theirs, and I eat thirty in a day. They were very small

NIAGARA FALLS FROM THE CANADIAN SIDE, 1793.

(From a Water-color by Mrs. Simcoe.)

and high flavoured. When tired of eating them raw, Mr. Talbot roasted them, and they were very good.

Fri. 5th—Francis has been very ill, and the extreme heat of this place is thought to be prejudicial to him. It is, therefore, determined that I shall take him to the camp on the mountain. I shall have an establishment of two marquees, a tent and two sentries. The Governor will come to see us whenever he has leisure; my dinner is to be sent every day from Navy Hall. This day I embarked at one o'clock on board the gunboat with Francis and Sophia, and Mr. Mayne, of the Rangers, attended me. I left the thermometer at 90, but it is pleasant on the water. It requires a strong, steady wind to carry vessels to the Landing, as the current runs four knots an hour against them. The gunboat, not having top sails, catches but little wind between the high banks. It blew fresh when we embarked, but soon became calm. Mr. Bouchette, for the honour of his vessel, declared we were going on, but as it was not apparent to Mr. Mayne and myself that we made the least way, we had the boat let down, and proceeded the remaining three miles in it. I was much fatigued in ascending the mountain; we reached the camp about five o'clock. I dined alone. The Governor came to supper. The mosquito net was not brought, and I passed a most wretched night. Mr. Talbot returned from the Miami, where a fort had been built by order of the Governor-General, Lord Dorchester. The Indians have sent a deputation to the Commissioners, to desire to converse with them at Niagara before they proceed to the Miami, as Wayne's army has advanced nearer to them than they expected.

Sat. 6th—The Governor returned to Navy Hall, as did the Commissioners and some Indian chiefs.

Sun. 7th—The Governor came to supper. The Indians have demanded whether the Commissioners have full powers to fix a boundary; they are to reply to-morrow. The " Mississaga " arrived with 270 Indians from St. Regis. They belong to the tribes called the Seven Nations of Canada. They speak French, are much civilized, and have a good deal of the manners of Frenchmen.

NOTE.—The term "Seven Nations" is an error. There were the "Six Nations" but not "Seven." The Mississagas were for a time encamped near the "Six Nations" and they were called by some people the "Seven Nations."

Mon. 8th—Another Indian Council held to-day at Navy Hall, at which the Commissioners declared that they had full power to fix a boundary.

Tues. 9th—It was determined in the Indian Council to-day that the Commissioners and Indian deputies shall go to Sandusky to treat. The Seven Nations having no conductor or officer with them, Mr. Talbot will accompany them to Sandusky. The House of Assembly (the second session of the first Legislature) was prorogued to-day.

My marquee commands the most beautiful view of the river and lake seen between the finest oak trees, among which there is always a breeze of wind. The music tent is at such a distance as to sound pleasantly. Mrs. Hamilton and Mrs. Richardson were with me in my arbour when we heard so violent a clap of thunder as made us all stoop our heads; the lightning followed instantly. We ran into the tent, and stayed until a violent torrent of rain had abated. On coming out I observed an oak, which had stood close to the arbour, was much blasted by the lightning. Mrs. Hamilton took Francis home with her, lest he should catch cold from the damp of the tents after the violent rain. I drank tea and slept at Mrs. Hamilton's.

NOTE.—The First Legislature of Upper Canada met from September, 1792, to June, 1796, at Navy Hall, Niagara. The following is a list of the Sessions with dates of meeting:—First Session, 17th

DIARY OF MRS. SIMCOE

September-15th October, 1792; second session, 31st May-9th July, 1793; third session, 2nd June-9th July, 1794; fourth session, 6th July-10th August, 1795; fifth session, 16th May-3rd June, 1796.

Mrs. Richardson, wife of Dr. Richardson, surgeon of the Queen's Rangers, was Madeleine Askin, second daughter by his first wife of Colonel John Askin of Detroit. They were married on the 24th of January, 1793, by the Rev. Robert Addison, who had been sent to Niagara by the Society for the Propagation of the Gospel, and was afterwards first Rector of St. Mark's Church there. Although the church was not opened until August, 1809, parish records were kept from 1792, and one of these shows that on "24th January, 1793, Dr. Robert Richardson, blr., and Madeleine Askin, spinr.," were married. Mrs. Richardson became the mother of Major John Richardson, Canadian novelist, author of "Wacousta."

Thurs. 11th—I walked to the camp. The Governor went to Navy Hall. I drank tea with Mrs. Hamilton, and saw the Seven Nations pass.

Fri. 12th—Mr. Talbot dined with me on his way to Fort Erie.

Mon. 15th—A wet day, which is very dismal in a tent; but to see the light again, and feel the air dry, is such a pleasure that none can judge of but those who have felt the reverse.

Tues. 16th—We dined in the hut, and Mr. Mayne, of the Rangers, drove me to Navy Hall in the afternoon in a gig we have had made, in which he drove two horses tandem; it is so light that we went to Navy Hall, which is seven miles, in three-quarters of an hour, and returned to the Landing by eight o'clock. The road is good but for the stumps of trees on each side, which it requires attention to avoid; but my charioteer left Westminster, the school for boys in Dean's Yard, Westminster, last year, so you may conclude him to be a steady person. He is a *protégé* of Lord Amherst's. He supplies Mr. Talbot's place when he is absent.

Thurs. 18th—The weather being very hot, we went again to the camp. In the evening we rode to Mrs. Tice's, a pleasant situation, like some in Epping Forest; it is three miles from the camp.

Fri. 19th—Went to Navy Hall; caught cold by going out this evening without a fur tippet, which the great dew renders necessary after the very hot days.

Sat. 20th—Capt. Shaw and 100 men set off in batteau for Toronto. Sometimes these batteau sail around the lake by the south shore to the head of the lake, and then by the north to Toronto, but in fine weather they cross the lake going direct. I drank tea at the fort (across the river).

Sun. 21st—Extremely hot weather. Rode to the camp this evening, and found it cooler and less damp than at Navy Hall. The mountain is covered with a sweet, purple flower, the roots of which, infused in brandy, make a wholesome cordial. It is called Oswego bitter. Mr. Russell (Hon. Peter Russell) says it is a wild balm of Gilead, and that an oil may be extracted from it. The leaves, dried, are good in pea soup or forced meat. By some mistake my dinner did not arrive from Navy Hall one day last week, but I had some of the excellent New York biscuits, which I eat, and said nothing about my dinner, feeling a pleasure in being able to be independent.

Mon. 22nd—We crossed the water to the Ferry House (Lewiston, N.Y.), opposite Queenstown, and breakfasted in an arbour covered with wild vines and beautifully situated on the bank of the river. We rode up the hill to the spot where the French had a fort built about 1750. We saw a very extensive view towards the head of the lake. On our return we found the arbour so cool and pleasant that the Governor sent for his writing-box, and we stayed here the whole day. After dinner I ascended

York (Toronto) Harbor, 1793.
North side of the Bay, near the Old Fort.
(From a Drawing by Mrs. Simcoe.)

12

the hill again and made a sketch. We supped in the camp. The "Caldwell" sailed, with Capt. Smith, for Toronto.

Tues. 23rd—Excessively hot weather. The Governor went to Navy Hall. Francis is much better, but weak. I see him almost every day, but did not choose to pay Mrs. Hamilton so long a visit, tho' I feel greatly obliged to her for keeping the child. I have just heard that the "Onondaga" is arrived at Navy Hall to take us to Toronto. Whether we shall remain there, and the regiment build huts for their winter residence, is not yet decided.

Thurs. 25th—Went this evening to Navy Hall.

Sat. 27th—I went to church. Drank tea at the fort. My Marvel of pine is in great beauty (evidently a plant or shrub).

Sun. 28th—An experiment of firing shells from cannon was made at the Fort by the Governor's orders.

Mon. 29th—We were prepared to sail for Toronto this morning, but the wind changed suddenly. We dined with the Chief Justice, and were recalled from a walk at nine o'clock this evening, as the wind had become fair. We embarked on board the "Mississaga," the band playing in the ship. It was dark, so I went to bed and slept until eight o'clock the next morning, when I found myself in the harbour of Toronto. We had gone under an easy sail all night, for as no person on board had ever been at Toronto, Mr. Bouchette was afraid to enter the harbour till daylight, when St. John Rosseau, an Indian trader who lives near, came in a boat to pilot us.

NOTE.—The Governor, it seems, was not one of the passengers on this occasion, for although Mrs. Simcoe uses the word "we," she continues by saying that "no person on board had ever been at Toronto." The Governor had visited Toronto on Tuesday, the 3rd May—his first visit—and was at that port until the 12th, when he returned to Navy Hall. He was in Niagara on the 28th July and in York on the 6th of August. There is no entry in the diary as to the date he left Niagara or of his arrival in York.

St. John (St. Jean Baptiste) Rousseau lived in 1793 on St. John's Creek, later known as the Humber. He settled in Ancaster in 1795, where he built the first grist and saw mill on the site of the present village. He was a member of Masonic Lodge, No. 10, in the township of Barton, known to-day as Barton Lodge, No. 6, Hamilton. He died in 1815.

Tues. 30th—The Queen's Rangers are encamped opposite to the ship. After dinner we went on shore to fix on a spot whereon to place the canvas houses, and we chose a rising ground, divided by a creek from the camp, which is ordered to be cleared immediately. The soldiers have cut down a great deal of wood to enable them to pitch their tents. We went in a boat two miles to the bottom of the bay, and walked thro' a grove of oaks, where the town is intended to be built. A low spit of land, covered with wood, forms the bay and breaks the horizon of the lake, which greatly improves the view, which indeed is very pleasing. The water in the bay is beautifully clear and transparent.

NOTE.—The "rising ground" where the party camped was east of the site of the present Old Fort, at the Queen's Wharf, Toronto. The "Creek" known now as the Garrison Creek ran from the northwest, along the east side of the Fort, but now the creek is drained. Bellwoods Park is a portion of its old bed. The grove referred to was situated on that part of Toronto bounded by George Street on the west, Parliament Street on the east, Queen Street on the north and Toronto Bay on the south. Early pictures of that part of the city show oak trees along the line of Palace Street, the present Front Street. The spit of land is the present island, in 1793 a peninsula.

Sun. Aug. 4th—We rode on the peninsula opposite Toronto, so I called the spit of land, for it is united to the mainland by a very narrow neck of ground. We crossed the bay opposite the camp, and rode by the lake side to the end of the peninsula.

NOTE.—The party crossed the bay of Toronto from their camp on the shore near the site of the Old Fort, and landed at the present Hanlan's Point, known in the early days as Gibraltar Point. This point is shown in all the Government maps from 1796 as "Gibraltar Point." When Mrs. Simcoe writes later on that the "Onondaga" on her way from Kingston to York was "off Gibraltar Point at York" when passing the present Lighthouse Point, she wrote in error. The peninsula in 1793 joined the mainland at the foot of the present Woodbine Avenue. In 1854 the waters of Lake Ontario broke through and created the present Island. Later the eastern channel was made, now used by the largest lake boats.

4th—We met with some good natural meadows and several ponds. The trees are mostly of the poplar kind, covered with wild vines, and there are some fir. On the ground were everlasting peas creeping in abundance, of a purple color. I am told they are good to eat when boiled, and some pretty, white flowers, like lilies of the valley. We continued our ride beyond the peninsula on the sands of the north shore of Lake Ontario till we were impeded by large trees on the beach. We then walked some distance till we met with Mr. Grant's (the surveyor's) boat. It was not much larger than a canoe, but we ventured into it, and after rowing a mile we came within sight of what is named, in the map, the highlands of Toronto. The shore is extremely bold, and has the appearance of chalk cliffs, but I believe they are only white sand. They appeared so well that we talked of building a summer residence there and calling it Scarborough.

NOTE.—The party rowed east on Lake Ontario, to the present highlands known from the name given them by Governor Simcoe as Scarborough Heights. The summer residence was not built at the Heights, but a couple of miles up the Don River at the place known as "Castle Frank."

4th—The diversity of scenes I met with this morning made the ride extremely pleasant. The wooded part of the peninsula was like shrubbery. The sands towards the lake reminded me of the sands at Weymouth, and the sight of the highlands presented a totally different country to anything near the bay, tho' I was not more than four miles from it. I was very near riding into what appeared a quicksand, which, with a little rain and wind we met with for half an hour as we rode from the shore to the Mississaga, were the only unpleasant incidents that occurred this day. After dinner we left the Mississaga, and slept to-night in the canvas house.

NOTE.—The canvas house was one of three or four large and small tents that Governor Simcoe bought in London at the sale of the effects of Captain Cook, the explorer. The original drawings of these tents

CASCADE ON THE SEVERN.
McDonald's Rapids, between Sparrow Lake and Ragged Rapids.
(From a Drawing by Lieutenant Pilkington, copied by Mrs. Simcoe.)

are in the British Museum, and facsimiles will appear in my biography of Governor Simcoe.

Mon. 5th—The children came on shore; this afternoon we walked two miles to the old French Fort, but there are no remains of any building there. It rained very hard, and I was as completely wet as if I had walked through a river, for being in a shower in the woods is quite different from being exposed to it in an open country; every tree acted as a shower bath, as the path was just wide enough to admit of one person. We passed some creeks and unhewn trees thrown across, a matter of some difficulty to those unaccustomed to them. I should think it might be done with less danger of falling with moccasins on the feet.

NOTE.—The "old French Fort" was Fort Rouillé, erected about 1750 and named after the French Colonial Minister of that name. It was a stockade trading post, popularly known as Fort Toronto, but officially as Fort Rouillé, and the site was at the foot of Dufferin Street, Toronto, now marked by a monument. Mrs. Simcoe's calculation of distance seems to have been erroneous, for it is less than a mile from the camp, which was east of Garrison Creek, to the ruins of the French Fort. Probably the pathway to the ruins was circuitous and as they were walking through the woods the distance may have led Mrs. Simcoe to the belief that they had gone two miles.

Tues. 6th—Having been wet thro' these last two days, I declined going with the Governor to see a mill on St. John's Creek, six miles towards the head of the lake. The Governor brought me some very good cakes. The miller's wife is from the United States, where the women excel in making cakes and bread.

NOTE.—In November of 1678, the Franciscan Friar La Motte and Hennepin sailed from Fort Frontenac for Niagara. On the 26th they arrived at the Indian village of Taiaiagon, near Toronto, probably a few miles west of the mouth of the Humber River, where they ran their vessel for safety into the mouth of the river, which Parkman says was "probably the Humber." The site of this Indian village is shown in a manuscript map sent to France by Intendant Duchesneau and is now in the Archives de la Marine in Paris. The word "Taiaiagon" means a portage or landing place, and it is very doubtful if Hennepin in its use intended to refer to the site of Toronto. There is no certainty as to the derivation or meaning of the word Toronto. In early maps Lake Simcoe is called "Lac Tarento" and "Lac Taronthé." Toronto evidently denoted Lake Simcoe and the surrounding region. In LaHontan's map the Humber River is marked Tanaouate. By others it was called Toronto River.

In the maps of 1756 the river Humber, two miles west of Toronto, is given as St. John's Creek. It is, however, given as the Humber by D. W. Smith, A.S.G., on 31st January, 1798, in a plan of Humber Mills, while State Papers H. 1, 1798, are entitled "Papers re Humber Mills." They contain a letter from John Wilson offering to purchase the Government Saw Mills on the Humber, and "a statement of annual income arising from the Government Saw Mills on the Humber, commencing May, 1794, and ending December 31st, 1797,"

DIARY OF MRS. SIMCOE

signed by John McGill, Superintendent Saw Mill Accounts. A map of the Province of Upper Canada describing all the new Settlements, Townships, etc., with the Counties adjacent, from Quebec to Lake Huron, compiled at the request of His Excellency Major-General John Graves Simcoe, First Lieutenant-Governor, etc., by David William Smyth, Esq., Surveyor-General, London, Faden, 1800, is the earliest map in the Archives Department, Ottawa, giving the name Humber. The Government Mill was situated about the site of the ruins of the present "old mill." It is believed that after the War of 1812-4 it was never used. The Surveyor-General spelt his name indifferently "Smith" and "Smyth."

Wed. 7th—I rode on the peninsula from one till four. I saw loons swimming on the lake; they make a noise like a man hollowing in a tone of distress. One of these birds was sent to me dead at Niagara; it was as large as a swan, black, with a few white marks on it. At a distance they appear like small fishing boats. The air on these sands is peculiarly clear and fine. The Indians esteem this place so healthy that they come and stay here when they are ill.

Fri. 9th—Some Indians of the Ojibway tribe came from near Lake Huron. They are extremely handsome, and have a superior air to any I have seen; they have been living among Europeans, therefore less accustomed to drink rum. Some wore black silk handkerchiefs, covered with silver brooches, tied right round the head, others silver bands, silver arm bands, and their shirts ornamented with brooches; scarlet leggings or pantaloons, and black, blue or scarlet broadcloth blankets. These Indians brought the Governor "a beaver blanket to make his bed," as they expressed themselves, apologized for not having done it sooner, and invited him to visit their country.

NOTE.—The territory occupied by the Ojibway nation was the largest in extent of any Indian possessions of which there is a definite knowledge. When the Champlain traders met the Ojibways in 1610, their eastern boundary was marked by the waters of Lakes Huron and Michigan. The mountain ridge lying between Lake Superior and the frozen bay (Hudson Bay) was the northern barrier. On the west stretched a forest, beyond which was a vast prairie. On the south, a valley, by Lake Superior, thence to the southern part of Michigan. The land within these boundaries has always been known as the country of the Ojibways.

Sat. 10th—I went to my favourite sands; the bay is a mile across. The Governor thinks, from the manner in which the sandbanks are formed, they are capable of being fortified so as to be impregnable; he therefore calls it "Gibraltar Point," tho' the land is low.

Sun. 11th—Lt. Smith of the 5th Regiment who is here as Acting Deputy Surveyor-General read prayers to the Queen's Rangers assembled under some trees near the parade. This evening we went to see a creek which is to be called the River Don. It falls into the bay near the peninsula. After we entered we rowed some distance among low lands covered with rushes, abounding with wild ducks and swamp black birds, with red wings. About a mile beyond the bay the banks become high and wooded as the river contracts its width.

Lt. Smith has drawn a fine map of the La Tranche River. From what has been surveyed, it is proved that Charlevoix, the French explorer's map, describes the country with great truth. If the line from the road

On the Severn River.
McLean's Bay, at the Outlet of Sparrow Lake.
(From a Drawing by Lieutenant Pilkington, copied by Mrs. Simcoe.)

to the river La Tranche was laid down according to its true bearings on any map but Charlevoix's, it would strike Lake Erie instead of La Tranche.

NOTE.—The Indian name of the Don River was "Wonscoteonach," signifying "back burnt grounds," that is, the river coming down from the back burnt country, which had previously been swept by fire. The term is merely descriptive and not a proper name. The creek which Mrs. Simcoe states is "to be called the River Don," was so named by the Governor on this visit to Toronto. He very often discussed the naming of places in the Province with his wife. This is gathered from letters at Wolford.

Sir David William Smith, only child of Lieutenant-Colonel John Smith, of the Fifth Foot, was born 4th September, 1764. He was ensign in his father's regiment and afterwards captain. He was a member of the Executive Council and of the three first Canadian Parliaments. He was also Surveyor-General of Upper Canada. In 1821 he was created a baronet. He died in England in the spring of 1837.

SIR D. W. SMITH.

Tues. 13th—An Indian named Wable Casigo supplies us with salmon, which the rivers and creeks on this shore abound with. It is supposed they go to the sea; the velocity with which fish move makes it not impossible, and the very red appearance and goodness of the salmon confirms the supposition; they are best in the month of June. I brought a favourite white cat, with grey spots, with me from Niagara. He is a native of Kingston. His sense and attachment are such that those who believe in transmigration would think his soul once animated a reasoning being. He was undaunted on board the ship, sits composedly as sentinel at my door, amid the beat of drums and the crash of falling trees, and visits the tent with as little fear as a dog would do. There has been a fever at Niagara. This place is very healthy, and I think it probable we shall spend the winter here. Mr. Talbot is still in Philadelphia; Mr. Grey at Quebec. He has broken his arm there. The Governor has the gout in his foot very slightly. He has just received a letter from Prince Edward, lamenting his not obtaining leave to go to England.

Sat. 24th—The Governor has received an official account of the Duke of York (1763-1827) having distinguished himself in an action in Flanders by which the French were dislodged and driven out of Holland. The Governor ordered a royal salute to be fired in commemoration of this event, and took the same opportunity of naming this station York. There are a few twelve or eighteen pounders, which were brought here from Oswegatchie or from Carleton Island. The "Mississaga" and "Onondaga" fired also, and the regiment.

NOTE.—It is doubtful whether this refers to Old Oswegatchie, the fort that was originally built by the French at Ogdensburg in St. Lawrence County, New York, on the banks of the Oswegatchie River. The name is a corruption of the Huron word meaning "black water." The fort was occupied by the French during the Seven Years' War, but was captured by the British in 1760, when they were en route down the St. Lawrence to attack Montreal. Directly opposite Ogdensburg is the Canadian town of Prescott, and northeast of Prescott is the township of Augusta in the County of Grenville, in which was situated a district known as New Oswegatchie. Near the present village of Maitland, in 1758, defensive works were erected by the French, and because timber was easily procured, a shipyard was established. The original French fort with its pickets was in existence in 1785. It is more than likely that the guns came from Carleton Island.

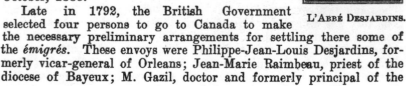

Sat. 24th—There were a party of Ojibway Indians here, who appeared much pleased with the firing. One of them, named "Great Sail," took Francis in his arms, and was much pleased to find the child not afraid, but delighted with the sound.

NOTE.—On the 26th August, 1793, was issued over the signature of E. B. Littlehales, the major of brigade, an official order to the effect that the Lieutenant-Governor having received information of the success of His Majesty's arms under H:R.H. the Duke of York, by which Holland was saved from the invasion of the French, the Governor had determined to change the name of "Toronto" to that of "York" in honor of the Duke. This order was effective from 27th August, when the two-cross Flag was raised and a salute of twenty-one guns fired to commemorate the event.

CANISE (Great Sail).

Sun. 25th—The Abbé des Jardins and a Monsr. de la Corne arrived here. They are sent by some French *émigrés* to examine whether a suitable establishment could be allotted for them in this country. The Abbé appears a cunning, clever man, whose manners are those of one accustomed to live in the best society in Paris. La Corne is a Canadian who has been some time resident in France. The Governor received them with great civility; has ordered a marquee to be pitched for them. He has recommended them to travel towards Burlington Bay, at the head of the lake, where the country is open and the climate very mild. The soil and local circumstances they may judge of when on the spot.

NOTE.—L'Abbé Philippe-Jean-Louis Desjardins was born in France 6th June, 1753. He became a priest in December, 1777, and was one of the forty-four priests who fled from France during the French Revolution. Shortly after his arrival in Canada in March, 1793, he was sent to Niagara. Afterwards he became a director of the Ursuline Convent in Quebec, where he was a well-known ecclesiastic. It was owing to his efforts that many valuable paintings were brought to Canada. He died in Paris on 21st October, 1883.

L'ABBÉ DESJARDINS.

Late in 1792, the British Government selected four persons to go to Canada to make the necessary preliminary arrangements for settling there some of the *émigrés*. These envoys were Philippe-Jean-Louis Desjardins, formerly vicar-general of Orleans; Jean-Marie Raimbeau, priest of the diocese of Bayeux; M. Gazil, doctor and formerly principal of the

ON THE SEVERN RIVER.

The Little Chute, near the Entrance to Gloucester Pool.

(From a Drawing by Lieutenant Pilkington, copied by Mrs. Simcoe.)

College of Navarre; and the Chevalier François-Josue Saint-Luc de la Corne, formerly post captain in the French Navy. These gentlemen were given £200 by the Government and £80 by the Relief committee. They were instructed to embark on His Majesty's packet for New York, and, having arrived there, to seek out His Majesty's agent, Sir John Temple, who was directed to give them all the needful assistance in prosecuting their journey to Quebec. The envoys reached that city on March 2nd, 1793, and presented their credentials to the Lieutenant-Governor. On August 3, 1793, M. Desjardins and the Chevalier de la Corne left for the Upper Province. They were received with great cordiality, were entertained for several weeks in the capital of the Province, Newark, now called Niagara, and apparently expressed a wish for land in this vicinity. They also visited York. As a result the Executive Council set aside for them a township at the west end of Lake Ontario near Burlington Bay.

Wed. 28th—I walked with the Governor on Gibraltar Point this evening.

Thur. 29th—The gunboat arrived from Niagara. An officer from Detroit came in her, who says the Indian Commissioners returned to the States without making peace with the Indians, as they refused to give up what the Indians had invariably made the terms of accommodation.

Fri. 30th—The "Mississaga" came from Niagara in four hours. Mr. Russell came in her.

Wed. 4th Sept.—I rode to St. John's Creek (the Humber River). There is a ridge of land extending near a mile beyond St. John's House, 300 feet high and not more than three feet wide; the bank towards the river is of smooth turf. There is a great deal of hemlock spruce on this river; the banks are dry and very pleasant. I gathered a beautiful large species of Polygala, which is a genus of annual and perennial herbs and shrubs of the order of Polygalacae.

I found a green caterpillar, with tufts like fir on its back. I accidentally touched my face with them, and it felt as if stung by a nettle, and the sensation continued painful for some time. It was extremely calm when we set out, but on our return we were almost seasick, the water was so rough. A little breeze on this lake raises the waves in the most sudden manner.

Fri. 6th—I have read Alfred's letters. I never expected to have been so much entertained by a political book or to have comprehended so much of the politics of Europe. Mr. Osgoode, the Chief Justice, suspects it to be written by Mr. Burgess. (A friend of Governor Simcoe's, whose portrait is at Wolford.)

I went to-day to ride to Gibraltar Point.

NOTE.—*Three letters (signed Alfred) to the people of Great Britain and particularly to those who signed the addresses on the late changes of administration and the dissolution of Parliament. London, 1785.*

Wed. 11th—We rowed six miles up the Don to Coons', who has a farm under a hill covered with pine. I saw very fine butternut trees. The nuts are better than walnuts; gathered berries of cockspur thorns. I landed to see the shingles made, which is done by splitting large blocks of the pine into equal divisions. We found the river very shallow in many parts and obstructed by fallen trees. One of them lay so high above the water that the boat passed under, the rowers stooping their heads. It looked picturesque, and a bald eagle sat on a blasted pine on a very bold point just above the fallen tree. The Governor talks of placing a canvas house on this point for a summer residence. Vencal rowed—a very intelligent man, born in Sweden.

NOTE.—Coon's farm was on the east bank of the Don River about where Chester is to-day.

Fri. 13th—Mr. Pilkington coasted the lake from Niagara, and arrived here in two days, about 100 miles.

NOTE.—Robert Pilkington (1765-1834) obtained his commission as second lieutenant in the Royal Artillery in 1787. He was transferred to the Royal Engineers in 1789 and was stationed at Quebec; was first lieutenant in January, 1793, and captain in 1801. He was on General Simcoe's staff from 1793-6 and built the fort on the Maumee by instructions of Governor Simcoe. The building of this fort was one of the causes of friction between Governor Simcoe and Lord Dorchester, the Governor-General at Quebec. The Governor had advised against the erection, but was ordered to carry out instructions. Pilkington remained in Canada until 1803. He became major-general in 1825 and was inspector-general of fortifications in England in 1830. He died in 1834. His wife was Hannah, daughter of John Tylee, and by her he had two sons, one of whom died shortly after birth, and four daughters. The surviving son, Robert John Pilkington, married Jane, daughter of Andrew Shaw, of Montreal, a daughter being Mrs. J. W. Molson of that city.

Sat. 14th—We walked to the spot intended for the site of the town. Mr. Aitkin's (the surveyor) canoe was there; we went into it, and himself and his man paddled. We went at the rate of four knots an hour. I liked it very much; being without the noise of oars is a great satisfaction. I gathered purple berries from a creeping plant, seeds of lilies and spikenard. To see a birch canoe managed with that inexpressible care and composure, which is the characteristic of an Indian, is the prettiest sight imaginable. A man usually paddles at one end of it and a woman at the other; but in smooth water little exertion is wanting, and they sit quietly, as if to take the air. The canoe appears to move as if by clockwork. I always wish to conduct a canoe myself when I see them manage it with such dexterity and grace. An European usually looks awkward and in a bustle compared with the Indian's quiet skill in a canoe.

NOTE.—Alexander Aitkin was the Deputy-Surveyor, who by order of Governor Simcoe, made the first survey and map or plan of the original town of York (Toronto). This plan was made in June, 1793, after the Governor had selected the site. The Governor, who retained the plan with other official documents, sent it to the war authorities in London, on his arrival in England from Canada in 1796. Many times during the past century search for this plan was made in the War Office, in the Colonial Office, and in the British Museum, but without avail. In October, 1900, however, I discovered it in the Public Record Office, Chancery Lane, London, just 107 years from the date of its making. Aitkin was a very active official and was a favorite with Governor Simcoe. During the latter years of his life he resided in Kingston, U.C., where he died about 1830.

ON THE SEVERN RIVER.

Head of the Big Chute, near Gloucester Pool.

(From a Drawing by Lieutenant Pilkington, copied by Mrs. Simcoe.)

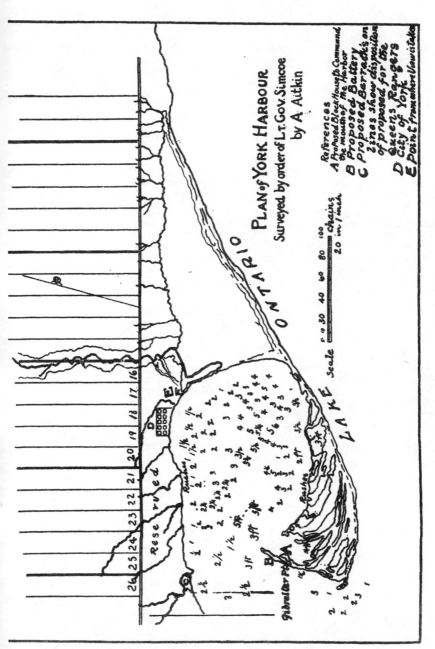

PLAN of YORK HARBOUR

Surveyed by order of Lt. Gov. Simcoe
by A. Aitkin

ONTARIO

LAKE

Scale 1. 10 30 40 60 80 100 chains
20 in 1 inch

References

A Proposed Block House the Command
the mouth of the Harbor
B Proposed Battery
C Proposed Barracks on
lines show disposition
of proposed for the
D Queens Rangers
E City of York
E Point from other View is take

FIRST OFFICIAL PLAN OF YORK (TORONTO), 1793.

(From the Record Office, Chancery Lane, London, England.)

195

DIARY OF MRS. SIMCOE

Mon. 23rd—I rode on the peninsula. My horse has spirit enough to wish to get before others. I rode a race with Mr. Talbot to keep myself warm. I gathered wild grapes. They were pleasant, but not sweet. Capt. Smith is gone to open a road, to be called Dundas Street, from the head of the lake to the River La Tranche. He has 100 men with him.

Tues. 24th—I hear that they kill rattlesnakes every day, yet not a man has been bitten, altho' they have been among them for six weeks. Capt. Smith sent two of the snakes in a barrel, that I might see them; they were dark and ugly, and made a whizzing sound in shaking their rattles when I touched them with a stick. We dine in a marquee to-day. It has become too cold in the arbour; the canvas house we use as a bed-room, but the other is going to be erected for a winter dining-room. I have gathered most beautiful white berries, with a black eye, from red stalks. I cannot find out its name.

Wed. 25th—The Governor set out, with four officers, a dozen soldiers and some Indians, to visit Lake Huron.

Sun. 29th—I walked on the sand bank and gathered seeds of Toronto lilies.

Wed. Oct. 2nd—The Governor's horses returned from the Mississaga Creek, now the Holland River, from whence he sent me some seeds. I received the outside garment sent from England by Mr. G. Davison. The ground mice are innumerable and most troublesome here. We want the edict published in Spain to excommunicate and banish them. I send you a bat remarkable for its size, and a beautiful black and yellow bird.

Fri. 25th—I send a map to elucidate the Governor's journey, which was attended with danger as well as with many pleasant circumstances. The western side of the lake is drawn from Mr. Pilkington's sketches, the eastern from former accounts. Mr. Pilkington, who was one of the party, says the scenery was fit for pictures the whole way, and from his drawings I should suppose so. They rode 30 miles to the Miciaguean—Mississaga—Creek, then passed a terrible bog of liquid mud.

The Indians with some difficulty pushed the canoe the Governor was in through it. The Governor went to the habitation of Canise, the Indian who held Francis in his arms during the firing when "York" was named. Canise and his eldest son were lately dead, and their widows and children were lamenting them. Young Canise gave the Governor a beaver blanket, and made speeches of excuse for not sooner having made his bed. The Governor went to see a very respectable Indian named "Old Sail," who lives on a branch of Holland's River. He advised him to return by the eastern branch of it to avoid the swamp. They proceeded about thirty miles across Lac aux Claies, now named Simcoe, in which are many islands, which Coll. Simcoe named after his father's friends and those gentlemen who accompanied him. The river from thence to Matchedash Bay afforded the most picturesque scenery, from the number of falls and rapids upon it. Some of them were avoided by carrying the canoes on the shores; others they risked going down.

NOTE.—There have been great changes in recent years on the Severn River owing to the placing of dams at the various water-falls. McDonald's Rapids have been almost obliterated by blasting, done by the Dominion Government and by the Town's power dam at the Ragged Rapids, but in the recollection of Mr. C. H. Hale of Orillia, who has kindly furnished me with information regarding the Severn pictures, the principal cascade of McDonald's Rapids was as shown in the sketch made by Lieutenant Pilkington in 1793.

Holland's River is named after Surveyor-General Samuel Holland. The town of Holland Landing, thirty-eight miles from Toronto, is situated on this river.

196

SPARROW LAKE CHUTE.
On the Severn River, below McLean's Bay.
(From a Drawing by Lieutenant Pilkington, copied by Mrs. Simcoe)

THE GOVERNOR AT LAKE SIMCOE.

Lake Simcoe, originally Ouentaronk Lake, sometimes called Sinion or Shiniong, afterwards called Lac aux Claies, was given its present name by Governor Simcoe out of respect for his father.

The three principal islands in Lake Simcoe are now known by the names of Snake, Georgina and Thorah Islands. Georgina and Thorah Islands were formerly known as Graves and Canise Islands, respectively, but have come to be called by the names of the townships to which they are adjacent. Snake Island, from the time of the earliest white traders down to the present, has had the name it now bears. There was an attempt more than a century ago to rename the islands after friends of Governor Simcoe, but none of the designations came into general use. Smith's Gazetteer, published in 1799, and in its second edition published in 1813, gives Snake Island as Darling's Island, named after Captain (afterwards General) Darling, one of the friends of Simcoe who accompanied him on this trip to Lake Simcoe and Matchedash Bay. These names, however, had only a temporary application on paper, and the names in use among the traders and early settlers were not superseded by the proposed ones.

Matchedash Bay is an inlet at the southeast extremity of Georgian Bay, Lake Huron—also spelled Machedash and Matadash—and means muskeg or marshy ground. Waubaushene is situated at its mouth, nearly opposite where the Severn enters Georgian Bay.

25th—In passing a rapid an Indian in the Governor's canoe fell over, and the canoe passed over him. He rose up on the other side and got in again without seeming discomposure. On returning one of the soldiers cut his foot near Holland's River. Mr. Alexander McDonnell and another gentleman stayed with him, as he was unable to travel. The "Old Sail" received them hospitably, and shot ducks for them. A small quantity of provisions being left with them, and an Indian who carried a large cargo quitting the party, reduced the stock so much that the Governor set out with only two days' provisions and the expectation of five days' march to bring them to York. The Indians lost their way, and when they had provisions for one day only they knew not where they were. The Governor had recourse to a compass, and at the close of the day they came on a surveyor's line, and the next morning saw Lake Ontario. Its first appearance, Coll. Simcoe says, was the most delightful sight, at a time they were in danger of starving, and about three miles from York they breakfasted on the remaining provisions.

NOTE.—The Big Chute is now being developed by the Simcoe Power, Light and Railway Company, and for many years there has been a lumbermen's dam at this point. At the right side of the river, going down stream, in the neighborhood of the Big Chute, there is considerable indentation caused by the dams raising the water. This indentation was not apparent in 1793, before the inroads of civilization.

25th—Had they remained in the woods another day it was feared that "Jack Snap" would have been sacrificed to their hunger. He is a very fine Newfoundland dog who belonged to Mr. Sheehan, near Niagara, but has lived at Navy Hall from the time of our coming there, and walked to Detroit with Coll. Simcoe. He has been troublesome enough on this excursion, as his size was very unsuitable to a canoe, but he is a great favourite.

DIARY OF MRS. SIMCOE

Coll. Simcoe had the satisfaction of finding Matchadash Bay such as gave him reason to believe would be an excellent harbour for very large ships. A bay near Prince William is called Penetanguishene, a fine harbour. The fever at New York and Philadelphia amounts almost to the plague.

NOTE.—There was a terrific visitation of yellow fever at New York and Philadelphia in 1791-2 and 1793. Many thousands of persons died of the pestilence.

Sun. 27th—A road for walking is now opened up three miles on each side of the camp. I can, therefore, now take some exercise without going to the peninsula. Mr. McDonell arrived with the soldiers from Holland's River. He brought some wild ducks from Lake Simcoe, which were better than any I have ever tasted; these birds are so much better than any in England from their feeding on wild rice. Capt. Smith is returned from cutting the road named Dundas. It is opened for 20 miles.

They met with quantities of wild grapes, and put some of the juice in barrels to make vinegar, and Capt. Smith told me it turned out very tolerable wine. They killed numbers of rattlesnakes every day, but nobody was bitten by them. Capt. Smith brought two in a barrel to show me, as I had never seen any alive.

NOTE.—This shows that the road known as Dundas St. was in October, 1793, opened for twenty miles, that is, as far as Port Credit. It was named after Henry Dundas, who became Home Secretary, 1791, and Secretary for War, 1794. He was raised to the peerage as Viscount Melville, December 24th, 1802.

Mon. 28th—The weather has been very cold for some days and the frost very severe, notwithstanding which we feel it quite mild in the woods. To-day we walked two miles to a pretty spot by the side of a creek, where we had a fire made of many large trees and wild ducks roasted by it, and we dined without feeling the least cold. Coll. Pickering's, the American Indian Commissioner's dish, chowder, is also easily dressed in the woods, being prepared in a kettle before we left our house.

NOTE.—Sparrow Lake Chute, two or three miles below McLean's Bay, has been considerably affected by dams built on the Ragged Rapids, to such an extent in fact, that at one time it was navigable by steamers.

Gloucester Pool is an enlargement of the Severn River five miles from its mouth. The Severn empties into Georgian Bay at Port Severn on the east side of the Bay at its southern extremity. Civilization has so completely altered the aspect of this landscape that it is a difficult matter after a hundred years to identify places.

"By Gloucester Pool," on the Severn River.

(From a Drawing by Lieutenant Pilkington, copied by Mrs. Simcoe.)

CHAPTER XIII.

BUILDING OF CASTLE FRANK, ON RIVER DON.

It was in the last days of October, 1793, that General Simcoe determined to select a site for a summer home near York. Frequent excursions by boat up the Don as far as navigable, and walks through the woods that skirted its banks, created a love for that part of the country, a sentiment which was always retained by the Governor and his wife. Years after their return to England she often spoke of "that pretty spot, Castle Frank." Mrs. Simcoe made many sketches of her summer home both from the high ground on which it stood and from the approach up the river. Two of these drawings have been preserved. She writes:

Tues. 29th—The Governor having determined to take a lot of 200 acres upon the River Don for Francis, and the law obliges persons having lots of land to build a house upon them within a year, we went to-day to fix upon the spot for building the house. We went six miles by water from the Fort and east along the bay shore to the Don, and up that river, landed, climbed up an exceedingly steep hill, or rather a series of sugar-loafed hills, and approved of the highest spot, from whence we looked down on the tops of large trees and, seeing eagles near, I suppose they build there. There are large pine plains around it, which, being without underwood, I can ride and walk on, and we hope the height of the situation will secure us from mosquitos. We dined by a large fire on wild ducks and chowder, on the side of a hill opposite to that spot. Our long walk made it late before we had dined, so that, altho' we set out immediately afterwards and walked fast, it was nearly dark before we reached the surveyor's tent. From there we went home in a boat, as the stumps and roots of trees in the road were so troublesome to walk among in the dark. Mr. Littlehales and some gentlemen lost their way in attempting to return to the camp after us. They slept in the woods about a mile distant.

The following description of Castle Frank is from Robertson's Landmarks of Toronto, Vol. 1, p. 3-5.

"During the spring of 1794, the Governor built Castle Frank as a summer residence and named it after his son Francis. It was in the woods on the brow of a steep high bank overlooking the valley of the Don, at a point just beyond the fence which is now the north bounds of St. James' Cemetery. A large portion of the land formerly belonging to Castle Frank is now part of the burying ground. Below and to the south of the dwelling was a deep ravine down which between hog-back formations ran a stream named Castle Frank brook, which flowed into the Don, just above a small island on the west side. The marshes gave way on the right at this point to good land covered with elm, butternut and basswood trees. The site of the building is marked with a stone. The ground on each side of it has a steep descent on its north side to the Don, and on the south

to the bottom of Castle Frank brook ravine through which the tiny
rivulet runs. The view from the dwelling was hemmed in by the
trees that covered alike the surrounding level land and the steep-

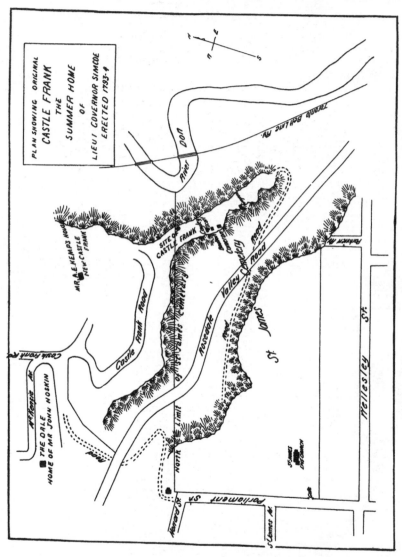

MODERN PLAN SHOWING SITE OF CASTLE FRANK.

(From a Drawing in the Crown Lands Department, Toronto.)

hillsides that could only be climbed with difficulty. No prettier spot could have been selected for a summer home. Some of the
white pines that stood there a century ago are still to be seen, but
many look as if they were second growth. To the east the view was

CASTLE FRANK, 1794.
(From a Drawing by Mrs. Simcoe.)

down upon the valley of the Don, and to the west over the ravine now in the cemetery. The modern entrance to the ravine is by Castle Avenue and Castle Frank Crescent.

"Castle Frank was not occupied permanently by the Governor and his family, but many excursions were made and week ends spent by the friends who enjoyed pleasant hours in the little settlement during Governor Simcoe's administration. The building was about fifty feet in depth and thirty feet in width, the latter being the frontage, which faced south. The front elevation was not unlike that of a Greek temple. The trunks of four large, well matched, unbarked pine trees answered for columns supporting the pediment or the projection of the whole roof. The main doorway was in the centre of the front, but no windows on either side. On the east and west sides were four windows with shutters of heavy double planks running up and down on one side, and crosswise on the other, and thickly studded with the heads of stout nails. Of a similar construction was the door. A chimney arose from the middle of the roof. The walls were built of rather small, carefully hewn logs, of short lengths, clap-boarded. They presented a comparatively finished appearance on the outside, but after a time took the weather-stained color that unpainted wood assumes. Inside the finish was rough, in fact the interior was never fully completed. A slight attempt at a division into rooms had been made, but was never entirely carried out. Entering the front door the visitor found himself at once in an apartment extending the width of the building and about half its length. On one side was a big fireplace. At the rear of this was another room of similar dimensions with a fireplace in the opposite wall. This cleared space in front of the building was but a few yards across, and from it to the site of the town ran a narrow carriage-way and bridle-path cut out by the soldiers and graded, traces of which may still be found.

"Castle Frank received its title from the five year old son of Governor Simcoe, although the Rev. Dr. Henry Scadding, one of my old school masters at Upper Canada College and from whom I obtained all the information here given in regard to the building, points out that there was a 'Castle-franc' near Rochelle, which figures in the history of the Huguenots. The Iroquois had honored the Governor with the title of 'De yonyn hokrawen,' signifying 'One whose door is always open,' and on his little son, who appears to have been a great favorite with them, as he sometimes was attired in Indian costume, they conferred the honour of chieftainship, and named him Deyoken, which means 'Between the two objects.' A warrior's fate befell the young chieftain, for at the age of twenty-one, while serving with his regiment during the Peninsular War, he fell in the breach at Badajoz in 1812. In spite of the unavoidable discomforts of life at Castle Frank and at York, many were the compensating pleasures, especially for the soldier pioneers who formed almost the entire male population. Governor Simcoe's mind was absorbed with schemes of government and war. Those who were fond of sport might gratify their desire to the full in the forest which surrounded York, where bear, deer and wolves and small game abounded. Woodcock and snipe were plentiful on the peninsula and east and north of the east end of Toronto Bay. In the early days salmon was speared at night in the Don, and the bay and Lake Ontario were filled with fish of all kinds. Until Governor Simcoe's departure in 1796, Castle Frank's rough roof covered many a gay party, brought up by canoes and rowboats from the Fort, or on horseback.

"After Governor Simcoe's return to England Castle Frank was occasionally used by President Peter Russell and his family for a picnic, excursion party or ball, when the guests were in summer taken up the Don in boats and in winter by the same route in sleighs. That these trips must have given great enjoyment to those concerned is evident, for there is a letter extant from Mr. Russell, written in December, 1796, in which he says: 'I hope the ladies may be able to enjoy the charming carioling (sleighing) which you must have on your bay and up the Don to Castle Frank, when an early dinner must be picturesque and delightful.' Captain John Denison, an officer in the English militia, came to Canada from Hedon, Yorkshire, in 1792. He first settled in Kingston, but in 1796 he moved to York, and during the summer months he lived at Castle Frank by permission of the Honorable Peter Russell."

NEAR CASTLE FRANK.
(From a Drawing by Mrs. Simcoe.)

Colonel Talbot in a letter to General Simcoe dated July 17th, 1803, writes of a trip to York and a visit to Castle Frank. He says: "I paid a visit of duty to Castle Frank, which I am sorry to add is uninhabited and going to ruin. Some rascals had, a few days before I saw it, broken off the window shutters and gone down to the lower apartment, where they broke down the chimney in order to carry away the bar of iron that supported it."

In 1807, Mrs. Simcoe, the widow of the late Governor, wrote to Sir David W. Smith, Bart., who resided at Alnwick and in 1798-9 was Speaker of the Legislative Assembly of Upper Canada, concerning the Scarborough lands of her late husband. Sir David replied that he understood that the Government long before he left Canada made some entry in the Council books, and that he considered Castle Frank as making up the residue of this land. But, added Sir David, the General told me that the person who made out the deed of the Castle Frank property mistook 'G' for Graves and called the property, registered in the name of Francis, 'Graves' instead of 'Gwillim.'

After 1807, Castle Frank was tenantless. The building began to show further signs of decay, and in 1829 it was accidentally burned through the carelessness of some amateur fishermen, and so a building that would to-day be a genuine relic of the olden time passed out. The only relic I know of in connection with Castle Frank is a Masonic gavel made out of a piece of ash, and which was presented to me by Orient Lodge A. F. and A. M., Toronto, in 1892, during my term as Grand Master of the Grand Lodge of Canada, in the Province of Ontario.

Wed. 30th Oct.—We have received from Montreal a birch bark canoe, such as is used by the North-West Company to transport their goods to the Grand Portage. It requires twelve men to paddle, is large enough to contain four or five passengers to sit very commodiously in the centre under an awning. An Indian woman came to-day with pitch, which is made by the Indians from fir trees, to gum the canoe if any part of it is worn off by bringing it hither. She held a piece of pitch in her hand, and melted it by applying a piece of burning wood. Her figure was perfectly wild and witchlike, and a little fire, with a kettle on it by her side, in a stormy, dark day, the waves roaring on the beach near which she stood, formed a scene very wildly picturesque.

Fri. Nov. 1st—I walked this morning. At eight this dark evening we went in a boat to see salmon speared. Large torches of white birch bark being carried in the boat, the blaze of light attracts the fish, when the men are dexterous in spearing. The manner of destroying the fish is disagreeable, but seeing them swimming in shoals around the boat is a very pretty sight.

The flights of wild pigeons in the spring and autumn is a surprising sight. They fly against the wind and so low that at Niagara the men threw sticks at them from the fort and killed numbers; the air is somewhat darkened by them. I think those we have met with here have been particularly good. Sometimes they fix a bullet to a string tied to a pole, and knock them down. Coll. Butler, of the Rangers, was observing that they build where there are plenty of acorns, but do not feed within 20 miles of the place, reserving that stock of provisions till the young ones can leave their nests, and then scratch the acorns up for them.

Pigeons have been shot with rice in their craws on the Mohawk River. Rice does not grow nearer than Carolina. Therefore, it is presumed (considering the supposed time of digestion) that they must have flown 200 miles a day.

Fri. 8th—We have had a week of incessant rain.

Sat. 9th—I went to-day for the first time in the North-West canoe. A beaver blanket and a carpet were put in to sit on. We carried a small table, to be used in embarking, for the canoe cannot be brought very near the shore, lest the gravel or pebbles injure her, so the table was set in the water and a long plank laid from it to the shore, to enable me to get in or out, the men carrying the canoe empty into the water and out of it up on their shoulders. We have less than "boards between us and eternity," for the canoe is formed of birch bark fixed on to thin ribs of very light wood with the gum or pitch the Indians make from fir trees, and of which they always carry some with them, lest an accident rub off any, or the heat of the sun melt it.

We dined in a meadow on the peninsula, where I amused myself with setting fire to a kind of long dry grass, which burns very quickly, and the flame and smoke run along the ground very quickly and with a pretty effect. I was delighted with the swift and easy motion of the canoe and with its appearance.

Thurs. 14th—I went again in the canoe until we came in sight of the Highlands, but it was so very cold I was very glad to walk part of the way back. We dined on the peninsula. I passed a spot on the peninsula where it was supposed an Indian had been buried lately. A small pile of wood was raised, a bow and arrow lay on it, and a dog-skin hung near it. Some Indians sacrifice dogs, other tribes eat them when extremely ill.

Tues. 19th—At this season of the year there is usually a fortnight of foggy weather; the air is perfectly dry and hot, and smells and feels like smoke; it is called Indian summer. I have never heard these smoky fogs well accounted for.

Wed. 20th—We dined in the woods and eat part of a raccoon; it was very fat and tasted like lamb if eaten with mint sauce.

Thurs. 21st—An owl was sent to me, shot at Niagara; it measured five feet from wing to wing when they were extended.

Fri. 22nd—Mr. Littlehales went on horseback to Niagara.

NOTE.—This journey was made by travelling west from York along Dundas Street and then through a track in the woods along the north shore of Lake Ontario to Burlington Bay, where a stop was made at the government inn known as "The King's Head." The journey from Burlington Bay to Niagara was made through the woods, skirting the south shore of the Lake.

Fri. 29th—An Indian came here who, by way of being in mourning for a relation, was painted black round his face.

Mon. Dec. 2nd—The "Great Sail," his wife and ten children came here; they grouped themselves like Van Dyke's family pictures. They brought us deer. Francis handed plates of apples to them. He shakes hands with the Indians in a very friendly manner, tho' he is very shy and ungracious to all his own countrymen. A Mississaga, called the "Man of the Snakes," was here also. The Mississagas dress very indifferently.

NOTE.—Earlier in the autumn, Canise, otherwise known as "Great Sail," and his son had died, for on 25th October Mrs. Simcoe writes that they are "lately dead." She also refers to "young Canise," no doubt a grandson, "who gave the Governor a beaver blanket and made speeches of excuse for not sooner having made his bed." The "Great Sail" here mentioned was in all probability a successor to the chieftainship.

Sun. Dec. 8th—The "Onondaga" was left under the care of a young lieutenant and ran aground. It is feared she cannot be got off until the spring, and then perhaps not without injury.

NOTE.—In 1793, the "Onondaga," 12 guns, 80 tons burthen, an armed vessel of the Provincial Government went ashore on the west side of Gibraltar Point, now Hanlan's Point. After being abandoned, the vessel was pulled off by Mr. Joseph Bouchette. For this act he was promoted second lieutenant in the provincial navy.

Mon. 9th—The Governor went to the west shore of the peninsula at Gibraltar Point to view the "Onondaga" in such rough weather that the waves came into the boat and made everybody wet.

Thur. 12th—Mr. Grey has just received orders to join Sir C. Grey in the West Indies. He is to go by way of New York. The Governor and

Mr. Talbot set out with him this morning to accompany him as far as Niagara. Fine, calm weather.

Note.—The foregoing entry has reference to Lieutenant Thomas Grey, who had come to Canada with Governor Simcoe, joining his father, Sir Charles Grey, first Earl Grey, who was in this year (1793) appointed with Jervis (subsequently Earl St. Vincent) commander of an expedition to the French West Indies. They reduced Martinique in March, and St. Lucia and Guadaloupe in April, 1794.

H.M. Schooner "Onondaga."

(From a Drawing by Mrs. Simcoe.)

Mon. 16th—An exceedingly rough day. At eight o'clock the Governor and Mr. Talbot returned. They left Niagara at one o'clock yesterday, rowed till four in the morning, slept a few hours at Jones' farm at the "head of the lake." They arrived at Niagara on Friday in such rough weather that there was great difficulty in turning Mississaga Point. (At the mouth of the Niagara River.)

Thur. 19th—I walked to the Don. There are great hopes of getting the "Onondaga" afloat.

Sat. 21st—A hard frost. The bay is half-frozen over. The "Man of Snakes" came here.

Sunday 22nd—The bay is quite frozen over. Mr. Talbot skated to the other side. I walked to-day.

DIARY OF MRS. SIMCOE

Mon. 23rd—Very cold weather.

Tues. 24th—Thunder and lightning last night. Extreme hard frost this morning.

Thur. 26th—Wright and Herring returned from Niagara in a boat. It is found to be practicable to walk and ride thither throughout the winter, therefore we are not in as isolated a situation as it was expected we should find it. We received news of Admiral Gardner's having taken two 44-gun ships off Sandy Hook and some privateers near Halifax.

NOTE.—Edward Wright emigrated to America before the Revolutionary War. On its expiration he returned to the old land, where he remained for several years, but in 1792 came to Canada with the

E. G. S. WRIGHT.

ADMIRAL GARDNER.

Queen's Rangers. His son, Edward Graves Simcoe Wright, who in after years kept the Greenland Fisheries Tavern, north-west corner of Front and John Streets, Toronto, was the first white child born at York, 1794. Edward H. Rodden, Toronto, is a great-grandson of Edward Wright of the Rangers.

Richard Herring, also a Queen's Ranger, was a juryman in one of the three memorable trials that took place in the York Court House in 1818 in connection with the North-West Company and the dispersion of Lord Selkirk's Red River Settlement.

Admiral Alan Gardner was prominent in many naval exploits and was created a baronet for his services in Howe's victory in 1794. As first Baron Gardner, he was created a peer of the United Kingdom in 1806.

Fri. 27th—The weather so cold that some water spilt near the stove froze immediately.

Mon. 30th—I walked to the "Old French Fort" and returned by the Creek. I caught cold.

CHAPTER XIV.

A WINTER AT YORK.

Castle Frank, although in an unfinished state, was habitable in 1794, for early in the year the Governor and his family resided there In the spring, however, Mrs. Simcoe returned to Niagara, where life at Navy Hall was more enjoyable and varied than at York.

York, Mon., Jan. 6th, 1794—The skin of a cross fox, marked yellow, black and white, with a dark cross on the back, was brought here and sold for four dollars; sometimes they are sold for two dollars.

I sketched a likeness of the "Great Sail," who came here to-day. The Indians call the stars we name Ursa Major, a marten (sable) with a broken tail. I received from Detroit a stone carved by an Indian into a head, and when it is known that they have no tools but the commonest kind of small knife, it is surprising to see it is so well done.

I sketched a Caughnawaga Indian to-day whose figure was quite antique. He was from the settlement of that tribe on the south side of the St. Lawrence, opposite Lachine. I have often observed (but never had more reason to do so than to-day) that when the Indians speak, their air and action is more like that of Roman or Greek orators than of modern nations. They have a great deal of impressive action, and look like the figures painted by the Old Masters.

Thur. 14th—There is a great deal of snow on the River Don, which is so well frozen that we walked some miles upon it to-day, but in returning I found it so cold near the lake that I was benumbed and almost despaired of ever reaching my own house, and when I came near the hill was frightfully slippery. Near the river we saw the track of wolves, and the head and hoofs of a deer. The workmen, who reside in a small hut near the place, heard the wolves during the night, and in the morning saw the remains of the deer. The Indians do not kill wolves; they seldom take trouble that does not answer to them, and the wolves are not good to eat and their skins are of little value.

Sat. Jan. 18th—The Queen's (Charlotte of Mecklenburg-Strelitz, Consort of George III.,) birthday. The weather is so mild that we breakfasted with the window open. An experiment was made of firing pebbles from cannon. A salute of 21 guns and a dance in the evening in honour of the day. The ladies much *dressed.*

Sunday 19th—The weather so pleasant that we rode to the bottom of the bay, crossed the Don, which is frozen, and. rode on the peninsula; returned across the marsh, which is covered with ice, and went as far as the settlements, which are near seven miles from the camp. There appeared some comfortable log houses, inhabited by Germans and some by Pennsylvanians. Some of the creeks were not frozen enough to bear the Governor's horse, but mine passed very well. He excels in getting over difficult places and in leaping over logs, which I like very much.

QUEEN CHARLOTTE.

DIARY OF MRS. SIMCOE

NOTE.—Mr. William Berczy was born in Saxony in 1749. He visited England in 1791 and became agent for an association that were owners of a large tract of land in Genesee, N. Y. The intention was to settle Germans on the lands of the association. But owing to differences between Mr. Berczy and the chief manager of the association in Philadelphia, Berczy withdrew his people from New York and settled them by arrangement with Governor Simcoe in Markham, near Toronto. Mr. Charles A. Berczy, son of William Berczy, was born at Niagara in 1794, and died in Toronto in 1858. He was an acting deputy assistant commissary general during the War of 1812, and was postmaster of Toronto from about 1840-52. He married Miss Finch of Greenwich, England, and by her had a large family. Two of his daughters were noted for their beauty.

JOHN SCADDING'S DWELLING.
(From a Drawing by Mrs. Simcoe.)

Sat. 25th—Two soldiers went to Niagara. These expresses are to go at regular periods by way of a post.

Sun. 26th—We went to the Don to see Mr. Talbot skate. Capt. Æneas Shaw's children set the marshy ground (the marsh at Ashbridge's Bay) below the bay on fire; the long grass on it burns with great rapidity this dry weather. It was a fine sight, and a study for flame and smoke from our house. At night the flames diminished, and appeared like lamps on a dark night in the crescent at Bath.

Mon. 27th—I walked below the bay and set the other side of the marsh on fire for amusement. The Indians have cut holes in the ice, over which they spread a blanket on poles, and they sit under the shed, moving a wooden fish hung to a line in the water by way of attracting the living fish, which they spear with great dexterity when they approach. The Governor wished me to see the process; we had to walk a half-mile to the place. There was no snow on the ice, and we were without cloth shoes. The Governor pushed a large limb of a tree before him which kept him

THE SCADDING FAMILY

steady, and with the assistance of Mr. Talbot I reached the spot where they were catching maskalonge, a superior kind of pike, and pickerell. I was almost frozen from looking on, tho' the apprehension of falling kept me warm while I walked.

Fri. 31st—One of the horses drawing hay across the bay fell into an airhole and was drowned. Mr. Scadding's cottage burned down.

NOTE.—This house was just over the Don at the Queen Street crossing—on the Scadding farm—site of the Toronto Jail. The Scaddings were one of the pioneer families of Toronto. They were of Devon origin and resided near Honiton. John Scadding was the manager of Wolford, the Simcoe estate, and emigrated to Canada in 1792, a few months after Simcoe's arrival. A brother, Thomas, living in Honiton, never emigrated. The brothers married sisters, the Misses Triges.

JOHN SCADDING, JR.

John Scadding was a man of excellent executive ability and one of the best informed in England on every branch of farm work. Wolford is an estate of about 5,000 acres and at one time part of it was divided into over twenty farms.

He had three sons, John, Charles and Henry. John married Emily Playter, daughter of John Playter. There was no issue by this marriage. Charles married Jane Bright, the issue being Henry, William, Edward, Charles, John and Sophia. Henry, eldest son of Charles Scadding, married Elizabeth Winder Wedd, daughter of John Wedd, and sister of William Wedd of Upper Canada College. Of their issue there were Charles, Bishop of Oregon, and Henry Crawford Scadding, the well-known physician of Toronto. Henry (Rev.), third son of John Scadding, of Wolford, married Harriet, daughter of John Spread Baldwin. They had a daughter, Henrietta, who married the late Robert Sullivan, a son of the late Judge Sullivan. Mrs. Sullivan lives in Toronto.

DR. SCADDING
AT 28 YEARS.

DR. SCADDING
AT 56 YEARS.

The Rev. Dr. Henry Scadding was more in the public eye than the other members of the Scadding family, and his familiar face will long be remembered by the people of Toronto. He was born in Devonshire in 1813 and came to Canada at the age of eleven years. His father after settling in Canada returned to England and brought out his wife and family. Dr. Scadding was educated at Upper Canada College and was the first head boy under Dr. Harris.

DIARY OF MRS. SIMCOE

He graduated at St. John's College, Cambridge, in 1837, and was an intimate personal friend of Mrs. Simcoe, widow of the first Governor. He was the incumbent of Holy Trinity Church, Toronto, for many years, and also principal of Upper Canada College. He died in Toronto on 6th May, 1901.

Sat. Feb. 1st—I am in great spirits to-day, as the Governor talks of going to Detroit in March and spending a month there very gaily; but the greatest amusement will be the journey. We shall ride to the Grand River, from thence to the La Tranche, where canoes will be built, in which we shall go down to Detroit in a few days, and we shall take Lake Erie on our return. This scheme particularly pleased me, as it will prevent our going to Detroit in July, which I had dreaded on account of the extreme heat of that season.

Sun. Feb. 9th—The weather damp, mild and dirty. When will the end of March arrive? I am quite impatient to set out for Detroit.

Thurs. 13th—We rode to town. I galloped on the sands several times. I saw a Chippawa woman carrying a linen bundle tied up like a doll. I was told it was customary for them to carry about this thing for some months after the death of their husbands. When an Indian intends to express his determination to get thro' any difficulty he says "Garistakaw," and after that always pursues the object.

Fri. 21st—Mr. Bouchette (son of the Commodore) has got the "Onondaga" off the shoal, and she is not injured by the ice. Mr. Littlehales came from Niagara.

Sat. March 1st—The news received of the death of the Queen of France. Orders given out for mourning, in which everybody appeared this evening, and the dance postponed.

NOTE.—Marie Antoinette was married to the Dauphin of France, afterwards Louis XVI. After the fall of the Girondists she was condemned to death by the Jacobins and guillotined October, 1793.

Mon. March 3rd—The weather extremely cold.

Tues. 4th—The weather extremely cold. Tho' I wore three fur tippets I was so cold I could hardly hold my cards this evening. This is the first time we have felt the want of a ceiling, which we have not had made in our drawing-room because the room was rather low.

Wed. 5th—Very cold. I divided the room by hanging across it a large carpet, which made it warmer. There has so little snow fallen this winter that it was scarcely practicable to track the deer, in consequence of which the Indians have been almost starved. A great many of their women and children come to our windows every day for bread, which we cannot refuse them, tho' having but a small quantity of flour until the spring supply arrives, it is inconvenient to give them what they require. There have been apprehensions that the French Republicans at New York would attack Lower Canada from Albany this winter, but a mutiny on board some of their ships carried them to France. If the Americans were to attack this province I should go to Quebec. I have just received your (Mrs. Hunt's) letters, in answer to which I can only say "Que diable avait elle a faire dans cette galere?" What nonsense about the books. Did people but consider their happiness, the first point of their creed would be, not to consider things as serious which are of no consequence.

NOTE.—"Qu'allait-il faire dans cette galère?" from Molière's "Fouberies de Scapin." Scapin pretends that his young master Leandre has been taken prisoner on a Turkish galley, and that the captain claims 500 crowns as ransom; Geronte, a miser, Leandre's father, half distracted at the idea of having to. lose either his son or his

216

money, repeats seven times during the scene, "What did he go into that galley for?" a proverbial French expression.

Fri. 14th—As I was riding across the bay I felt the horse sink under me, and supposing there was a hole in the ice, I threw myself off; the horse lay down to roll in the snow, and as I was falling I struck him with my whip, and I believe that prevented him from rolling over me. I was not hurt, but much afraid he would repeat the trick. I dreamt some time since that the Governor, Mr. Talbot and I were passing a wood, possessed by an enemy, who fired ball at us as fast as possible. I was so frightened that I have never since liked to hear a musquet fired, and I am quite nervous when I hear of the probability of this country being attacked. In a magazine we met with a very pretty hymn sung by Sicilian mariners. It sounds charming played by a band on the water. The master of the

A VIEW ON THE MIAMI RIVER, 1794.
(From a Drawing by Lieutenant Pilkington, copied by Mrs. Simcoe.)

band is a German, who boasts of having performed before the King of Prussia in the great church at Strasburg.

Sat. 15th—An express is arrived from Lord Dorchester, who orders Governor Simcoe, as soon as the navigation of the lakes is open, to go and establish a fort on the River Miami, in a country claimed by the Americans some distance below Detroit.

The Governor thinks the order may be put in execution so much earlier if he goes down the La Tranche to Detroit that he intends setting out to-morrow for the Grand River. This order of Lord Dorchester puts an end to my scheme of going to Detroit, which is an exceeding great disappointment to me.

NOTE.—In September, 1793, Lord Dorchester, the Governor-General, who had been on leave of absence in England, returned to

DIARY OF MRS. SIMCOE

Canada. He sent Governor Simcoe to erect a fort on the Maumee River, in that part of the Indian territory now in the State of Ohio. Simcoe was strongly against the establishment of this fort, but he had to carry out the instructions of Lord Dorchester, who was commander-in-chief. Maumee and Miami are, it is said, the same word differently spelled by English and French phonetic renderings. Its meaning is "Walkers," the term being applied to a tribe of Indians who roamed from Wisconsin to Ohio. They preferred to travel on foot rather than by canoes. Two rivers, at least, also bore the name, but it

SITE OF FORT MIAMI (MAUMEE).
Fortification looking south across the River.
(From a Drawing in the J. Ross Robertson collection.)

is only in recent years that the different spelling has been used with regard to the rivers. "Miami" designates a river which joins the Ohio in the southwestern part of the State of that name, while "Maumee" is a river running into Lake Erie, five miles northeast of Toledo. Many historians have, however, written the name of the latter river as "Miami," as did both Simcoe and Dorchester.

Clearly, the fort built by Simcoe was on the north bank of Maumee River, five miles from its mouth, where the first rapids occur. Mr. Avern Pardoe is of this opinion, and in a paper on "The First Chapter of Upper Canadian History" in the Ontario Historical Society Papers and Records, Vol. VII., points out that "There is a

218

THE SITUATION OF FORT MIAMI

general misapprehension as to the situation of the Fort which Simcoe built in the Indian territory. Because it was called Fort Miami some have supposed it was on that Miami River which is a tributary of the Ohio River. The fort was situated on the Maumee River, not far from Lake Erie, into which the river flows. The Maumee is called the Miami on some maps of a date subsequent to Simcoe's operation." "A History of the Maumee Valley," published in Toledo about sixty years ago, says:—

"The fort was built on the left bank of the Maumee (the Maumee of Lake Erie) near the lower limits of the present village of Maumee, Lucas County, Ohio. Indian Superintendent McKee's agency and supply house was a mile and a half above this fort and near the lowest rapids of the Maumee. The British also built another fort on Turtle Island just outside of Maumee Bay, twenty miles or more northeast from their Fort Miami."

Sun. 16th—I walked half-way to the town with Mr. Talbot. The day very windy; returned before evening prayers. Mr. Pilkington walked from Niagara. I copied some sketches he made going to Lake Huron. He says the thermometer was 5 degrees below zero the 5th of this month at Niagara. Are you not shocked at the siege of Valenciennes (taken by the Allies in 1793) or any real action that has lately occurred, being represented on the stage in London? If English minds become hardened by seeing such sights as amusements, they will in time be as well able to become their friends' executioners as the French have been.

Mon. 17th—A dance to-night.

Tues. 18th—The Governor and Mr. Talbot set out at half-past seven for Detroit.

Wed. 19th—This is the month for making maple sugar; a hot sun and frosty nights cause the sap to flow most. Slits are cut in the bark of the trees, and wooden troughs set under the tree, into which the sap—a clear, sweet water—runs. It is collected from a number of trees, and boiled in large kettles till it becomes of a hard consistence. Moderate boiling will make powder sugar, but when boiled long it forms very hard cakes, which are better. I saw a number of trees slit to-day as I rode with Mr. McGill to his farm.

In a month's time, when the best sap is exhausted, an inferior kind runs, of which vinegar is made. Cutting the trees does not kill them, for the same trees bear it for many years following. Dr. Nooth, at Quebec, showed me some maple sugar which he had refined, and it became as white as West India sugar. The sap of birch trees will make vinegar.

NOTE.—The location of this farm is not known. There is no record of land granted to McGill in or near York until July, 1809, when he was granted Park Lot No. 7, one hundred acres extending from Queen to Bloor Streets and from the west side of Mutual to the east side of Bond Street. Land has increased in value in Toronto since the days of 1809. In that year the hundred acres would probably be worth about a pound an acre. The present assessment of the lot is $2,016,075 for the land and $2,680,412 for the buildings, or a total assessment of $4,696,487. Add thirty per cent. and the real present-day value of this hundred acres is $6,105,433. The McGill Square portion of the lot bounded by Bond, Shuter, Church and Queen Streets was sold about 1871 to the Metropolitan Church for $25,000. The land is now assessed for $308,280 and buildings $138,000, a total assessment of $446,280. These prices show the extraordinary increase in value of lands that were part of the primeval forest a century ago. Mrs. Simcoe, up to the time of her death, was much interested in the progress of York. Some letters in her manuscripts refer to the development of the town that her husband founded.

Fri. 21st—The weather extremely warm. Mrs. Richardson spent the day with me.

Sat. 22nd—Abundance of geese and ducks seen, which denotes the approach of spring.

Sun. 23rd—A very hot day.

Tues. 25th—I had a party at cards this evening. Some white fish were sent me to-day from Niagara and dressed for supper; they were the best I ever tasted.

Thurs. 27th—A strong, easterly wind. All the ice went out of the harbour in two large sheets, each above half a mile long.

Fri. 28th—Mr. Gamble, the surgeon of the Queen's Rangers, returned from the Mohawk village on the Grand River, where he had been to attend Chief Brant. He brought a letter from the Governor, who went from the head of the lake to Niagara, sending Mr. Talbot to the Grand River to order the canoes to be prepared. The Governor expected they would be in readiness for him to leave Brant's on the 26th. The ice would not allow them to move sooner. Mrs. Richardson spent the day with me.

NOTE.—John Gamble, born in 1756, was son of William Gamble, of Duross near Enniskillen, Ireland. He came to America in 1779, serving as regimental surgeon during the Revolutionary War, after which he settled in New Brunswick. He resided there until 1793, when he was appointed surgeon to the Queen's Rangers stationed at Niagara. After the regiment was disbanded at Toronto in 1802 Dr. Gamble moved to Kingston. He died in 1811 and his family returned to York in 1820. He married Isabella Elizabeth, daughter of Dr. Joseph Clarke. One of their sons was the late Joseph Clarke Gamble, barrister-at-law, Toronto, who married, first, Mary Sayre, daughter of D'Arcy Boulton, a daughter being Miss Sarah Gamble of Toronto. He took as his second wife Harriet Eliza, daughter of Honorable John Henry Boulton, and of their issue the following survive:—F. C. Gamble, Deputy Minister of Public Works, Victoria, B.C.; A. W. Gamble, H. Dudley Gamble, K.C., and A. G. Gamble, Manager of the Sterling Bank, Toronto; Mrs. C. E. Bowker (Elizabeth Sophia), of London, England; and Mrs. I. F. Hellmuth (Harriet Emily), of Toronto.

Sat. 29th—Rain and damp weather.

Sun. 30th—I walked on the sands.

Tues. April 1st—I rode to the town; a delightful evening.

Wed. 2nd—I rode.

Mon. 14th—I rode. I saw a fine eagle.

Tues. 15th—A boat came from Niagara, where the river is still full of ice. I received some excellent white fish from thence. A boat arrived from the Bay of Quinte with pork.

MRS SIMCOE AGAIN AT NIAGARA

Wed. 16th—Walked towards the old French Fort.

Fri. 18th—The "Caldwell" arrived from Niagara. She left it the 16th. The harbour was open on the 10th of this month.

NOTE.—There is no entry in the diary from Friday, 18th April, until 2nd May. It was a time of sorrow for the Governor and his wife, for their little daughter Katherine, born in Niagara on 16th January, 1793, was buried on the 17th April, 1794. It is rather peculiar that Mrs. Simcoe makes no reference to the sad event.

Fri. May 2nd—Governor Simcoe arrived at six this evening from Niagara. He rode from the Grand River to the La Tranche, where he embarked the 29th of March in canoes, and that day he reached the site intended for New London. The 30th he slept at the Delaware village; the 31st at the Moravian village; the 1st of April at an Indian trader's; the 2nd arrived at Detroit; two days the snow fell incessantly, so that they were wet thro' in the canoe, which repelled a slight attack of gout the Governor was seized with. He saw wild turkeys and eagles, and shot a deer which the wolves drove down the river. The Governor stayed four days at Detroit, and then went to Captain Elliott's at the River au Raisin; from thence rode 30 miles to the River Miami, in Ohio, and stayed at Coll. McKee's, of Detroit, a little distance from thence.

On the way they passed an Indian fort, and swam the horses over some creeks. At Coll. McKee's there were very good wild turkeys. On his return the Governor saw Turtle Island, at the entrance of Miami Bay, and was detained some days among the Bass Islands, at the west end of Lake Erie, by contrary winds. They went on some of the islands, and it being St. George's Day, gave one of the islands that name. The Governor killed seven rattlesnakes with a small stick on one of the islands, and Mr. Pilkington shot a sturgeon. The Governor arrived at Fort Erie the 25th of April.

NOTE.—Captain Matthew Elliott was Assistant Agent of Indian Affairs in 1790 at Detroit. In 1795 he became Deputy and in July, 1796, Superintendent. In 1812 when the British entered the fort at Detroit, the regiment of Indians was led by Colonel Elliott. He was an intimate friend of Tecumseh and fought at the Battle of the Thames, where the latter fell. At eighty years of age he took the active command of the Indians at the assault on Fort Niagara in 1813. His death took place in 1814. One writer said regarding Elliott that "His Majesty has lost one his most faithful and zealous servants."

Fri. 9th—At seven this morning we set off in a boat for Niagara with the children and Mr. Talbot, intending to reach the head of the lake to-night, but a very stiff breeze rising ahead about four o'clock, we put on shore 12 miles short of it. The tents were pitched and fires made. The Governor and I walked some distance on the beach, and Mr. Talbot amused himself by barking elm trees as the Indians do, and covering his tent with it, for it proved a very wet night. The children and Junk, a nurse, slept on the office boxes in the tent.

Sat. 10th—We rose at daylight, breakfasted and set off, but the weather was so misty that I saw less of the country towards the "Head of the Lake" than I had expected, and was prevented going into Burlington Bay. After some hours of wet weather it blew very fresh and cleared up. A wave washed into the boat, of which no notice was taken, but Collins, a nurse, laid her cloak on the other side. People sometimes cross from the

16-mile creek to the 40-mile creek (Grimsby), but the Governor does not like meeting those breezes which rise suddenly on this lake.

NOTE.—These creeks are designated by their distance from Niagara, if on the south side of Lake Ontario, and from Burlington if on the north side. Oakville on the north shore is situated at the mouth of the Sixteen-Mile Creek.

NIAGARA TO THE "FORTY."
(From a Drawing by Mrs. Simcoe.)

10th—We coasted to the forty-mile creek, forty miles from Niagara, and passed in at three o'clock. The mouth of this creek forms a very fine scene; a very bold spur of the high land appears beautiful in the distance. It is about three miles off. Some cottages are pretty placed on the banks of the river, and a saw mill affords a quantity of boards, which, piled up in a wood, makes a varied foreground. It was about six before we reached the 20-Mile Pond, the mouth of another creek.

NOTE.—Twenty-Mile Creek runs into Twenty-Mile Pond before it reaches the lake. Jordan, Ontario, is situated three miles from the lake shore, on high ground, having on its left a deep valley through which flows the "twenty-mile creek."

10th—A small inlet from the lake carries you into this pond, which is two miles long. The banks are very high, of a fine verdure, and the summit covered with wood, which was now reflected with the deepest shade in the water and had a most beautiful appearance, which was soon heightened by the rising moon, giving more force to the shadow. Two houses of Coll. Butler's, of the Rangers, were distinguished at a distance.

We had not eaten since eight this morning. I was, therefore, desirous to get something for the children, and while some salmon we bought of an Indian as we passed Burlington Bay was preparing for our supper, we walked half a mile with the children to a farmhouse, which we found inhabited by some Pennsylvanians, whom Governor Simcoe had assisted last year at Niagara; we had here excellent bread and milk and butter. We then returned to the tents, and Francis lay down on his greatcoat on the grass and went to sleep till his tent was ready for him. We supped by starlight amid this fine scenery of wood and water; the bright fires of the soldiers below the hill, contrasted with a dark sky, now and then brightened by a gleam of moonlight, had a beautiful effect.

Sun. 11th—We left this beautiful spot about eight o'clock. The entrance to the Seventeen, Sixteen, Fifteen and Twelve Mile Creeks appeared pretty as we passed them. It blew so fresh we were afraid of losing the awning from the boat. It was too showery for me to venture in the canoe. It was a pretty sight to see how swiftly she glided through the water. We arrived at Niagara at twelve, and before two I wished to return to York; the heat here was so great, and looking on the land seemed to me to add to the heat, and was quite disagreeable after having been accustomed to look on the bay at York, and the river here, tho' half a mile wide, appears narrow after leaving that expanse of water.

WATERFALL NEAR BURLINGTON BAY, 1794.

(From a Drawing by Mrs. Simcoe.)

AN EARLY NIAGARA MANSION

NOTE.—There is no Seventeen-Mile Creek. In all probability Mrs. Simcoe referred to the Eighteen. There are no villages at the Fifteen, Sixteen or Eighteen, while what was known as the Twelve-Mile-Creek is now St. Catharines.

Tues. 13th—I went to see Major Smith's house he has built on this side of the river. It is a very good one. The town here is enlarged and called Newark.

NOTE.—The house referred to by Mrs. Simcoe as Major Smith's (afterwards Lieutenant-Colonel Smith), was built about 1793, by his son, D. W. Smith, Surveyor-General of Upper Canada. In his

TWENTY-MILE CREEK (JORDAN, ONT.), 1794.

(From a Drawing by Mrs. Simcoe.)

"Tour Through Upper Canada" in 1795 La Rochefoucauld writes of the house as follows: "In point of size and elegance, the house of Colonel Smith, lieutenant-colonel in the Fifth Regiment, is much distinguished. *It consists of joiners' work, but is constructed, em-*bellished and painted in the best style; the yard, garden and court are surrounded with railings, made and painted as elegantly as they could be in England." D. W. Smith owned what is now called Court House Square or Market Square, Niagara, his house being situated on the west side of King Street between Queen and Johnson. In 1798 the house was offered for sale for a free Grammar School, with four acres as endowment, and again in 1800 at a reduced price. Governor Hunter, however, opposed the purchase on the ground that the house was in too exposed a position, being opposite Fort Niagara. Miss

15

Janet Carnochan says it is not known what became of the house, but its site was occupied in 1812 by the Government House, which was burned in 1813.

Niagara was called "Newark" by Lieutenant-Governor Simcoe in 1792, but both names were used either from habit or fancy. In 1798, however, by Act of the Legislature the name again became "Niagara."

RESIDENCE OF D. W. SMITH, NIAGARA.

(From a Drawing by Mrs. Simcoe.)

Wed. 14th—Mr. Pilkington goes to-morrow to see and to give orders for fortifying the new post at the Miami, the fort Governor Simcoe built by order of Lord Dorchester. He gave me some sketches taken on Lake Erie.

Thurs. 16th—Some ladies dined here from the Garrison. After they went I drove out in the open carriage towards the Landing. The apprehension of the war with the United States engages my attention very disagreeably; at the same time I reflect that I should not have less anxiety in any other part of the world. Had we remained in England probably the Governor would now be going on the European continent, where campaign follows campaign without a prospect of peace, and here, if a war takes place, the result must be speedily decisive.

Fri. 16th—Drove this evening, after dining at Mr. Peter Russell's, the Receiver-General's, towards the two-mile creek; the road horribly bad.

NOTE.—Two-Mile Creek and Pond, where Honorable Peter Russell lived, is two miles from the mouth of the Niagara River, due west, and has been a favorite resort for sportsmen. The new military quarters lately purchased by the Canadian Government are close to it.

Sat. 17th—So cold an east wind that I had a fire; a large party at dinner. The new merchant vessel, called the "Governor Simcoe," arrived. She sails remarkably well.

NOTE.—The schooner at first known as the "Governor Simcoe" and latterly simply as the "Simcoe," was built at Kingston in 1794 and was of only eighty-seven tons burthen. She was at first intended for the North-West Company's lake trade, but in the end her career appears to have been purely local and confined to Lake Ontario, as she is frequently referred to in the Gazettes of 1797 and 1798 as plying between Kingston and Niagara, the latter place being at that time of considerably more business importance than the capital of the province, the town of York. The "Simcoe" was so constructed that in case of necessity she could be armed with eight four-pounder guns and a similar number of swivels. The "Simcoe" was the first vessel built for trade on Lake Ontario. Her first captain was Captain Murney. John Clarke says in his "Memoirs" (Vol. VII., Ontario Historical Society Papers), with regard to Captain Murney:—"I recollect a Captain Murney building a schooner in the County of Prince Edward, of red cedar, in the year 1800 or 1801, which vessel was named the 'Prince Edward.' I was on board the following year, and crossed from Kingston to Niagara. He was a noble captain of a staunch, good ship. I believe Captain Murney married a Miss Smith of Kingston. The captain was father of the late Honorable Mr. Murney, of Belleville. In the year 1812 this schooner was in good condition, and was employed as a Government armed vessel on Lake Ontario."

Sun. 18th—Very cold.

Mon. 19th—The wind changed and the weather warm.

Tues. 20th—I am always glad to have large parties at dinner, for when I sit alone I do nothing but think of the threatened war in this country. After the ladies leave me, Mr. Talbot drives me in the gig towards the Landing, the weather being usually too warm to walk, and the Governor employs two or three hours on writing in an evening. This evening a cow was lying in the road, and Mr. Talbot did not turn out of the way, expecting she would, and, before he was aware of it, one wheel went over her back, but as she lay quite still the carriage did not overset.

Wed. 21st—A large party at dinner.

Thurs. 22nd—The Governor and I dined alone. We fished near the wharf at Niagara.

Sat. 24th—We rode in the morning, and were prevented going to the garrison in the evening by a great fog.

Sun. 25th—I persuaded the Governor to ride this evening. We had not ridden a mile before there came so violent a shower that we were wet through in three minutes, and the claps of thunder were so loud as to make the horses start. After changing our clothes we sat down to tea, and agreed with Mr. Talbot that the rain had been the pleasantest mode of taking a shower bath, and the extreme violence with which it fell rendered us less liable to catch cold than we should have been under a gentle shower.

Wed. 28th—All the ladies from the garrison, the fort on the east side of river, and Newark, drank tea here previous to the ball which is to be given on the 4th of June.

Thurs. 29th—The "Mississaga," the "Caldwell" and the gunboats arrived, bringing some of the members of the House of Assembly from the lower townships. Capt. John McDonell, of Glengarry, the Speaker, etc., etc., dined with us.

Mon. June 2nd—The House of Assembly met to-day. We went to the garrison in the evening and drank tea with Mrs. Smith. The "Mississaga," "Caldwell" and gunboats sailed. Capt. Brooking, of the 17th Regt., went in the "Mississaga."

Tues. 3rd—The Governor goes to the fort on the east side of the river almost every day, to see the works which the Engineers are repairing. I am glad to take the opportunity of crossing the water (and glad he is induced to take this little exercise) and walking on the common behind the fort, as I consider the air so near the lake, and where the ground is high, to be much healthier than our side of the water. The Governor stayed so late with the Engineer this evening that it was dark, and Francis fell asleep on the common before he returned to us.

NOTE.—Fort Niagara on the east side of the Niagara River was not handed over by the British to the Americans until 1796.

Wed. 4th—The ball was held in the Council Chamber. The Governor and I and Mr. Talbot went into the room after all the company were assembled. There were 22 couple. I did not dance. The ladies were all well dressed. We supped at twelve in a room as large as the ballroom, and we came away at two o'clock. The whole was extremely well managed, as Mr. Talbot ordered it himself.

NOTE.—There is no information extant as to the location of the Council Chamber. It is believed, however, that it was in a building which was an addition to Navy Hall.

Thur. 5th—I was tired by sitting up late, and went to take an early dinner at the Fort with Mrs. Smith. The Governor had a large party of gentlemen to dinner. Mr. Talbot came for me in the evening, and it was so cold we were obliged to wrap ourselves up in great coats and tippets.

Fri. 6th—The Governor went to the Fort Chippawa, and returned at night wet through. Mrs. D. W. Smith, wife of the Surveyor-General, has added a boy to her family to-day.

Sat. 7th—Francis' birthday was not kept yesterday, as the Governor was from home. To-day the little cannon Mr. McDonell gave him fired a salute of 21 guns, and tho' they are not two inches long, made a loud report and pleased him much. Being three years old, he was dressed in a rifle shirt and sash, which gave him somewhat the air of an Indian. He found a dead snake, and gave it as a present to one of the gentlemen with us. I went to the Fort this morning, and walked in the evening. Mr. Talbot went towards the Queenstown Landing in his canoe.

Tues. 10th—Some Seneca Indians came here from the northern part of the State of New York. Francis went to see them dance, and afterwards imitated their dancing and singing surprisingly well.

Wed. 11th—I rode in the morning, and went to the Fort in the evening, to walk on the common.

Fri. 13th—Mrs. Smith, Commodore Grant and I went to the Landing in a boat and dined with Mrs. Hamilton; we carried Francis with us. Mr. Talbot came to meet us in his canoe in the evening.

Sat. 14th—The "Mississaga" arrived from Kingston. Mr. Brooking came in her.

Mon. 16th—Company at dinner. The "Onondaga," 12 guns, sailed for Kingston. Capts. Fitzgerald and Cleddowe went in her, by whom I wrote letters.

NOTE.—Captain Augustine Fitzgerald had rank in the regiment, 13th July, 1791, and in the army the previous January.

Tues. 17th—Capt. Charlton, of the 5th Regt., went in the "Mississaga."

DINNER AND BOATING PARTIES

NOTE.—Captain Edward Charlton of the 5th is given in the army list as having rank in the regiment 21st July, 1783. He received rank as major, 1st March, 1794.

Thur. 19th—I went in a boat this evening.

Sun. 22nd—Capt. Talbot sailed in the "Governor Simcoe." I dined at the Fort, and rode on horseback after I came home.

Mon. 23rd—A large party of the members of the House of Assembly dined here.

Tues. 24th—Mrs. Mason, wife of Mr. J. M. Mason, of the 5th, and a party from the Fort, dined here. We went on the water in the evening.

NOTE.—John M. Mason, ensign in the 5th, became lieutenant on 18th October, 1793.

Wed. 25th—A large party to dinner, and on the water in the evening. Mrs. Mason saw a rattlesnake in her garden under some radish leaves.

Fri. 27th—I dined at the garrison.

Sat. 28th—Mrs. D. W. Smith dined with me.

Sun. 29th—A rattlesnake seen under the wharf not 100 yards from our house, and it is supposed that there is a nest of them there.

Thurs. July 3rd—Mr. Tukel arrived from England.

Sat. 5th—We dined at Major Smith's, and his grandchild was christened.

Mon. 7th—The House of Assembly (the third session of the first Legislature) prorogued. General Wayne, of the United States, has insinuated to the Six Nations that the western nations poisoned those of their chiefs who died at the meeting at Sandusky last year.

NOTE.—Mrs. Simcoe must have been in error as to the date of the prorogation of the third session of the first Legislature, for official records show that it took place on the 9th July and not on the 7th.

Wed. 9th—Went this evening to the Fort. Mr. Darling stuffed a bird for me called a Recollect. The appearance of red wax on its brown wings and the tuft of feathers on its head make it very pretty. (Probably a waxwing.) The Indians shoot small birds with such blunt arrows that their plumage is not injured.

Sun. 13th—Mr. C. Justice Osgoode sailed for Quebec. The Governor dined at the mess.

Mon. 14th—A large party at dinner.

Tues. 15th—Rowed in a boat towards the Four-Mile Creek. Mrs. Smith and Mrs. Mason went with me.

Wed. 16th—The weather very hot. We went out in a boat. While we were walking in the garden this evening about 50 Indians, men and women, landed from their canoes and encamped outside the paling, brought on shore their luggage and made fires; they were met by a party of Senecas, who sat round their fire. All this passed with so little noise or bustle that we scarcely heard there were people near us. What a noise would the encampment of 50 Englishmen have made! But "Rien de trop" should be the motto of these people. Those who draw best and make no smoke without producing a marked effect may be compared to Indians who never appear to make one motion that does not effect the purpose they intend. We sent some bread and meat to this party. There is always an appearance of distinctions among these savages; the principal chiefs are usually attended by apparently inferiors, who walk behind them. I call them aide-de-camps. I observe none but the chiefs shake hands with the Governor.

Thur. 17th—We dined in a boat a half-mile from hence, under a steep rock on the shore of the Niagara River, which affords shade, and to which the boat is fastened. Down the side of the rock a fine spring pours rapidly and as clear as crystal.

The Governor was walking on the hill this evening when his shoulder and finger were struck by a shot fired by a soldier belonging to the guard tent, who fired at an Indian dog which had taken away some pork. A shot remained in the Governor's finger, and was very painful. A gentleman walking with him was struck and the dog severely wounded, which caused great concern to the Indian women. An Indian was also struck by the shot. The Governor immediately gave him the soldier's gun to appease him, and reprimanded the soldier.

Fri. 18th—Major and Mrs. Smith dined under the rock with us.

Sat. 19th—The weather still excessively hot, tho' some rain fell.

Sun. 20th—A cold, east wind. I breakfasted at the garrison.

THE SERVOS HOUSE, NIAGARA, 1783-1911.
(From a Drawing by Owen Staples, in the J. Ross Robertson collection.)

Sat. 26th—As I much wished to visit the Forty-Mile Creek, the Governor allotted two or three days for this party of pleasure. Mr. Mayne was chosen to accompany us, and Francis was one of the party. At two o'clock we embarked with a fresh east wind, which fell almost immediately, but has occasioned so much surf that we could not go on shore at the Four-Mile Creek; about two miles further we landed and dined (Mr. Servos has a house at the mouth of the creek). We passed Mr. McNab's house at the Eight-Mile Creek, and beyond the Twelve-Mile Creek we encamped on a point without noticing that the field abounded with a coarse weed, which is such a harbour for mosquitos that the tent was filled with them, and we were glad to rise and breakfast at half after three in the morning.

NOTE.—The oldest house in Niagara Township is that owned by Miss Mary Servos, daughter of the late Colonel Peter Servos. It is built on an eminence commanding a view of the Four-Mile Creek, now known as Virgil. The house has been altered, but the principal room, with its heavy rafters, dates back to 1783. This room was used at one time as a Government store. The Servos family were of Prussian

THE FIFTEEN-MILE CREEK, 1794.
(From a Drawing by Mrs. Simcoe.)

origin. Some of the sons were present at the siege of Niagara (1759) while grandsons served in Butler's Rangers. Four generations of the Servos family have served in capacities as ensign, lieutenant, captain and colonel. In 1779, Governor Haldimand gave Daniel Servos a commission as lieutenant in Colonel Johnson's company of North American Indians, and in 1788 he received a commission from Lord Dorchester, to be captain of the first regiment of militia in the District of Nassau. Mrs. Jarvis, wife of William Jarvis, Provincial Secretary, 1792-1817, writes of the Four-Mile Creek, "There is a great mill upon it, and the family that it belongs to are Dutch."

INTERIOR VIEW OF SERVOS HOUSE.
(From a Drawing by Owen Staples, in the J. Ross Robertson collection.)

Allan Macnab, born 1768, was ensign in the 71st Regiment and afterwards lieutenant in the 19th Hussars. He served with General Simcoe in the Revolutionary War, at the conclusion of which he settled in Canada. He was subsequently Sergeant-at-Arms in the House of Assembly. His wife was Anne, daughter of Peter William Napier. Macnab died in 1830. The late Colonel (the Honorable Sir) Allan Napier Macnab of Hamilton, Ont., who was the first Queen's Counsel appointed in Canada, was a son of Allan Macnab. The name Eight-Mile Creek has been replaced by that of Macnab.

Sun. 27th—The weather misty, damp and disagreeable. Francis caught cold, and was so ill that v.e went on shore at the Eighteen-Mile Creek and stopped at Sail's, the Indian's house, half an hour.

DIARY OF MRS. SIMCOE

We stopped at the Fifteen-Mile Creek, and took a sketch of the mouth of that river. We dined on the beach at the Twenty-Mile Creek, and went across the pond to one of Coll. Butler's houses, where we slept, after taking great pains to smoke the house and fix the mosquito net well, for this place abounds so much with mosquitos that the farmer does not sleep in his house from June till September, but sleeps in his barn to avoid them. The pond is full of wild rice, a marshy weed. The N.E. wind has filled up the inlet so much that the boat was obliged to be drawn over sand.

Mon. 28th—We rose at six, left Francis with a servant, and set off for the Forty-Mile Creek. By the time they had drawn the boat over the sand into the lake, a strong N.W. wind sprung up, which was exactly ahead of us and prevented our getting to the Forty till two o'clock, tho' with a fair wind we should not have been two hours; the fog excessively thick, and perfectly counteracted our schemes of seeing the country. However, we walked thro' the village and beyond Green's Mills a little way up the mountain, far enough to see where the stream dashes over very dark rocks, surrounded by hemlock, spruce and other picturesque trees. Green ground the corn for all the military posts in Upper Canada. His mill stood five miles east of Hamilton, on the Stoney Creek road.

A mile further is a mill and small waterfall, and at a season when the water is higher the scenery must be wonderfully fine; at present it is well worth seeing. I drank tea at Green's, and unwillingly left this fine scenery, of which I had so slight a view. We were no sooner in the boat, expecting a rapid passage up the Twenty-Mile Creek, when the wind veered and came right ahead, so that it was ten o'clock before we arrived at the inlet. It was quite dark, and we were another hour getting the boat over the sand and rowing to the house. Mrs. Green advised me to give Francis crow's foot boiled with milk till it becomes red and thick, which she said would cure the present complaint in his stomach.

There are 100 people settled at the Forty, and there have been but seven graves in five years. The Governor promises that I shall ride on the mountain above the Forty this season.

NOTE.—In writing of the Forty-Mile Creek, where Green's Mills were situated, Rochefoucauld, who visited the place in travelling through Canada in 1795, says:—"Forty-Mile Creek was one of the chief objects of our tour. This stream, which intersects in a straight line the range of mountains extending from Queens' Town, flows, with a gentle fall, into the plain, and affords some wild, awful, yet very pleasing prospects among the mountains. Before it empties itself into the lake, it turns a grist mill and two saw-mills, which belong to a Mr. Green, a Loyalist of Jersey, who six or seven years ago (1788-9) settled in this part of Upper Canada. This Mr. Green was the constant companion of the Governor on this journey (along the shore of Lake Ontario). He is apparently a worthy man, and in point of knowledge far superior to the common caste of settlers in this neighborhood. His estate consists of three hundred acres, about forty of which are cleared of wood. He paid one hundred and twenty-five dollars for forty acres, through which the creek flows that turns his mill, on account of the greater value they bear for this reason, the common price being only five shillings ($1) per acre. Land newly cleared yields here, the first year, twenty bushels of corn. The soil is good, though not of the most excellent quality. They plough the land, after it has produced three or four crops, but

THE GORGE NEAR FORTY-MILE CREEK (GRIMSBY), 1794.
(From a Drawing by Mrs. Simcoe.)

AN EXCURSION FROM NIAGARA

not very deep, and never use manure. The price of flour is twenty-two shillings (4.40) per hundredweight; that of wheat from seven to eight shillings ($1.60) per bushel. The bushel weighs fifty-two pounds upon an average. Labourers are scarce and are paid at the rate of six shillings ($1.20) a day."

Tues. 29th—Embarked at nine, rowed a little up the creek among the wild rice, and then turned to the lake, the wind exactly contrary and so very fresh that we were obliged to go on shore at the Seventeen-Mile Creek, where we dined and walked to Schram's farm, where the women were making straw hats. I gathered crow's foot. Mr. Mayne had a fit of the ague—in short, everything went *au contraire* during the expedition. We arrived at Niagara before eleven. A fine, clear evening now we are returned from our tour.

Fri. Aug. 1st—The weather insufferably hot at Niagara. We walked to Mr. Smith's and supped there, which was very pleasant, as the rooms are so much larger than ours at Navy Hall. Mrs. Smith now resides on this side of the water, for the change of air for a sick child.

Sat. 2nd—The heat extreme. We dined in the boat under the rock. A thunderstorm drove us into Mrs. Smith's house.

Sun. 3rd—The Governor went early this morning to the Tuscarora village, which is about two miles above Lewiston, N.Y.; dined on the water and returned early. The thermometer 96.

Mon. 4th—The thermometer 96, but Mr. Vandeleur, who is just arrived from Detroit, calls it cool weather. The thermometer was 101 in Fort Lernoult (Detroit). The heat and mosquitos do not affect me in the violent manner they used to do.

Tues. 5th—A storm and cold wind.

Thurs. 7th—Rode in the evening. The whortle berries of this country are larger than in England, quite black, and if dried in the sun make as good puddings as Levant currants, quite as sharp. The Indians live in the woods where they grow at this season of the year, and boil quantities of them into cakes.

General Washington was seen last year at the theatre at Philadelphia; lights were carried before him to the stage box, where he sat in a front row, Mrs. Washington and the aide-de-camps on the seats behind him, the music playing "God Save George Washington," to the tune of "God Save the King." The gentlemen who gave this account went to the theatre this year and discovered General Washington in a back row of the front boxes, without attendants, the Vice-President and Mrs. Washington in the same bench, and no notice taken when he came into the theatre. The next day a paragraph in the papers asserted that if Washington did not take the fort at Presqu'ile he ought to be guillotined.

NOTE.—The projected expedition of the Six Nations to clear out the settlers at Presqu' Isle was abandoned as the President of the United States interposed to prevent further encroachments by the Pennsylvanians in that quarter.

Fri. 8th—The "Onondaga" called, with Mr. Vandeleur on board. The "Mississaga" arrived, with the Bishop of Quebec, his brother, Mr. Mountain, and his son, who is the bishop's chaplain. Mr. Lemoine arrived in his decked boat from Kingston across the lake. She left Kingston on Wednesday.

NOTE.—The Bishop of Quebec to whom Mrs. Simcoe referred was the Right Rev. Jacob Mountain, D.D. (the name was originally Montaigne), first Protestant Bishop of Quebec. He belonged to a

237

DIARY OF MRS. SIMCOE

French Protestant family who settled in England, in Norfolk County, upon the revocation of the Edict of Nantes. He was educated at Wyndham and Norwich, and afterwards went to Cambridge. At

the time of his selection for the see of Quebec he was examining chaplain to the Bishop of Lincoln. In 1793, George III. erected the Canadas into a diocese of the Church of England, and Dr. Mountain was appointed to take charge. He arrived in Quebec 1st November, 1793. The outlook was anything but encouraging, for there were but six clergymen in Lower Canada and three in Upper Canada. However, by indefatigable diligence and energy, obstacles were overcome, and Bishop Mountain may well be called the father and founder of the Anglican Church in Canada. He labored here for thirty-two years,

BISHOP MOUNTAIN. his death taking place on 16th June, 1825, at Marchmont, near Quebec, the seat of the late General Sir John Harvey, Bart. Three of Bishop Mountain's sons followed the profession of their father.

In the register of St. Mark's Church, Niagara, an entry on 5th June, 1793, records the marriage of Ensign Lemoine to Susan Johnson, who was Susannah, the seventh daughter of Molly Brant and Sir William Johnson.

Sun. 10th—I went to church. The Bishop preached an excellent discourse, Romans 1, 16 v., "I am not ashamed of the Gospel of Christ, for it is the power of God unto salvation to everyone that believeth, to the Jew first, and also to the Greek."

Tues. 12th—An express from Detroit. It is now decided that I am to go to Quebec next month. The hostile appearance Gen. Anthony Wayne's conduct bears makes the continuance of peace with the United States very doubtful.

Thurs. 14th—The Governor went with the Bishop to see the Falls of Niagara.

Fri. 15th—The Bishop sailed for Kingston. I wrote to Mrs. Caldwell to take a house at Quebec for me. Should the French and Americans assault Quebec this winter I shall find more comfort in Mrs. Caldwell's society than in that of most others, as such a scene would not be new to her. She was in the town when besieged by Montgomery, 1775. Coll. Caldwell was one of the most active of the defenders of it.

Sat. 16th—I went to the garrison this evening.

Sun. 17th—An express from Detroit.

NOTE.—This means that the Government messengers had arrived with letters and official documents.

Mon. 18th—The Governor and myself have colds, which is very unusual. Notwithstanding, we crossed the water and rode to the Landing at Lewiston. I had not ridden on that side of the river before. We dined in the boat opposite Mr. Hamilton's, at whose house we drank tea, and returned to Navy Hall in the boat.

Tues. 19th—The Governor had the shot extracted from his finger. It was so near the joint that it is feared the finger will always be stiff; it was a large shot.

238

SPRAY OF THE FALLS OF NIAGARA, AS SEEN FROM THE CHIPPAWA RIVER.

(From a Drawing by Mrs. Simcoe.)

ARRIVAL OF GEN. SHANK

Wed. 20th—A wet day. Mr. Hamilton dined with us; the cannon sent to Fort Erie.

Thurs. 21st—Mrs. Hamilton and Mrs. Richardson here.

Sun. 24th—Mr. Crooks' new vessel, named "The York," sailed for Kingston, and Mr. LeMoine's decked boat accompanied her.

NOTE.—Mr. Crooks was the brother of the Honorable James Crooks of the Legislative Council, and a member of the firm of W. and J. Crooks, West Niagara. His vessel "The York" was afterwards wrecked at the Genesee River.

Mon. 25th—Capt. David Shank arrived with the detachment from York, to go to the Miamis.

NOTE.—David Shank was gazetted lieutenant in the Queen's Rangers, March, 1777, obtaining his captaincy October, 1778. He served throughout the Revolutionary War, and when his corps was disbanded in 1783, he was placed on half pay. In 1791, he was recalled to full pay, when he joined the Light Infantry battalion, which was also given the name of Queen's Rangers, raised in that year in England for services in Canada under Colonel Simcoe. Shank became brevet-major, 1st March, 1794, and on Simcoe's

GEN. SHANK.

returning to Europe assumed command of the troops in Upper Canada in the summer of 1796. He became lieutenant-colonel in January, 1798, and took command of his regiment in the following April. He remained in the corps until it was disbanded at the Peace of Amiens. On September 3rd, 1803, he was appointed to the command of the Canadian Fencibles. He became major-general, 1811, lieutenant-general, 1821, and died in Glasgow, 16th October, 1831. He acquired in York a large tract of land in what is now

the north side of Queen Street, Toronto, near Trinity College. The portrait is from the original oil painting at Wolford.

Tues. 26th—I received the finest red water melons from York I ever saw.

Wed. 27th—More detachments from York for the Miamis.

Thurs. 28th—Mr. Sheaffe returned from Oswego with news that Lord Howe has taken seven sail of French ships.

NOTE.—Mr. Sheaffe was Lieutenant Roger Hale Sheaffe of the 5th Regiment. He was born in 1763 in Boston, and was a son of Mr. William Sheaffe, Deputy Collector of Customs at that port. He entered the army as an ensign in 1778 and rose to the rank of lieutenant in 1780. He served

GEN. SHEAFFE.

in Canada from 1787-97, and did important work. Under instructions from Dorchester and Governor Simcoe, Sheaffe was entrusted with a mission in connection with settlements by Americans on the

DIARY OF MRS. SIMCOE

south shore of Lake Ontario. Both the Governor-General and Governor Simcoe protested against these settlements. Sheaffe was made a captain in 1795. In 1811 he became major-general. In recognition of his services at Queenston Heights he was made a baronet in 1813. He was in command at York in April, 1813, and was severely and, in the opinion of many, justly criticized for his conduct in not remaining in York and assisting the local militia, just before the attack of the Americans. He was made a general in 1828. In 1810 he married Margaret, third daughter of Mr. John Coffin of Quebec, cousin of Admiral Coffin. Sheaffe died in Edinburgh in 1851, and his wife a few years later.

Fri. 29th—An express from Detroit announces that General Anthony Wayne has retired from the Miami Fort after having summoned it to surrender. He came within shot of it, and found it stronger than he expected and that there was cannon. The match was lighted to have fired if he had not retired. Major Campbell, who commanded, showed great discretion and propriety of conduct. If the Governor had waited until the opening of the navigation of the lakes to have gone to the Miamis, as Lord Dorchester proposed, the fort would not have been rendered defensible enough by this time to have intimidated General Wayne, and war would not have commenced with the United States.

NOTE.—After the battle of Fort Recovery, General Wayne, "Mad Anthony," marched to within thirty miles of Fort Miami, recently built by Governor Simcoe, and on August 20th drove away the Indians who, to the number of two thousand, had gathered nearby under the command of Little Turtle. After this engagement, Major Campbell, who commanded the fort, wrote to Wayne expressing surprise at the appearance of an American force at a point almost within sight of the British guns. General Wayne in reply denounced the erection of the fortress on American territory as the highest act of aggression. Then he set fire to and destroyed everything within sight of Fort Miami.

Governor Simcoe proceeded with Captain Brant and 150 warriors to encourage the Indians, but they had no relish for another brush with General Wayne's forces. Finally in October, 1794, the United States Secretary Randolph communicated with the legation in the United States and matters were arranged satisfactorily by a withdrawal

GEN. WAYNE.

of the troops and the abandonment of the fort. Major William Campbell, who commanded at Miami, was of the 24th Regiment. He had rank in the army 1st December, 1778, and in the regiment, 31st May, 1781. He became lieutenant-colonel in 1795.

General Wayne was brevetted major-general in 1783 and in 1792 was appointed major-general and commander-in-chief of the army in the United States.

MACKENZIE THE N. W. EXPLORER ARRIVES

Mon. Sept. 1st—The merchants gave a dinner to commemorate Lord Howe's victory of the 1st of June. The Governor and the officers of the garrison dined with them. Mrs. Smith and some ladies dined with me.

NOTE.—Lord Richard Howe obtained a decisive victory off Ushant, 1st June, 1794, for which he received the thanks of Parliament, and two years after he was made admiral of the fleet.

Thurs. 4th—The militia officers dined with the Governor. I dined with Mrs. Smith.

Mon. 8th—Mr. Mackenzie, who has made his way from the Grand Portage to the Pacific ocean, is just returned from thence, and brought the Governor a sea otter skin as a proof of his having reached that coast. He says the savages spear them from the rocks, as the Indians here do sturgeon. These animals are amphibious, but generally in the sea. Mr. McKenzie went down the River of Peace near two degrees north of Lake Superior, and came to the Rocky Mountains, on which rise some rivers that fall into the Atlantic, and others which empty themselves into the Pacific ocean. He went down a river which falls into the latter and rises not 700 yards from the River of Peace. He afterwards travelled 17 days by land. There are a kind of large sheep on the Rocky Mountains, their horns the size of a cow's. The Indians near the coast live on fish, which they are very dexterous in catching; they dry salmon in boxes in a kind of upper story in their huts. They prepare the roes, beating them up with sorrel, a plant with acid taste, till it becomes a kind of caviare, and, when the salmon are dried, boil and mix them with oil. These savages never taste meat, and think if any was thrown into the river the fish would go away. One of Mr. McKenzie's men having thrown the bone of a deer in the water, an Indian dived and fetched it out, nor would they suffer water to be ladled out in a kettle in which meat had been boiled. Are these not veritable fish eaters? Mr. McKenzie observed those Indians who inhabited the islands on the coast to be more savage than the others. The otter skins are sold at a great price, by those who trade on the coast, to the Chinese.

SIR ALEXANDER MACKENZIE.

NOTE.—Sir Alexander Mackenzie was born in Inverness, Scotland, about 1755. He emigrated to Canada in his youth and became a clerk in the North-West Fur Company. From 1781 to 1789, he traded with the Indians at Lake Athabasca, and in the latter year discovered the river which bears his name, and traced it from its source to its entrance into the Arctic Ocean, where he arrived in July, 1789. In 1792, he led another exploring party westward to the Pacific. On his return to England in 1801, he published his "Voyages from Montreal to the Frozen and Pacific Oceans." He died in 1820.

CHAPTER XV.

MRS. SIMCOE VISITS QUEBEC.

There was always war or rumor of war in these pioneer days in Canada. Peace between the United States and Canada had been declared years before, when the War of the Revolution gave independence to the American people. But disquieting rumors were always floating in the air, and Niagara was a centre where the pros and cons were always a ready subject of conversation. Mrs. Simcoe had her fears. She had resolved upon a visit to her friends in Quebec, and while she felt that she might return to Upper Canada, she was not too certain, for if the question of peace or war was not speedily settled it would be too late for her to return without considerable discomfort and possibly danger.

However, she said good-bye to her friends, the ladies of the garrison at Niagara, whom she had invited to tea a day or two before she determined to sail, but owing probably to adverse winds it was not till the morning of the 13th September, 1794, that the anchor of the Government schooner "Mississaga" was weighed and Mrs. Simcoe and her family left Niagara wharf.

Tues. Sept. 9th—Mrs. Smith and the ladies of the garrison drank tea with me. The Governor sets off for Detroit to-morrow, and I shall sail for Quebec the next day. If I hear, with official certainty, at Quebec that peace with the United States is agreed on in England, I may return here this autumn, but if that news does not arrive very speedily it will be too late for me to return.

KEY TO ILLUSTRATION ON OPPOSITE PAGE.

No. 1.—The building on the right represents a building on Ontario Street, near the piano factory, foot of Princess Street (Store Street).

No. 2.—A building on the site of the late ex-Mayor Gaskin's residence, south-east corner Ontario and Princess Streets.

No. 3.—The old Macaulay House, now a butcher shop, standing on southwest corner of Princess and Ontario Streets, west side of Ontario Street, and south side of Princess Street.

No. 4.—The Protestant Church, back of Masonic Hall of 1792, opposite the present Market-place.

No. 5.—In front is a building now in Market-square, and on the site of General Bradstreet's batteries.

No. 6.—Indian storehouse, near the water's edge, now the site of Folger and Richardson's wharves.

No. 7.—Beyond is vacant space, at present occupied by the Kingston and Pembroke R.R., and in front of the City Hall. West of vacant space are buildings on Ontario Street.

No. 8.—Site of Swift's wharf at the foot of Johnson Street, near the Grand Trunk Railway depot.

KINGSTON, U.C., IN 1794. (See p. 244.)

(From a Drawing by Mrs. Simcoe.)

THE SISTER OF THAYENDANEGEA

Fri. 12th—The Governor set off this morning for Detroit. Mrs. Smith came to take leave of me. The " Mississaga " is to sail as soon as the wind is fair; that not being the case this afternoon, I was dissuaded from going on board, but having so often seen a wind lost by not embarking before it had risen, I determined to go on board and wait for it, which I did at six o'clock. Capt. McGill accompanies me, in order to see that the batteau are properly prepared and attended.

Sat. 13th—On board the "Mississaga." At six this morning we weighed anchor. The Fort and Newark looked very pretty under a rising sun as we left Niagara River. The wind is fair, and we keep the south shore, so I hope to discern the entrance to the Genesee River. At twelve the wind changed, and we kept the north shore. Orders were given for my accommodation that no person should have a passage to Kingston in the "Mississaga," but I relented in favour of Brant's sister, who was ill and very desirous to go. She speaks English well, and is a civil and very sensible old woman.

NOTE.—About 1748, Colonel Johnson (Sir William) contracted an Indian marriage with Miss Mary Brant, " Miss Molly," sister of Thayendanegea (Joseph Brant), and by her had eight children, Peter, Elizabeth, Magdalene, Margaret, George, Mary, Susannah and Anne. Elizabeth married Dr. Robert Kerr, an eminent surgeon, who settled at Niagara. Susannah, as already stated, became the wife of Lieutenant Lemoine of the 24th Regiment, while three other daughters married Captain Farley of the 16th Regiment, John Ferguson of the Indian Department and Captain Earle of the Provincial Navy. The records of the first Protestant Church (afterwards St. George's), Kingston, show that on 16th April, 1796, Mary Brant was buried by Rev. John Stuart, but no mention is made of the place of burial.

Mrs. Grant in her entertaining book speaks of Molly, and says that Sir William "connected himself with the daughter of an Indian sachem, who possessed an uncommonly agreeable person and good understanding and whether ever formally married to him according to our usage or not, continued to live with him in great union and affection all his life." Colonel Johnson, in his private diary, always mentioned Molly kindly. By thus forming an alliance with the family of an influential and powerful chief, Colonel Johnson evidently aimed at a more extended influence over the Indians. Nor did the result disappoint him.

In his will, Sir William ordered the remains of his " beloved wife Catherine " to be deposited in his burial-place, and provided most liberally for his "prudent and faithful house-keeper, Mary Brant" and for all her children, whom he calls his "natural children." He divided the remaining part of his money and lands between Colonel Claus and Colonel Johnson and their wives, his estate at Fort Johnson going to his son, Sir John Johnson.

Sun. 14th—We have had a very rough night and a head wind, and nothing but being on deck the whole day prevented my being very sick. In the afternoon, being in the centre of the lake, I discerned both the N. and S. shores. I also discerned a high point on the south shore, called the Thirty-Mile Creek from Niagara, in sight of the Duck Islands, a few miles off Point Traverse (in Prince Edward County) and N.E. of it.

DIARY OF MRS. SIMCOE

NOTE.—These are two islands, known collectively as The Ducks. The larger island is the further to the east in the lake and is called the Main Duck, while the smaller island, close to the south-eastern extremity of Prince Edward County, is called the False Duck. Sailors frequently speak of the islands as the "Main Ducks" and "False Ducks," but the name should not be pluralized. The two are properly spoken of as The Ducks. They are so named either from their shape—at a distance they roughly resemble ducks in the water--or from the fact that wild ducks formerly abounded in the vicinity. The trip was slow and must have been rough, for the vessel did not reach Kingston until 8 a.m. on the 15th, or fifty hours from Niagara to Kingston, a distance of nearly 200 miles.

Mon. 15th—A very rough night. At eight this morning we anchored in Kingston harbour. Capt. McGill went on shore and engaged the only King's batteau which was there, and hired one of the merchant's for my baggage. Capt. Porter came on board to know my commands, and some ladies called upon me. At twelve we got off in the batteau, which had a comfortable, low awning of twisted osiers or willow whose twigs are used for making baskets, which was more convenient at this season, when the weather becomes cold, than the high wooden awnings. In less than half an hour it began to rain, and continued the whole day. We went only 18 miles to Gananowui. Carey's house being shut up, we went to Fairfield's, close by the mill. Mr. (Colonel) Joel Stone, a Loyalist, who settled in Gananowui about 1790, is building at the mouth of the Gananowui River. Capt. McGill slept in the boat. Fairfield accommodated me with a room.

NOTE.—Captain Richard Porter of the 60th was captain from 26th November, 1784, and major from 1st September, 1795.

A coincidence in the history of the 60th Regiment in North America is that the 2nd and 3rd battalions, as part of the *first* English garrison at Quebec, were present in September, 1759, when the British ensign was hoisted over the captured city by an officer of the Royal Artillery; and in November, 1871, one hundred and twelve years later, a detachment of the 1st battalion of the 60th, the remnant of the *last* English garrison of Quebec, consigned the Imperial flag to the keeping of another artillery officer, whilst the flag of the Dominion of Canada was hoisted in its stead.

William Fairfield, a U. E. Loyalist, was one of the pioneers of Ernestown, in all probability settling there about 1788. In 1794 he appears to have been in the vicinity of Gananoque, where he had a grist mill. He was not the original holder of the land at Gananoque, but must have rented it from Sir John Johnson, whose grant of land was on the east side of Gananoque River. The first document registered in the Registry Office at Brockville was on the 13th December, 1797, at eight o'clock in the evening, S. Sherwood, Deputy Registrar. There could be no deed of land until 1796 or 1797 because the first patents were issued then. William Fairfield was for many years on the Commission of the Peace and was a member of the Provincial Parliament. He died in Ernestown in 1816.

COL. JOEL STONE OF GANANOQUE

Joel Stone, a U. E. Loyalist, afterwards known as Colonel Stone, was born in Guilford, Conn., 7th August, 1749. He was a descendant of William Stone, one of the emgirants who sailed from London, Eng., in May,1639, landing at New Haven, Conn., in July. He served under  Sir William Howe in the Revolutionary War and remained in New York until the evacuation of the British in 1783. In July of that year he sailed for England to recover a legacy to which his wife was entitled. His stay there was prolonged, for he did not return until 1786, arriving in Quebec on 6th October. In 1792, he settled at the junction of the Gananoque and St. Lawrence Rivers, the Crown having given him a grant of land on the west side of the Gananoque River. He founded the town of Gananoque.

COL. JOEL STONE.

In 1793, his wife died, and in 1799, he married a second time. Stone was the first Collector of the Port, and on 2nd January, 1809, he was appointed colonel of the 2nd Regiment of Militia, County of Leeds. He did not remain long in command, feeling obliged on account of declining years to resign. This he did in 1812. His death took place in Gananoque on 20th November, 1833.

By his first wife, Leah Moore, Colonel Stone had a son and a daughter; the former died unmarried, but his daughter, Mary, married Charles McDonald, of Gananoque (an elder brother of the Hon. John McDonald), and of this marriage one of the descendants, a grandson, is Mr. Charles McDonald of Gananoque, Civil Engineer.

Stone's second wife was Abigail Coggswell, widow of Abraham Dayton. There were no children by this marriage, but Henrietta Maria Mallory, a grand-daughter of the Colonel's second wife, became a member of the family, and in due course married John McDonald (afterwards Hon. John McDonald). He was a member of the Legislative Assembly of Upper Canada, and, at the Union in 1841, was called to the Legislative Council of the new Province of Canada. Of this marriage the sole male representative of the name of McDonald is Judge Herbert S. McDonald of Brockville, Ont. Herbert M. Mowat, K.C., of Toronto, and John McDonald Mowat of Kingston are grandsons on their mother's side.

Mon. 15th—The baggage boat was not arrived at Gananowui, and my boudet or canvas stretcher being in it, I was at a loss what to sleep on, till I recollected some planks I had in the boat. I laid one of these, supported by a small box at each end, and put a carpet over it, on which I slept admirably. Collins had a small room within mine for herself and the children. Fairfield built the little vessel I saw lying in Kingston Harbour. She contains 120 barrels, and is gone for flour to the Bay of Quinte. Fairfield told me he had been 36 miles back in the country towards the Ottawa River; the Gananowui runs within half a mile of a river that falls into the Ottawa. The Indians carry over that portage. He saw many lakes eight

or ten miles long. He went to catch whitefish, but having no means of
taking them but spearing he only killed 23. They are very difficult fish
to spear, and he had not nets. The land above this house is considerably
higher than any in this part of the country, and falls every way from this
height. Here are abundance of ground squirrels, but the men do not take
the trouble of skinning them when killed, tho' the fur is beautiful. Mr.
Stone is building a saw mill here, opposite Sir. J. Johnstone's. It will
work 15 saws at once. Stone's grant of land is on the west side of the
river and Johnstone's is on the east side.

HOUSE AND MILL, NEAR GANANOQUE, 1794.
(From a Drawing by Mrs. Simcoe.)

NOTE.—Judge McDonald, of Brockville, is under the impression
that this view is on the St. Lawrence and not on the Gananoque
River, 1794, as it would appear that the latter is shown at the right,
where it enters the St. Lawrence, and yet there could not have been
a mill on the bank of the St. Lawrence, there being no water from
that source. It is just possible that the buildings shown were erected
by Colonel Stone along the bank of the St. Lawrence at this spot,
and that there is an error in calling one of them a mill.

Tues. 16th—This morning Mr. Stone sent me excellent cream and
butter. We did not embark till ten. This morning was so wet that the
Canadians were unwilling to move. The sun shone a little while, but the
afternoon proved wet, and it was dark before I came to Capt. Cowan's,
opposite Oswegatchie. Here I had a large room with six windows in it.

Wed. 17th—We embarked at six. The tea kettle was boiled, and I
breakfasted in the boat; showery weather. Passed the rapid called Les
Gallettes (Gallops rapids off Pointe Galloppe in Edwardsburgh). The
waves, dashing against the bottom of the boat, sounded as if she struck
on rocks, and their appearance more agitated than those we see in a ship-
wreck on the stage. A mile before we came to the Long Sault there was a
violent storm of thunder, lightning and rain, and as we were about to
descend the rapid another violent storm arose, which was a good accompaniment to a terrific scene. This rapid is very long, but it did not appear
to me so frightful as Les Gallettes, tho' the current is so strong for the
space of some miles that we went nine miles in the hour without sailing.
One man steers; the rest row occasionally, but the Canadians are so
accustomed to the navigation that with empty boats the man who steers
is often the only one awake.

I dined in the boat; at three stopped to deliver a letter at Glengarry
House, where Major McDonell lives. At four a thunderstorm occasioned
us to stop at the boat-house on Lac St. Francis, in that part of the St.
Lawrence which widens above Coteau du Lac, where Mr. McGill was for
staying the night; but I thought it too early, and sailing across the lake
a good way from shore a violent gale of wind arose when we were in a
line with Pointe Mouille. It thundered, rained, and became perfectly
dark; the boat tossed violently, the children crying and Collins sighing.
The wind blew so strong off shore that I feared being driven out into the
lake and lost, or driven to the United States shore. Capt. McGill thought
there was some difficulty, as he promised the men rum if they exerted

themselves to get to the shore, which they at last did, and I waited half an hour, intending to sleep in the boat rather than proceed in such weather five miles to the Pointe au Bodet. There was no house nearer. The weather then clearing up and growing calm, I consented to proceed, provided they kept close to the shore, which they did, and about ten we arrived at Pointe au Bodet. Mr. John McDonell, the Adjutant-General of Militia of Upper Canada, had arrived there, and he gave me up his rooms, in which were large fires, very comfortable after the cold, rough evening I had been out in.

NOTE.—Mr. J. A. Macdonell of Glengarry states that John Macdonell "was appointed by Lieutenant-Governor Simcoe to be first adjutant-general of militia in Upper Canada, and was the founder of our militia system."

I find among my Simcoe manuscript an account of part of the journey, in the handwriting of Mrs. Simcoe, though the heading is not written by her. It reads:—

A SIMCOE RELIC.

"A Short Journal, with Rough Sketches contained in a letter addressed by Mrs. Simcoe to her husband, the Lieutenant-Governor, in 1794, when on her way in a covered boat from Kingston to Montreal and Quebec."

It is in the form of a letter to Governor Simcoe written on the 17th September, 1794, and really a more extended account than what appears in the diary proper for the 15th-17th September. The first paragraph is undated. It refers to Mrs. Simcoe's friends who were evidently visiting Kingston and who desired to go east to Montreal, and states that:

"Miss M'Donell, Miss Bouchette, Capt. Porter and Mr. Salmon came on board the 'Mississaga.' Capt. Bouchette wanted to refuse the ten guineas. He say'd it was too much. I believe he was very well satisfied."

Mon. Septr. 15th—Left Kingston at half-past twelve in a boat with a comfortable awning of hoops and oil cloth, accompanied by another batteau with the baggage; a fine and strong wind, delightful sailing. At four the wind came ahead, and we were obliged to row. In half an hour after we left Kingston it began to rain hard, and continued to rain the whole night.

Cary's house shut up, as he was gone to Kingston. Rained too hard for me to pitch the tent or sleep in the batteau. Slept at Fairfield's house, close by the mill at Gananoqui. He is the farmer's son who built a small vessel at Gananoqui. She is now gone for a load of flour to the Bay of Quinte. I think I saw her in the harbour at Kingston. She has carried 120 barrels; looks not much larger than the "Onondaga." Mr. M'Gill stayed in the batteau.

NOTE.—The vessel which Mrs. Simcoe mentions as having been built by Fairfield was no doubt built by him for Colonel Joel Stone. This contention is borne out by the fact that a letter dated 2nd February, 1793, at Gananoque, written by Stone to Governor Simcoe, says:—"Permit me to inform your Excellency that I have recovered my health some time in November last from a fever I took at the head of Lake Ontario last July, since which I am commissioned to build

a schooner of 40 tons burthen, on my premises here. She is to sail out of this river and is to be called the 'Leeds Trader,' and I expect will sail by the first of July next." As all the land on the west side of the Gananoque River, near Gananoque, was granted by the Crown to Colonel Joel Stone and that on the east side to Sir John Johnson or his heirs, it would appear that Fairfield must have been a "squatter" or an employee, and therefore may have been captain of Colonel Stone's vessel.

FAIRFIELD'S HOUSE AND MILL.

(From a Drawing by Mrs. Simcoe.)

Fairfield say'd he had been 35 miles back from his present house to catch whitefish, but having no means but spearing, and they are remarkably swift and difficult to spear, he took but 23. Was out two nights. There are many lakes eight or ten miles long. The land at Gananoque is very bad between, fit for nothing, but twelve miles back becomes very good.

NOTE.—Mr. Charles Britton, a resident of Gananoque for many years, fixes the site of Fairfield's mill on the east side of the river on lot 1027 in the village of Gananoque back of Skinner and Company's factory. The Gananoque River runs northwest from the St. Lawrence and a mile north of the town it inclines east and continues northeast from Kingston.

VIEW FROM FAIRFIELD'S HOUSE.

(From a Drawing by Mrs. Simcoe.)

Tues. 16th—A very wet morning after a night of incessant rain; the Canadians would not stir, so I waited to breakfast. Mr. Stone, who is building a mill opposite Fairfield's, came, and was extremely civil; brought butter and milk. About nine the rain ceased. I walked to look at the mill, and embarked. Gave a dollar to the people. Mr. M'Gill said Stone was too much of a gentleman to offer anything to. The mill he is building is to have 15 saws. He says there is a portage of only half a mile from the Gananoqui to the Rideau. The Indians carry over it, that is, 50 or 60 miles to the Grand River. He say'd the hill behind Fairfield's house is the highest ground anywhere about the country, the land descending

POLITENESS IN THE OLDEN TIME

from it every way. Fairfield say'd there is a fall 30 miles up the Gananoqui 50 feet high, and many slight rapids. About twelve the day grew fine and pleasant. Our Canadians are old and do not sing; however, I made them sing "Trois Filles d'un Prince," tho' indifferently.
Capt. Porter say'd to Mr. M'Gill the "Sophia" might be two weeks in one trip to Oswegatchie. Rain in the afternoon. Got on to Capt. Cowan's, just opposite Fort Oswegatchie, an admirable large room, six large windows in it, 12 feet high. Capt. Cowan spoke much of the weakness and unprovided state of the inhabitants in case of war with the States; he particularly mentioned as dangerous the circumstances of settlers who call themselves residents under the King's Government (but some whose loyalty is very doubtful), building saw mills on the opposite shore. One, Honeywell, in particular, who had been a notorious rebel, and since his residence under the King's Government was once confined at Kingston for improper behaviour. This man has a saw mill directly opposite this house, with many thousand boards cut. Capt. Cowan says these mills afford ample provision for rafts, on which the Americans might pop over and ravage this country. A well-known road thro' the woods from Oswegatchie to Crown Point, in Lake Champlain, or to Lake George, is so passable that 30 or 40 head of cattle pass with ease in eight days.

NOTE.—Captain David Cowan, R.N., was one of the early settlers of this part of the country. His home "opposite Fort Oswegatchie" (Ogdensburg), would be Prescott, in the County of Grenville. In 1819 he lived in the Township of Charlotteville, County of Norfolk, but owned some 450 acres of land in the Township of Pittsburg, six miles west of Gananoque, which was granted him in recognition of his services during the War of 1812. He was an uncle of Mr. Alexander Cowan of Pittsburg Township, Frontenac County, U.C. Miss Margaret Cowan, a daughter of Mr. Alexander Cowan, married the late George B. Holland, of Toronto, whose descendants live in Toronto, Gananoque and Brockville.

An interesting mention is made of Captain Cowan in the Memoirs of John Clark, of Port Dalhousie, in Volume VII. of the Ontario Historical Society Papers and Records. It reads:—

"There were two worthies amongst us equal, if not superior, to Beau Nash, in the old times. These were Captain Cowan, of the navy, and Staff-Surgeon Fleming of the army. They in every particular were the essence of politeness. The Chippewa (sic) Bridge in that day was nearer the mouth of the Chippewa (sic) River than the present bridge, consequently was of greater span. One fine morning these two gents being at Chippewa, were crossing the bridge at opposite ends, and both being somewhat halt in their legs, when they stepped on the bridge, commenced to bow to each other and did not stop bowing till they met each other in the centre when they took a most cordial grip and passed on. So much for Captain Cowan and Dr. Fleming of bygone days' politeness."

Wed. 17th—Embarked at six; fine wind, showery. Passing the first rapid at Chimney Island the water is very frightful. A little below John's Town saw a deer crossing the river, a canoe trying to overtake it. The deer swam up the stream and got ashore. At half-past nine passed Matilda township and the Rapid Plat, 20 miles. At half after three Mr. M'Gill wanted to give a message from you to the Speaker (John Macdonell), so we stopped for him to deliver it, and I take the opportunity of sending this book, that you may know we got safe and well so far and had a pleasant journey. Fray give this book to Mr. D. W. Smith, to send back to me immediately, for I mean to make some pretty drawings from these rough sketches.

I should not have sent you this rough one, but that I know you will be glad in any way to know myself and the children are well, and as comfortable as is possible to be anywhere in your absence.

We have had a good deal of thunder and rain to-day. A thunderstorm was hardly passed when we entered the Long Sault. Had it continued, what a fineward element. The Long Sault Rapid was less alarming than I expected, but very grand and fine, and nothing but reason would keep one from being afraid. Your sight must be terrified, tho' knowledge makes you rest satisfied.

Ever most attachedly yours,

E. Simcoe.

The going down the river is so fine a thing altogether I wish for you every moment. I should be in ecstasies if you were here to partake of them.

Thurs. 18th—Embarked at six, and reached the Cedar Rapids, opposite the village of that name, at ten; from thence I went in a calèche to the Cascades between Grand Island and Isle Perault, from whence I was two hours going in the boat to La Chine, eight miles above Montreal. I waited there two hours for a calèche, and set out in it with Francis, but the road was so rough and the carriage so indifferent that I was obliged to stop and take Collins with me to hold the child, or we should have been shaken out. I was so fatigued with this eight miles to Montreal that I determined never to go in a post calèche again. The carriage was driven tandem, the first horse tied to the other by a rope, which did not in the least confine him. The horses generally went different ways and at a great rate.

I went to Mr. Gray's at Montreal, but his house being under repair, Mr. Frobisher, another merchant, requested me to be at his house, where I should be better accommodated, and indeed it is elegantly fitted up. He sent his carriage for me.

NOTE.—Edward William Gray was a man well known in military, civil and social circles in Montreal. He was born on the 4th December, 1742, in England and came to Montreal in the autumn of 1760 in the "Vanguard," man-of-war, and was initiated into Freemasonry on 2nd October, 1760, when the ship was in the St. Lawrence, in front of Quebec. His Masonic certificate is in the Archives Department at Ottawa, and it is the earliest certificate known to the craft in Canada. In the Masonic institution there were in the olden time three kinds of warrants given to lodges. A civil warrant was for a lodge composed of citizens of a certain place. Another warrant was known as a "sea warrant," for members on board a British man-of-war, while a third warrant was known as a "field warrant" given to soldiers in a British regiment. It is permissible to hold these lodges either in the quarters of a regiment or on board a man-of-war "in the most convenient place adjacent to the ship." In January, 1760, a warrant was issued for a lodge on board the "Vanguard," man-of-war, of which Thomas Dunckerley was W.M. The lodge on the occasion of this initiation was held no doubt in a lodge room in the city of Quebec, for there were a number of military

COLD WEATHER IN THE ST. LAWRENCE

lodges stationed in the fortress, that possessed Masonic warrants. William Gray was postmaster of Montreal for many years, and sheriff of the District of Montreal. His Commission as Deputy-Provost-Marshal, corresponding to that of sheriff, is dated 15th June, 1765. He was appointed Deputy Public Appraiser and Vendue Master on 11th August, 1766, and was promoted to the office of Provost-Marshal on 1st May, 1775. He was appointed major of a corps of volunteers raised amongst the merchants of Montreal at the time of the American invasion, and for services rendered was afterwards given the rank of colonel, commanding the English militia in the city and suburbs of Montreal. He died on 22nd December, 1810.

Fri. 19th—Mrs. Frobisher came from her country house to dine with me. I saw the large sheep's horn Mr. Mackenzie, the North-West explorer, brought from the Rocky Mountains. Major Duke called to enquire whether I would have men from the 26th to row my batteau, but I preferred the Canadians. Mr. Smith, of the 7th Fusiliers, brought me letters from England.

NOTE.—Major George Duke's first commission in the 26th is dated 10th September, 1779, with rank of captain. In October, 1793, he was in command, as major, at St. John's and Isle-aux-Noix, Lower Canada. In the army list his name is given also as "Charles" Duke, with the statement that he "sold out," though the date is not given.

The 26th, or Cameronian Regiment, was formed in 1689, deriving its popular designation of "Cameronians" from the sect (named after one of its first preachers, Richard Cameron). The regiment was formed at the time when the religious persecution by the Stuart family led many of their subjects of the Presbyterian persuasion in Scotland to take up arms. In 1787 the regiment was stationed at Quebec, in 1789 at Montreal, and in 1790 at Niagara, and at various other stations in Canada until 1800, when it returned to England. The unfortunate Captain John Andre, who joined the 26th from the 44th Regiment, was commissioned on 18th January, 1777. He was executed on 2nd October, 1780. Andre was a personal friend of Governor Simcoe.

Sat. 20th—A very wet day, so I stayed at Mr. Frobisher's.

Sun. 21st—I left Montreal at nine, with a good many buffalo skins in the boat, as the weather grows very cold, and every ten leagues I feel it more so; the weather very windy and disagreeable; an unpleasant squall near Varennes, on the river near Montreal. We afterwards passed St. Sulpice, on the north shore of the St. Lawrence, and La Valtrie, a pretty village among oaks, and reached D'Autray, thirteen leagues from Montreal, at six o'clock. I walked the last half-mile to warm myself. I had a good fire at the Post House, and wrote till eleven. I was charged six shillings for rooms, fire and milk. I carried tea, cold tongue and fowl, or herrings, which composed our supper.

NOTE.—Dautrey, spelled Dautré on old maps, is on the north shore of River St. Lawrence, about half-way between the village of Lanoraie and the River des Chaloupes.

DIARY OF MRS. SIMCOE

Mon. 22nd—Set out at six; passed Berthier, a village on the north shore, at twelve; came to N. York, missed the house we were directed to go to, stopped at another while the men lighted their pipes; previous to passing Lake St. Pierre had a distant view of Maskinonge, in the county of that name, Rivière du Loup (the county town of Maskinonge) and Machiche; at seven arrived at Three Rivers, one of the oldest towns in the province, founded in 1618, and had a good fire at the Maison de poste, and very cheap (a much better house than the inn kept by an Englishman, where, instead of two dollars, I might have paid eight).

NOTE.—The MSS. reads N. York. The map drawn by Mrs. Simcoe shows "N. York" on Lake St. Peter. There is no trace of the name now.

After drinking tea (or supper) and the children are gone to bed, I dress my hair, which I have not time to do in the morning, change my habit, and lay down on a boudet (or folding bed) before the fire, covered with a

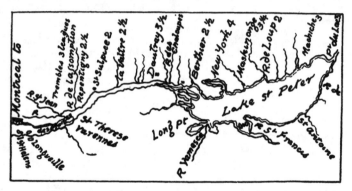

MONTREAL EAST TO POINT DU LAC, 1794.
(From a Drawing by Mrs. Simcoe)

fur blanket. I do not undress when I have not my bed, which is the case at present. I came 21 leagues to-day, and felt it very cold, but the children mind it so little that Francis will not keep on his gloves.

Tues. 23rd—Left Three Rivers after breakfast. In the afternoon the weather was particularly fine, and the scenery between Grondines and Cap Santé was peculiarly beautiful, illuminated by the setting sun. The churches of Deschambault and Cap Santé are very picturesque objects among the wood, and the high ground near the latter is of the finest verdure, covered with large, detached trees, has a very fine appearance; indeed, going down the St. Lawrence affords the most delightful scenery, whether it be between Kingston and Montreal, among the numberless wooded islands of all sizes, or the woody, rocky shores bordering the rapids, and the transparent clear waters.

NOTE.—Deschambault, a village in Portneuf County, P.Q., on north shore, forty miles above Quebec. Cap Santé is 31 miles from Quebec. During the French *régime* it was a French post and after the Battle of the Plains the army was quartered in the vicinity for several months.

ARRIVAL AT QUEBEC

Tues. 23rd—From Montreal to Quebec the country is more diversified by villages and houses, and is very pretty, excepting a part of it in passing Lake St. Peter, which is flat and low, but from Deschambault it again becomes fine. The opposition of a strong current makes the voyage up the river very tedious, but the velocity with which the boat passes down affords incessant variety of objects, and nothing can be pleasanter. I cannot tho' but regret leaving the climate of our upper country (Upper Canada), the warmth of which gives an idea of comfort to the most uninhabited scenes.

We came 19 leagues to-day, and arrived at six at Cap Santé, and I found myself at the house where I had met with so much civility on my way from Quebec. The woman recognized and welcomed me with her usual French politeness; by great industry she had saved some money to make the miserable cottage it had been formerly fit for the reception of travellers. She said my calling there accidentally had made her think of so doing. Her husband is quite uncivilized, but she had been educated at a convent. An orchard full of fine apples was in great beauty, just ready to

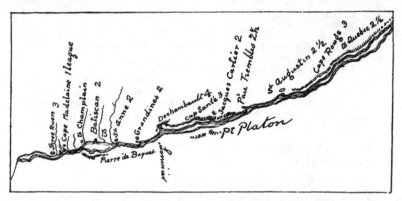

MAP OF ROUTE FROM THREE RIVERS TO QUEBEC.
(From a Drawing by Mrs. Simcoe.)

be gathered. I had much satisfaction at seeing the progressive state of improvement making here. I was made happy in receiving a letter to-night from Mrs. Caldwell, pressing me in the kindest manner to reside with her till my house at Quebec could be prepared for me.

Wed. 24th—The tide prevented my leaving Cap Santé till nine o'clock. Fine weather. Passed the mills at Jacques Cartier; landed at a romantic spot named Cap Rouge, three leagues above Quebec. I walked a mile to the Maison de Poste, dressed myself, and went in a calèche four miles to Belmont, where I met with the most friendly reception that was possible.

Thur. 25th—I received a great many visits from my acquaintances at Quebec, who all appeared glad to see me.

Fri. 26th—Many more visitors. Coll. Caldwell and Miss Johnson dined at St. Foix (St. Foye), but I could not prevail on Mrs. Caldwell to leave me, and I could not accept Lady Dorchester's invitation, as my clothes had not arrived.

Mon. 29th—The Bishop's family and Coll. and Mrs. Despard dined here.

NOTE.—Mrs. Despard was the wife of Lieutenant-Colonel John Despard of the 7th Regiment who had brevet rank as colonel from 13th July, 1791.

17

DIARY OF MRS. SIMCOE

Tues, 30th—Coll. Caldwell proposed my taking his house at "Sans Bruit," which I felt disposed to do. I went to see it to-day. The weather was very cold and some snow fell, which gave me an unfavourable idea of Sans Bruit, and I did not like the thoughts of so cold a place. I called on Mrs. Mountain, wife of the Bishop, at Powell Place, and on Mrs. Despard at Woodfield. It is said that peace is settled between Great Britain and the United States, but as I have not heard it officially (or even in that case could I tell how Gen. Wayne may previously have acted at the Miami) I cannot venture to return with Mr. McGill to Niagara. He sets out to-day. Some snow fell.

Wed. Oct. 1st—Coll. and Mrs. Caldwell went to their mill. Miss Johnson and I drove to Quebec.

Thurs. 2nd—I breakfasted with Mrs. Murray, and went to the house offered me in Palace Street, which I liked very well. Coll. and Mrs. Caldwell returned to dinner. We drank tea at Mr. Nathaniel Taylor's, Deputy Commissary General.

Note.—Mrs. Murray was the wife of Richard Murray, who is given in the list of Protestant house-keepers as a Justice of the Peace in 1794.

Tues. 7th—We dined at the Bishop's; a very large party there, and Coll. and Mrs. Despard.

Wed. 8th—Miss Johnson and I went to Quebec.

Sun. 12th—Coll. Beckwith and several friends dined here. Coll. Caldwell, having found that I was the daughter of his old friend, Coll. Gwillim, who fought at Quebec under Wolfe, and with whom he stayed some time in London after the death of Genl. Wolfe, is now doubly kind and interested about all my concerns.

Note.—(Colonel) George Beckwith was Acting Adjutant-General at Quebec in 1794.

Mon. 13th—I took possession of my house in Palace Street. Dined at the Chateau.

Thurs. 16th—Quebec—I have bought a covered carriole, but until the snow falls I cannot use it. Coll. Caldwell sends a calèche for me to go to Belmont, as it does not seem worth while to buy one for so short a time as I suppose it will be possible to use it.

Fri. 17th—Dined and slept at Belmont.

Sat. 18th—Came home; 22 visitors this morning.

Wed. 22nd—Dined and slept at Belmont.

Thurs. 23rd—Came here; a great many visitors this morning. The certainty of peace relieved me from so much uneasiness that I scarcely seem to feel the banishment from the upper country as much as I expected to have done. Yet at times I have doubts whether an American mob may act in opposition to their executive government.

I have been amused by a play called "Carthusian Friar," written by a lady, an emigrant. Coll. Caldwell calls almost every day to know whether offers of service other people make, they premise with saying, "If Coll. I want anything, and is so attentive to all my business that whatever Caldwell has not done it already." Coll. Beckwith has been very civil. I have added a horse, a cow and a cat, and a Canadian driver to my establishment. Patras drives admirably. I have heard from the Governor, but the letter was dated Fort Erie, six days after he left Niagara.

Sun. 26th—Dined at M. Bàby's (Hon. Francis Bàby). Baron de Rue, M. D'Anoilt and many others there. The office ordered to be shut on Sunday.

Thurs. 30th—Dined at the Chateau

PLEASANT DAYS AT THE CAPITAL

Tues. Nov. 4th—I have heard that all was well at Detroit on the 13th of October, and Governor Simcoe returned to Niagara. Instead of the usual frost and snow at this season, we have damp, mild weather, which disagrees with everybody. I have a cold, which keeps me at home. The wind is east, and has prevented the Fusiliers sailing for Halifax; they have been on board ship for a week. An east wind at this season is most extraordinary.

Thurs. 6th—The "Eweretta" and convoy sailed to London this morning.

Note.—Ship "Eweretta," Alex. Patterson, master, sailed to and from London.

Tues. 11th—I attempted to go to Belmont in my carriole, but the roads were too bad. I drank tea at the Chateau.

Wed. 12th—Dined with Madame Bàby.

Thurs. 13th—Spent the evening at Mrs. Ogden's, wife of Isaac Ogden, Judge of Admiralty.

Fri. 14th—Dined at Mrs. Winslow's.

Sat. 15th—The weather so bad I put off going to Powell Place.

Sun. 16th—Some snow. Francis and I went to Belmont in an open carriole.

Tues. 18th—Drove from Belmont to Powell Place; went to Quebec at four; dined and went in the evening to the Chateau. When I left it, called at home for my great-coat, and went with Miss Murray in an open carriole at ten o'clock at night to Belmont; a little snow, but very mild.

Thurs. 20th—Letters have been received from Governor Simcoe dated Niagara, Oct. 30th.

Tues. 25th—A heavy fall of snow and the thermometer five degrees below. I dined at Mr. Ainslie's, Collector of Customs. Baron de Rue there; he was promised letters of recommendation by Coll. Harping (at Quebec, Nov., 1794), who died. The Dauphin, eldest son of Louis of France, is dead.

Fri. 28th—I dined at Mr. Dunn's. The stoves so heated that the thermometer in the room must have been at 90. Ice and fruit were in great request.

Note.—Honorable Thos. Dunn was a member of the Executive Council, Lower Canada. As senior member he was administrator on two occasions, first in 1805, on the departure of Sir Robert Shore Milnes, and again during the interval between Governor Craig and Sir George Prevost.

Sat. 29th—A violent snowstorm, and very severe, cold weather; but in Miss William's room, daughter of the Clerk of the Executive Council, where I dined, the thermometer must have been at 86.

Sun. 30th—I dined at Belmont; returned in the open carriole.

Tues. Dec. 2nd—Dined at the Chateau; supped at Mr. Taylor's.

Wed. 3rd—I dined at Belmont.

Thurs. 4th—I dined at the Chief Justice's (Osgoode); a pleasant French party there.

Note.—Chief Justice Osgoode had, after leaving Upper Canada, been appointed Chief Justice of Lower Canada. Chief Justice Smith had died 3rd December, 1793.

Fri. 5th—Went to breakfast at Belmont; drank tea with Madame Bàby.

Sat. 6th—Dined at Thomas Grant's, of the Surveyor's Office. I have had letters from Governor Simcoe, tho' nearly a month after the time I

259

ought to have received them. Mr. Gray kept them at Montreal till he had an opportunity of sending them by a gentleman, in order to save the postage of so large a packet. The Governor proposed my meeting him at Pointe au Bodet, which is the boundary of this province, in January or February, as soon as the ice is good. As I had not thought of moving till the weather communication was open, this scheme is doubly delightful

LADY DORCHESTER.
(From a copy of a miniature in England.)

to me as being an unexpected pleasure, and I think I shall like travelling *en carriole* very much. Mr. Mayne, of the Rangers, is to meet me at Montreal. I desired he may not come further.

Lady Dorchester was so obliging to insist on sending me one of her open carrioles—mine, being a covered one, was disagreeable in a morning—

and this will greatly add to my amusement; indeed, she and Lord Dorchester have been uniformly polite and obliging to me; she is one of those few who appear to act upon principle, and with a consistency which is not to be moved. I think her a sensible, pleasant woman, and I like the parties at the Chateau excessively, for there are forty or fifty people in an evening, and I think it is very amusing to walk about the room and have something to say to everybody without a long conversation with any.

NOTE.—The following interesting incident in connection with the marriage of Sir Guy Carleton and Lady Maria Howard is given in the Life of Dorchester, Morang's "Makers of Canada":—

"Almost immediately on the passing of the Quebec Act Carleton sailed for Canada and landed on September 18th, 1774. During his long stay in England he had married the Lady Maria Howard, daughter of the Earl of Effingham, who with her two children born of the marriage accompanied her husband across the Atlantic. The lady was less than half Carleton's age, which was now forty-eight. A family tradition attributes the fact of Carleton's remaining so long unmarried to an early disappointment in a love affair with his cousin, Jane Carleton. The circumstances of his marriage were somewhat singular, and were given to me by the present representative of the family. Lord Howard of Effingham, then a widower, was a great personal friend of Carleton's, and of about the same age. On this account and also foreseeing for him a distinguished career, he cordially accepted his overtures for the hand of his eldest daughter, Lady Anne. She and her younger sister, Lady Maria, had seen a great deal of Sir Guy at their father's house, and doubtless regarded him as a benevolent uncle rather than a potential lover. In time, however, they became aware that other schemes were abroad, and on a certain occasion when Carleton arrived at the house and was closeted with his Lordship it seems to have been pretty well understood what he had come for. The two young ladies were sitting together in another apartment with a relative, a Miss Seymour, and when a message came to Lady Anne that her presence was required by her father its purport seems to have been well known. When this young lady returned to her friends her eyes were red from tears. The others, waiting impatiently for her news, were the more impatient as well as perplexed at her woe-begone appearance. 'Your eyes would be red,' she replied to their queries, 'if you had just had to refuse the best man on earth.'

"'The more fool you,' was the unsympathetic rejoinder of her younger sister, Lady Maria. 'I only wish he had given me the chance.'

"It appears that Lady Anne was already in love with Carleton's nephew, whom she afterwards married, and who served under his uncle in Canada.

"There the matter rested for some months till Miss Seymour one day confided to Sir Guy what Lord Howard's younger daughter had remarked on hearing of his discomfiture. This so much interested the middle-aged lover, who, no doubt, had recovered from a perhaps

DIARY OF MRS. SIMCOE

not very violent passion, that in due course he presented himself as
a suitor for the younger daughter, who proved herself as good as
her word. Miss Seymour, who lived to old age, used to tell the
story to members of the Dorchester family who only passed away
in comparatively recent years.

" Lady Maria was small and fair, upright and extremely dignified,
and was ceremonious to a degree that in her old age almost amounted
to eccentricity. She had been brought up and educated at Ver-
sailles, which may be held to account for her partiality for the French
at Quebec, and may possibly have influenced her husband in the
same direction."

Tues. 9th—I drank tea at the Chateau.
Wed. 10th—Went to Belmont and to Powell Place, where I dined and
slept.
Fri. 12th—Went to Belmont.
Sat. 13th—Lord and Lady Dorchester called upon me. Mr. D. W.
Smith writes me word from Niagara that the Governor went to York on
the 13th of November, and was to proceed immediately from thence to
Kingston in a boat coasting by the Bay of Quinte.
Tues. 16th—At the Chateau. I am also sure to meet Madame Bàby
there, who is one of the most agreeable people at Quebec.
Wed. 17th—At Mr. Craigie's (John Craigie).

NOTE.—Honorable John Craigie, brother of Lord Craigie, Lord
of Session in Scotland, was Commissary-General and Provincial
Treasurer. He married Susannah, second daughter of John Coffin,
a descendant of Tristram Coffin, and a Loyalist who left Boston in
1775, and settled with his family in Quebec.

Thur. 18th—The last ship that sailed, the "Bridget," is lost. The
August packet is taken by the French, and three officers of the 4th Regiment who were on their way hither in her. One of their wives desired
to preserve a book of drawings, and the captors immediately threw it into
the sea.
Fri. 19th—I supped at Mr. Plenderleath's.

NOTE.—John Plenderleath, afterwards lieutenant-colonel of the
49th Regiment, was assistant storekeeper-general at Quebec in 1794.
He served in the War of 1812, receiving many wounds while in action.
He returned to England in later years, where he died.

Sat. 20th—Wed. 24th—At home on account of Francis' illness, which
Dr. Nooth cannot define, whether it was worms, gravel or plum stones, or
what.
Thurs. 25th—I heard an admirable sermon preached by the Abbé des
Jardins at the French church, and afterwards an excellent one by our own
Bishop.
Fri. 26th—Mr. Coffin gave a dinner and ball on the marriage of Mr.
(Herman Witsius) Ryland, Lord Dorchester's secretary. He had been
engaged to the lady ten years, but pecuniary circumstances would not
allow them to marry before he left England last year with Lord Dor-
chester; those difficulties being removed, she had last had dependence enough
on him to come this winter under the conduct of his friend, Mr. Finlay

HERMAN WITSIUS RYLAND

(Dep. P.M.G.). I was so fatigued with having sat up with Francis for some nights that I did not enjoy the ball.

NOTE.—Herman Witsius Ryland was born in England in 1770. He took part in the American War, returning to England with Sir Guy Carleton. On the latter's appointment as Governor-General, Mr. Ryland, as Civil Secretary, accompanied him to Canada, filling the position not only while Dorchester was in office, but during the terms of succeeding Governors. He resigned in 1811, continuing to fill, however, his position as clerk of the Executive Council until his death in 1838. His son, George Herman Ryland, then held the office until the union of the Canadas. Mrs. Henry J. Low, of Montreal, and Mr. Herman Ryland, of Quebec, are grandchildren of Herman Witsius Ryland, and Mr. H. Ryland Low, of Montreal, is a great-grandson.  HERMAN W. RYLAND.

Mon. 29th—Met Lord and Lady Dorchester at Mr. Grant's, so I did not go to the concert.

Tues. 30th—Drove in my open carriole to Belmont; returned after dinner and went to Mr. Ainslie's; won five rubbers at whist, having been braced and brightened by the cold drive this afternoon.

Wed. 31st—Drove to Fort Louis Gate, and walked on the plains with Lady Dorchester; supped at Mrs. Ogden's.

CHAPTER XVI.

RETURN TO UPPER CANADA.

Mrs. Simcoe, satisfied that the war trouble she feared was not imminent, determined to return to Upper Canada notwithstanding her aversion to a winter journey west, as expressed in some of her letters. She resolved to make the trip by the only available route, a land journey along the north side of the St. Lawrence. Her stay at Quebec had been a round of pleasure and gaiety. Those in official circles, as well as the leaders in the social life of the ancient city, had welcomed her return, and as her diary shows, had paid her respect and kindly courtesy, for every day functions, some of the major character and others of a minor, occupied her time. Mrs. Simcoe was a most affectionate wife, and every express to Upper Canada carried letters to the Governor telling him of her daily doings at Quebec. She left Belmont on the afternoon of 6th February.

Late in the fall of 1794 the Governor had left Niagara for the purpose of making a personal inspection of different parts of the province. He visited York and from thence proceeded to Kingston, where he arrived on 4th December. The journey, owing to the lateness in the season, was stormy and hazardous, but was accomplished, however, without mishap. His time in Kingston was fully and actively employed, and the early part of February found him at Johnstown, a hamlet east of Prescott. Here he laid plans for a road to the forks of the Rideau, for the establishment of settlements previously surveyed, and for personally investigating the water communication with the Ottawa. All schemes were perforce set aside. In March Mrs. Simcoe joined her husband at New Johnstown (Cornwall), and after spending a few days at Johnstown they repaired to Kingston, where the Governor became very ill and was unable to travel for several weeks. On the 15th May they left for York.

Thurs. Jan. 1st, 1795—I dined at the Chateau. There were about forty persons. In the evening there was a rout or assembly, for introducing strangers. These routs used to be held frequently, but since Mr. Carleton's death, which is many months since, there has not been any.

Note.—Thomas Carleton, a son of Lord Dorchester, born in 1774, died in 1794.

My having dined at the Chateau without having been formally introduced is a compliment not usually paid. There were 63 ladies this evening. I won a rubber at whist; there was but one card table. The people are unaccountably formal when they come to the Chateau, tho' Lady D. proposes cards and wishes them to be amused.

Fri. 2nd—At Madame Bàby's; the thermometer ten degrees above. I preferred coming home in the open carriole.

A ROUND OF ENJOYMENT

Tues. 6th—I went with Lady Dorchester in her carriole beyond Wood-field. The carriole was large and pleasant, and a seat in front for children. Her drivers are Canadians and, therefore, will not wear liveries. The Canadian coats, with capots and sashes, look very picturesque. I drank tea at the Chateau, and Miss Carleton danced.

NOTE.—Miss Carleton was a daughter of Lord Dorchester.

Wed. 7th—I dined *en famille* at the Chateau, carrying the children. Supped at Mrs. Taylor's.

Thurs. 8th—I went to Belmont.

Fri. 9th—I went to Powell Place in a snowstorm, and returned to Belmont at night.

Sun. 11th—Coll. Beckwith mentioned Governor Simcoe having the rank of Major-General. (He received this rank in October, 1794.)

Mon. 12th—Dined at Madame Bàby's; went to the concert. Thermometer 10 degrees below.

Tues. 13th—Dined at the Chateau; a "rout" in the evening. Miss Carleton is very ill and Lady Dorchester the picture of misery.

Wed. 14th—I went to Belmont in the open carriole; dined and returned in time to go to Mrs. Le Maistre's, where I played cards and supped. Spent two or three days at Powell Place.

Tues. 20th—A ball at the Chateau, as the 18th was Sunday. The ladies much dressed. Miss Williams the most so. Miss Carleton stayed a very short time in the room, having been excessively ill for this last week.

Thurs. 22nd—Mild weather and a S.E. wind, which occasions a good deal of illness, and also inconvenience, for the meat, bought as usual in large quantities in the autumn, will not keep.

Sat. 24th—I walked on the plains with Lady Dorchester, and have learned to wrap myself up enough to defy the cold, but the weight of clothes is very fatiguing. Dined with Mrs. Taylor. Drank tea at the Chateau.

Sun. 25th—At Belmont.

Mon. 26th—Drank tea with Miss Mountain. Lord Dorchester sent his dormeuse, a travelling carriage adapted for sleeping, that I might see whether I should like that sort of a carriage to travel in to Upper Canada. It is like an open carriole, with a head made of sealskin, and lined with baize; a large bear or buffalo skin fixes in front, which perfectly secures you from wind and weather, and may be unhooked if the weather is fine or mild; a low seat, and feather bed to keep one's feet warm. I drove a mile or two in it and like it much, and bespoke one to be made the same.

Tues. 27th—I dined at the Chateau. Francis is ill.

Wed. 28th—I dined at Mr. George Longmore's. Francis is worse. A letter from the Governor.

NOTE.—Mr. George Longmore was an apothecary on the Hospital staff, and a surgeon in the Ordnance Department.

Thurs. 29th—Dined at the Chateau, and carried the children there.

Fri. 30th—Dined at Mr. Taylor's; supped at Mr. Coffin's.

Sat. 31st—Lady Dorchester came to see me. I dined at the Chateau and supped at Madame Bàby's. Mr. Mayne is arrived at Montreal, and the Governor on his way to Coll. Gray's to meet me. Sent off my baggage on a traineau, a sled used for that purpose, to Montreal.

Sun. Feb. 1st—Dined at Mr. Taylor's. Drank tea at the Chateau.

Mon. 2nd—Dined at Mr. Taylor's. Went to Miss Williams'. It was her birthday, and there was a ball. Danced with Capt. Archdall, of the King's Own Regiment of Foot.

NOTE.—Captain Archdall received his rank in the 4th, or King's Own, Regiment of Foot on 2nd September, 1795.

DIARY OF MRS. SIMCOE

Tues. 3rd—Dined at the Chateau.

Wed. 4th—Drove to Powell Place, drank tea with Mrs. Craigie; went with her to the concert; returned; played three rubbers at whist and supped.

Thurs. 5th—Lady Dorchester called to take leave of me. I slept at Belmont.

Fri. Feb. 6th—I left Belmont at two o'clock; the children, Collins and a great deal of baggage in a heavy dormeuse or carriole, with a head built after that of Lord Dorchester's. I went six leagues to Pointe aux Trembles. It was quite dark before I arrived there; a tolerable Post House.

Sat. 7th—I set off at seven; the weather bright and pleasant, tho' the wind E. At Jacques Cartier the ice was so rotten I was obliged to go a league higher to cross the river with safety; when I came to Ste. Anne's the sun shone so bright I thought I should have time to go two stages further to Cap Madeleine, near Three Rivers, where I was advised to sleep if I went further than Ste. Anne's; but when I came to the next stage, Champlain (75 miles S.W. of Quebec), I was frightened at the ice cracking on the river, and when I stopped at the Post House it was so perfectly dark that I could not reconcile myself to going further.

Sun. 8th—The house at Champlain was wretched, and the people said that travellers never slept at it, but on my repeating a request for a room they gave up their sitting-room, which appeared so dismal that I could not sleep, tho' I lay down on a boudet. In the night a great dog crept in from under the stove, and people were talking continually. The children went to bed. I would not allow them to stay to breakfast in a place I had wished to quit from the moment I entered it. The people looked as if they belonged to the cave dwellers. When I came to Cap Madeleine I had the expectation of passing very bad ice within a mile, which intimidated me so much that I would not stay to breakfast. We went two leagues above the usual place of crossing, and even there saw water on each side of the carriage. We were driven by so very old a man that they sent another to take care of him over the most dangerous part of the road. I wanted to detain him the whole stage, but he would not stay to affront the old man; he said he had driven over 60 years. He was very near overturning us before we came to Three Rivers. It was Sunday and the streets filled with people, so I would not go out to breakfast, but kept Collins (who never liked losing a meal) without her breakfast till five in the afternoon, when we arrived at a very comfortable Post House at Maskinonge, a village on the north shore, where I had a very good dinner and stayed that night. We had travelled twenty leagues and a half.

Mon. 9th—The Dep. P.M.G. at Quebec having sent orders to all the Post Houses on the road to keep horses ready for me, and told the courier to pay for them, I had not the least trouble of waiting or paying. "Labadie (the courier) pave tout," and they ask me no further questions. The weather has been delightful to-day. I thought the expanse of miles of ice from Pointe aux Trembles to Montreal looked very formidable, but it was good ice, and we arrived at Mr. Edward Gray's at five o'clock, having travelled twenty-four leagues and a half since we left Maskinonge at five this morning. The post horses are very good; they drive tandem, and change every three leagues.

Tues. 10th—I set off at eight this morning in my dormeuse. Mr. Mayne followed in a carriole, and servants in a third. When I was told we were to go with the same horses to Pointe au Bodet, 63 miles, I thought we should have a very tedious journey, but it was far from being so; the ice was excellent.

It was a delightful drive across the wild part of the St. Lawrence below its junction with the Ottawa to the Cedars, where we rested the horses two hours, and they brought us to the Pointe au Bodet by six o'clock. When we were on Lake St. Francis my driver left the carriage and walked behind with the other drivers; every half-mile he came and whipped the horses violently, and I saw no more of him till we had gone another half-mile, the horses steadily pursuing a slight track on the snow; but had there been air holes in the track they pursued, as sometimes happens on the ice, what would have become of us? It put me in mind of the reindeer, who travel self-conducted. The Governor came half-way to Pointe au Bodet to meet me to-day, and returned to Coll. James Gray's, as I was not arrived.

Wed. 11th—I set out by seven, and by eleven had the pleasure to see the Governor quite well at Coll. Gray's, where we stayed.

Fri. 13th—Mr. Mayne returned to Montreal. The Governor and I set out towards Kingston; stopped an hour at a good inn, where the sessions are held—the last house in Stormont; went about 35 miles to Mr. Patterson's at the Rapide Plat, where we slept—a damp room. The roads to the west of Montreal are excellent, because they drive the horses abreast and make the carrioles wider.

NOTE.—Mr. Patterson was a son-in-law of the Honorable John Munro and lived in what has been known for more than a hundred years as " The Old Blue House," about four miles east of Iroquois. It stood on a bluff of the river at "Flagg's" at the head of Rapide du Plat, but has been moved twice within the past twenty years, and now stands on the north side of the road. It is only half the original size, a wing having been removed and the front altered in changing the old house from place to place. Within its walls were entertained almost every noted man of the first forty years of the history of Upper Canada.

Sat. 14th—Came to dinner at Johnstone, opposite Oswegatchie, fifteen miles from the Rapide Plat.

This place was laid out for a town, but there are but a few houses built; one of them is intended for an inn. The Governor has been residing at it for a fortnight, expecting me here. I intend to stay here ten days. Major Littlehales is with him, and they keep a very good house, promising to give me turkeys and venison every day. There are two comfortable rooms, and what I most desire are the stoves in them. The weather is severely cold and bright. We play at whist in the evening. The journey has quite established Francis' health, tho' he was so ill when we left Quebec.

NOTE.—Johnstown is just east of Prescott, the scene of the Battle of the Windmill of 1837. It is not to be confused with "New Johnstown," the name by which Cornwall was first known.

Thurs, 19th—I had not been here two days when I felt the violent effects of a cold I caught by sleeping in a damp room at the Rapide Plat; it has particularly fallen into my eyes and affected them, so much so that I think I shall never recover totally. I was obliged to-night to throw off most of the wrappages I had bound about my eyes and head, and go to a ball given by the inhabitants of the province to the Governor; people came 40 miles to it in carrioles. I was really so ill I could scarcely hear or see, and possibly neglected the very people I meant to be most civil to.

Fri. 20th—Drove seven and a half miles to dine at Mr. Jones'; returned by nine o'clock.

NOTE.—Ephraim Jones, ninth son of Colonel Elisha Jones, was a United Empire Loyalist who settled in the township of Augusta, county of Grenville. He is stated in Lord Dorchester's list to have

DIARY OF MRS. SIMCOE

been a Commissary. After the Revolutionary War Mr. Jones had charge of the supplies granted by the British Government to the settlers in Upper Canada. He was a Justice of the Peace and a member of the first House of Assembly. In 1890 he received a grant of three hundred acres of land in the township of Augusta, now owned by Thomas Murdock.

Sat. 21st—Dined at Mr. T. Frazier's (Fraser).

Sun. 22nd—Dined at Mr. W. Frazier's (Fraser).

Mon. 23rd—Thurs. 26th—A great deal of snow fell these days, and the inhabitants endeavoured to persuade the Governor not to set out till the snow was beaten; but a gentleman residing with us had business at Kingston, and assured the Governor it would be excellent travelling. So we set off at eight, and met two Mr. Jones', who were coming to request the Governor not to undertake the journey yet. When they found him determined to proceed, they said they would go also, to beat the way and to hasten our journey; they took us into their lighter carriages, or we never should have got on, the snow was so heavy. We stopped at another Jones', where there was the largest wood fire I ever saw; he also set out to beat the road, and so did several other people. One gentleman came some miles below Oswegatchie for that purpose, and with this assistance we went 19 miles to Mr. Jessup's house in the woods, where we slept, but the people who so civilly travelled with us had to go back again, as there was no accommodation for them and their horses. It was six before we arrived. It was the coldest day remembered in Upper Canada. Mr. Jones' finger was slightly frost bit; he was speaking of a very pretty pond near one of his mills. I asked him of what size. He said 300 acres.

NOTE.—Mr. Jessup was Major Edward Jessup, born in Stamford County, Conn., in 1735. After the failure of the Burgoyne expedition in 1781 the provincials were re-organized, and the corps known as the Loyal Rangers was formed. Major Edward Jessup was in command. He spent several years in England and on returning to Canada settled in Grenville, in the township of Augusta, the pioneer town of Prescott having been begun on his property. His son, Lieutenant Edward Jessup, was elected as member for Grenville in the second Legislature. The son died in Prescott in 1815, while the father died at the same place in the following year. The site of Major Jessup's house is now occupied by the entrance to Fort Wellington, Prescott. The surviving descendants of Major Edward Jessup are Mr. Edward Jessup, until recently Collector of Customs at Prescott, and Misses Clarendon and Zaire Jessup.

Fri. 27th—We left Mr. Jessup's at nine, drove nine miles through the woods to a small cottage; then proceeded 18 miles to Cary's, beyond the Gananowui. We went four miles on the ice before we came to that river, at the mouth of which the ice is very bad, so we drove as fast as possible, as that is thought the safest way on rotten ice. I was very much frightened, for it was dark, and I knew that if they did not keep exactly the right track, which could scarcely be seen, we were in the greatest dangers.

When we arrived at Cary's we heard that Mr. Forsyth had lost both his horses three days ago at the mouth of the Gananowui, by keeping too far from the shore; they saved the carriole by cutting the traces, but neither he nor his companions were dexterous enough to save the horses. The people of the States are particularly expert in saving horses from

268

drowning; they travel with ropes, which they fasten round the horses' necks if they fall into the water; pulling it stops their breath, and then they float and can be pulled out; then they take off the rope as quickly as possible, and the horse travels on as well as before.

When Governor Simcoe was driven by Swayzie to Detroit he carried these "choke ropes," and had occasion to use them. A "choke rope," or check band, is a small strap of rope or leather by which the bridle is fastened around the neck of a horse.

Sat. 28th—Cary's an indifferent house, but warm. We left Cary's at nine, drove near the mills at Gananowui; stopped at a farm at Howland's, half-way to Kingston, where we arrived at six o'clock, having travelled 20 miles thro' woods. I was amused by observing the various barks of trees —the most deeply indented and light coloured white ash, the rugged shag bark hickory, the regular marked iron wood, the perpendicular ribbed cedar, the bass wood, the varieties of white and black oak, the maple, chestnut, etc; the strong lines on the pine, particularly the Norway, which is of a yellow brown, and when cut approached to a bright orange colour; among all this the smooth bark of the beech looked as naked as a frog, and had a very mean appearance amongst the rest of the trees.

The following verses were found in the MSS. of the diary. They are dated "Kingston, January 1st, 1795," and were evidently composed by Governor Simcoe in anticipation of his wife's return to Upper Canada.

"Kingston, January 1st, 1795.

"Twice six revolving years have run their course thro' yonder azure plains, diffusing joy.
Gladness and light has discontinuous mov'd,
Since thou, Eliza, overflowing source of happiness domestic, dost employ
My wedded thoughts, most honour'd, most belov'd.
And if the gathering clouds of fleeting life
Besides, thy presence soon illumines the scene,
And pleasure draws from elemental strife;
And now when Night and Absence intervene
O may my wishes wing thy speedy way;
Return, thou source of joy; return, thou source of day."

Sun. March 1st—We are very comfortably lodged in the barracks at Kingston. As there are few officers here, we have the mess room to dine in and a room over it for the Governor's office, and these, as well as the kitchen, are detached from our other three rooms, which is very comfortable. The drawing-room has not a stove in it, which is a misfortune, but it is too late in the winter to be of much consequence. We have excellent wood fires. I went to church to-day and heard an excellent sermon by Mr. Stuart.

NOTE.—The barracks where Mrs. Simcoe stayed were the Soldiers' or the old Tête du Pont barracks, located on almost the same site as the present barracks, Kingston. There are none of the buildings standing now, but on the square are the remains of the foundations of the buildings erected towards the latter part of the eighteenth century.

Tues. 3rd—A thaw. Mr. Frazier, who drove my carriole, set out yesterday to return home.

Sat. 7th—Dined at Mr. Stuart's, the Rector of Kingston.

Sun. 8th—An express from York.

Mon. 9th—We are desirous of seeing the Bay of Quinte; the ice is as smooth as possible and, I am told, very pleasant to drive upon, and possibly the change of air may abate the violent cough I still have. We therefore determined to set out to-day. We called at Mr. Booth's farm, 11 miles distant; the next 11 miles brought us to Mr. Macdonell's, where we dined and slept.

NOTE.—The "King's Sawmills," subsequently known as Booth's Mills, were situated on Lot No. 18 in King's Township.

Tues. 10th—Set off and drove four miles on this delightful ice to Mr. Fisher's, in Hay Bay. He was not at home. We proceeded 15 miles further to Mr. Cartwright's mills, on the Appanee River, and slept at his house, a romantic spot.

NOTE.—Hay Bay is in the township of Fredericksburg, running S.W. into East Bay, making the fork of the north channel of the Bay of Quinte. Mr. Fisher of Hay Bay was probably Judge Fisher, who lived in that district at the time.

The Appanee River is in Lennox County, Ont. The original spelling was "Appanee," or variations, such as "Appanea," "Appanie." On a map of 1815 it is to be found "Apannee." In the Clark Record book it is given twice as Napanee, once in 1788 and again in 1789. On the original Crown Lands map the river is named "Appannee," and the following legend on the map, "Mills built on the Appinnie River under the sanction of Lieutenant-Governor Hamilton," locates the site on the left bank in Fredericksburg Township. Since Naw-paw-nay is the Indian (Mohawk) for "flour" this is sometimes given as the origin of the name, but since the original name has not the initial "N," and as the name was there before the flour mill was erected, we must look elsewhere. An intelligent Indian student suggested that it is related to "opining," which means "potato." The suggestion has also been made by a student of Canadian history, Mr. W. S. Herrington, K.C., of Napanee, that the Indian name for flour (Naw-paw-nay) may have been derived from or may have originated from the name Napanee after flour milling began at the Falls.

Mr. Robert Clark was instructed by the Government to build a saw and also a grist mill at the Falls on the Napanee River, the work being under the direction of Honorable Richard Cartwright. Mr. C. C. James, Deputy Minister of Agriculture, states that in a record book in his possession the first entry, "Appenea Falls, 8th November, 1785," marks the beginning of construction. The saw mill was set up March, 1786, and the grist mill on 25th May, 1786. The latter is the mill shown in Mrs. Simcoe's picture. Grinding wheat began in December of 1786, or early in 1787. For some years the mill was in charge of a Government officer named James Clarke, who, by the way, was in no way related to Robert Clark, the builder. In August, 1799, the Government transferred the mill and lots 18 and 19 in the 7th concession of Fredericksburg to Honorable Richard Cartwright. The mills were situated on the left bank of the river just below the

MILL ON THE APPANEE RIVER, 1795.
(From a Drawing by Mrs. Simcoe.)

THE CARTWRIGHT FAMILY

Falls. Until recent years the old Joy sawmill occupied, in all probability, the exact site of the original sawmill, and the Ross grist mill, just below it and situated under the hill, which was in operation some years ago, was the successor of the original grist mill. Whether it occupied the exact site cannot now be determined, but if it was not the original mill reconstructed, it must have occupied approximately the same site.

Richard Cartwright, great-grandfather of Sir Richard Cartwright, was born in 1720. He came to America and settled in New York about 1742, removing to Canada after the Revolutionary War. His son (Honorable) Richard Cartwright, who owned the mills at Napanee after 1799, was born 2nd February, 1759, and died 1815. He served in Butler's Rangers 1778-9 and was a member of the Legislative Council of Upper Canada from 1792. He was also a Justice of the Common Pleas.

Two of the sons of Honorable Richard Cartwright were Robert David and John Solomon. Reverend Robert David married Harriet, daughter of Conway Edward Dobbs of Dublin, Ireland, a son being Sir Richard Cartwright, and a grandson A. D. Cartwright, secretary of the Railway Commission, Ottawa. John Solomon married Sarah Hayter Macaulay, daughter of Dr. James Macaulay of the Queen's Rangers. James S. Cartwright, K.C., Master in Chambers, and John R. Cartwright, K.C., Deputy Attorney-General, are surviving sons.

Wed. 11th—We are now half way up the Bay of Quinte. Had we set out a week sooner we might have gone 50 miles further, but a general thaw is so soon expected that we do not venture. We are now travelling on a coat of upper ice formed about a fortnight since, and between that and the original ice is two feet of water. The rapidity with which a thaw comes on is incredible; from the ice being excellent, in six hours it is sometimes impassable.

We set out at eleven and drove 14 miles to Trumpour's Point, so named from a man of that name who lives there. He was formerly in the 16th Dragoons, and lives by selling horses; his wife gave me some good Dutch cakes, as I could not wait to eat the chickens she was roasting in a kettle without water. This house commands a fine view. We passed a village of Mohawk Indians at Mohawk Bay, opposite the Appanee River.

From Trumpour's we went to Mr. McDonell's and slept there. This bay is about a mile across, thickly inhabited on the north side. The farms are reckoned the most productive in the province. The journey has been of great benefit to my health.

NOTE.—Paul and Haunts Trumpour, who were brothers, appear to have been the only pioneers of this family in the Bay of Quinte District; and the latter, it would seem, came direct to Prince Edward County, while the former settled at Adolphustown. There is no record of Haunts having lived at the latter place, but the name of Paul is to be found in the "Annual Return of the Inhabitants of Adolphustown," continuously from 1794 to 1812.

The Mohawk Settlement was on the Bay of Quinte, west of Richmond, and between the river Shannon and Bowen's Creek.

18   273

DIARY OF MRS. SIMCOE

Thur. 12th—Left Mr. McDonell's, called at Booth's, and arrived back at Kingston at three o'clock.

Sun. 15th—An express by land arrived from Niagara, and went by York and the Bay of Quinte, for the navigation is not yet open across the lake. Mr. Mayne arrived from Montreal; he says the roads are now very good. Mr. Stuart preached one of the most impressive and best sermons I have ever heard, the text—" Now is the accepted time, now is the day of salvation."

Wed. 18th—An express went to Niagara. A person lately crossing Lake Champlain passed a large hole in the ice and an infant, alive, lying by the side of it. By tracks it appeared that a sleigh had fallen in, and it was known that a heavy-laden sleigh, with families in it, left the country on the opposite shore the day before; probably the mother threw the child out as the sleigh went down. The gentlemen carried the infant to Montreal, where a subscription was raised for her maintenance—a good circumstance this for the commencement of a heroine's life in a novel.

Fri. 20th—A severe frost. Mr. Mayne drove me on the harbour, and Lt. Frasier, of the 60th Regiment, drove the Governor. A large party to dinner.

Sat. 21st—The Governor so ill to-day he could not leave his room to dine with Mr. Breakenridge.

NOTE.—James Breakenridge settled in Bennington, Vt. He was lieutenant of militia; born in 1721, died 1783, leaving issue, besides others, two sons, David and James, who were officers in the Royalist Army (Roger's Rangers), in the Revolutionary War, at the conclusion of which they came to Canada. Mr. Breakenridge of whom Mrs. Simcoe writes was James, colonel of militia and lieutenant of County of Leeds, who settled in Elizabethtown. The late Mr. Walter B. Read, K.C., Toronto, son of the late D. B. Read, K.C., was a great-grandnephew of James Breakenridge of Elizabethtown.

Tues. 31st—Capt. Parr came to take command of the garrison; he relieves Capt. Porter, of the 60th Regiment.

NOTE.—Captain Parr was the son of John Parr, Governor of Nova Scotia in 1782. Rochefoucauld, in writing of a visit to Kingston in July, 1795, says that he and his party "had a letter from General Simcoe to the commanding officer in Kingston, who, at our arrival, was Captain Parr of the 60th Regiment. Six hours after, the detachment commanded by that gentleman was relieved by another of the same regiment, under the orders of Major Dobson. This circumstance, however, did not prevent Captain Parr from giving us the most obliging proofs of civility and kindness. He is the son of the aged Governor of Nova Scotia."

Fri. April 24th—The Governor has been so ill since the 21st of March that I have not left his room since that day. He has had such a cough that some nights he could not lie down, but sat in a chair, total loss of appetite, and such headaches that he could not bear any person but me to walk across the room or speak loud. There was no medical advice but that of a horse doctor who pretended to be an apothecary. The Governor, out of consideration for the convenience of the staff-surgeon, had allowed him to remain at Niagara, and his not being made to attend his duty has caused me a great deal of anxiety to see the Governor so ill without having proper attendance. Capt. Brant's sister prescribed a root—it is,

A GALE ON LAKE ONTARIO

I believe, calamus, a genus of palm, one species of which yields a resin called dragon's blood, the root of which is the sweet flag—which really relieved his cough in a very short time.

Sat. 25th—Walked out this morning.

Sun. 26th—I went to church. It rained. My umbrella was forgotten, and the wet through my sleeves gave me a cold, which perhaps I was more susceptible of from not having been out of the house so long.

Mon. 27th—I had a fit of the ague. The first boats went down to Montreal.

Wed. 29th—I had a fit of the ague.

Fri. May 1st—The first boats arrived from Montreal to-day. The unusual mild weather occasioned Lake Champlain to freeze very late. Mr. Frobisher's sleigh was lost in crossing it; it contained many bags of dollars and valuable things.

Sun. 3rd—The ague again.

Mon. 4th—As I am going away so soon, I am obliged to invite the ladies to dinner, but I am ill and weak. I was obliged to sit in the drawing-room while they went to dinner.

Tues. 5th—The ague.

Wed. 6th. Ladies dined here. I walked in the evening.

Thurs. 7th—Very ill indeed.

Mon. 11th—I drank tea with Mrs. Stuart, and much fatigued by that drive—only a mile.

Tues. 12th—I went on board the "Onondaga," the Government schooner, but the wind coming ahead, we could not sail.

Thurs. 14th—I saw "The Mohawk" launched, a Government boat of 80 tons. She is the size of the "Mississaga." She came with such rapidity that it appeared as if she would have run down the ship we were in, which was at anchor ahead of her. I went on shore, and walked on Point Frederick and the hill above it. Miss Bouchette, daughter of Commodore, dined on board with me. I have not had the ague since I have been in the ship.

NOTE.—Point Frederick is between Kingston Harbour and Haldimand Cove.

Fri. 15th—We weighed anchor at twelve. After sailing five miles a head wind and a stiff gale arose; we returned to the harbour. At two the wind changed and we sailed again; a wet afternoon.

Sat. 16th—Unpleasant, cold weather, little wind.

Sun. 17th—About 5 p.m. we were off Gibraltar Point at York. It blew extremely hard from the shore; the Captain chose to turn the Point without shifting a sail; he was supposed to be not sober, and the Governor ordered the English lieutenant to give orders, and he brought us safely into York Harbour. We were certainly in great danger, for the "Onondaga" is so built that she would overset sooner than carry away anything. I was unusually frightened, having dreamt twice following the other night that I was lost in the "Onondaga." My servant came several times to tell me we were going to the bottom. I told her to shut the door and leave me quiet, for the motion of the ship made me sick.

Mon. 18th—At one o'clock we went on shore.

Thurs. 21st—A moor-hen—a kind of water fowl, which lives on rushes in marshy ground—was brought to me to-day, and repeatedly pecked at the reeds represented in the tapestry, not touching any other part.

York, Sun. 24th—Some ladies dined with me. Walked in the evening. The weather damp and cold.

Mon. 25th—I went with the Governor to the mill (the Government mill) on the Humber, and gathered a beautiful species of polygala or milk wort. I was slightly attacked by the ague.

Wed. 27th—The ague.

DIARY OF MRS. SIMCOE

Mon. June 1st—I went in a boat to Francis' estate, Castle Frank. I drank tea at Playter's.

NOTE.—Immediately beyond the Castle Frank woods, on the property later known as Drumsnab, was the estate of Captain George Playter, and directly across, on the opposite side of the river, that of his son, Captain John Playter, both of whom emigrated from Pennsylvania after the Declaration of Independence. Official records show that Township Lot No. 20, in the 2nd Concession on east side of Yonge and north side of Bloor, was granted to Captain George Playter on 20th August, 1796. Captain George Playter's house stood on the present site of Mr. A. E. Kemp's residence, No. 2, Castle Frank Crescent. This residence was built in 1902, and when the excavations were being made the laborers came upon the stone foundation of Captain George Playter's residence of 1795.

One of Captain George Playter's sons was James Playter, who had a son James. His children are Edgar Manning, manager of a branch of the Canadian Bank of Commerce, Queen and Bathurst Streets, Toronto; Nelson, of Toronto; Catherine Louisa and Mary M. Playter, while Mrs. Barlow Cumberland of Port Hope is a direct descendant of Captain George Playter of early York, through his daughter Mary, who became the wife of Thomas Ward, a barrister at York, afterwards of Port Hope, Ontario.

Thurs. 4th—Company at dinner, and a ball in the evening as usual.

Sat. 6th—Francis gave a dinner on his birthday to the soldiers' children. The Shaws dined with him at an upper table.

Tues. 9th—We sent the children and servants in the "Onondaga," and intend going ourselves to-morrow in the canoe. Dined at Commissary McGill's.

Wed. 10th—The weather so bad we could not move.

Thurs. 11th—The weather continues adverse to our quitting York. We had a dance this evening.

Mon. 15th—We set out in a canoe at seven, dined at the Sixteen-Mile Creek, and arrived at Jones', three miles beyond Burlington Bay, at seven in the evening. I was delighted with the canoe, the motion so easy, so pleasant, so quiet, like what I should suppose being in a palanquin. We sat on cushions in the bottom of the canoe. The Indians brought us strawberries not quite ripe. Jones' sister put them in a saucepan with water and sugar, and boiled them, and I thought them very good with my tea.

NOTE.—Mr. Augustus Jones was Deputy-Surveyor. The family emigrated from Wales to America, and settled on the Hudson River. He was recommended to Governor Simcoe by Mr. Cobden and at the Governor's request came to Canada and practised his profession as surveyor in different parts of the province. His house was built on the shore near Stoney Creek, presumably the site of what was known as the "Salt Works Farm." Augustus Jones and Brant were friends, and owing to the proximity of their homes, exchanges of hospitality were frequently made, and many pleasant hours spent together.

Tues. 16th—We left Jones' at seven, dined near the Twenty, and arrived at eight o'clock at Navy Hall.

CHAPTER XVII.

VISIT OF DUKE DE LA ROCHEFOUCAULD.

In 1795, Mr. Hammond, the British Ambassador at Washington, had informed Governor Simcoe in an official letter that the Duke de la Rochefoucauld-Liancourt, who was on a visit to the United States, proposed paying a visit to Upper Canada and to Niagara. Letters to the same effect came from the Duke of Portland, who was a personal friend of Rochefoucauld's.

The Duke was an eminent man in France. He was born in 1747 and lived beyond the allotted span, for he was eighty years of age when he died in 1827. His loyalty to the unfortunate Louis XVI. was his undoing, for he was compelled to seek other climes while his native France was in the throes of revolution. He spent several years in England and America, but returned to France under the Consulate. There he resumed the active part he had played in education, benevolence and reform.

The Duke was welcomed by the Governor in June, 1795, and accepted his invitation to "remain with him, to sleep in his house and consider ourselves as at home." The visit of the Duke and what he wrote concerning his visit to Upper Canada are not pertinent to the contents of this volume, and will be found in the biography of Governor Simcoe, now in course of preparation. Suffice it to say that the Duke wrote a work on his travels in North America, the contents of which were severely criticized. He seemed to have no appreciation of the fact that he and his party were guests, and he violated all the rules of hospitality by relating private conversations and gossip, coloring and garbling and distorting incidents and conversations as if his purpose was to sow the seeds of discord and ill-feeling. He apparently had no consideration of personal delicacy, and instead of

DUKE DE LA
ROCHEFOUCAULD.

writing in a friendly manner he seemed to regard himself when writing concerning the British Government as a "foreigner and a foe," as the English translator of his volume admits. The Duke was in Canada from the 20th June until the 22nd July, 1795. The Governor, Lord Dorchester, had doubts as to the advisability of his visit, and refused to permit the Duke to descend the St. Lawrence and visit Lower Canada. His remarks about Mrs. Simcoe show he lacked the predominant characteristic of a French gentleman and that he forgot that he was the guest not only of the Governor but of his charming wife, who, with true British hospitality, were both doing all they could to make his visit a pleasant one. He says:— "Mrs. Simcoe is a lady of thirty-six years of age. She is bashful and speaks little; but she is a woman of sense, handsome and amiable, and fulfils all the duties of the mother and wife with the most scrupulous exactness. The performance of the latter she carries so far as to act the part of a private secretary to her husband. Her talents for drawing, the practice of which she confines to maps and plans, enable her to be extremely useful to the Governor."

As an "Anglo-Canadian" (D. W. Smith), who reviewed that part of the Duke's work referring to his visit to Upper Canada, wrote after the death of General Simcoe in 1806, " Was it well done of the *ci-devant* Duke de la Rochefoucauld (while he was fostered by an English Governor, in a country where he was received with as much attention as if he had then actually enjoyed his honours and his prosperity) to publish to the world that this exemplary lady performed the duties of a wife with so much scrupulous exactness as to act the part of a private secretary to her husband? Was she thus to be metamorphosed into a clerk because she sometimes copied her husband's confidential despatches? Fye, sir—you should have respected the lady's delicate feeling; although you had none such for her lord. But Mrs. Simcoe is well known to all who loved and followed the General's fortunes, and no reflection on her conduct, whether powerful or puerile, can shake their attachment to the relict of their friend, or induce the world to believe or form any opinion on the Duke's assertions, except that of ill-nature and ingratitude in his own breast."

Dr. Scadding in his work of "Toronto of Old" writes that the Duke in his statement about Mrs. Simcoe might have added "that her skill, facility and taste were attested by numerous sketch-books and portfolios of Canadian scenery in its primitive condition, taken by her hand, to be treasured up carefully and reverently by her immediate descendants, but unfortunately not accessible generally to Canadian students."

Mrs. Simcoe was not favorably impressed with her visitors. She thought "their appearance is perfectly democratic and dirty," and this conviction was evidently a settled one, for she writes, "I dislike them all."

Mon. 22nd—The Duke de Liancourt arrived, strongly recommended by the Duke of Portland, Mr. Hammond, etc.; therefore Genl. Simcoe is obliged to pay every attention to him. He is attended by Mr. Gilmard, an Englishman, a French naval officer named Dupetit-Thouars, and M. de Blacons. Their appearance is perfectly democratic and dirty.

Wed. 24th—Monsr. Blacons returns immediately to the United States, where, I hear, he keeps a shop. Monsr. Dupetit-Thouars and Gilmard are going to visit York.

Mon. 29th—The Governor took the Duke de Liancourt to see Forty-Mile Creek. I dislike them all.

Thur. July 2nd—The Governor returned. Mrs. McGill came to stay a few days with me during the Commissary's absence.

MRS. TICE'S HOUSE, NEAR QUEENSTOWN, WHERE MRS. SIMCOE SPENT PART OF THE SUMMER OF 1795.

(From a Drawing by Mrs. Simcoe.)

THE POWELL FAMILY

Sun. 12th—The thermometer 95 in the shade.

Tues. 21st—Mrs. McGill returned to York.

Fri. 24th—Coll. and Mrs. Campbell, from Detroit, dined with me.

Sat. Aug. 1st—Excessive hot day. Coll. and Mrs. Campbell went in our boat to Queenstown; we rode. From thence they drove up the mountain, and we dined in the arbour by the side of the river, from which we were driven by a violent shower. We drank tea at Mrs. Hamilton's, and came home in the boat.

Wed. 5th—We went to the Queenstown landing with Mrs. Macaulay, and dined by the rock which Hennepin mentions; a very pleasant day.

NOTE.—Father Louis Hennepin, a missionary, arrived at Quebec in 1675, and joined the party of La Salle in 1678. When they reached the Illinois River La Salle was forced to return and Hennepin proceeded without him in 1680, exploring the Upper Mississippi. His picture of the Falls of Niagara is the earliest picture of the cataract known. He mentions a rock at Niagara, and calls it "le Gros Rocher." It is between the two falls.

Mon. 10th—The House of Assembly (the fourth session of the first Legislature) prorogued to-day.

NOTE.—It is true that York was now the official capital, but there was no building in York that would accommodate the Legislature, so it continued to be held at Niagara.

CHIEF JUSTICE
POWELL.

Tues. 11th—We rode to Judge Powell's; dined at Mrs. Tice's, and obtained her consent to our staying a fortnight at her house. She is to give us two rooms, and we are to have a tent pitched for the servants. The situation is peculiarly dry and healthy, on the mountain five miles from the Falls of Niagara. There is a shed or gallery before the house, and some oak trees close to it. Therefore there is always shade and cool air here when we were suffering from intense heat at Navy Hall. We rode home in the evening.

MRS. POWELL.

NOTE.—Chief Justice William Dummer Powell was born in Boston in 1755. The grandfather of the Chief Justice came from England as Secretary to Lieutenant-Governor Dummer. The family was an old Welsh one, their estate in Wales being known as Caer-Howell. When a lad of nine, William Dummer was sent to England to be educated, and from there went to Holland to acquire a knowledge of French and Dutch, and in 1772 returned to Boston. In 1779 he was called to the bar by the Middle Temple, and in 1789 appointed a Commissioner of the Peace of the Province of Quebec. In this year he left Montreal with his family for Detroit, which was still in possession of the British. In 1791 he was appointed Commissioner of Oyer and Terminer and Jail Delivery for Quebec, and in 1792 to the same office in Upper Canada. Up to the War of 1812,

281

DIARY OF MRS. SIMCOE

Powell had been a Puisne Judge, but in 1815 was promoted to the Chief Justiceship. The Chief Justice married in 1773 Ann, daughter of Dr. J. Murray of Norwich, England, of the family of Murray of Philiphaugh. He retired from the Bench in 1825, and died in Toronto nine years later. The living descendants of the Chief Justice bearing the Powell name are the families of John Bleecker Powell, Collector of Inland Revenue, Guelph; Arthur Wellesley Powell of Montreal, and Dr. Robert Winyard Powell of Ottawa, Ont. Brindley Powell and William Dummer Powell reside in the United States.

Wed. 12th—We sailed in the boat to the Queenstown landing, and arrived at Mrs. Tice's to dinner. In the evening we walked to the whirl-pool.

Thur. 13th—The Governor drove me in the carriage for the first time; we went to the Falls and returned by starlight, tho' the road has many stumps of trees on the sides, of which I was a little afraid.

Fri. 14th—We breakfasted at six and called on Mrs. Hamilton (wife of Capt. Hamilton) at the Chippawa. On our return stopped at Canby's Mill. From thence the rapids above the Falls appear very grand. Near this mill, about a year ago, a burning spring was discovered, which, if a candle is held to it, will continue flaming a great while.

NOTE.—Captain James Mathew Hamilton, son of Rev. Nicholson Hamilton of Donoghadee, County Down, Ireland, born 1768, was ensign of the 5th Northumberland Regiment of Foot in 1786. He

received his lieutenancy on 16th July, 1794, and his captaincy on 11th August, 1799. He served with his regiment in Canada, being stationed at Mackinac for some time. While there he married Louisa, daughter of Dr. David Mitchell, surgeon-general to the Indian Department, who performed the ceremony, there being no minister of any denomination in that part of the country in those early days. They were remarried by Rev. Robert Addison at Niagara. In

CAPTAIN HAMILTON.   MRS. HAMILTON.

St. Mark's Register the marriage is third on the list, and is thus quaintly recorded: "August 24th, 1792, Captain James Hamilton to Louisa Mitchell his wife. They had been married by some commanding officer or magistrate and thought it more decent to have the first repeated." From the time of Rev. Robert Addison's arrival he kept the register, which became the St. Mark's Church register in 1809, when the church was opened. In 1795, Captain Hamilton was in command at Chippawa and about 1800 he returned to England, where he sold his commission. His wife died in 1802, and he remarried, his second wife being Louisa Jupp. He returned to

282

FORT CHIPPAWA, ON THE RIVER WELLAND, 1795.

(*From a Drawing by Mrs. Simcoe.*)

AN OUTING AT THE FALLS

Canada about 1828. Ann Elizabeth, eldest daughter of Captain James Hamilton by his first wife, married Thomas Gummersall Anderson. One of their daughters is Mrs. W. H. Rowe of Toronto. Mr. Basil G. Hamilton of Wilmer, B.C., is a grandson of Captain Hamilton, being descended from the latter's second wife.

Between the village and the falls of Chippawa there were three mills; the lower for the manufacture of flour; the two upper mills, which were near to each other, and adjoining to the road, were for the purpose of sawing timber into boards, and for manufacturing iron. The latter mills are referred to as Canby's and Burch's, as Benjamin Canby and John Burch had mills in this locality.

About three miles from Chippawa, in the township of Willoughby, there is a spring of water whose vapor is highly inflammable, and is emitted for a time with a considerable degree of force. If collected within a narrow compass, it is capable of supporting combustion for nearly twenty minutes, and of communicating to water placed over it in a small confined vessel the degree of boiling temperature.

Fri. 14th—I went to see it to-day, but it has not been cleared out for some time, and the cattle having trod in it and made it muddy, it did not deserve the name of the burning spring. We had our small tent and some cold meat hung under the carriage. We pitched the tent near the Falls and dined, after which, being fatigued by the heat, I lay down in the tent and slept, lulled by the sound of the Falls, which was going to sleep in the pleasantest way imaginable. After tea we had a very pleasant drive home.

Sat. 15th—The Governor drove the children to the whirlpool, and I rode part of the way; we carried our tent and provisions as yesterday, and dined on a point from whence the whirlpool and the opposite bank of the river, on which is a mill, form altogether a very fine scene; the mill appears like a part of the perpendicular flat rock on which it stands. In the bay (or whirlpool), formed by two immensely high points of land, are now a number of logs collected by Canby at his saw mill above the Falls; the dam which confined them having given way in a flood, the logs came down the Falls and were stopped here by the various strong eddies in this agitated pool, where they whirl about, and probably will continue so till the end of the world, for they never appear to go beyond the circle of a certain distance, and sometimes are set quite upright by the currents; it is a curious scene.

Sun. 16th—A most excessive hot day. The Governor went to Navy Hall.

Mon. 17th—The weather extremely warm; the Governor returned at eleven. This evening we drove to a farm inhabited by Painter. It is just opposite the Fort Schlosser Fall. I was so delighted with the sight of the Falls from this spot, just above what is called the "Indian ladder," which gives so different a view of them from what I saw at the Table Rock that I am determined to return here again. The road is tolerable for a carriage. It was quite dark before we got home.

NOTE.—The Indian Ladder was on the Canadian side, and a second ladder was made near it for Mrs. Simcoe more easily to descend. The ladder consisted of a tall cedar with the branches lopped off about a foot from the trunk and placed against the face of the cliff. By some it was said to be about half a mile below, or north of Table

Rock, by others a mile. It is said there was also an Indian ladder on the American side. Colonel John Clarke in his Memoirs (Ontario Historical Society Records, Vol. VII., 1906) says "I, however, remember the Indian Ladder (so called), having often gone down on it, being only a long pine tree with the branches cut off, leaving only enough to place your foot on, to hold to, when ascending or descending."

Wed. 19th—At home all day—a thunderstorm.

Thurs. 20th—A wet morning. The Governor went to Navy Hall. A cold evening. Mr. Pilkington called.

Sat. 22nd—The Governor drove towards the Falls in the evening.

Sun. 23rd—In the evening we rode to the mill near the whirlpool. I made a sketch, in which a large, living birch tree, suspended by the roots, with the head downwards, hanging between a bold rifted rock near a cascade, if well drawn, would have a most picturesque appearance. The miller who lives here has a project of finding means to drag these logs on shore, in which case it will answer him to build a saw mill here, for it is not unusual for floods to bring down a quantity of logs from Canby's mill, and the timber is not at all injured by having passed the great Fall.

Mon. 24th—Mr. Pilkington, having been desired to put one or two short ladders to make the descent easy from rock to rock by the side of the "Indian Ladder," which is a notched tree, we set out to-day, determined to make our way to the bottom of the rocks below the Falls. We stopped near Painter's house to look at the Fort Schlosser Fall, and then descended the hill, which I found much easier than had been represented, and very little more difficult than the usual way to the Table Rock, altho' it carried us so many feet below it. I rested half-way, and sketched the rock and ladder above me. The view from the margin of the water is infinitely finer than from the Table Rock. We were near a mile distant from it. The Governor walked with a guide nearly underneath it, but as the path over the rocks was bad and not one picturesque scene to be gained by it, I did not attempt going, but sat endeavouring to sketch the scene till my paper was quite wet by the spray from the Fort Schlosser Fall. The quantity of cypress and cedar with which the sides of the rocks are covered adds greatly to the beauty and richness of the scenery. We dined on the rocks beneath the overhanging cedars. A man speared a large sturgeon this afternoon near where we were working. As we ascended the hill again, when near the top of it I stopped to observe a most picturesque view of the Falls, seen in parts thro' the rough spreading branches of hemlock spruce trees, which formed a noble foreground, and the setting sun added richness to the scene. I rested myself at Painter's house, where they prepared, besides tea, those cakes, baked in a few minutes on an iron before the fire, which the people of the States make so well; eggs and sweetmeats, and bacon or salt fish, they usually offer with tea. I believe it is a more substantial meal with them than their dinner, which is slight.

I came home by moonlight after a most pleasant day. All the time I have been at Mrs. Tice's has been filled up with seeing the most delightful scenery, and nothing to interrupt the pleasure of dwelling on the sights. The waggons arrived to carry the General's baggage to Fort Erie. He is going as far as Long Point, on Lake Erie.

Tues. 25th—The Governor and I and Francis went in the carriage to Fort Chippawa, but finding the baggage had not arrived, could proceed no further; dined and slept at Capt. Hamilton's, who commands here.

We walked this evening, and I made some sketches. Weather excessively hot; the Governor very ill. We slept in a room in the Block House, where the logs were some distance apart. Without this contrivance, used

MOUTH OF THE WELLAND RIVER, AT CHIPPAWA, ONT.

(From a Drawing by Mrs. Simcoe.)

A DAY AT FORT ERIE

as loopholes in the case of attack, as well as for admitting air, I think the heat would have been insufferable; as it was, I left my bed and lay on the floor.

Wed. 26th—Went out early in the boat with Capts. Darling and Smith. The latter brought me a thermometer I had been long wishing for, and the Governor bought it of an officer going to England; almost immediately it fell out of my hand and was broken, to my great vexation. The Governor set out on horseback, but finding himself very ill, made signs to come ashore, which we did half-way between the Chippawa and Fort Erie, and at a very good farmhouse he stay'd the whole of the day till six in the evening, when we proceeded in the barge to Fort Erie. We ordered dinner and made ourselves quite at home here, supposing it an inn, and afterwards found we were mistaken. It was not an inn, but the home of a very hospitable farmer. The whole of the shore we passed to-day is flat and uninteresting. About Fort Erie the verdure is greater than I have seen in Canada, and, being unaccustomed to green without being enriched by warm brown tints, it gave me such an idea of damp and cold that I immediately put on a fur tippet and thought it quite comfortable, tho' there was no particular change in the weather, but only in the tints. I saw some of the vessels which are built on this lake and rigged like scows, a large, flat bottomed boat. They are better painted, and have a more respectable appearance than those on Lake Ontario.

We slept in an indifferent house, two miles beyond the Fort, kept by very dirty people, but it has the advantage of being very near the lake.

NOTE.—Fort Erie is in Welland County, on Lake Erie. It was first fortified during the French occupation and greatly strengthened during the War of 1812. Since then it has gone gradually to decay and has long been dismantled.

Thurs. 27th—An excessive hot day. We pitched the tent among some trees near the beach, which is a very pleasant spot, and the house is too dirty to stay in. I dined in my tent, the Governor at the Fort. The beach is covered with flat rocks, among and upon which are cray fish in very shallow pools of water. I amused myself by catching them. The lake is narrow here, and has not the sea-like appearance of Ontario. The opposite shore is seen and some rising land beyond it, but a flat horizon, without fine-shaped or pointed hills.

Fri. 28th—The heat intense; if my thermometer had not been broken I might have ascertained it. I sat in my tent; the flat rocks and shallow water extend a prodigious way into the lake. One of the servants went to the lake to wash his clothes. Francis followed him up to his knees in water and sat on a rock by him; presently an Indian went to wash his clothes, and the group looked very picturesque. Francis came back completely wet to fetch a loaf of bread he desired to give to the Indian. Commodore Grant arrived to-day from Detroit in the " Chippawa," the largest of the King's vessels on this lake. There was an Indian council to-day. *The Governor had company at dinner. I dined in my room.*

Sat. 29th—Breakfasted in the tent. The Governor went to an Indian council; he returned to an early dinner, intending to go this evening to Point Abino on his way to Long Point. I accompanied him in his carriage to Fort Erie, from whence I went in a boat to the Chippawa. Mr. Bing, having just arrived from Detroit, went with me. I slept at Capt. Hamilton's, who is commandant at the Chippawa, where we arrived about nine. Mr. Bing went on to Niagara.

NOTE.—Fort Chippawa was dismantled after the War of 1812.

Point Abino, or Bertie, or Ridgeway, is in Welland County, nine miles from Buffalo. It was here that the Fenians crossed into

DIARY OF MRS. SIMCOE

Canada West in 1866. Mr. Bing was probably the man who afterwards became major-general and who fought against Bonaparte.

Sun. 30th—The weather was so hot I gave up my intention of riding to Mrs. Tice's, but having no gentleman with me I was obliged to drive the carriage myself, which I had never done, and the roads were excessively rough till after passing by the Falls. I tied Francis into the carriage and drove him very safely, altho' he complained of being much bruised and shook. A violent rain began just as I arrived at Mrs. Tice's.

Mon. 31st—A Moravian woman, married to a farmer near here, brought me a loaf of bread so peculiarly good that I could not but enquire about it. She said that it was made with rennet and whey, without yeast or water, and baked in wicker or straw baskets, which is the method taught at the Moravian School at Bethlehem (on the Lehigh River, in Pennsylvania), in the States, where she was educated. The bread was as light as possible and rich, like cake. This woman brought a wild turkey here during my absence; another has been seen. Mrs. Tice has the finest melons imaginable. I prefer water melons, and eat two or three every day. The Indian corn is just now in proper state for boiling or roasting; it begins to turn yellow. Francis and I dine upon it. All the vegetables are particularly good, and I eat little else. The Asiatics eat no meat in the summer, and I daresay they are right, and the heat here nearly approaches to that in the east. The people here in the summer live chiefly on vegetables and a little salt pork. Now the wild pigeons are coming of which there are such numbers that, besides those they roast and eat at present, they salt the wings and breasts of them in barrels, and at any time they are good to eat after being soaked. There is a pond before this house where hundreds of them drink at a time; it is singular that this pond rises and falls as a river does, tho' it is such an immense height above it. The May apples are now a great luxury; I have had some preserved, and the hurtleberries are ripe. Baron La Hontan says the root of the May apples (or, as the French call them, *citrons sauvages*) is poisonous.

Tues. Sept. 1st—I rode to the little mill near the whirlpool; while I sat sketching, the trees around were covered with pigeons.

Wed. 2nd—A very wet day; notwithstanding, I rode in the evening to drink tea with Mrs. Powell, wife of Chief Justice Powell, who was alone. She is a very sensible, pleasant woman. It was very dark and wet coming home. Elderflower leaves take off the pain of the gout or rheumatism.

Fri. 4th—Dined at Mrs. Powell's; met Mrs. Richardson, wife of Dr. R.

Sat. 5th—Capt. Hamilton called. No news from Fort Erie yet.

Sun. 6th—I walked to Mrs. Powell's this evening.

Mon. 7th—I walked a mile this evening to the spring from whence this house is supplied with drinking water. I gathered two kinds of yellow flowers, which are sweet after sunset. I believe it is salep. Cat mint in tea is a good stomatic, and sweet marjorie tea for the headache. Sweet briar and boiling water poured over it, put into jars, milk pans or anything that is to be washed out, purifies them sooner and better than anything else. Mrs. Tice uses it constantly in her dairy.

Tues. 8th—Mrs. Smith dined with me. I walked in the evening to Mrs. Powell's. I was feverish, and felt great relief from a saline draught taken in the effervescent state, a little salt of wormwood water and two teaspoonfuls of lemon juice. I hear the people in the Lower Settlement (Queenstown) are suffering severely by the ague. There are a great many sassafras trees in the woods near Navy Hall, and they are very beautiful and sweet. There are also a great many sumach shrubs by the river. I gathered the branches of flowers of the sumach last year and poured boiling water upon them, which tastes like lemonade; it has a very restringent, hard taste.

A GLIMPSE OF THE LAKE AND BEACH NEAR FORT ERIE.

(From a Drawing by Mrs. Simcoe.)

MINERAL SPRINGS ALONG NIAGARA RIVER

Wed. 9th—I walked this evening into a field which was clearing, to see the immense large fires.

Thurs. 10th—I dined with Mrs. Powell, whose company is very pleasant to me.

Fri. 11th—I walked two miles thro' the woods below the mountains to see a spring which has been lately discovered, which is said to cure lameness, blindness and every disorder. The water tasted like ink and looks very dark. It smells very sulphurous, and so does the earth all around it extremely strong of brimstone.

Sat. 12th—The Governor returned, and is far from well. He was pleased with Long Point, which he called Charlotteville; the banks on the lake 150 feet high; on the shore grew weeping willows, covered with vines; he gathered some grapes already sweet. He returned up the Grand River, from thence crossed a short portage into the Welland, which he descended to Fort Chippawa. He went part of the journey on horseback, and was much annoyed by passing wasps' nests. The wasps stung the horses terribly.

NOTE.—Years before a settlement was made at or near Long Point Lieutenant-Governor Simcoe proposed to found there a military establishment to aid in the defence of the new province of Upper Canada, for he claimed that at Long Point was "the only good roadstead on Lake Erie" and "admirably adapted for settlements." Here he laid out a site for Government buildings and called it "Charlotte Villa," and the township of Charlotteville was named in honor of Queen Charlotte. The township fronts on Long Point Bay. Lord Dorchester, however, objected to this founding of a military settlement. In 1812 Fort Norfolk was built at Charlotteville, but nothing except the trenches remain.

Mon. 14th—We walked to the mineral spring.

NOTE.—Along the boundaries of the River Niagara, and behind the Falls, the elevated and rocky banks were everywhere excavated by sulphurous springs, the vitriolic acid uniting with the limestone rock, and forming plaster of paris, which was here and there scattered amid the masses of stone composing the beach beneath. These excavations extended in many places to a distance of fifty feet underneath the summit of the bank. With reference to the mineral spring, an old resident of Niagara-on-the-Lake states that it was near the old military hospital, which information he gives on the authority of the doctor of the Royal Canadian Rifles at Niagara-on-the-Lake in 1850-6. The military hospital was formerly the Indian Council House marked on a map of 1799 as well as on later maps. The Council House was converted into a hospital in 1822. It lies on the common near Butler's Barracks almost a mile from Navy Hall, and on the line between the two.

Tues. 15th—The Governor much worse. The heat excessive. I fell thro' a trap-door in my room into a cellar, but was not very much bruised.

Sat. 19th—We walked to Mrs. Powell's.

Tues. 22nd—We walked with Francis to the school, where he goes every day, a mile from this house. He carries some bread and butter or cheese for dinner with him, and returns in the evening.

DIARY OF MRS. SIMCOE

Thurs. 24th—Rode to the mill. The Governor very ill. His disorder is bilious fever.

NOTE.—This mill was in all probability the Servos mill, situated on the Four Mile Creek.

Fri. 25th—Very hot weather. Rode to Lutes' farm this evening. Mrs. Tice has a number of standard peach trees; some produce small fruit, others large, quite green, but very well flavoured, tho' they look unpromising.

NOTE.—This farm near Niagara was owned by Samuel Lutes, or Lutz, as it is also spelled. In the first census of Niagara in 1782 Samuel Lutz is given as having cleared eighteen acres of land, and in the list of farms on the Niagara River and back from it, near St. David's, mention of three farms belonging to Samson Lutes is made.

Sun. 27th—A wet day and very co'd.
Thurs. Oct. 1st—Mrs. Powell drank tea with me.
Fri. 2nd—Left Mrs. Tice's; went to Navy Hall; a very cold night.
Sat. 3rd—A sultry day.
Thurs. 15th—A most violent storm on Lake Erie. Mr. Tukel lost.
Sun. Nov. 1st—A little snow fell.
Wed. 4th—Fine weather. We breakfasted with Mrs. Hamilton.

BASS ISLAND, WEST END OF LAKE ERIE.
(From a Drawing by Lieutenant Pilkington, copied by Mrs. Simcoe.)

CHAPTER XVIII.

VISIT TO NEW CAPITAL OF UPPER CANADA.

Late in the autumn of 1795 Mrs. Simcoe again went to York, leaving Navy Hall on 13th November. The trip across the lake occupied nine hours and was made in the schooner "Governor Simcoe," which was considered a fast sailer. Although the Governor is not mentioned as one of the party, he was at York on 1st January, 1796, and apparently recovering from an illness, for Mrs. Simcoe writes on that day, "The Governor infinitely better, can walk four or five miles without fatigue."

There are no entries in the diary between November 13th and the 1st December, while record of happenings was kept with irregularity until the following March. Indeed, it would appear that the diary was only kept at intervals when Mrs. Simcoe was away from Navy Hall. This visit to York was a prolonged one. It covered five months, for Mrs. Simcoe did not return to Navy Hall till the 29th of April, 1796.

She writes on leaving Navy Hall in November:—

Fri. 13th—We left Navy Hall at eight o'clock in the "Governor Simcoe," and arrived at York at five; drank tea with Mrs. McGill. Mr. Lawrence is come with us; he is lately from the States. The Hessian fly has destroyed much of the crops in the Bay of Quinte.

NOTE.—A biographer writes:—"John Brown Lawrence of New Jersey was a member of the Council, and a distinguished lawyer. He was born in Monmouth County. His inclination was to take part in the Revolution; but, suspected by the Whigs from the first, because of his official relations to the Crown, he was finally arrested and imprisoned in the Burlington jail for a long time. Accused of treasonable intercourse with the enemy, he was tried and acquitted. His imprisonment proved a fortunate circumstance. Lieutenant-Colonel John G. Simcoe, commander of the Queen's Rangers, was a fellow prisoner, and when exchanged, said at parting, 'I shall never forget your kindness.' He did not; and when appointed Lieutenant-Governor of Canada, he invited Mr. Lawrence to settle there. The invitation was accepted, and, favored by the Governor, he acquired a large tract of Crown land. . . . Mr. Lawrence died, I conclude from circumstances, in Upper Canada about the year 1796."

Tues. Dec. 1st—A summer day.
Tues. 8th—Mr. Lawrence says the tough skins from the inside of wild pigeons' gizzards, hung up to dry, and grated to a fine powder, is an infallible cure for indigestion.
Fri. 18th—Francis brings all the wood I burn in my stove from the woodyard; I think the exercise is of service to him. He has to-day a

DIARY OF MRS. SIMCOE

little sledge to draw it upon. Mr. Jones, the surveyor, says seven hundred rattlesnakes were killed near Burlington Bay this summer. They live in caves, and in very dry weather go down to the lake to drink; they are sluggish, and, as they move in numbers at a time, probably would be easier destroyed than many other reptiles. The man is quite recovered who was bitten by one last August.

Sun. 20th—A boat going to the "Head of the Lake" with letters lost her bottom near the River Credit, but the men were saved, being near the shore.

Tues. 22nd—I walked towards the town; the snow deep enough to drive a sleigh.

Fri. 25th—A frost. Mrs. Shaw dined with us.

Sun. 27th—A slight shock of an earthquake was felt this morning about five o'clock by the Governor and almost every person in the garrison but myself. The weather is calm, and there is no appearance of the lake having risen. An express from Kingston.

Mon. 28th—Walked to the town. A party began to-day to cut a road from hence to the Pine Fort, near Lake Simcoe. Mr. Jones, the surveyor, says the Indians killed over 500 deer in a month within a fence of seven miles; they cut down trees and laid them in a circle of that extent; the deer were afraid to pass the apparent fence and were easily shot.

NOTE.—At the Holland River was the Pine Fort called Gwillimbury, after "Gwillim," Mrs. Simcoe's maiden name. In 1799, Yonge Street ended at this Pine Fort.

Fri. Jan. 1st, 1796—The Governor infinitely better, can walk four or five miles without fatigue, probably owing to the cold season of the year. An express from Kingston. Mrs. Macaulay came to see me and we had a dance. There are ten ladies here, and as they dance reels we can make up a ball.

Mon. 18th—A ball and firing, as usual on this day (Queen's birthday). A very cold night.

Tues. 19th—I walked with Mrs. Macaulay; a bear killed by "The Man of the Snakes." I do not like the meat. It is like pork. Mr. McGill drinks tea made of hemlock pine. It is not pleasant, but thought wholesome.

Sat. 23rd—We walked on the ice to the house which is building on Francis' 200 acre lot of land. It is called Castle Frank, built on the plan of a Grecian temple, totally of wood, the logs squared and so grooved together that in case of decay any log may be taken out. The large pine trees make pillars for the porticos, which are at each end 16 feet high. Some trees were cut and a large fire made near the house, by which venison was toasted on forks made on the spot, and we dined. I returned home in the carriole. Several people were fishing on the River Don thro' holes cut in the ice; the small red trout they catch are excellent. I gathered black haws; the roots of the trees, boiled, are a cure for complaints in the stomach.

NOTE.—This entry shows that Castle Frank was used as a camp not only in the summer, but also in the wintertime. The building was not completed till June, 1796.

Sun. 24th—A very cold day. I walked to Major Smith's lot, on which I gathered keys of the sugar maple and partridge berries. They are scarlet, growing on a creeping plant like stone cress.

Mon. 25th—Very cold weather; the bay frozen across.

Thurs. 28th—Drove again to Castle Frank, and dined again in the woods on toasted venison. The ice is excellent. The berries of the moun-

298

SITE OF CHARLOTTEVILLE, AT LONG POINT, 1795.
(From a Drawing by Lieutenant Pilkington, copied by Mrs. Simcoe.)

tain tea or winter green are now in great beauty, their bright scarlet berries peeping thro' the snow and the rich colour of their green leaves; they taste like orgeat (or barley syrup), but are of a very warm nature and raise the spirits.

Fri. 29th—Excessive cold weather. I walked to the town; the Governor drove round the bay to Gibraltar Point.

NOTE.—The route was east along the present Queen Street to Woodbine Avenue, thence over the peninsula to the site of the lighthouse. There were too many small lagoons for pleasant walking north of this to the actual spit of land known as "Gibraltar Point."

SKINNER'S MILL, DON RIVER.
(From a Drawing by Mrs. Simcoe.)

Tues. Feb. 2nd—Mrs. Richardson went with me to Castle Frank; it is not yet floored; the carpenters are building a hut for themselves. I gathered fox berries. They grow like small red currants on a delicate plant. The water elder berries are here called tree cranberries, and are less bitter than in England. We had an immense fire to-day, and dined on toasted venison.

Wed. 3rd—We drove on the ice to Skinner's Mill, a mile beyond Castle Frank, which looked beautiful from the river. The ice became bad from the rapidity of the river near the mill. At the mouth of the Don I fished from my carriole, but the fish are not to be caught, as they were last winter, several dozen in an hour. It is said that the noise occasioned by our driving constantly over this ice frightens away the fish, which seems probable, for they are still in abundance in the Humber, where we do not drive; 15 dozen were caught there a few days ago. The Governor finds great benefit by driving out this cold weather, and likes my dormeuse very much. The children sit in front of it.

NOTE.—Timothy Skinner's grist mill was on the east bank of the Don River. To reach it one had to drive down the old Don Mills

Road, a continuation of Broadview Avenue. The mill is just below Todmorden. It was built in 1794, on Lot 13, township of East York, for lots 13 and 14 belonged to the Skinner family. Parshall Terry, a member of the first Legislature, helped to build the mill, which was operated by Mr. Timothy Skinner for some years, and then by Mr. Colin Skinner, who took Mr. John Eastwood into partnership, and they used the building as a paper mill. It is claimed that the first paper in Upper Canada was made in this mill in 1826. Skinner and Eastwood both married into the Helliwell family, and on Mr. Eastwood's death the property came into possession of Thomas, Joseph and William Helliwell. In 1847 it passed into the hands of the Taylor Bros. During their time it was twice destroyed by fire, and once during the ownership of the present owner, Mr. Robert Davies. The walls, which were of stone, stood, however, and a new roof and floors made the building as it was first built.

Thurs. 4th—We drove three miles to the settlement below the town (across the Don River), and at Mrs. Ashbridge's saw calabashes, the fruit of the calabash tree, a vessel made of a dried gourd or shell—a gourd plant, which have holes cut in them as bowls to ladle out water, having a natural handle. I brought away some of the seeds, which are to be sown in March, in rich ground. Might not the use of these calabashes, which are in shape like skulls, have given rise to the story of the southern Indians drinking out of the skulls of their enemies? I saw Mr. Richardson's infant laid in a box, which he held by a cord, and was skating up the bay; this gave the child air and exercise.

NOTE.—George Ashbridge emigrated from Yorkshire, England, to the United States and settled in Pennsylvania near Philadelphia in 1698. He had several sons and daughters. His eldest son, John, born in 1702, married Hannah Davies, of Pennsylvania. Their eldest son, Jonathan, born 1734, married Sarah James. After Jonathan Ashbridge's death his widow and family settled in York. She died 13th June, 1801. There were two sons, John and Jonathan, and several daughters, two of whom were Sarah, who married Mr. Heron of Niagara, and Mary, who married Mr. Parker Mills, of York. The descendants of Jonathan Ashbridge are Jesse Ashbridge and Miss Hannah Lambert of Toronto, Jonathan of Scarboro and W. T. Ashbridge of British Columbia. Of John's descendants in Toronto there are Albert J. Ashbridge and Mrs. R. Short, also Mrs. Hagerman of Victoria Square. The original Ashbridge home was on Township lots 8 and 9 in the First Concession from the bay, now No. 1470 Queen Street East, just west of the corner of Morley Avenue and Queen Street, Toronto.

Fri. 5th—Mrs. McGill, Miss Crookshank and a large party drove with me in carrioles to dine on toasted venison by a large fire on the beach below the settlements. We sat under the shelter of the root of an immense pine, which had been blown up by the wind, and found it very pleasant, and returned six miles in 32 minutes. Had a card party in the evening.

Sat. 6th—The ladies did not catch cold, and were delighted with the novelty of dining in the air in winter, so to-day we went to Castle Frank.

QUEBEC CARRIOLES ON TORONTO BAY

Mrs. Macaulay joined the party. The ice was not quite so good, and the snow melted. It was so mild we could not wear great-coats. Francis has a small sleigh, which the servants have taught a goat to draw; he is the handsomest goat I ever saw, and looks very well in harness. It is a very pretty sight to see Francis drawn in this car. They used the animal to draw the sleigh by making him draw it full of wood. At first he was very untractable.

Mon. 8th—We set out on the ice with three carrioles brought from Quebec, but driving too near a large crack in the ice near the shore the horses in the first carriole broke in, but being quickly whipped, recovered their footing on the ice and drew the carriole over the crack. We got out of our carriage, and Mr. Givins thought he would drive better and pass safely, but the horses plunged much deeper and could not extricate themselves. With difficulty the harness was unloosed, and they were set free without injury, the water not being above five feet deep.

We walked over to Mr. Macaulay's lot and dined in that part of the woods, and in the evening I walked home; but the carrioles went very safely across the bay, keeping further from the crack, and perhaps the night air made the ice harder. John Macaulay, who is but four years old, cut through some large pieces of wood with an axe, which made Francis emulous to become an axeman also; he is going to begin to-morrow.

NOTE.—On September 1st, 1797, by patent from the Crown, Dr. James Macaulay became the owner of Park Lot No. 9, consisting of a hundred acres having a frontage of 660 feet on Lot (Queen Street) from Yonge Street west and extending from Lot Street to Bloor, a distance of 6,600 feet on the west side of Yonge. On the same date David W. Smith, Surveyor-General, became the owner of Park Lot No. 10, lying to the west of the Macaulay lot, with the same frontage and depth. On October 16th, 1797, Mr. Smith traded his lot, No. 10, to Chief Justice John Elmsley in return for other lands which are not named.

The Chief Justice was anxious to have a frontage on Yonge Street, and on May 30th, 1799, he traded the south half of his lot to Dr. Macaulay for the north half of Lot No. 9. Thus Dr. Macaulay became the owner of the entire block of property extending from the north-westerly corner of Lot Street to the present College Street and from Yonge Street to a point 132 feet west of Elizabeth Street. On the front portion of this block fronting on Lot Street Dr. Macaulay laid out a plan of 41 lots, which he called "Teraulay." On this plan James, Teraulay and Elizabeth Streets are shown running from Lot Street north 380 feet to Macaulay Lane, now Albert Street. The entire block owned by Macaulay gradually became settled and was given the local name of Macaulay Town. This property at the issue of the patent was worth a few hundred dollars. To-day it is worth about $30,000,000.

The youthful axeman to whom Mrs. Simcoe refers was John Simcoe Macaulay, born in October, 1791, eldest son of Dr. Macaulay.

The dwelling of Dr. Macaulay in Toronto was a commodious colonial cottage, known as "Teraulay Cottage," where Holy Trinity Church now stands. Sir James B. Macaulay, second son of Dr. Macaulay, built about 1843 a fine brick residence on the south side of College Street near Yonge. The site is now occupied by the Bishop Strachan School for girls.

LIEUT. GIVINS.

Lieutenant James Givins, afterwards Colonel Givins, was Superintendent of Indian Affairs. He married Angelique, daughter of Captain Andrews, of the Lake Ontario armed fleet, and he had six sons and three daughters—Henry; James, who was a Judge in London, Ont.; Saltern, who was at one time Rector of St. Paul's Anglican Church, Bloor St., Toronto; Adolphus, Halton and George, of the Medical

CAPT. ANDREWS.

Staff in India; Caroline, who married Colonel Hillier; Cecil and Elizabeth. Judge Givins had five sons and four daughters, James, Warren, Hillier, John and Henry. James and Hillier had commissions in the British Army. Captain Hillier and Henry are the only surviving sons of the late Judge Givins. Of the four daughters, Eliza of Elgin, Ill., the eldest, and Maude, the youngest, of Toronto, are living. The only living descendants of the Rev. Saltern Givins, the third son of Colonel Givins, are Robert C. Givins, his son Robert, and Charlotte C. Givins of Chicago, Ill.

Tues. 9th—A strong easterly wind; a vast quantity of ice driven by it out of the bay—half a mile of ice that we drove over last night is totally gone. A Mohawk, named Jacob, and his wife came here. They are handsome and well dressed. She works any pattern given her in beads remarkably well; they brought Francis a present of cranberries.

Wed. 10th—A wet day. The post arrived from Niagara.

Thurs. 11th—A wet day.

Fri. 12th—There is very little ice left in the bay. Fine weather.

Sat. 13th—Mr. Pilkington, of the Engineers, arrived from Niagara. The sudden thaw obliged him to wade across the inlet at the "Head of the Lake."

NOTE.—This means that Mr. Pilkington walked around the Burlington Beach and waded across the original entrance to Burlington Bay, which had been known as Geneva Lake or Macassa Bay up to 1792, when by proclamation on 16th June of that year the name was changed to Burlington Bay. In the "Topographical Description of Upper Canada," issued in London in 1813, under the authority of Sir Francis Gore, it is stated with regard to Burlington Bay that it was "perhaps as beautiful and romantic a situation as any in the interior of America, particularly if we include with it a marshy lake which falls into it, and a noble promontory that divides them." The picture, which is the only one known of the entrance to the bay, shows the original entrance at the extreme north end of the beach. It was almost landlocked in 1796. It was about a mile and a half north of the present canal begun in 1825 and opened in 1832.

ORIGINAL ENTRANCE TO BURLINGTON BAY, 1796.

(From a Drawing by Mrs. Simcoe.)

HOW WINTER DAYS WERE PASSED

Wed. 17th—The thermometer 15 degrees higher than it was yesterday.
Thurs. 18th—We walked to the town, and from thence drove on the ice to dine at Castle Frank; the ice was good. I made a small sketch of the house. The winter express arrived from Quebec. The party who went to cut the road from hence to Lake Simcoe, called the Yonge Street, are returned after an absence of seven weeks. The distance is 33 miles and 56 chains; they brought two trout from Lake Simcoe weighing about 12 pounds each, but they are not as good as the smaller trout. There are plenty of black bass, maskalonge and whitefish in that lake. I heard an anecdote of black bass which, if true, renders it probable they remain in a torpid state during the winter. An old hollow tree, which lay on the margin of the lake, half under water, being stopped and taken out, 30 black bass were taken out of it. Mr. Lawrence, who went with the party from motives of curiosity, speaks well of the apparent quality of most of the land; 20 miles from hence, near Bond's farm, he saw two small lakes near each other, from whence many fish were taken. He saw no wild animals.

Mr. Lawrence met with some Indians, who invited them to feast on bear's meat. They appeared to use many ceremonies on this occasion, which he did not understand. The head is always presented to the chief of the party, and they make a rule that all that is dressed of bear's meat must be eaten at the feast. Mr. Lawrence brought me two wooden bowls and spoons; they are made by the Indians from the knots or excrescences growing on pine and other large trees; they are stained red by the juice of the inner bark of the hemlock pine, of which they make a decoction on purpose. The children will use these bowls as basins at breakfast when travelling.

Note.—William Bond was a sergeant in the Queen's Rangers. He had a farm on Yonge Street near the Oak Ridge (Lots 62, 63), 1st Concession Whitchurch, east side of Yonge Street. On this property is a crescent-shaped sheet of water called Bond Lake. He had the first nursery garden in York.

Fri. 19th—Mr. Pilkington went in a boat to the "Head of the Lake." We dined in the woods on Major Shanks' farm lot, where an arbour of branches of hemlock pine was prepared; a band of music stationed near. We dined on large perch and venison. Jacob, the Mohawk, was there. He danced Scotch reels with more ease and grace than any person I ever saw, and had the air of a prince. The picturesque way in which he wore and held a black blanket gave it the air of a Spanish cloak; his leggings were scarlet; on his head and arms he wore silver bands. I never saw so handsome a figure.

Mon. 22nd—I went to Castle Frank. The ice on the river was good.
Tues. 23rd—A boat crossing the bay to the storehouses on Gibraltar Point was driven among the ice by a strong east wind, and could not be extricated until eight at night, when a boat carried planks to lay where the ice was rotten, and assisted the men on shore.

Last Sunday I rode to Mr. McGill's lot, above three miles from here, where I was surprised to see the land rise so suddenly; a narrow pine ridge was on a steep ascent; a quantity of good building stone near it. The weather very cold. It snowed fast.

Note.—The blockhouse at the Point stood exactly on the spot where the Toronto Water Works crib stands, just north of the north dock of the Toronto Ferry Company. The formation of the old Gibraltar Point (Hanlan's) has, of course, been entirely changed during the last forty years. At that time the beach was a hundred feet to

DIARY OF MRS. SIMCOE

the east of the Ferry cribwork, and in 1792-1818 there was a large area of beach on which was built the blockhouse. The "storehouses" stood about five or six hundred feet south of the blockhouse, and on the west shore of Blockhouse Bay—hence the name of that stretch of water.

As to the McGill property, some pioneers to the fore forty years ago claimed that McGill had in addition to a hundred acres bounded by Queen, Mutual, Bloor and Bond Streets, land north of Davenport Road. This height of land was originally crowned by a pine grove along its entire face, and portions of the original pine growth still stand west of Bathurst Street and at the head of Dufferin Street.

Thurs. 25th—I went with a party of ladies to Castle Frank. The ice is still good, tho' the weather is warm and hazy like an Indian summer. The young Shaws dined with us.

Fri. 26th—Mild weather. We regret losing the cold, clear air. A boat arrived from the "Head of the Lake" in four hours.

Tues. March 1st—A card party to-night.

Wed. 2nd—The weather very cold. I gathered partridge berries.

Thurs. 3rd—Frost and snow.

Sat. 5th—The winter express set off for Quebec. An Indian and a Canadian came from Matchadash Bay in five days, and said they could have travelled the journey in four. We rode up the Yonge Street and across a pine ridge to Castle Frank.

Sun. 6th—Rode to Castle Frank.

Mon. 7th—Very cold weather.

Sat. 12th—Mrs. Macaulay came; a dance in the evening.

Sun. 13th—Geese and blackbirds seen, which denotes the approach of spring.

Mon. 14th—Rain.

Tues. 15th—Thaw and rain.

Fri. 18th—A great deal of snow.

Sat. 19th—A thin ice covered the bay.

Sun. 27th—Easter Day. The ice went out of the bay this morning, driven by a strong east wind; in the evening the wind changed to the west and drove it back, and as it beat against the shore in a floating surface of very small pieces it made an uncommon and fine sound, which I listened to a great while from the terrace before the house.

Wed. 30th—Wild pigeons arrived.

Thurs. 31st—Walked to Castle Frank and returned by Yonge Street, from whence we rode. The road is as yet very bad; there are pools of water among roots of trees and fallen logs in swampy spots, and these pools, being half frozen, render them still more disagreeable when the horses plunge into them.

Sat. April 2nd—The "York" packet sailed for Niagara and the Genesee River.

Sun. 3rd—Some Indians brought maple sugar to sell in birch bark baskets. I gave three dollars for 30 pounds.

Mon. 4th—Capt. Mayne arrived from New York in 18 days. Some Indians brought some excellent wild geese from Lake Simcoe, and several kinds of ducks, which were very pretty as well as very good. The large black duck is esteemed one of the best. The abundance of wild rice, off which they feed, makes them so much better than wild ducks in England.

Sun. 10th—A little snow. A man arrived from Kingston. He left it the 1st of April; the bay was then entirely frozen. We walked to Castle Frank and rode home. The air was full of pigeons. I think they are fatter and better here than at Niagara.

CAMPING IN APRIL

Sat. 16th—Commissary McGill went to Kingston.

Sun. 17th—Mrs. McGill dined with me. We walked to Mrs. Macaulay's in the evening. Came home by nine o'clock.

Mon. 18th—Francis has not been well. We therefore set off to Castle Frank to-day to change the air, intending to pass some days there. The house being yet in an unfinished state, we divided the large room by sail cloth, pitched the tent on the inner part, where we slept on wooden beds.

It is quite a summer's day. Mosquitos arrived at three o'clock. A large wooden canoe was launched here to-day, built by one of the men who ought to have been busy working at Castle Frank.

Tues. 19th—A letter from Major Littlehales, dated Niagara, 17th of April, mentions the river being full of ice.

Wed. 20th—The porticos here (Castle Frank) are delightfully pleasant, and the room cool from its height and the thickness of the logs of which the house is built; the mountain tea berries in great perfection. Francis is much better, and busy in planting currant bushes and peach trees. There is an insect which is not to be got rid of; it bores into the timber and is heard at night; it is like a very large maggot. I have seen them taken from under the bark of trees to bait fishing hooks.

Sat. 23rd—A strong east wind. Went to the garrison in the evening, as we are soon going to Niagara.

CHAPTER XIX.

A TRIP ACROSS LAKE ONTARIO.

Governor Simcoe had not good health during his term of office in Canada. While he was most careful in his living, yet he had never fully recovered from the strain of the American campaign when he led the Queen's Rangers in its most active work as one of the gallant regiments in the British service. Frequently throughout this diary there are references to his illnesses, as on the occasion of his leaving York for Niagara he was "too ill to go on board." The trip too was a severe one, for the cold was extreme. Yet it was five hours shorter than when Mrs. Simcoe crossed the lake in the "Governor Simcoe" in November; for on that occasion it took nine hours to make a trip that was covered on April 29th in less than four hours. The visit to Niagara extended to the 7th of June, when a return was made to York.

Fri. April 29th—The wind and weather unfavourable for the canoe. Therefore we determined to sail in the "Mohawk." The Governor was too ill to go on board before two o'clock. The wind blew very hard N.N.W. We reached Navy Hall in 3 hrs. ¾. It was so excessively cold I could not remain on deck, and so rough that I was sick in the cabin, and wished I had gone in the canoe.

Sat. 30th—Still very cold and snow. The vessel lately built on Lake Erie, and named by Lord Dorchester the "Francis" (after Mrs. Simcoe's son), is arrived at Fort Erie.

Tues. May 3rd—"The Ottawa," a government boat, left Detroit the 27th of April and came to Fort Erie in 36 hours. Commodore Grant say'd peas were stuck at Detroit, tho' not sown here; but probably that snow-storm which fell as "The Ottawa" left the Detroit River, killed them. It does not answer here to sow seeds in the gardens till May, for tho' the weather may have been long good, when ice comes down from the Upper Lakes in April it occasions the air to be so cold that gardens near the river suffer very much. Major Dodgson made those soldiers who would otherwise have kept a cur keep a sporting dog, by which means he was enabled to hunt hares and deer last winter at Kingston.

NOTE.—Peas in the garden were probably of sufficient height to be trained on sticks, which is quite a common custom.

Major Richard Dodgson of the 60th was captain from 14th July, 1790, and major from 1st March, 1794.

In 1755, Parliament authorized the raising of a regiment of foot in British North America, and the 60th or King's Royal Rifle Corps, formerly the 62nd or the Royal American Regiment of Foot, was formed in 1756. It fought in 1758 at Louisbourg and in 1759 at Quebec, and in 1760 at Montreal. Some of the battalions of the regiment were in various stations in North America and the West Indies from 1760-1876. In 1794 rifles were introduced into the English army, and were first issued to a battalion of the 60th Royal

DEATH OF COLONEL BUTLER

American Regiment of Foot. In 1852, one sergeant and forty privates were lost in the wreck of H.M. troopship "Birkenhead."

Thurs. 5th—Sultry weather.

Sun. 8th—A very cold night; we always feel the N.E. wind severely, being so much exposed to it. At York we are only open to the north. Snow fell last night. Mr. and Mrs. Hamilton dined here.

Mon. 9th—A wet, cold day.

Thurs. 12th—Received a cap from Miss Bond from Philadelphia.

Sunday 15th, Whit-Sunday—Coll. Butler buried (His Majesty's Commissioner for Indian Affairs).

Mon 16th—The House of Assembly opened.

NOTE.—This was the fifth session of the first Legislature.

Tues. 17th—Rode before breakfast. Felt agueish.

Sun. 22nd—Went to the garrison. Mr. Todd dined here. Miss Russell, sister of Hon. Peter Russell, has preserved some winter cherries which are very good.

NOTE.—Miss Russell was Honorable Peter Russell's sister, Elizabeth, who lived with him at Niagara and at York after the latter place was selected by Governor Simcoe as his capital. Their residence was known as "Russell Abbey" near the bay shore on Palace (Front) Street, at the foot of what is now Princess Street, Toronto. Miss Russell, who was her brother's heiress-at-law, survived him by several years. She was a most charitable woman and respected by all who knew her.

Tues. 24th—I rode with Mr. and Mrs. Jarvis to the mountain, to call on Mrs. Powell. I gathered sassafras, a shrub in bloom. I have been drinking the buds in tea, and it has removed the symptoms of ague. Mrs. Powell mentioned about the weather at Detroit, that it was not unusual to see calèches on dusty roads, carrioles on the ice, and ships sailing at the same time.

NOTE.—William Jarvis, fifth son of Samuel Jarvis and Martha Seymour, was born in Stamford, Conn., on 11th September, 1756.

WILLIAM JARVIS.

He was a cornet in the Queen's Rangers, and was engaged during the Revolutionary War. In 1789, he was commissioned as a lieutenant in the Western Regiment of Militia of the County of Middlesex, and on 1st January, 1791, received the commission of captain in the same Regiment. In July, 1792, he was appointed Secretary and Registrar of the Records of the Province of Upper Canada. William married in England in 1785, Hannah Owen Peters,

MRS. JARVIS.

daughter of Samuel Peters, D.D., of Hebron, Conn. Peters was a Loyalist and was spoken of as first Bishop of Upper Canada, but was appointed Bishop of Vermont. He did not take office however, as he was such a dyed-in-the-wool Loyalist that he would not live in the United States.

There were seven children by the marriage of William Jarvis and Hannah Owen Peters:—1. Samuel Peters, who died in childhood. 2. Maria Lavinia, married George Hamilton, the founder of the city of Hamilton. 3. Augusta, married Thomas McCormick. 4. Samuel Peters (2) after whom Jarvis Street, Toronto, was named, married Mary Boyles Powell, daughter of Chief Justice Powell. 5. William Munson, Sheriff of Gore, married Anne Racy. 6. Hannah Owen, married Alexander Hamilton. 7. Ann Elizabeth, married W. B. Robinson, a brother of Chief Justice Robinson.

One of the children of Samuel Peters Jarvis and Mary Boyles Powell was William Dummer Powell, who married Diana Irving, a sister of Sir Æmilius Irving, and had four children:—Mary Æmilia, William Irving, Augusta Lavinia and Edward Æmilius, who is of the firm of Æmilius Jarvis & Co., Toronto. Portraits in oil of Secretary Jarvis and his wife, from which these pictures are taken, are in possession of Mr. Æmilius Jarvis, of Toronto.

Wed. 25th—Walked in the woods. May apples, ladies' slippers in bloom, and a beautiful shrub here called dogwood; it is more like a gum cistus, which yields laudanum.

Sat. 28th—A wet day; the Governor ill.

Wed. June 1st—News received of the Treaty being ratified between Great Britain and the United States.

CHIEF JUSTICE JAY.

NOTE.—The treaty referred to was Jay's Treaty. A writer says:—"Alarmed at the rising spirit of hostility towards Great Britain, Washington determined to make a great effort for peace, and, with the consent of the Senate, sent Chief-Justice John Jay to London, with the offer of a treaty of amity and commerce. Jay undoubtedly did the best that could be done, and on 19th November, 1794, signed a treaty of amity and commerce, which the President and Senate approved in July, 1795. The treaty provided that the pre-revolutionary debts owed to British subjects should be paid by the United States, and that the British Government should indemnify Americans for losses sustained by illegal captures. A large sum of money was afterwards paid on this account. The treaty was assailed in the United States by the party favorable to France. But Alexander Hamilton defended the treaty and it carried by a vote of fifty-eight to fifty-one." Under its terms the fort at the east side of the Niagara River was given up to the United States.

Fri. 3rd—The House of Assembly prorogued. I went with some ladies to hear the Governor's speech on the dissolution. Miss Russell has a collection of plants dried by merely shutting them in books; I wish I had thought of doing so.

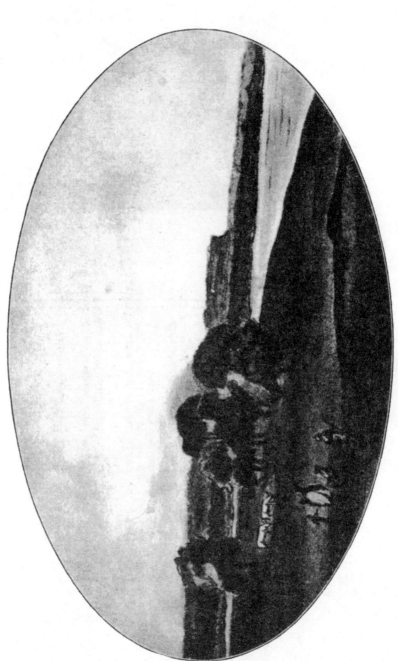

VIEW FROM THE KING'S HEAD INN, 1796.

(From a Drawing by Mrs. Simcoe.)

BALL AND SUPPER AT NAVY HALL

NOTE.—The function at which Mrs. Simcoe was present on 3rd June, 1796, was the prorogation at the end of the fifth and last session of the first Legislature. The dissolution would follow afterward by proclamation.

Sat. 4th—Mr. Pilkington has erected a temporary room adjoining our house for the ballroom to-night. It is 60 feet long, and the end ornamented by colours. We danced 18 couple and sat down to supper 76.

Sun. 5th—Mrs. Smith dined here. I rode in the evening as far as Mr. Sheehan's.

NOTE.—A Captain William Sheehan married Miss Anne Butler in Gosport, England, about the middle of the 18th century. He was an officer in the British army. The only issue of this marriage was Walter Butler Sheehan, who was clerk in the Indian department at Niagara and was in 1793 Sheriff of the County of Lincoln. He married a Miss Andrews, a daughter of Captain Andrews of the Lake Ontario Navy during the War of 1812-4, the issue of this marriage being Walter Butler, Henry Ford, George Hill, James Muirhead, and William, and one daughter, Anne. Walter Butler Sheehan, the eldest son of the sheriff, was Collector of Customs at Dunnville, where a number of his descendants still reside.

Mon. 6th—Francis five years old to-day. Mr. Pilkington drew his picture. The Governor drove me to the Queenstown landing, to take leave of Mrs. Hamilton; it was very cold returning. I drank tea at Mrs. Smith's, and met Mrs. Montigny, wife of Capt. Montigny, on the staff at Detroit, and Miss Hay, a relative of Lieut. Henry Hay, serving at Detroit.

Tues. 7th—We left Navy Hall at ten o'clock in the canoe, followed by a boat. Dined at Twelve-Mile Creek.

Some heavy showers in the afternoon induced us to put into the Twenty-Mile, where, after being tolerably wet and climbing up a hill covered with wet grass, we found an empty house. We had a fire made, dried our clothes and beds, drank tea, and slept well without mosquitos, but the smell of musk-

FRANCIS G. SIMCOE.

rat skins, which had been drying in the house, was disagreeable. Some strawberries ripe, and the fields covered with blue lupines, a kind of gay flowering pulse.

Wed. 8th—We set off at seven, but the men paddled as idly as they did yesterday, so that we did not reach the Forty-Mile Creek (nine miles) till twelve o'clock. I was out of patience that the canoe was so disgraced. We encamped on the Point, where the boards are piled that are brought from the saw mill; the plank afforded a shed for the tent. We walked to John Green's, and as a room was prepared for us we slept there, but dined at the Point. They eat pumpkin pie, which, with lemon juice, was very good. Francis dipped in the lake. Breakfasted at seven and set out.

NOTE.—This house stood about three-quarters of a mile from the lake on what is now Patton Street, being a part of Lot 10, Con. 1, of the township of North Grimsby. It was built north and south, and the wings were added to the main or centre part ten years after the first erection. The north wing was within the past ten years removed to a fruit farm, two miles west of Winona, while the south wing and centre were used later as a waiting room for the Hamilton, Grimsby and Beamsville Railway. The building was subsequently torn down and the site is now occupied by the Presbyterian Manse and the residence of H. H. March.

The Green brothers owned a grist and saw mill which stood on the west side of the road, almost midway between John Green's dwelling and Lake Ontario, the grist mill being on Lot 10 and the saw mill on Lot 9. The frame of the old grist mill is now used

JOHN GREEN'S DWELLING AT THE "FORTY."
(From a Drawing by William Forbes, Grimsby, Ont.)

as a planing mill in connection with a lumber yard, while the saw mill was demolished about fifty years ago.

Thurs. 9th—I saw very grand rocks in going towards the mountain and passed three water falls, the first sombre and beautiful from the water falling from various directions over dark, mossy rocks. The second was pretty from the fine scenery of tall trees, thro' which it shone —the third, just below an old saw mill, falls smoothly for some feet, and is a bright copper color, having passed through swamps; it then rushes into white foam over regular ledges of rocks spreading like a bell, and the difference of color is a fine contrast. The course of this river is a series of falls over wild rocks, the perpendicular banks on each side very high, covered from top to bottom with hemlock, pines, cedars and all forest trees of an immense height. By camping near the bank the water is seen below. There are stones in this water which appear like petrified shells, but Green was not at home and I could not get any fetched to me. Returning we noticed a scene of rocks, the lake below towards Burlington

THE TWENTY-MILE CREEK, JORDAN, ONT., 1796.

(*From a Drawing by Mrs. Simcoe.*)

AT "THE HEAD OF THE LAKE"

Bay, and half a mile to the east an extensive distant view towards the Genesee River and overlooking the country from hence to Niagara. I saw a cream-colour'd hawk, with black-tipp'd wings and a scarlet tail. We saw a rift in the rocks, a narrow pass where wolves descend from the mountain to commit depredations on the sheep below. The woods are full of sarsaparilla. I gathered some wild flax at Green's. In his garden he has quantities of melons near the river, and last year cut 800 pumpkins from three-quarters of an acre of land; they are esteemed excellent food for cows, making the butter particularly good. We dined to-day at our encampment and slept at Green's.

Fri. 10th—A very wet night. I rode to-day towards Anderson's, and dined at one at the encampment, and sent the children and servants to the "Head of the Lake" in the canoe. Mrs. Green went as a guide to conduct us on horseback across the mountain. Green has lately, at the Governor's request and expense, cut a road thro' the wood, making it passable for me to ride. The Governor thinks the country will derive great benefit by opening a road on the top of the mountain (where it is quite dry) from Niagara to the "Head of the Lake," instead of going a most terrible road below, full of swamps, fallen trees, etc. We crossed the creek by the old saw mill at the head of the waterfalls I mentioned yesterday after leaving the Forty-Mile Creek, and found the whole of the way very dry and good; stopped frequently on the edge of the bank to look over the extensive wooded plain below us, which is bounded at four miles distance by Lake Ontario, and the opposite north shore with Flamborough Head discernible.

NOTE.—This is the bend of the mountain north of Burlington, and is quite a feature in the northern horizon, looking from Burlington Beach.

The steep cliffs of the mountain, on the top of which we were, are rocky, covered with wood, the view enlightened by fleeting gleams from a setting sun, the view to the west terminated by Burlington Bay.

The spot that most engaged our attention was named by Green "the Tavern," because when cutting the road the men generally met there to dine, and more wood being here cut down, the view was less obstructed by the trees; from hence we observed the canoe with the children in it. After we had passed these nine miles it grew dusky, and Mrs. Green rather misled us, but at last we found a way, tho' a very steep one, to descend the mountain. A mile before we came to this descent we passed Stony Creek, seven miles from the "Head of the Lake," so named from the stony nature of its bottom. It's a small stream that falls 97 feet in an amphitheatre of bare red rocks, which looked as if they ought to have been covered by a falling lake instead of so small a stream. At the foot of the mountain we came to Adam Green's Mill.

It was eight o'clock, and we had five miles of that terrible kind of road where the horses' feet are entangled among the logs amid water and swamps, to ride by moonlight, rather in the dark, for in the woods the glimmering of the moon is of little use, but rather throws shadows which deceive the traveller, tho' to a picturesque eye they are full of indistinct and solemn beauty, but little serviceable to horses who plunge to their knees in mud pools half full of loose logs.

By daylight I much fear these roads, and had particularly dreaded this, but not being able to see or try to avoid the danger, and my nerves braced by this cold and dry night, I went thro' it not only well but with a degree of pleasure, admiring the unusual brightness of the stars, and the immense apparent height given to the trees by the depth of shade. I was so engaged by the scene that I did not much advert to the cold, which was very great in passing the swampy grounds.

319

DIARY OF MRS. SIMCOE

After three miles we came into good galloping ground on fine turf by the side of the lake, till we came to the "King's Head Inn," at the "Head of the Lake."

Here Walbekanine and a number of his tribe, who are encamped a mile distant, were assembled to compliment the Governor, and fired muskets in our horses' faces, their usual mark of respect, which frightened me and my horse very much; he started and I shrieked, but the sound was lost in the whoops of the Indians. They gave us the largest land tortoise I ever saw.

Sat. 11th—At the King's Head Inn. This house was built by the Governor to facilitate the communication between Niagara and the La Tranche, where he intended to establish the seat of government, and its situation was not without reference to a military position.

THE "HEAD" OF LAKE ONTARIO.
(From a Drawing by Mrs. Simcoe.)

NOTE.—The King's Head stood near the southeast or southerly end of Burlington Bay, near the present filtering basins of the Hamilton Waterworks, and north of the pumping house. The house was two miles south of the Burlington Canal, 200 feet from the bay shore, and its front faced north or northwesterly looking towards the Brant homestead. It stood at the junction of the Hamilton and Stoney Creek road on the west side, between Burlington Bay and Lake Ontario. In connection with the King's Head Inn and its situation, "Topographical Description of Upper Canada" says:— "At the head of Lake Ontario there is a smaller lake, within a long beach, of about five miles, from whence there is an outlet to Lake Ontario, over which there is a bridge. At the south end of the beach is the King's Head, a good inn, erected for the accommodation of travellers, by order of His Excellency Major-General Simcoe, the

COOTE'S PARADISE, NEAR BURLINGTON BAY, 1796.

(From a Drawing by Mrs. Simcoe.)

lieutenant-governor. It is beautifully situated at a small portage which leads from the head of a natural canal connecting Burlington Bay with Lake Ontario, and is a good landmark."

Another inn was intended to be built at the Grand River. There are eight rooms in this house, besides two low wings behind it, joined by a colonnade, where are the offices. It is a pretty plan. I breakfasted in a room to the S.E., which commands the view of the lake on the south shore, of which we discern the Point of the Forty-Mile Creek, Jones' Point and some other houses. From the rooms to the N.W. we see Flamborough Head and Burlington Bay. The sand cliffs on the north shore of Burlington Bay look like red rocks. The beach is like a park covered with large, spreading oaks. At eight o'clock we set out in a boat to go to

THE KING'S HEAD INN, BURLINGTON BAY.
(From a Drawing by Mrs. Simcoe.)

Beasley's, at the head of Burlington Bay, about eight miles. The river and bay were full of canoes; the Indians were fishing; we bought some fine salmon of them. When we had near crossed the bay, Beasley's house became a very pretty object. We landed at it, and walked up the hill, from whence is a beautiful view of the lake, with wooded points breaking the line of shore and Flamborough in the background. The hill is quite like a park, with large oak trees dispersed, but no underwood.

Note.—The location of this point of land was on the north shore of the lake, east of Burlington, Ont.

Richard Beasley was an Indian trader. He was the first settler at the "Head of the Lake." He owned the land now known as Dundurn Park. It is stated by the Beasley descendants that the house of Richard Beasley was west of the present site of Dundurn Castle and that the building was afterwards incorporated in the present castle, but this is not at all likely as the first dwelling must have been built of logs. The so-called castle is a substantial residence, built of brick and well proportioned. The late Senator McInnes, the last owner, informed me that the stone building at the western part of the castle, now used as a gymnasium, was built prior to the main structure. It shows indications of having been incorporated in the main building. The descendants of Beasley's family state that Richard Beasley moved to his house at Dundurn immediately after his arrival at Hamilton, or more properly speaking, Barton Township, and that his sons, Richard, George, David C., and Henry Beasley were born in the house, the latter in 1793. Without documentary evidence it is believed that Richard Beasley's, the U. E. Loyalist's, first house, was at Dundurn, and that his elder sons were born in a house on this site.

KING'S HEAD INN, FROM THE SOUTH-EAST.
(From a Drawing by Mrs. Simcoe.)

Sat. 11th—We walked two miles on this park, which is quite natural, for there are no settlements near it. Beasley's, the Indian trader, can scarcely be called such, trading being his only occupation; but the country appears more fit for the reception of inhabitants than any part of the province I have seen, being already cleared.

The Governor says the country on the banks of the La Tranche is like this, but the plains infinitely more extensive. Further west of this terrace we saw Coote's Paradise, so called from a Capt. Coote, who spent a great deal of time in shooting ducks in this marshy tract of land below the hill we are upon. It abounds with wild fowl and tortoises; from hence it appears more like a river or lake than a marsh, and Mordaunt's Point in the distance takes a fine shape. I was so pleased with this place that the Governor stay'd and dined at Beasley's. A strong east wind prevented our sailing back. We therefore arrived late, and found a salmon and tortoise ready dressed for our dinner. Walked on the beach in the evening. Beasley gave me a weed, somewhat like a milkwort, a small white flower with a long root, which tastes hot and aromatic, which he called rattlesnake plantain. I think it is what Charlevoix calls senega. There are several different plants called rattlesnake, from being supposed

LAKE ONTARIO AND ORIGINAL ENTRANCE TO BURLINGTON BAY, 1796.
(From a Drawing by Mrs. Simcoe.)

to cure the bite of that snake. (Senega or seneca, snake root, antidote for bite of rattlesnake.)

NOTE.—Captain Coote, formerly of the 8th Regiment of Foot, was so keen a sportsman and spent so much of his time in the marsh shooting ducks that it was called Coote's Paradise. The marsh was between the head of Burlington Bay and Dundas, Ontario.

Sun. 12th—Riding near Jones' house (Augustus Jones, the Surveyor) and pond, we saw three deer, I suppose going to the pond. They stood still some time. We went to Adam Green's. He showed us a spring of salt water, which look'd thick and blue as it fell into a tub, from whence I tasted it. He and his daughter guided us to see the Fall of Stoney Creek from the bottom.

THE SHORE AT THE "HEAD OF THE LAKE."
(*From a Drawing by Mrs. Simcoe.*)

NOTE.—Stoney Creek is a village in Wentworth County, on Lake Ontario, six miles east of Hamilton. This place was the scene of a battle between the British and Americans in 1813, in which the latter were defeated.

Sun. 12th—We went through pathless woods over rocks, logs—and, in fact, the most difficult walk I ever took, and if the girl had not preceded me I should have given it up. We came too near the fall to see it in a picturesque view. I crossed the river on stones. A man climbed a considerable height up part of the red amphitheatre to get me a piece of the stones. He had no apparent footing, it was so perpendicular. He formed a singular appearance.

This part of the mountain is said to abound with rattlesnakes, and why I did not meet them in these unfrequented places I do not know. I gathered a great many plants. Green gave them all names, and I stopped

327

at his house to write them down. Ginseng, a root highly valued as a tonic, which the merchants tell me they send to England, and in some years has sold at a guinea a pound; sarsaparilla, golden thread—the roots look like gold thread. When steeped in brandy they make a fine aromatic tincture and liquorice; consumption vine, a pretty creeper. Green's daughter was cured of consumption by drinking tea made of it. Poison vine, in appearance much like the former, but differs in the number of leaves; one has five, the other seven. Madder, toothache plant, a beautiful species of fern; sore throat weed; dragon's blood; Adam and Eve, or ivy blade, very large, which heals cuts or burns; droppings of beach; enchanter's night shade (a slender, erect herb, with small white flowers, inhabiting cool, damp woods); dewberries; wild turnip, which cures a cough—it is like an aram.

They prepared me some refreshment at this house, some excellent cakes, baked on the coals; eggs; a boiled black squirrel; tea, and coffee made of peas, which was good; they said coffee was better. The sugar was made from black walnut trees, which looks darker than that from the maple, but I think it is sweeter.

Green's wife died a year ago and left ten children, who live here with their father in a house consisting of a room, a closet and a loft; but being New Jersey people, their house is delicately clean and neat, and not the appearance of being inhabited by three people, every part is so neatly kept. I sent a boy to gather a flower I forgot to bring from the mountain, and he met a rattlesnake. We rode back to the "King's Head" to dinner.

Mon. 13th—The wind being against our going to York, we rode on the beach, and had a sweet view of Burlington Bay. We passed the Indian encampment. Their huts and dogs among the fine oak trees they were under, formed a picturesque appearance. Afterwards we sailed to the north shore of Burlington Bay and pitched our tents near a house, where we had the tea kettle boiled, but we found the sand flies very troublesome. I found a pretty small tortoise, but boiling it took off the polish from the shell.

Tues. 14th—The wind is high and contrary; we could not attempt going to York. This place is so delightful I do not regret it.

Wed. 15th—Capt. Brant (Thayendanegea) the Indian Chief, called on horseback on his way to Niagara, but left his sons and attendants here till the wind proves fair for them to proceed. The boys are going to school at Niagara. They are fine children about ten years old. They dined with us and gave Francis a boat. Francis gave the Mohawks a sheep for their dinner, and afterwards they danced and played at ball. A violent east wind and terrific surf—a prodigious sea this evening. I stood for some time under an umbrella to admire its grandeur. It proved a very wet night. Brant's sons slept in our house, and the Indians found shelter under a number of planks; these are here to finish the house.

Thurs. 16th—Rode to the inlet and embarked in the boat, for the continued east wind had raised such a swell we thought the canoe would not be pleasant. The wind was light. It soon became calm and continued so until 12 o'clock, when it rose violently from the west, which coming against the late swell formed a terrifying sea.

The motion of the sea was disagreeable and my fears awoke also, till we landed at 3 o'clock at the River Credit, 12 miles from York. We were surprised to see how well the canoe made her way through this heavy sea. She rode like a duck on the waves. After dinner we walked by the River Credit. Numbers of Indians resort here at this season to fish for salmon, and the Governor wishing to go some way up it, which our boat was too large to do, he made signs to some Indians to take us into their canoe, which they did; there were two men in her, which with ourselves and Sophia completely filled the canoe. They

THE RIVER CREDIT, NEAR YORK, 1796.
(From a Drawing by Mrs. Simcoe.)

carried us about three miles, when we came to rapids and went on shore.

The banks were high, one side covered with pine, and a pretty piece of rocky country on the other. On our return to the canoe a small snake was in it, and the Indians took it out with caution and abhorrence. They hate snakes, which they seem to dread more than the Europeans do. We returned to our boats, where, not having any provision left, or money, the Governor made signs to know that they should be recompensed for their trouble if they came to York. There is abundance of salmon caught in this river. About five, the weather being calm, we set out and arrived at York at nine.

THE BEACH NEAR THE KING'S HEAD INN.
(From a Drawing by Mrs. Simcoe.)

NOTE.—The "Rapids" near the mouth of the river Credit still exist, being situated at Streetsville. They are, however, now greatly reduced in volume as compared with what they were even sixty years ago. These rapids were to a certain extent navigable, as venturesome lumbermen from the earliest days of the province used to run their timber rafts down them during the spring. The Credit River empties into Lake Ontario, thirteen miles west of Toronto.

CHAPTER XX.

LEAVETAKINGS OF FRIENDS.

The 16th of June, 1796, was not a very favorable day for a water trip along the north shore of Lake Ontario, but the Governor having waited for a favorable wind since the 13th, determined to make an effort to reach York on the 16th. The party were in a sailboat while a canoe followed, and by three o'clock in the afternoon they landed at the River Credit. The trip was varied by an excursion three miles up that river in a large canoe which had room enough for the Governor, his wife and daughter, and two Indians. The weather calming about five o'clock, a start was made for York, which was reached by nine o'clock.

The Governor had early in the year determined upon returning to England. His relations with Lord Dorchester had not been of a harmonious character, and his opinions so differed from those of the Governor-General, especially on the subject of the building of Fort Miami, that Governor Simcoe preferred to ask for leave of absence. This request was answered about the middle of July, for on the 14th the official letter came to York stating that the frigate "Pearl" would be at Quebec to take him home in the beginning of August.

Wednesday, July 20th, was the last day at Castle Frank and on the 21st Mrs. Simcoe said good-bye to her friends, but "was so much out of spirits" that she was unable to dine with Mrs. McGill, and to make matters worse she "cried all day." At three o'clock on the afternoon of the 21st the "Onondaga" weighed anchor, and the guns at the Fort saluted the Governor as the Provincial vessel started on its journey around the peninsula and east on the lake to Kingston.

Of these last days at York Mrs. Simcoe writes:—

Fri. 17th June—Very warm day. Mrs. McGill and Mrs. Macaulay, wife of Dr. Macaulay, dined with me.

Mon. 20th—Part of the regiment (Queen's Rangers) embarked for Niagara.

Sat. 25th—We intended to have gone to the Humber in the canoe, attended by music, and spend a pleasant day there, but Francis being ill with fever prevented it.

Wed. 29th—Very ill and feverish, having been alarmed about Francis.

Thurs. 30th—Sent the children to Castle Frank in a boat. We rode there through those pleasant shady pine plains, now covered with sweet scented fern. There is no underwood under the pines, so it is good riding.

Fri. 1st July—A large party from the garrison to dinner. A boat with music accompanied them; we heard it in the evening until they had passed the town. It sounds delightfully.

NOTE.—The favorite route by water from the garrison or Fort was from the Fort through Toronto Bay to its east end and then up the Don River.

THE GARRISON AT YORK (TORONTO), 1796.
Showing First Houses in the Fort and Magazine on the Shore.
(From a Drawing by Mrs. Simcoe.)

FIRST BRIDGE OVER THE DON

Sun. 3rd—The Governor went to the garrison and returned to supper. Some heavy thunder showers fell this evening and the mosquitos more troublesome than ever. It is scarcely possible to write or use my hands, which are always occupied in killing them or driving them away. This situation being high does not at all secure us from mosquitos or gnats.

Mon. 4th—I descended the hill and walked to Skinner's Mill through the meadows, which looked like meadows in England. Playter was haymaking. Going down the hill some dragon's blood seed fell out as I passed, which I collected.

Wed. 6th—I passed Playter's picturesque bridge over the Don; it is a butternut tree fallen across the river, the branches still growing full leaf. Mrs. Playter being timorous, a pole was fastened through the branches to hold by. Having attempted to pass it, I was determined to proceed, but was frightened before I got half way.

NOTE.—This was the first bridge over the Don River at York at the foot of the present Winchester Street, Toronto, placed there about 1794.

Thurs. 7th—The weather excessively hot and we find the underground room very comfortable; the windows on the side of it are cut through the side of the hill.

The winter we were at Kingston, deer were continually seen about here, but the noise made by the carpenters at work upon the house last winter, prevented them from coming. A fine eagle shot at the town.

Sun. 10th—Rode very pleasantly through the pine plains; gathered tea berries. I saw mosquito hawks' nests, at least the eggs and young birds lying on pieces of bark on the ground. Query, whether the mosquito hawk is not the "whipper will" (whip-poor-will), so called from the resemblance of its notes to the words—which makes such a noise every night. We had company at dinner. I walked down the hill in the evening and gathered dragon's blood, a plant or dragon root, from which you get resin of darkish red color; Lychnis de Canada, a plant with scarlet flower; tryliums, which resemble lilies; toothache plant, like toothache grass. It has a pungent taste. Licorice, wild lilies, etc.

Mon. 11th—A very wet day and the mosquitos so numerous that smoke would not drive them away; when it grows dark I take my candle and sit to read on my bed under the mosquito net, which is the only protection from them.

Tues. 12th—We rode to the town by the new road opened by the Government farm, and through the town; it is the shortest way in point of time. The road is so much better than Yonge Street. Dined with Mrs. McGill. Returned to Castle Frank.

Wed. 13th—The Governor rode to the garrison this morning. In the evening we went in a boat, caught a sun fish.

Thur. 14th—Walked through the meadows towards Coon's farm on the Don—saw millions of the yellow and black butterflies, New York swallow tails, and heaps of their wings lying about. Gathered wild gooseberries, and when they were stewed found them excellent sauce for salmon. In the afternoon the Governor received his leave of absence, and information that the frigate "Pearl," Capt. Ballard, is at Quebec, and is to take him to England. She sails August the 10th.

Fri. 15th—Rode to the Garrison and slept there.

Sat. 16th—Hot and sultry weather.

Mon. 18th—Rode to dine at Castle Frank; so heavy a shower of rain that we were obliged to quit the lower room, the windows of which are not glazed—slept here.

DIARY OF MRS. SIMCOE

Tues. 19th—Mrs. McGill and Mrs. Macaulay breakfasted here. I returned to the garrison with them in Mr. Bouchette's boat, and rode back to dine at Castle Frank. Mr. Pilkington came in the evening. It was very damp and cold. I was glad to stand by the fire.

Wed. 20th—Took leave of Castle Frank, called at Playter's, dined with Mrs. McGill. Mentioned my spinning wheel. Slept at the garrison.

MRS. SIMCOE'S SPINNING-WHEEL.
(From original in possession of Mrs. Stephen Heward, Toronto.)

NOTE.—Mrs. Simcoe had brought with her to Canada a spinning wheel which was made by order of Queen Charlotte, consort of George III., for the Marchioness of Buckingham, and given by her to Mrs. Simcoe, who on leaving Canada in 1796 gave the spinning wheel to Mrs. McGill, aunt of Mrs. Stephen Heward, Toronto.

Thur. 21st—Took leave of Mrs. McGill and Miss Crookshank. I was so much out of spirits I was unable to dine with them. Mrs. McGill sent me some dinner, but I could not eat; cried all day. The Governor dined with Mr. McGill and at three o'clock we went on board the "Onondaga," under a salute from the vessels. Little wind, soon became calm.

Fri. 22nd—Light wind and contrary.

Sat. 23rd—We were opposite the 50-mile creek from Niagara.

NOTE.—Probably about in line with Cobourg harbour.

Sun. 24th—Opposite Presqu-isle head.

NOTE.—Near the Carrying Place from Lake Ontario to Bay of Quinte.

Mon. 25th—A side wind towards evening, fair and fresh; at half past eleven at night we anchored in Kingston harbour.

After a stay of about eighteen hours the King's bateaux were ready and the Governor and his family on the 26th commenced their journey to Montreal, at which place they arrived on the evening of the 30th. The trip was much like the trip up the river in 1792, and to Mrs. Simcoe it had many charms, so that the notes in her diary are most interesting. She writes:—

Tues. 26th—A cold day. The Governor breakfasted on shore; at eleven we embarked in a batteau; at six stopped at a rocky island six miles from Gananowui, where we made a fire and boiled a tea kettle; there is a pretty bay here. I called the island "Isle au trippe," from gathering *trippe de roche* on the rocks. It is a kind of liverwort plant good for diseases of liver, which the Canadians going to the Grande Portage boil and eat on very hungry days, but it is bitter and not wholesome. We proceeded three miles to a beautiful rocky island (as

336

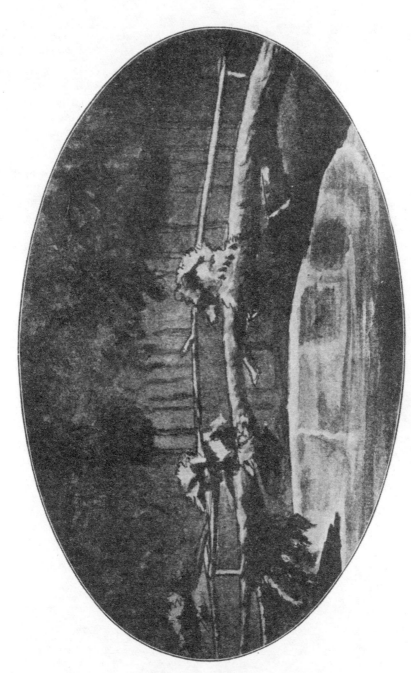

PLAYTER'S BRIDGE OVER THE DON RIVER, AT YORK.

(From a Drawing by Mrs. Simcoe.)

we thought, but it proved to be the main shore) among the thousand Islands. I called it "Bass Island," for the number of black bass I saw swimming in shallow water near the shore. We supped at ten, the stars shining unusually bright. We placed the beds on the trunks in one of the batteau, which was covered with sail cloth over the awning. We slept extremely well and so cool that we determined to keep that batteau so fitted up for the rest of the voyage rather than go into houses, now the Governor is so unwell, and suffers from the heat, besides the fresh breeze on the water keeps away the mosquitos. We heard a wild kind of shriek several times in the night; we thought it was loons, which scream in that way. An American said he guessed it was the painters (so they call panthers), as the sound came from the shore of the United States, where those animals abound.

CASTLE FRANK IN THE SUMMER OF 1796.
(From a Drawing by Mrs. Simcoe.)

Wed. 27th—We breakfasted and set off at seven—it rained. Passed Toniata Isles and the river of that name, then the Isles au Baril, on one of which we landed. The wind and sea so high we had difficulty in turning the Point, from whence we had a pretty view of the islands. Dined here and gathered hurtleberries. We afterwards came to Capt. Jones', the prettiest point on the river; he has a fine farm and garden, and water melons, though so much to the N.E. Here we waited until the tea kettle was boiled, and then proceeding, passed Commissary Jones' saw mill, E. Jones' windmill and Mr. Cowan's pot ashery, near Johnstone.

NOTE.—Toniata Island is five leagues from Pointe au Baril near the present village of Maitland, now known as Grenadier Island. In a map William Chewett made for Governor Simcoe and enclosed

339

DIARY OF MRS. SIMCOE

in a despatch to the Duke of Portland, 29th July, 1795, Toniata Island is shown opposite Leeds County, about ten miles west of Grenville River. Pointe au Baril is near the present village of Maitland between Brockville and Prescott.

Stopped for the night at Pt. au Cardinal, just below Les Geolettes (the Gallops, seven miles above Iroquois), which terrifying rapid we passed in a minute. Here Mr. Hugh Munro is building a mill. The

KINGSTON FROM THE HARBOUR, 1796.
(From a Drawing by Mrs. Simcoe.)

KEY TO ILLUSTRATION.

No. 1—Is Cartwright's wharf and storehouse, built on the Horn which turned in toward the ground now occupied by the Montreal Transportation Company's shipyard, there being formerly a bay on the site of the shipyard and extending in close to the present site of the Haymarket. It is now occupied partly by the military stables on the south side of the road leading to and across the Cataraqui bridge, partly by the road itself and partly by Knapp's boathouse. It is on the north side of the road and close to the end of the bridge.

No. 2—These buildings were storehouses, formerly occupied by the Quartermaster-General's department. They have long since been swept away, their site being occupied by officers' quarters within the walls of the barracks. The foundation walls are still visible in the barrack square.

No. 3.—This is Forsyth's wharf, now called the Queen's Wharf, in the barrack yard, on the south side and on the line of Barrack Street.

No. 4—The flag on Fort Frontenac, probably the S.E. bastion, where there was a round tower, the foundations of which are visible in the barrack square.

No. 5—Probably the gable of the present Central Hotel, corner Queen and Ontario Streets.

BRIDGE OVER THE DON RIVER AT YORK, 1796.

(*From a Drawing by Mrs. Simcoe.*)

timbers are uncovered and it has the appearance of a sketch of a ruin in Italy. Some merchants' batteaux were drawing up round the point with the greatest labor, exertion and difficulty, and the velocity with which a boat appeared flying downwards with great rapidity formed a contrast well worth seeing. We supped at ten on a fine piece of dry ground under a plum tree and sheltered by some boards belonging to the mill; a cold windy night. A stiff breeze astern kept off the mosquitos. I was only afraid the cable of our boat, which was tied to a tree, should by this fresh breeze get loose and leave us drift down the rapids.

Thur. 28th—We breakfasted at seven. I made a sketch and embarked. Passed Frazier's farm and Pt. Iroquois, where the Indians formerly fought a battle, Pt. aux Pins, a fine place for a fortification, Pt. Acolo, where Mr. Munro's sawmill stands near the Rapid Plat, Capt. Duncan's, Grosse Point, Pointe au Gobelet and then we came to the Long Sault, which extends nine miles.

NOTE.—Point Iroquois, a beautiful point of land jutting out into the St. Lawrence from the Township of Matilda, is now incorporated in the village of Iroquois, Dundas County. When General Williamson passed down the river with the United States army in November 1813 (shortly before the battle of Chrysler's Farm) he met with obstruction upon reaching Point Iroquois, as a picket of about a dozen men, among whom were Jacob and Peter Brouse, were

POINT IROQUOIS, DUNDAS COUNTY.
(From a Drawing by Mrs. Simcoe.)

posted at this point, which commands an extensive view of the river. The first Methodist Church in Dundas was built in 1797 upon Point Iroquois. Croil in his "History of Dundas" writes:—"A more beautiful site could not have been chosen. The point upon which it stood was the highest and most picturesque headland upon the St. Lawrence between Brockville and Montreal, and is said to have been a favorite spot with the Indians when holding their councils of war

THE RIVER BELOW POINT IROQUOIS.
(From a Drawing by Mrs. Simcoe.)

in days of yore. It commanded a view of the river above and below for many miles." Below Point Iroquois is situated Point aux Pins, the narrowest part of the river; and Rapid du Plat is in front of the township of Williamsburg, above Morrisburg.

DIARY OF MRS. SIMCOE

Honorable John Munro's mill was built on a magnificent scale for those days. It was on the point below Flagg's, just opposite the first rough water in the Rapid du Plat.

We descended the Long Sault in an hour without sailing and seldom rowing, though near particular currents they rowed with great exertion. The most agitated part is towards the end of the rapids, where the river becomes wider; here I had an opportunity of seeing the boats which followed us; they appeared to fly. I compared them to race horses trying to outrun each other. The velocity was extreme; sometimes the whirlpool turned them round; at others the head of one and stern of another boat appeared buried under the waves. I sketched the boats. These rapids did not appear formidable to me last year. I suppose my mind was then more engaged by the cause of my voyage, and the Governor's

A BEND IN THE RIVER ST. LAWRENCE.
(From a Drawing by Mrs. Simcoe.)

situation at the Miami; then I thought not of myself; now I had nothing to think of but the present danger, and was terrified.

In the entrance of Lake St. Francis we went to a small island south of our course; we had the tea kettle boiled and walked about for some time; there were many wild vines, nut, gooseberries and sumach trees; one of the latter we carried away to make chessmen of it, as the wood is said to be beautiful. The weather immoderately hot, and no wind since we left the rapids. The clouds foretell rain.

We stopped at Pointe Morandiere, which stretches a great way into the lake; we were agreeably surprised to find it a stony, dry piece of land; the swamps are to the north of it.

NOTE.—Pointe Morandiere is on the St. Lawrence, east of Cornwall, on the northwestern end of Lake St. Francis.

THROUGH THE RAPIDS OF THE CEDARS

Thur. 28th—I was very hungry and impatient for supper, but much afraid from the dark appearance of the sky that I would have to leave the ducks untasted, for I must have retired to the boat immediately if the rain began, for I never could have passed the slippery rocks I had to cross after they were wet. However, the sky cleared, we supped and sat admiring the stars till after eleven o'clock. A prodigious number of moths or flies here, which burnt themselves and lay in the fire in large heaps, but I did not see mosquitos.

Fri. 29th—Breakfasted at six in the morning and set off with a fair wind; passed Pte. au Bodet at nine; then Pte. au Foin, a very pretty spot; passed the rapids near the Coteau du Lac; passed Pte. au Diable near the Long Sault, and stopped at Pte. au Biron, on a hill from whence the view towards Coteau de Lac is very pretty.

There is a good Seigneurie House falling to ruins. We saw batteaux drawing round this point where the current is particularly strong. They

ISLE AUX SOEURS, NOW NUN'S ISLAND.
(From a Drawing by Mrs. Simcoe.)

used great exertion in poling and drawing with a tow line and pushing the boat, being above their knees in water. We embarked after dinner, and notwithstanding the immoderate heat they insisted on taking off the awning to go down the Rapids of the Cedars. The preparation seemed formidable but the ensuing journey more so. People usually go from hence in calèches four miles to the cascades, but the Governor wished to see all the rapids and would not go on shore.

This rapid is much more frightful than the Long Sault. I cannot describe how terrifying the extent of furious, dashing white waves appeared, and how the boat rose and plunged among them, the waves sometimes washing into the boat. Our keeping rather too near the shore made it worse. There is a place called "the run" near the locks, which is like going down the stream of an overshot mill, and I really thought we never should have risen out of it. The men rowed with all their might, and in passing it called out "Vive le Roi." We passed a rock which really seemed to fly from us. The children called out "How fast it runs." We did not leave this agitated and agitating scene till we came in sight of Pointe Claire and Isle Perrot and had seen the junction of the transparent St. Lawrence with the dirty waters of the Ottawa.

We slept to-night at the Isle aux Soeurs. The island consists of a table-shaped hill of fine turf, from whence are three fine views: To the north-west, looking over the immense width of the St. Lawrence, which is like a lake, is seen the Isle au Paix, Isle Perrot, Pointe Claire—in the distance Lac des deux Montagnes (the Lake of Two Mountains), the country about the Rideaux and Ottawa rivers, and some distant blue highlands. To the north-east, a rich, woody foreground with a pretty sandy beach, and the blue mountain of Montreal in the distance.

NOTE.—The Isle aux Soeurs was the French name for Nun's Island, now St. Bernard's Isle, at the mouth of the Chateauguay River, and is washed by the Chateauguay on two sides and by the St. Lawrence on one.

To the south, the village and river of Chateauguay (on the river of that name and 24 miles south of Montreal) winding along woods and cultivated country to a great distance, the Seigneurie House, and the river falling into the St. Lawrence forms the near view. This island and a house on it belong to the nuns, who reside at Montreal, and here they take care of insane persons. We pitched the tent at the foot of the hill and near the house.

NOTE.—Bouchette in his Topography states that the Seigniory at Chateauguay belonged in 1815 to the Grey Nuns. It was originally granted, in 1673, to Le Moyne, Sieur de Longueuil. In connection with the house Bouchette uses the word "Mansion," for it could not be designated a convent, as there were only two nuns. Being the owners of the Seigniory, the nuns resided in the Manor House.

Sat. 30th—A little rain. I walked to the Seigneurie House, which looks like a Flemish building, examined a raft lying in the Chateauguay River and thought its construction very curious.

At nine we embarked, and at eleven stopped at La Chine (Lachine) to take a pilot to conduct us to Montreal thro' the rapids, which extend almost the whole way, and are thought to be most dangerous of any, as the water is so shallow; the great width of the river adds terror to the scene, which presents miles of foaming waves. We stopped a little while, that we might not overtake or run foul of an immense *radeau* or raft that was going down. However, she struck on a rock and we passed her. It was a wild accompaniment to the scene we were in. The distant view was fine; on one side the mountain of Montreal and the town extending below, the island of St. Helen's opposite the east end of Montreal, and near to us that of St. Paul's, with some ruins of burnt houses upon it. On the other side the town of La Prairie (on the south shore seven miles from Montreal), with the blue hills of Chambly and Beloeil Mountain in the distance.

The Governor desired me to sketch the rapids of La Chine. I believe he wished to take off my attention from the rapids. I was more disposed to have cried than to have talked; reason told me there was no danger, because Canadians pass the rapids safely so many times every year, but one has to resist all that can affright the senses of seeing or hearing, so the pilot, to make himself appear brave, was perpetually reminding us of the great danger, which only his knowledge could save us from. We arrived at Mr. Gray's, at Montreal.

BY BATEAUX AND CALECHE TO QUEBEC.

Sun. 31st—Went to church in Lieut.-General Christie's coach.

NOTE.—General Gabriel Christie, born 1722, died in Montreal, 1799 ; he was a brevet-major under Amherst in 1759, and commander-in-chief in Canada, 1798. He was also a Justice of the Peace and a member of the Legislative and Executive Councils.

Francis' surprise at a room on wheels was great. He had never been in any carriage but an open one. This house of Mr. Gray's is very pleasant, from venetian blinds being fixed into all the window frames, which throws such a sombre light that all the women who have called have looked handsome, tho' they were not so in broad daylight; *et je me sentit valoir dix fois plus qu'un autretemps* (and I feel worth ten times more than at other times).

GENERAL CHRISTIE.

We drank tea at Mr. Frobisher's country house. It commands a noble view towards La Prairie, St. Helen's, Chambly and Beloeil, the town of Montreal, and a cultivated country in the near view. Francis, being accustomed to sentinels, asked, when he saw Mr. Frobisher's dogs' houses before the door, whether the people here kept dogs as sentinels. Mrs. Frobisher has an excellent garden; there was strawberry spinach, which she showed me as a pretty but very poisonous plant. I assured her I had often eaten it in Upper Canada. I have not caught cold the whole of the journey, which I attribute to living so totally in the air. At Kingston my trunk fell into the water in taking it from the ship, so I have had none but damp clothes to wear since, and no opportunity of airing them, as I have met with no fire but where the men were cooking.

Mon. Aug. 1st—I dined at Mr. Frobisher's; immoderate hot weather and a little rain.

NOTE.—The stay in Montreal was not prolonged. The Governor had official matters, as a record says, to attend to, and he was anxious to leave the affairs of his Province in good order. The accounts of the Province in connection with the military expenditure were all sent in duplicate to the authorities at Quebec, and some of these had to be adjusted. So after three days had been spent in Montreal the bateaux were on the 2nd of August in readiness, and on the fifth of the month the party landed at Cap Rouge, nine miles from Quebec, and after a strenuous journey in calèches, arrived at Belmont, near Quebec, the residence of Colonel Caldwell, where they were received by their friends, who were delighted to see the Governor and his wife again.

Mrs. Simcoe writes:—

Tues. Aug. 2nd—Left Montreal at eight; passed Long Pt. (N.E. of Montreal and on the island), Pointe aux Trembles (three leagues from Montreal and on the island), Varennes (on the south shore, six leagues below Montreal), St. Sulpice (on the north shore, eight leagues below Montreal), with a strong, fair wind; dined in the boat near La Valtrie (on the north shore, N.E., and twelve leagues from Montreal). Soon afterwards fell a heavy thunderstorm. They furnished the boat at Montreal with so miserable an awning that it let the water through, and sent very inexperienced batteau men, who scarcely knew how to manage the

347

boat. We were quite wet, but being near D'Autray, went on shore and determined to sleep there. Having been there twice already, I knew we should be well accommodated. A very cold night. The Maitre de Poste, La Fontaine and his wife, very old people, were perfectly Flemish figures. They supped in the room next to ours. I observe they eat onion broth, fat bacon, and finished by drinking sour milk; after supper they played a game at cards they called "le grand Brisque," which they seemed to be much amused by.

Wed. 3rd—Left D'Autray at eight, wrapped up in that fleecy hosiery which has been the companion of all my travels. At five this evening we came to Pte. du Lac St. Pierre, which is a widening of the St. Lawrence, a league from Three Rivers (30 leagues below Montreal), where the batteau men wished to go; but the Governor, being determined not to lodge in a town, insisted on their going into this little bay, which, doing unwillingly, they struck us against rocks; it was very shallow water, as they had said. We found the beach very pleasant, and walked from thence to a rising ground, where are the remains of Pte. du Lac barracks, built by Sir F. Haldimand in 1789. Gathered very fine wild raspberries. We were overtaken by a thunder shower that wetted me thro', but what was worse, on our return found the canvas and awning of our boat had not been properly fixed and that the beds were quite wet; there was no remedy, so I sat by the fire and dryed my habit, eat my supper, and slept in my clothes on the damp bed, without catching any cold.

Thur. 4th—Drew a plant of wild rice which was in blossom; gathered cardinal flowers, a beautiful purple flower, sand cherries and some raspberries. We went out of the bay without touching a rock, stopped five minutes at Three Rivers to speak to Mr. Mountain. At five this afternoon we went on shore at a most beautiful point, St. Pierre les Becquet. It is a very steep ascent from the beach to the village, among wood and rock. We went to the Cure's, who very civilly shewed us his house and garden and the church, which is very neat. From the garden is an extensive view. The mouths of the rivers Batiscan and St. Anne are seen on the opposite shore, with distant blue hills. This is the finest point on the river and a good military position. Madame Bàby (wife of Hon. François Bàby, of Quebec) has lands here.

NOTE.—Mr. Mountain was the Bishop's elder brother, Dr. Jehoshaphat Mountain, formerly rector of Peldon in Essex. He and his wife, with their son and two daughters, were amongst the party who accompanied the Bishop to Canada in 1793.

Batiscan River rises in the county of Quebec and falls into the St. Lawrence at Batiscan Bridge. St. Anne River is in Montmorency County, Que., and falls into the St. Lawrence at the east corner of the parish of St. Anne.

Thur. 4th—Descending the hill, we gathered nuts and wild fruits. Farther down the river the view of Richelieu (in Rouville County, about seven leagues S.E. of Montreal and south of the St. Lawrence), Deschambault (a village on the north shore of St. Lawrence, 14 leagues S.W. of Quebec), Grondines (a village in Portneuf County, on the north shore of the St. Lawrence and about 15 leagues above Quebec), in the distance, with bright lights from the setting sun very beautiful. We slept at Grondines in a room belonging to Mr. McCord, of Quebec. (He represents this village in the Parliament at Quebec.) We could not sleep on the water, as the tide obliged the boat to be brought on shore. A very cold night; we supped upon the beach.

Fri. 5th—We set off at seven; I was extremely delighted with the high banks and beautiful scenery in passing Deschambault, Richelieu and Cap

WITH OLD FRIENDS AT BELMONT

Santé on the north shore, opposite to which is Pt. Platon (on the south shore 13 leagues above Quebec), where we went on shore and admired the situation, which is fit for a fine house; there is a good farm belonging to the Convent des Ursulines at Quebec.

We dined in the boat opposite the pretty village of St. Augustine (four leagues from Quebec), and then went ashore at Cap Rouge (three leagues from Quebec). The Commissary at Montreal ought to be ashamed of sending such batteau men. They frequently asked me how far we were from Quebec, and many such questions. The only man at all accustomed to the way was dying of ague and of no use. From the St. Lawrence we walked a mile (the tide being out) over wet ground like marsh, interspersed with rock, which brought us to a house where we got a calèche, which carried us a mile to a kind of Post House, where we dressed and set out in a calèche, ascending a prodigious steep but winding road among red rocks and wood, and four miles brought us to Belmont, where we found our friends well and happy to see us. They have just finished an addition to their house, which makes it very comfortable.

As a proof of how much the Governor has suffered from the illness he had last autumn (the fever lasted from August till November), he was excessively fatigued by the exercise of driving four miles in the calèche.

CHAPTER XXI.

HOMEWARD BOUND.

The Governor on his arrival at Quebec found that the "Pearl" had gone on a cruise, and was expected back on the 10th of August; but, as the stay at Quebec after his business had been transacted was, as he said in a private letter, "a very pleasant one," he was glad to do nothing more than await the arrival of the ship on which he and his wife were to sail to England.

Lord and Lady Dorchester had left Quebec on 9th July, 1796, for England, in the "Active" man-of-war, but unfortunately this ship was wrecked off Anticosti on the 15th July. Simcoe was afraid that the "Pearl," which had gone down the Gulf to save the stores, would be ordered to take the Governor-General to England and so cause further delay. The "Pearl," however, arrived in Quebec on the 6th September, and on Saturday, the 10th, sailed for England with Governor Simcoe and his family, and after a somewhat eventful voyage anchored off the Downs on the 13th of October.

Mrs. Simcoe writes:—

Sat. 6th—A wet morning. Mrs. and Miss Prescott called on me. Bishop Mountain's youngest child died last night; they sent a very polite message requesting us to use their house at Quebec and their carriage. The Bishop's family are going immediately to Three Rivers, to visit his brother.

NOTE.—Mrs. and Miss Prescott were the wife and daughter of General Robert Prescott, who succeeded Lord Dorchester. The latter did not know he was to be recalled until Prescott's arrival in Quebec in June of 1796. Although Lord Dorchester left for England in July of 1796, he retained office until the following April, during which time Prescott performed the actual duties of Governor. General Prescott then formally became Governor-in-Chief, remaining in Canada until 1799, when he was recalled. He died in England in 1815.

Mon. 8th—Went to Quebec; called on Miss Mountain; dined at the Château; returned to Belmont in Mrs. Prescott's carriage. A heavy thunder shower when we were at dinner, but the weather still sultry. The country about Quebec is charming. The Governor, not having seen it in summer, is surprised at its beauty; the distant mountains appear more grand when the wooded country below is discerned, interspersed with the villages of Charlesbourg (four miles from Quebec), Montmorency (six and a half miles) and Lorette (eight miles). The "Pearl" frigate has gone on a cruise, but expected here on the 10th.

NOTE.—Miss Mountain was one of the Bishop's sisters who came to Canada with him.

Tues. 9th—The Governor went with Coll. Caldwell to his mills, and returned much fatigued.

LAST DAYS IN THE ANCIENT CITY

Wed. 10th—General and Mrs. Prescott dined here. I am very ill from the heat. I never felt the air so oppressive in Upper Canada.

Thur. 11th—Left our hospitable friends at Belmont and went this evening to reside at the Bishop's house at Quebec, where we are very comfortably lodged. Our obligation to Bishop Mountain is great, for there are no tolerable accommodations here for travellers, and no lodgings to be hired but what are very miserable, as Mrs. Prescott experienced before the Château was vacant.

Fri. 12th—There is a fog like our Indian summer, with insufferable heat. In the evening we walked upon Cape Diamond and to our favorite walk on the terrace. There is a cherry or grape tree in the Bishop's garden, as large as an apple tree. The fruit is the size of a large currant.

Sat. 13th—We dined at Chief Justice's Osgoode. Met Mrs. Prescott.

Sun. 14th—Went to church. Sat in the Governor's seat. Called on Mrs. Dalton and saw her beautiful drawings. I read a poem called "Caissa" in Jones' collection of Asiatic poems.

NOTE.—"Caissa," a poetic introduction to the game of chess, by Sir William Jones (1746-1794), the celebrated Oriental scholar.

Mon. 15th—Walked to Cape Diamond before breakfast.

Tues. 16th—News arrived of the "Active," Capt. Leveson Gower, on the way to England, being wrecked off the Isle of Anticosti. The crew got safe on shore, and Lord and Lady Dorchester were taken from hence to Gaspé in a schooner which, fortunately for them, was passing Anticosti a day or two after they were wrecked. From Gaspé they were to go to Halifax, probably in the "Pearl," which detains her from being here.

NOTE.—Captain Leveson Gower was born in Maryland in 1750. He served in the Revolutionary War, and died in 1818.

Wed. 17th—Dined at Belmont; sultry weather.

Thur. 18th—The ship "Adriatic" arrived from Halifax. Dined at the Château; thermometer 88. We were under great anxiety lest Lord Dorchester should take the "Pearl" to carry him to England from Halifax.

Fri. 19th—So ill I could not dine with Madame Bàby.

Sat. 20th—So ill I could not dine with Mrs. Dunn.

Sun. 21st—So ill I did not go to church. Mrs. Prescott called.

Mon. 22nd, Tues. 23rd—Dined at home; the heat insufferable. The only hours which are tolerable are from eight till ten at night, when we walk upon the ramparts.

Wed. 24th—Drank tea with Mrs. Winslow; in the night the wind changed and it became very cold.

Thur. 25th—The Bishop and Mrs. Mountain called on their return from Montreal, where they had spent the last fortnight. I drank tea with Mrs. Smith. It was too cold to walk with pleasure in the garden.

Sat. 27th—Madame Bàby obtained the Bishop's order for our admission to the Convent of Ursulines. The nuns were very civil, and pleased at my recollecting those I had seen before.

Mon. 29th—Dined at Woodfield. Two ships of those destined to go under convoy of the "Pearl" sailed to-day. Tired of waiting for her.

Tues. 30th—Dined at the Château.

Wed. 31st—Dined at Belmont.

Thur. Sept. 1st—We dined at Mr. Finlay's, the Deputy Postmaster-General, at Woodside. It is a very pretty situation. Quebec and Charlesbourg are good objects from it, but the weather was hazy. I walked thro' pretty grounds in the afternoon.

NOTE.—A residence on the St. Louis Road, built on part of the land of the old country seat of Thornhill.

DIARY OF MRS. SIMCOE

Fri. 2nd—A wet day.

Sat. 3rd—Drank tea with Miss Mountain. The "Pearl" arrived from Halifax in 14 days.

Sun. 4th—Coll. and Mrs. Caldwell dined with me.

Mon. 5th—Dined at Woodfield. Walked in the evening towards Sillery and saw a beautiful view of Cape Diamond, the Isle of Orleans, etc., under setting sun.

NOTE.—Sillery was originally a mission founded in 1637, named after Commandeur Noël Brûlart de Sillery, Prime Minister of Louis XIII., who gave 12,000 livres (or pounds) for the purpose. The old Sillery settlement was within the limits of the parish of St. Foye. The mission was about four and a half miles from Quebec, on the north shore of the St. Lawrence.

Tues. 6th—As I was getting into the carriage to go to the Château the street was full of smoke, which we supposed to be from a chimney on

THE RECOLLET CHURCH, QUEBEC.

(From an Engraving in the J. Ross Roberts on Collection.)

fire. Soon after we arrived at Mrs. Prescott's the gentlemen were informed that the fire, which had begun in a barn of hay, was raging furiously in St. Louis Street and approaching the Bishop's house. Gen'l. Simcoe immediately went there and remained the whole afternoon, giving directions to some of the crew of the "Pearl," by whose exertions the Bishop's house and houses adjoining were saved, tho' they several times caught fire. Mrs. Prescott and I were looking out from the upper window, when we saw a spark alight on the Recollet Church, and in a few minutes the whole building was in a blaze.

The churches and houses, being covered with shingles (wooden tiles), burnt rapidly, and the shingles being light, were also easily blown by the wind, which was high, and had it not changed probably the whole town would have been destroyed. The ships in the river weighed anchor. Some papers were blown to Pt. Levy, on the opposite side of the river. Our trunks being sent to the Chief Justice's, I went there to change my clothes, for we were all in full dress, as Mrs. Prescott was to have had a ball in the evening. I was terrified in passing the Parade. The heat was so great from the Recollet Church, engines kept playing on the Château, which was in great danger. I afterwards took the children into Palace Street, and sat with Mrs. Roslyn, of the Fifth Regt., till eight o'clock, when Gen'l. Simcoe came to fetch us to the Chief Justice's, where we slept, for tho' the danger was at an end the sight of everything still burning around the Bishop's house made me wish not to sleep there.

Wed. 7th—Drank tea with Mrs. Taylor and supped at the Chief Justice's, our baggage being sent on board the "Pearl."

The ruins of the Recollet Church, brightened from within by fire, not yet extinguished, had an awful, grand appearance as we walked home in a dark night; the effect of colour was very rich.

I sent an enquiry after the health of the Ursulines since their alarm and the exertions they had made in carrying water to the top of their house, which was endangered by the fire; I received a very polite note from the Superieure and a basket of plums from their garden.

Thur. 8th—Breakfasted at Woodfield; returned to Quebec with Mrs. Caldwell and dined with Coll. Barnes.

Sat. 10th—At eleven embarked on board the "Pearl." The cabin is larger than that in the "Triton," but the guns are very incommodious. I was busy arranging my trunks, and kept as few as possible with me, because I was informed if we met French ships we must clear for action, and all the baggage would be tossed below in confusion. I met with one trunk of the Bishop's clothes, but had an opportunity of a boat passing to send it to Quebec.

I find nothing missing but a very pretty Indian basket, in which were shoes. Capt. Leveson Gower, H.M.S. "Active," takes his passage to England with Capt. Ballard, and four of his lieutenants—Mr. Bond, Mr. Merriott, Mr. Worth, Mr. Deighton, master of the "Active." Capt. Gower lives in the cabin. About five we struck ground. The sensation was unpleasant, but we were instantly off. We anchored at night.

Sun. 11th—Weighed anchor at five. At nine passed a brig going to Quebec. Passed the Kamouraskas, rocky islands in the St. Lawrence, opposite mouth of Kamouraska River; and Pilgrim Islands, four islands, only rocks, near the south shore of the St. Lawrence (below L'Islet).

Mon. 12th—The wind west, fair, but obliged to lay to for the merchantmen under our convoy. There are ten. The "Brook Watson" and "Earl of Marchmont" are very bad sailers.

Tues. 13th—Fair wind and cold. We cannot carry sail enough to keep the ship steady, on account of those bad sailing merchantmen.

Wed. 14th—Wind south-east. Standing for the Bird Islands, north of the Magdalens.

Thurs. 15th—A head sea, hauled close to the wind. I was unwell all day.

Fri. 16th—A very wet morning after a rough night, and hauled close to the wind. It cleared up at twelve. At six the Captain spoke with the merchantmen and agreed to bear away from the Straits of Belle Isle, about 50 leagues off. We are now in sight of St. George's Bay, on the coast of Newfoundland, and a fine leading wind.

Sat. 17th—A fine wind; passed Scaring Islands at twelve. Rather sick; I found myself better by eating orange marmalade. A great swell to-night.

NOTE.—Between Cow Head and Shallow Bays, on the western coast of Newfoundland.

Sun. 18th—During the night I heard the officer on watch tell Capt. Ballard there was a sail in sight, and he ordered ammunition to be got ready. I got up, and tho' it was dark, contrived to collect my things and

DIARY OF MRS. SIMCOE

lock them up in the trunk, as I thought we might be suddenly called upon and the cabin cleared. I then went to sleep again. The next morning I heard that the sail was a brig from Quebec which had overshot her port. Capt. Ballard said we had been in great danger during the night. It was very calm, and a very heavy swell set us on the breakers, which we were quite near; everybody was quite alarmed and went upon deck, and a sudden breeze springing up from the breakers saved us from going upon them. We had entered the Straits of Belle Isle and passed an island of ice. At nine I saw an island of ice at a great distance. It was near Green Island, Newfoundland, about nine leagues from Cape Norman.

NOTE.—Green Island is between North and South Heads in the Bay of Islands.

At twelve we passed Portreau Bay. I looked at it through a glass and made a sketch of it. The country appears to be ledges of rocks, with a few scrubby pine, scarce able to grow on so harsh and dismal a soil. I discerned two waterfalls near the coast. After passing Portreau Bay, at entrance to Strait of Belle Isle, near Green Island, a fishing boat with Jersey men came alongside to inform the captain that two days ago three large vessels, supposed to be French, went into Temple Bay on the southern coast of Labrador, and about forty miles distant, opposite Belle Isle. The boat brought fish, and while we lay to some exceeding fine cod were caught. A slight breeze and excessive cold weather. This afternoon we sent the trunks below, and the cabin was partly cleared to prepare for meeting the French.

Mon. 19th—A head wind all night; towards morning a heavy gale and great fog. We were driven back between Portreau Bay and Green Island. At one time it cleared, grew calm and the wind fair, but a very great swell.

Tues. 20th—This morning at eight we were opposite Temple Bay, but it was too hazy to see any distance. A fair wind. At eleven we were abreast of Belle Isle, which is one entire dismal, barren rock. At twelve two French frigates and a brig were seen. They soon took six of our merchantmen, who, not having obeyed the "Pearl's" signals, were a great way ahead of us. We cleared for action. Capt. Gower conducted me down two flights of steps into the bread room, which just held me, the children and my servant; there I spent six hours in perfect misery, every moment expecting to hear the guns fire, as we lay for the enemy. Never having been in real danger before, I had no idea what it was to be so frightened. Some refreshment was sent me, but I could not eat. The sailor who brought it said, "You had better take it now, for there is no knowing when you may be able to get any more." I presently was informed that "The Progress," in which Genl. and Mrs. England were, was taken. At six o'clock Capt. Malcolm, of the Marines, very obligingly offered me his room, tho' only six feet long and four wide. I lay down with an excruciating headache, which essence of peppermint relieved.

Wed. 21st—As this room, cabin or cupboard is below decks, I heard people talking all the night, and could not help listening, even to the cabin boys. I heard half-sentences and supposed the rest, and it seemed inevitable for us to escape being taken. However, the next day at twelve I was persuaded to go into the gun room (the cabin being cleared and bulkheads thrown down), and I found that a more cheerful place, and the officers of the "Active," having no duty, played at back-gammon or cards with me all day long, for it was the only relief I found. Some gentlemen were continually coming down from deck, and various were the opinions; some thought the French would come up with us, others did not. The French were following at three leagues distance. We are now a mile to the northward of Belle Isle, between that and the Labrador coast. Islands of ice were passing all the day, which made the air very cold.

FEAR OF ATTACK BY FRENCH FRIGATES

I wished to see them, but did not have spirits to go upon deck, and I was told we should probably see them for some days to come.

It is supposed the "Ephron" got away from the enemy after she was taken, but she has not joined us. A fine breeze towards evening. The "Pearl" took the "Brook Watson" in tow twice, and her master let the hawser go. I was glad when we got rid of her. The "Adriatic" is with us, and the "London" was this morning, but guns were heard to-night off the north shore, and it is feared she is aground. Mr. Deighton, the master of the "Active," says he knew a ship which had her bottom knocked off by the ice, and yet she came safe into port. I played at backgammon and cards till half after ten.

Thurs. 22nd—A fine day, but very cold. We are still in the gun room, where the motion is so little felt that I like it much better than the cabin. I played backgammon or cards, which tranquilizes my mind, but it will be a great while before I recover from my fright. It is supposed the French ships are commanded by Citizen Barney, a famous rebel during the late American War. He drinks nothing but water, and as he lives hard we suppose he will fight hard. The New York paper mentioned his cruising off this coast.

NOTE.—Joshua Barney, born in Baltimore in 1759, was an American naval officer in the Revolutionary War. He became lieutenant in 1776, was captured by the British in 1777 and again in 1781. Having command of the "Hyder Ali," he captured the "General Monk" in 1782. In the autumn of that year he was sent to France with despatches for Franklin, and subsequently received a commission in the French service, resigning in 1800. He commanded a flotilla in Chesapeake Bay in 1813, was wounded at the battle of Bladensburg in 1814, and died at Pittsburg 1st December, 1818.

JOSHUA BARNEY.

Fri. 23rd—I slept more quietly last night, as it is thought we are safe from the pursuit of the French. We breakfasted in the cabin. It seems a fortnight since we left it, so much has the agitation of mind apparently lengthened the time. The cabin appears dull. It is excessively cold. We are in Lat. 53-54. We ran 150 miles since yesterday in the latitude of Cape Charles (at the entrance to the Strait of Belle Isle). If we are still driven on to the northward by these winds we shall soon get to Greenland. Mr. Hill, one of the lieutenants, went to the North Sea, and was obliged to eat salt pork raw, for if it was boiled it presently became a cake of ice. This man relates so many terrifying adventures that I scarcely feel safe to be in the same ship, for it seems impossible he can perform any voyage in a quiet way.

Sat. 24th—A south wind. At three o'clock hazy weather, raw, but rather less cold; Lat. 54-55. I copied the action of the 1st of June from Capt. Ballard's drawings, taken on the spot.

Wind S.W. An exceedingly heavy gale all night, and this day put in the dead lights, the weather so bad. Meat could not be roasted, but we had a pork pie, and tho' I dislike pork on shore, it is very good on board ship, and an excellent salt-fish pudding. The fish, having been boiled the day before, was now chopped up with potatoes, parsnips, herbs, pepper, salt, and boiled in a bag.

Mon. 26th—A sail in sight, which proved to be the "London." A fresh breeze still sending us northward. Wind S.W. I copied nine plans of the action of the 1st June.

NOTE.—Every search has been made for these drawings. It is supposed that they were given away by Mrs. Simcoe on her return to England, for there is no trace of them in the portfolios at Wolford.

Tues. 27th—A head wind; damp, disagreeable weather.

Wed. 28th—A dreadful night; a very heavy gale. We did not breakfast till twelve o'clock. The forestay sail split; a heavy sail all day. Lat. 56-10.

Thurs. 29th—Drank raspberry vinegar instead of tea and slept better. A great sea, little wind, very cold.

Fri. 30th—Lat. 55-56.

Sat. Oct. 1st—Lat. 54-55.

Mon. 3rd—Wind north.

Tues. 4th—Wind N.W., squally; in the long. of the Western Isles.

Wed. 5th—A very rough night; wind N.E.; from 5 p.m. it blew N.W. and an immoderate gale. The windows of the ports were broke, and the sea came into the cabin without measure.

Thurs. 6th—The gale continued all night, the sea washing in at the ports, and deep water under the beds and until six o'clock p.m. this day. They did not give us any breakfast, and we got up to dinner at two; the dead lights and doors to the quarter galleries put up. We have run 300 miles in the last 24 hours. Last night went 13 knots an hour under bare poles; parted with the "London," "Adriatic" and "Brook Watson" in the gale.

Fri. 7th—A sail seen this morning; they began to clear the ship, but the vessel proved to be the "Hope," of New London; these are the first American colours I have seen. A calm after one o'clock; wind S.S.W. this evening.

Sat. 8th—The ship in soundings on the Great Sole Bank, off the English coast. At eight the wind changed and blew fresh from the N.W. Some ships seen. The cabin was begun to be cleared, but this having happened two or three times, and no further ill consequences ensued, I now see this preparation with indifference, which had before inspired me with so much terror. I had continued drawing as long as they left a table in the room. The ships were soon discovered to be India-men. In the evening we passed another, to whom we spoke. She was from Jamaica; had parted from her convoy in a dreadful gale of wind four days since, in which her top sails were split. We ran nine knots an hour under bare poles.

Note.—Great Sole Bank lies in latitude 49° 23' north, longitude 10° 16', and continues 30 miles northeast by east. It is 7 miles long by 7 miles wide and lies 120 miles southwest of the Fastnet Light and 130 miles west of the Scilly Islands Lights. Its greatest depth is 70 fathoms.

Sun. 9th—We spoke to a West India vessel, called "The Lioness," and took her under convoy. She parted company from 130 sail in the late gale. A fair wind to-day, and we ran eight knots an hour. I went on deck to-night to see the lead heav'd and the ship lay to. It was a terrific sight when she turned her side to the wind. The waves seemed as if they would overwhelm the ship, and the noise was frightful.

IN SIGHT OF OLD ENGLAND

Mon. 10th—Passed the Islands of Scilly this morning; three or four sail seen; we spoke to one under Danish colours; the Land's End seen at one o'clock.

Tues. 11th—We stood close for Berry Head, on south coast of Devon, intending to go on shore at Tor Bay. This landing would have been more convenient for Gen. Simcoe, as he desired to go to Exeter. But the wind freshened so much it was impossible to get on board the fishing boats, which we saw at a little distance. Two hours sooner it might have been done, but we lay to for two or three hours in the morning to press men out of the India-men, and since that the wind has risen. Sophia wishes to be on shore, but Francis, never having been sick, thinks it a pity to quit the ship he is so fond of, and leave Beau and Bell, the captain's dogs, who are his constant playfellows. He is determined to be a sailor.

Wed. 12th—A fine day and fair wind, but we lay to so long for the convoy that we did not pass Dover till late. We anchored in the Downs, off the coast of Kent, at eight o'clock. It is difficult to go on shore here if the weather is not very calm, notwithstanding the extreme skilfulness of the Deal boatmen. We passed Beachy Head, where the cliffs are white, and Hastings, a brick town, this morning. In the afternoon the "Diamond" and "Melampus," frigates, passed us. It was a very fine sight to see those large frigates cut thro' the waves with so much swiftness, and they are handsomer objects than a line of battleships, which are heavier; they were painted black and yellow, with white figure-heads. A pretty, light, small vessel followed them, supposed to be Russian built.

Thurs. 13th—We anchored very near a large Indiaman. I was waked in the night by hearing a sailor call out that we should be aboard the Indiaman, and having heard of such accidents in the Downs, I did not like the alarm.

This morning I was much pleased with seeing the number of vessels in the Downs. The "Ville de Paris" got under weigh and passed close to us, but being under jury masts she looked extremely heavy and clumsy and of an immense size. I liked the frigates better. A wet morning; we landed at one o'clock. Capts. Ballard, Gower and some officers of the "Pearl" dined with us at the inn at Deal.

We took a friendly leave of men in whom we were much interested, having lived so much in their company for seven weeks; they both offered their best services for Francis. From my experience of people, I am as anxious he should be a sailor as he is to be one. Francis came downstairs in the inn backwards, as he used to descend the ladder on board the "Pearl." I felt it a great happiness to find the rooms steady, and not roll like the ship.

Fri. 14th—Genl. Grinfield came to breakfast with us, and invited us to dine at Dover with Mrs. Grinfield, which place we set out for after breakfast, and drove eleven miles thro' a bleak, barren country, and when I came to the hill at Dover I was amazingly struck with the grandeur of the scene, the grand appearance of the castle on those very high cliffs, part of the building in good and habitable preservation, the rest in ruins; a grand site and a building adapted to it. The bold cliffs, the town and beach beneath, form a charming picture, and the horizon of the sea was terminated by the fleet, which sailed yesterday, the "Ville de Paris" towering above the rest; we sailed round her before we came on shore, but a large frigate, such as the "Diamond," is a finer sight to my taste. The fresh east wind has probably sent them back.

We walked round the works, which are enlarging about the castle. Capt. Bruyere, of the Engineers, went with us; he has been long in Canada, to which country he was much attached, therefore I was delighted to talk with him.

We noticed the Roman brick very visible in one of the towers which is in ruins. We distinguished the coast of France, a part of which looks like Beachy Head. I was shown the church at Calais and the entrance

357

of Boulogne harbour. Saw the brass cannon given to Queen Elizabeth by the Dutch; it is 24 feet long, beautifully carved with figures of Britannia and the "God of the Scheldt." We went thro' the communication lately cut underground thro' the hill from the castle to the town; it is a handsome stone staircase of twelve hundred steps; at the bottom of every two or three hundred feet it is lighted by a passage and window at the extremity of the rock; we descended with a lanthorn; it cost £700. I was much pleased with Capt. Bruyere, for he talked with delight of Canada. He married a sister of Mrs. Selby's, of Montreal.

It was extremely cold walking on the hill. We spent some hours very pleasantly with Mrs. Grinfield, and at seven at night set off for Canterbury. A very violent rain this morning. Canterbury is fifteen miles from Dover. We arrived in the dark, very much fatigued.

NOTE.—William Grinfield, colonel of the 8th Regiment of Foot, 16th May, 1787, became major-general, 13th June, 1793, and lieutenant-general, January, 1798.

Captain Bruyere of the Royal Engineers was one of the military Land Board at Niagara in 1791. He died of exposure in the War of 1812. Mrs. Selby, wife of Dr. George Selby, of Montreal, was formerly Miss Dunbar, daughter of Major Dunbar. Dr. Selby, who was born in England and educated at the College of St. Omer, came to Canada about 1781. He died in 1835.

Sat. 15th—Damp, raw weather. Went to see the cathedral, which I greatly admired; the style of building is peculiarly grand and simple, and the ascent to the choir by steps has a grand effect. There is a monument of Edward, the Black Prince, in brass, in great preservation. The armour, helmet and gloves he wore at Cressy are hung over it.

A head of Dean Watson carved in stone, done in Italy, is a fine piece of sculpture, and there are many pieces of stone work curiously executed; there is a great deal of painted glass; a good picture of a Pope, but it has been shot thro' during the civil wars in Cromwell's time.

Thomas à Becket's tomb is plain. The stone around is deeply worn by having been knelt upon, as is said. There is a good monument of Henry IV. and his Queen. The ship called the "Great Harry," with four masts, built in Henry V.'s reign, is represented in stone. This cathedral has the advantage of Salisbury in not having been modernized.

The country from Canterbury to Dartford (18 miles below London on the Thames) is woody and beautiful; some views of the Medway and Thames.

The weather is damp, raw and unpleasant. I could not but observe, as we passed many houses, that those mansions appeared very comfortable habitations, in which people might live very happily, but it could not be supposed they could ever be induced to go out of them in such a damp climate, for the fields looked so cold, so damp, so cheerless, so uncomfortable from the want of our bright Canadian sun that the effect was striking, and the contrast very unfavourable to the English climate. We slept at Dartford.

Sun. 16th—A beautiful country from Dartford to London. On the road I passed a remarkable fine Cedar of Lebanon. Arrived at the hotel in Cork Street, London, at ten o'clock.

CHAPTER XXII.

AGAIN AT WOLFORD—SIMCOE'S DEATH.

Mrs. Simcoe's sojourn in Canada was always regarded by her with pleasurable recollections. She had made many friends in the land across the sea. Her husband had had the honor of establishing the first Provincial Government when Upper Canada was marked upon the map as the western Province of the old Province of Canada.

Nor did she forget the kindness and courtesy that had been so gracefully accorded to both herself and her husband, from the day in October, 1791, when they landed at Quebec, till that day in September, 1796, when they were homeward bound from the same port. True, she had two of her children with her, but there were four others at home. She longed to see them, for although their daily lives were recorded by monthly letters from Mrs. Hunt, yet her desire for her little ones gave her hours of depression. Then she remembered with tears the green knoll in the military burying ground at York that covered the little one, the first Katherine, who, born at Navy Hall, Niagara, in January, 1793, died and was buried at York (Toronto) in April, 1794.

When the "Pearl" anchored in the Downs, within sight of the white cliffs of England, Mrs. Simcoe realized that she was not far from the home of her childhood. She spent a few hours at Deal, a day with friends in Dover and Canterbury, a couple of days in London, and then proceeded southwest by coach to Exeter.

Glad was the welcome at Wolford. A letter written from Quebec in July had informed Mrs. Hunt that probably at the end of August the General and his wife would sail for England. Then a second letter in August said that they would sail about the end of the first week in September so as to arrive in England about the middle of October; and almost within a day of the promised time did the family carriage and pair, which had been sent down to Exeter to meet the home-comers, drive up to the door of Wolford.

Never was there a happier meeting. Mrs. Hunt and her daughter were as eager to see them as were the children, who waited eagerly for their father and mother and for the brother and sister whom they had not seen for five long years. The delight was mutual. The old home looked bright and cheerful on that October afternoon, and the day closed with worship read by the master surrounded by his household. The countryside knew of the General's return and the County families, glad to renew their friendships, were not long in calling at Wolford.

The old home life was quietly resumed. Much of the General's energy was thrown into the improvement of his estate, for but little along that line had been done during the years of his absence. The family were early risers, always up with the lark. The General was usually around with Mr. Scadding as early as six o'clock in the morning, and Mrs. Simcoe and one of her daughters frequently took a five-mile ride before breakfast.

Eliza Simcoe was now a girl of twelve years of age, while her sister, Charlotte, was eleven. Both girls showed extraordinary interest in their studies. They were lovable children, and as their governess said "excellent examples in every way" for Henrietta and Caroline and Sophia, who were nine, eight and seven years respectively.

Then the little ones from Canada were a welcome addition to the family circle which had been broken for five years. Francis Gwillim was a sturdy little fellow of five years, who in his own esteem was most important, for he had "talked to the Indians," and his sister, Sophia, who was two years his senior, did not forget to tell those who came her way that she too had shared the honor of being introduced to the "great red Chief Brant" when he came to see her father at Navy Hall.

In December of 1796, the General determined to accept the appointment of Commander-in-Chief at San Domingo. The announcement came as a shock to Mrs. Simcoe, who felt that her husband was not a robust man and the climate of the West Indies would not improve his health.

This was emphasized in a letter that the General wrote to the authorities at the end of the year, asking an assurance from the Government that it would provide for his family in case he should "perish in the mission which he was about to proceed upon." He had pointed out that twice in his life he had been "obliged to quit a Southern climate even without contagion to preserve life" and asked for the consideration of his claim.

That it was acceded to is shown by a letter written on December 6th, 1796, to the Honorable William Pitt, thanking him for giving the guarantee that in case of death his family would be provided for.

In January arrangements were made for his departure for San Domingo in the following month; and his new and arduous duties commenced when in March of 1797, he landed at Port au Prince. The climate of San Domingo was not propitious; for the scourge of yellow fever had played havoc not only with the inhabitants, but with many men in the British forces. But the General, as is shown in his biography, did much in a short time to re-establish the British character in an island that was rank with revolution and insurrection, and returned to England in September of 1797 to secure a force sufficient to make paramount the authority of British arms.

His reception at Wolford was a welcome long to be remembered. Mrs. Simcoe was delighted to see her husband again in the family home. She was anxious that his health, which had not been improved by residence in a West Indian clime, should be thoroughly recuperated by the balmy air of Devon and the regular life at Wolford, and it came about as she had wished.

Just two years had passed when another son was born at Wolford, in July, 1798—John Cornwall, the second son of the household. Wolford was a centre from which all sorts of enjoyment radiated. In the years that followed, the calling days were more like miniature court receptions, and a score of carriages of county people at the one time was not an unusual sight in front of Wolford Lodge.

A letter written in 1800 by a Devon lady says, "The drawing-room at Wolford on a reception day is most enjoyable, for it is filled with well-dressed men and women, for the county people always liked the Simcoes." Another letter states that "going to Wolford was like going to Court."

Though small in stature, Mrs. Simcoe was proud and somewhat autocratic in manner, most dignified, and commanding respect. Her daughters recognized these characteristics in their mother. They had been early taught that absolute obedience was a pre-requisite and that what the father and mother ordered was a law unto all concerned. Even on entering a room if their mother was present they would not dare, so states a Wolford chronicler, who knew Mrs. Simcoe, "to sit down without permission."

In October, 1798, Major-General Simcoe was gazetted a lieutenant-general and in 1801 was appointed to the command of the garrison at Plymouth in the absence of the Governor and of Lieutenant-General Grenville. This new charge took him away from Wolford, but as he returned frequently his wife, anxious that he should have every opportunity of building up his health, did not look with disfavor on this new appointment.

In the year 1800 a third son was born, Henry Addington, and for him Mrs. Simcoe had always a particular affection. The after-life of this pattern among men bore silent testimony to the tender care and upbringing by a Christian mother. This gifted son was born at Plymouth, where the Governor and his wife had been resident during December of 1799 until February of 1800.

Family responsibilities again increased in 1801, when the second Katherine was born at Wolford, and in 1804 Anne was born. She always declared that she remembered her father, although she was less than three years of age when he passed away.

But from 1800 until 1806, the daily routine of Mrs. Simcoe's life was not very varied. She occasionally visited London and was generally accompanied by one of her elder daughters. A favorite residence in town was at 53 Welbeck Street, fashionable lodgings patronized by leading Devon families when visiting town.

The General's position as commander of the Western Military District, which consisted of Dorset, Somerset, Devon and Cornwall, brought many people to Wolford. The threatened invasion of Britain by France had given special importance to his District, and all orders were issued from Wolford.

As John Bailey, an old servant who wrote an account of the General and his family, says in his narrative, "there were often ten or fifteen carriages there in a day, as all the head gentry in Devonshire visited Wolford and so many officers came on duty for orders. I have known three or four Lords staying at Wolford at one time."

The activities of the day at Wolford always opened with family prayer, at which all the household were present. The general read the service. "It was somewhat imposing," as a visitor of a century ago remarked, "to see the maid-servants headed by the housekeeper, and the men-servants, headed by the butler—seventeen in all—file into the dining-room morn and eve and hear the master or the mistress of the house read and comment on the chapters selected for daily worship." To-day the daily routine is the same—just as it was a hundred years ago when the general and his wife read the Holy Writings and knelt at God's altar with their household.

It is a matter of surprise that the General did not seem to know of the condition of his health when he was appointed in July of 1806 as commander-in-chief in India. If he did, he said nothing to his wife about it. The General had hardly accepted the position of commander-in-chief in India when orders came from Downing Street for him to proceed to Portugal, to act with the Earl of Rosslyn and the Earl of St. Vincent on a special mission to the Court of Lisbon; for the British Government had been informed of the intention of France to invade Portugal.

This caused Mrs. Simcoe to delay her preparations for India. The General had sailed for Portugal and had arrived at Lisbon on the 26th of August, 1806. Here he was taken ill, but he was not thought to be in a serious condition until the third week in September, when he was ordered to return to England by his physicians.

Mrs. Simcoe in the meantime proceeded about the end of September to London to purchase her outfit for her voyage to the East. She was accompanied by her daughter Eliza. But they had hardly got settled in London when a letter came from Exeter, stating that the General had returned from Portugal and was seriously ill at Archdeacon Moore's house in the Cathedral Close at Exeter. A hurried departure was made and in less than twenty-four hours by coach the mother and her daughter had covered the distance between London and Exeter, arriving at the Archdeacon's house a day or so before the General's death.

The story of the journey from Lisbon, his landing at Topsham, his arrival and death at Exeter and his burial when the shades of evening had fallen at the chapel at Wolford, will be told in another volume. It was as a bolt out of the blue for Mrs. Simcoe and her family. The daughters Eliza, Charlotte, Henrietta, Caroline and Sophia, were old enough to give some comfort to their widowed mother, and cheering too was the declaration of Francis Gwillim, then fifteen, that it would always be his aim to take pattern from the life of his father. John Cornwall, the second son, born in 1798, had died in infancy. The other surviving son, Henry Addington, was but five years of age as he stood with his sisters and held the hand of Katherine, his four-year-old sister, at the burial in the twilight of that November evening at Wolford.

CHAPTER XXIII.

MRS. SIMCOE AND HER CHILDREN.

The death of General Simcoe brought to Mrs. Simcoe many expressions of sympathy. Those high in position, military and civil, paid to her their sad tributes for the great loss she had sustained. The rich and poor knew that in the passing away of the General they had all lost a kindly and generous friend.

The old-time visitors who had spent pleasant days and weeks at Wolford manifested in their letters of sympathy the deep regard in which they had held the General and how much grief they felt for the widowed mother and her children.

But deep and genuine as was the sympathy, it did not lessen the sorrow at Wolford. From what I have been able to learn from those who knew Mrs. Simcoe, the death of her husband marked a great change in her life.

She had the younger children to bring up and educate, and occupied her time in looking after the welfare of her family. Her deep interest in those who lived on her estate was constant. She was continuous in good works and her endeavors in that direction earned for her the respect, regard and love of all those who lived in the country surrounding Wolford.

Francis Gwillim, whose ambition had been to follow in the path of his late father and enter the army, was educated with that intent, and secured a lieutenancy in the 27th Regiment of Foot in 1811, when he was in his twenty-first year.

His regiment was ordered to the Continent under the Viscount Wellington, but the service of young Simcoe was not a lengthened one; for he was killed in April, 1812, at the siege of Badajoz, and was buried upon the field of battle.

For some years Mrs. Simcoe did not journey far from Wolford. Once or twice she visited her birthplace, "Old Court," near Whitchurch, in Herefordshire; but from about 1825 her favorite touring spot was North Wales, which she generally visited once a year.

Sometimes her daughter Caroline accompanied her, and in all these excursions she was attended by her faithful servant, John Bailey, whose narrative gives so many incidents and experiences in travelling with his mistress.

After her son, the Rev. Henry Addington, had reached manhood's estate and married and had purchased the ancient manor of Penheale in Cornwall, Mrs. Simcoe paid him regular visits; but the house was not large, the guest chambers were few, so that Mrs. Simcoe spent her day with her son and stayed at Launceston, four miles from Penheale, every night.

DIARY OF MRS. SIMCOE

His first wife was Anne, daughter of Rev. Edward Palmer of Moseley, County Worcester. After her death he married Emily, daughter of Rev. Horace Mann of Mawgan, County Cornwall. A

REV. H. A. SIMCOE.

daughter by this second marriage is Emily, known as Mother Emily Clare, Superior of the Wantage Sisters Mission, Poonah, India.

Penheale Manor is mentioned in the Doomsday Book. It was improved by Mrs. Simcoe about 1830. The dwelling was in two distinct divisions with a courtyard, dividing two parallel wings, which were, in fact, two houses of different periods and of architecture. It

MOTHER EMILY CLARE.

is probable that at the time of Mrs. Simcoe's visits only one part of the house was in use. But after the improvements the Rev. Henry Addington Simcoe used both parts. He had a printing press in the part they called "across."

PENHEALE MANOR.
(From a Picture in the J. Ross Robertson collection.)

Mr. John Henry Vowler-Simcoe, eldest son of the late J. N. Vowler of Parnacott, Cornwall, who married Mary Northcote, second daughter of the Rev. Henry A. Simcoe, has assumed by Royal License the additional surname and arms of Simcoe, and succeeded on the death of his uncle, Mr. Samuel Simcoe, to Penheale Manor, Cornwall.

John Bailey's description of the tours with Mrs. Simcoe and her daughters in North Wales would do credit to the pages of a modern travel book. His drive of forty-two miles when Miss Harriet desired to go from Beddgelert, on the borders of Carnarvonshire, to Bala in Merionethshire, and his return on foot, shows how devoted he was to his mistress and her family.

Cheltenham in Gloucestershire was another favorite place of Mrs. Simcoe and her daughters. It was the only place where she made lengthened stay from Wolford. Bath was a popular resort in the thirties and forties and the daughters of the family always favored

DUNKESWELL ABBEY CHURCH.
(From a Drawing by Miss Harriet Simcoe.)

it. Eliza, the eldest daughter, and Caroline, the third daughter, resided there about 1852, and both died there.

Mrs. Simcoe had strong opinions upon the marriage question. She herself had not hesitated to enter matrimony when she was sixteen years of age, but when it came to a question as to the marriage of any of her daughters, for some reason or other she always opposed it. It must be remembered that all the daughters were clever, prepossessing and well-educated women.

One suitor who pressed his claim without success was the late Sir Thomas Dyke Acland of Devonshire, a man of admirable character; and two members of the nobility from other counties shared a similar fate. Mrs. Simcoe was obdurate. Her word was law, and her daughters, rather than incur her displeasure, accepted the situation, and all, with one exception, died unmarried. Some years after Mrs. Simcoe's death Anne married a Mr. Alford, who resided in Herefordshire, but left no issue.

The three daughters, Eliza, Caroline and Anne, were not only proficient in domestic economy, but they inherited a good deal of the commonsense that was a feature in the character of both their father and mother. In parish work they were indefatigable. Each daughter had her own parish—one that of Dunkeswell Abbey, another Luppit and the third that of Dunkeswell. Every parish had its schoolhouse and its teachers, and many of the generations that surround Wolford to-day, although their lives have fallen into the sere and yellow leaf of old age, remember most gratefully what "the young ladies" did for ·them when the primer and the slate pencil were essentials in their early training.

A RESTFUL SPOT AT PENHEALE.
(From a Picture in the J. Ross Robertson collection.)

"Holy Trinity," Dunkeswell Abbey Church, was built by Mrs. and the Misses Simcoe in 1842. It is in the Early English style, and with the burial ground occupies the site of the ancient abbey, which was founded by Lord de Brewer in 1201 for Cistercian monks, who were endowed with the manor and other lands. Only a fragment of the Abbey now remains. The interior of the church is very handsome, with several stained glass windows and columns, the capitals of which were carved by the Misses Simcoe. The altars are of carved stone by these ladies.

DEATH OF MRS. SIMCOE

The Rev. Henry Addington Simcoe, of Penheale Manor, the heir to the estate, made frequent visits to Wolford. For him his mother had a most affectionate regard. His loving disposition, his exemplary character and his earnestness in carrying on Christian work in Egloskerry, were most gratifying to her. During the last years of his mother's life his delight was to spend a few days at Wolford, when parish work would permit his absence, and when her end came he was with her. As John Bailey in his quaint way writes, " So her last day came and she died in a good old age—full of days, riches and honour."

During the last years of her life Mrs. Simcoe did not make any prolonged tours. She had always favored Cheltenham, but in 1848-9 she preferred Sidmouth on the South Devon coast, thirteen miles from Wolford, and these trips were not prolonged ones. At Wolford during the last summer of her life, when the weather was fine, an hour's drive on the estate and its neighborhood refreshed her.

In the autumn of 1849 her strength began to fail. If weather permitted she enjoyed an hour in a wheel chair guided by the faithful Bailey, but as the old year passed out and the new year entered, her family began to see that that day which never changes must soon come to her who had sixty-eight years before stood at the altar in Buckerall Parish Church.

On the 17th of January, 1850, at the age of eighty-four years, twenty-four of which were in married life and forty-four in widowhood, Elizabeth Posthuma Simcoe passed away.

The announcement of her death was not unexpected in the county. It brought many messages of sympathy from the large circle of family friends and expressions of grief and sadness from the tenantry on the estate, and from the people of the parish, all of whom had the deepest regard and respect for the family of Simcoe. The funeral was attended by the leading families of the county.

The clergy of the neighboring parishes, the tenantry on the estate, the laborers from the farms and the household servants, formed in line as the coffin, carried from the main entrance of Wolford, followed by the seven surviving children, Eliza, Caroline, Sophia, Henry, Katherine, Charlotte and Anne, was borne through the garden walks to the private chapel.

The impressive service for the dead was read by the Rev. Mr. Muller, the Vicar of Dunkeswell, the clergyman who had been most attentive to Mrs. Simcoe during her last illness, after which the silent gathering re-formed and followed the coffin to the east end of the chapel, where in a grave close by that of her husband the body was buried.

Mrs. Simcoe was a genuine Christian. She took a deep interest in all matters pertaining to religion and endeavored to practise in her daily life the works that are characteristic of a Christian woman. She constantly thought not of her own happiness but of the happiness of others, and the deep regret in the country-side at her passing away justified the expression that she was indeed much loved as the Lady of the Manor.

Her daughter, Anne, in writing to the present Mrs. Simcoe, shortly after her mother's death, said:—

"A prominent factor in my mother's character was humility—humility before God and man. Her retrospect of life would only have led her more gratefully to rest all on Christ, feeling she owed all to Him. As she says, 'I could not offer a prayer or praise that would be accepted but through Jesus Christ our Lord. May I feel daily more and more trust in this Saviour, and may He quicken and support me at the hour of death and on my approach to death.' And again, 'Strengthen me, Lord, for my dying hour; may the strength of the Lord be my support in that hour of trial.'

"But for inability now to fathom the unpacked boxes of books, I should like to have given some extracts shewing still more strongly her feelings on the approach of death, and how entirely she merged all feeling of self-reliance on her Saviour, and how completely she renounced all goodness and righteousness but His, in whom was all her hope."

After the death of Mrs. Simcoe, the daughters continued to reside there for a few months, after which Eliza, Caroline, Sophia and Katherine took up their residence at Bath. Charlotte went to Leamington and Anne remained at Wolford.

The Rev. Henry Addington Simcoe, the only surviving son of General Simcoe, inherited Wolford, but never lived there. He let it from 1851-66.

The Rev. Henry Addington Simcoe died in November, 1868; and as his eldest son, Henry Walcot, died in 1848, Captain John K.

Simcoe, his second son, inherited Wolford. He died in 1891, without issue. His widow, who resides to-day at Wolford, is the only one of the name related to this family, living.

In 1867, when Captain John Kennaway Simcoe, R.N., the second son of the Rev. Henry Addington Sim-

CAPT. J. K. SIMCOE.

MRS. SIMCOE.

coe of Penheale, married Miss Mary Jackson, second daughter of Colonel Basil Jackson, of Glewstone Court, Herefordshire, and an officer of the late Royal Staff Corps, Wolford once more had a Simcoe as the master of its household, for after his marriage Captain Simcoe rented the estate from his father for one year. At the time of his marriage, Captain Simcoe retired from the Navy and settled down as a country gentleman, generous in his hospitality, with a large circle of friends. Miss

ESTATE OF MRS. J. K. SIMCOE

Eliza Simcoe had previously left £30,000 for the upkeep of Wolford. The estate on the death of Mrs. Simcoe, widow of Captain John K. Simcoe, passes into the possession of Mr. Arthur Linton, who is descended from the Rev. H. A. Simcoe's eldest daughter, Anne Eliza, who married Sedley Bastard Marke, of Woodhill. Their daughter, Olive Ann, married Rev. George Linton, Vicar of Corsham in Wiltshire. Their eldest son, Arthur Henry Linton, is heir of the late Captain John Kennaway Simcoe, and will succeed to the estate. A condition of the inheritance is that he has to take the name and arms of Simcoe.

CHAPTER XXIV.

LOVING WORDS FROM THE PULPIT.

Sunday, the twenty-seventh of January, one thousand eight hundred and fifty, was a day that was never forgotten during the lifetime of the children of Mrs. Simcoe and of the parishioners who made up the congregation in the parish church of Dunkeswell, when loving testimony was paid to the life and works of her who had so recently passed away. Every family in the parish was represented, in fact

DUNKESWELL PARISH CHURCH BEFORE RESTORATION.
(From a Drawing by Mrs. Simcoe.)

every parishioner was present. It was on the occasion when the Rev. John Blackmore, A.M., the rector of Culmstock in Devon, an old and esteemed friend of the family, preached a sermon entitled "The Christian in Life and Death," on the death of Mrs. Simcoe. It was an appreciation well deserved and most acceptable to so many—not only to those in her family circle but to the people of the parish, who were devoted in their esteem for the late Lady of the Manor.

The sermon was (subsequently) privately printed at the Penheale Press, Launceston, by Mrs. Simcoe's only surviving son, the Rev. Henry Addington Simcoe.

AN APPROPRIATE TEXT

The text was:

"Blessed are the dead which die in the Lord from henceforth; yea, saith the Spirit, that they may rest from their labours; and their works do follow them." Rev. xiv., 13.

The preacher said:

"I feel, and doubtless you will feel with me, that the occasion of my standing in this holy place to-day is one of a deeply solemn and affecting character, the death—the departure rather—of a friend esteemed, revered, beloved—most justly esteemed, most justly revered, most justly beloved by us all. Well indeed may we mourn the loss of such a friend. But it is our privilege, through the grace and mercy of God, 'not to mourn as those without hope'; oh, no; we think of the departed, we look back at the piety of her life, and see the humble Christian living 'in the Lord'; we look at the peacefulness of her death, and see the trusting

INTERIOR DUNKESWELL PARISH CHURCH BEFORE RESTORATION.
(From a Drawing by Miss Harriet Simcoe.)

Christian dying 'in the Lord'; and we look at the volume of God's unerring Word, and we hear 'a voice from heaven' proclaiming, 'Blessed are the dead which die in the Lord.' 'Blessed are the dead which die in the Lord!' Oh, brethren, it is at such seasons as this that the heart feels the unspeakable preciousness of such a message from heaven. When the thoughts have been dwelling with some departed one in the sufferings of sickness, the solitude of the coffin, the silence of the grave, with what a sweetness and power of consolation does this 'voice of the Spirit' break upon the soul. 'Blessed are the dead which die in the Lord; even so, saith the Spirit, that they may rest from their labours'— their labours in the Christian warfare, their labours of faith and love— 'and their works do follow them'—widening the reality of their faith and the sincerity of their love. Here is comfort, instruction, encouragement for us all; comfort respecting the dear friend whom we lament, in the assurance that 'our loss is her eternal gain,' that from sojourning with us in the flesh she has passed to a blessedness such as mortal 'eye hath not seen, nor ear heard, nor heart conceived'; instruction and encouragement respecting ourselves still left for awhile pilgrims in this earthly wilderness, instruction as showing how we may attain the same heavenly blessedness, and encouragement in the certainty that we shall attain it if we seek it rightly 'in the Lord.'

"And may the power of the Spirit apply this Word of the Spirit effectually to each of us for comfort, instruction and encouragement! May the Almighty Spirit be to each of us, as He was to our 'blessed' friend, a Spirit of light and life and holiness and peace! 'Awake, awake, and arm of the Lord, put on'—put forth—'thy strength'; if there be souls here spiritually 'dead in trespasses and sins,' by Thy life-giving energy 'raise them from the death of sin to the life of righteousness,' and those whom Thou hast thus raised vouchsafe to strengthen, establish, sanctify more and more; and grant that we may all know, in our own eternal experience, how 'blessed are the dead which die in the Lord.'

"'In the Lord.' How much is implied in these three words!—baptism and the great change, and the living faith, and the mighty blessings signified and sealed by Christian baptism. We find the expression used in the New Testament Scriptures to denote the Christian's union with Christ as signified and sealed by baptism. Thus Christians are spoken of as 'baptized into Christ,' the word 'into' denoting their entering and being admitted into that state, being used in connection with baptism, and Christians so baptized are spoken of afterwards as being 'in Christ,' 'in the Lord.' But the expression implies also the reality—through the inworking power of the Holy Ghost—the reality of that 'death unto sin and new birth unto righteousness' of which the baptismal rite is the figure, the reality of that cleansing by the blood and Spirit of Christ, of which the application of the water is the sign; the reality of that faith in Christ, as the Son of God, the Prophet, Priest and King of His people, of which baptism is the profession, the real acting out of that living faith in Christ through which the believer cleaveth to Christ and followeth Christ 'in newness of life,' according to His Word; that faith through which 'the inner man,' receiving 'nourishment' from Christ, bringeth forth 'the fruits of the Spirit' of Christ, even as the branch in the vine, receiving living sap from the vine, produces the fruits of the vine. Thus was our departed friend 'in the Lord,' baptized with water, and with the Holy Spirit, having not only the sign, but also 'the thing signified,' showing not only the possession, but also the possession and the power of true faith. And thus, living 'in the Lord,' she died 'in the Lord,' and 'in the Lord' she 'liveth for evermore.'

"In thus speaking of the departed I speak not to her praise, but to the praise of that 'grace of God' by which she was what she was; praise while living she would have disclaimed and deprecated; praise when dead she needeth not; in the sight of God and in the memory of man 'her works do follow her.' And oh, how utterly less than nothing must be all praise or dispraise from man when the blessed spirit has heard from the adorable Redeemer, the everlasting Judge, 'Well done, good and faithful servant, enter thou into the joy of thy Lord.'

"But I would direct your attention to a few particulars respecting her, the consideration of which may tend, with God's blessing, to promote an object which lay near her heart while she lived, and which, if the spirits above can take any interest in things below, she would now desire most especially to have promoted, namely, the welfare—the spiritual and eternal welfare—of her fellow-creatures. And for this purpose I shall speak not of her powers of mind, or soundness of judgment, or decision

CHARACTER OF MRS. SIMCOE

of character (natural endowments given perhaps in the same measure but to few), but rather of those 'fruits of the Spirit' to which, through the same Divine Spirit, all Christians should aspire, and in seeking, cherishing and manifesting which we are all called to 'follow her good example.' The subject indeed is large, important, holy and glorious; and I feel myself utterly unequal to it, unable to do anything like justice to it; but I would desire to look humbly to Him whose 'strength is made perfect in the weakness of man,' and who alone can work in any of us that 'power of godliness' which we are privileged to contemplate in remembering our honoured friend.

"You know that the grand leading feature in her character was religion—true, practical godliness. In the ordering of her affairs, the management of her household, the employment of her means, the habits of her daily life, might be seen the guiding, governing influence of religion; there was evidently a higher principle and a nobler object than merely temporal things could supply, evidently a looking to something beyond the applause of man, the gratification of sense, the possessions of earth; a looking to things spiritual, invisible, eternal; a regard for the will, the favour, approval and glory of God in Christ Jesus, flowing forth in works of piety towards God, and of benevolence and beneficence to men, 'adorning the doctrine of the Saviour,' and the church of which she was a faithful member. I believe that the finest type, the highest exemplification, of the Christian character is to be found in the true, sound, consistent member of the Protestant Church of England, and such was our revered friend, a true Church of England woman and, as such, a true Christian in principle and in practice, in faith and in works. Her works, her practice, you all know, approve, admire; trace them to their sources, the principles from which they sprung; and let us remember, it is only as we have the same principles that we can have the like character on earth, the like blessedness in heaven. These principles, then, in her case were those religious principles which are called evangelical. On this point we have her own testimony. I am privileged to hold here a statement, written by herself more than thirty years ago, by which 'tho' dead she yet speaketh' for our instruction and profit; and a most valuable testimony it is, not only to the fundamental importance of those scriptural truths which the world so often despises, but also to the soundness of her own faith and the unquestionable certainty of her present and eternal blessedness. Hear her words: 'Now while my senses are perfect, I will declare that I trust and expect to die in those evangelical principles which form the happiness of my life, and I trust and hope will do of my death.' Observe this remarkable declaration made, as from a special regard to God's glory, 'while her senses'—all her powers of mind and judgment—'were perfect'; intellectual faculties there were of a high order, the tastes of an elegant, cultivated and accomplished mind, ample means for their gratification, the possession of earthly affluence, the enjoyment of domestic life, the affection of dutiful children, the attachment of numerous friends, the respect and esteem of all the neighbourhood, the consciousness of a life spent in the paths of honour, virtue, integrity and usefulness; yet none of these things are spoken of as especially constituting her happiness, but those religious principles which are called evangelical. Nor are we left in doubt as to what she meant by 'evangelical principles'; her own statement is in substance this: 'By evangelical principles I mean a humiliating estimate of our moral condition as radically corrupt, and of ourselves unable even to think a good thought; a condition also that the death of Christ is an all-sufficient sacrifice and atonement for our sins, whereby those who believe in Him are saved from the curse of God's broken law, and have His righteousness imputed to them; and a conviction that by the power of the Holy Spirit we are alone enabled to feel any good desires, or to do those works

373

which are the evidences to ourselves that our calling is sure, and that we have been blessed by divine grace with a living faith.' These 'evangelical principles,' comprehending (be it remembered) a deep, heartfelt conviction of three great truths, namely, our utterly corrupt and lost state by nature, justification through the atoning sacrifice and perfect righteousness of Christ, and sanctification by the regenerating power of the Holy Ghost—these are the very principles revealed in Holy Scripture, maintained in the Articles and Homilies of our reformed Church, and inwrought into the substance of all our Church services. Wherefore? Doubtless that by God's blessing they might be inwrought in all our hearts, and become the substantial elements of our character. God grant they may be so more and more! The following language of our dear friend, respecting the individual she was then addressing, just expresses what, I am sure, would have been her desire for us all: 'I earnestly pray that the power of God may (for no other power can) make you to taste of these principles.'

"And now observe the effects, the actual manifested influence, of these principles in our departed friend, whose heart and mind were impressed with them and made, in her own expressive language, 'to taste of them.' You know her habitual happy cheerfulness of mind, her happy freedom from carking care and disquieting anxieties. Mark, then, the source and support of that happiness. You remember her own words, that her 'evangelical principles formed the happiness of her life, and her hope and trust were that they would form the happiness of her death.' Nor was that a vain hope, that trust was not disappointed; those divine principles, which dissipated the dark clouds and let in the full, cheerful sunshine on her pathway of life, shed a bright and beautiful radiance along 'the dark valley of the shadow of death'; 'the Lord,' her well-known and beloved 'Shepherd,' who for many a year with unfailing care had 'fed her in the green pasture and led her forth beside the waters of comfort,' He was still with her, and gave her to know and feel the truth of those words which she had often uttered with the lips in this place, and which we have heard again this morning—

'I pass the gloomy vale of death,
From fear and danger free,
For there His aiding rod and staff
Defend and comfort me.'

But observe her testimony further on this point :' Before these principles were, by the blessing of God, impressed on my mind, I thought of death with terror, and was never composed in my mind respecting either temporal or eternal concerns.'

"There may possibly be persons here who make light of what are called 'evangelical principles,' speaking of them perhaps, as I have heard them spoken of, with a sort of scornful contempt as indicating weakness of mind. Consider this remarkable testimony. You know something of the mind which gave it—a mind distinguished by superior acuteness, clearness, strength, solidity, soundness, soberness—yet, according to its own deliberate and unquestionable testimony, 'until these evangelical principles were, by God's blessing, impressed on it,' that mind was 'never composed respecting either temporal or eternal concerns, and never thought of death but with secret feelings of terror.' And that was perfectly natural and reasonable; such were reasonably the feelings of the human heart knowing something of its sinfulness and of the holiness and justice of the Almighty Judge. And if you think at all seriously of your sins, and of the infinite holiness and justice of Him who is coming to be your Judge, such would be your feelings. I am speaking perhaps to some whose feelings are such; disquieted midst the uncertainties of life, shrinking with secret dread from the prospect of death. The time was when our 'blessed' friend felt even so; but she found relief, deliverance, from such tormenting fears, and composure, peace, happiness, were her portion in life and in death. How? From the power of those religious principles which are called evangelical. And it is only from the influence of the same principles that you can find the like deliverance, the like rest for your own soul.'

"We read in the 13th Chapter of the Book of Numbers that among the Israelites in the wilderness of Paran were exhibited a large, magnificent cluster of rich grapes, and beautiful pomegranates and figs; but they did not grow in that wilderness; a Caleb and Joshua had been in the promised land, and plucked them in the valley of Eschol, and brought them to stimulate and cheer and encourage their brethren in the wilderness with such earnests of the goodness of that land: so the happiness, cheerfulness and peace which adorned our dear friend's earthly course were not of earthly origin; they sprung, not from the natural stock of mental endowments or moral virtue, but from the spiritual root of evangelical principles; her faith had laid hold on the Saviour, and through Him had penetrated the land of promise and gathered of the heavenly fruits, and showed them as beautiful specimens of the richness and blessedness of that inheritance. Wherefore? That we might be stimulated and cheered and encouraged to 'press toward the prize of our high calling in Christ,' to seek and cherish a 'like precious faith with her,' that we also might be 'filled with peace and joy in believing.' Oh, seek that faith; seek the living power of those 'evangelical principles' of the blessedness of which we have seen such delightful evidence; seek more and more, from the teaching of God's Word and Spirit, a humbling conviction of your utterly corrupt, lost and helpless state through sin, a realizing knowledge of the fulness and freeness of salvation 'by grace through faith in Christ,' and an experimental acquaintance with the enlightening, renewing, sanctifying power of 'the Spirit of life in Christ Jesus.'

"If you are a stranger to these things, if your 'mind has not been impressed,' if your heart has not been made in any measure 'to taste of these principles,' what hope have you? What peace, what happiness in prospect of death, judgment and eternity? I may possibly be speaking to some who know nothing practically of these principles, living just as they might have lived if Christ had never died for them, having, it may be, 'the form of godliness, but denying the power thereof'; while some perhaps are altogether careless, thoughtless, indifferent, worldly; and some perhaps outwardly and openly ungodly—oh, as a minister of that Saviour who hath loved you and given Himself for your redemption, let me speak a word to you, and may the Holy Spirit enable me to speak 'a word in season'; may the Spirit carry the word with power to the heart, to the soul, to the conscience, that there may be an awakening, an alarm, a conviction of danger, a fleeing to the Saviour, a 'laying hold upon the hope set before us in Christ.' You know that you have a soul, an immortal soul, which must either be saved or lost; you know that you must live forever in the perfection of happiness, or in the perfection of agony; and doubtless you sometimes think of this when some friend or neighbour dies, when you see the grave open, or hear the bell tolling for the funeral of another, then perhaps the thought arises that you also must die, that your turn will come, that the hour is drawing near—how near you cannot tell—when death will lay his hand on you, when your limbs will become cold, motionless, stiff in death, your heart cease to beat, your breath cease to be drawn, your ears be closed, your eyes dimmed and darkened in death; when your body will be wrapped in the shroud, nailed up in the coffin, buried in the grave, and your soul will have returned to God, the Judge of all. And then come thoughts of the resurrection day and the final judgment day, the outbursting of the divine glory in the heavens, the appearing of the Lord Jesus in the clouds, 'revealed in flaming fire,' and the showing of the heavenly host and the 'trump of the archangel,' and above all the mighty voice of the Lord Himself penetrating the depths of earth and sea; and the opening of the graves, and the rising of the dead—the rising of your body reunited to the soul, and yourself standing before 'the great white throne,' and 'the books opened,' and 'every secret thing brought to light," and the eye of the Judge fixed on you, and the sentence of the Judge pronounced on you, and your eternal portion declared, assigned, entered on—where? With the saved or lost? With the blessed or the damned? Oh, when such thoughts arise, when such solemn events are present to your mind, do you not feel that the one thing, the one great object which above all others most deeply concerns you, is to escape the damnation of hell, to attain the blessedness of heaven? Shall it be so?

DUNKESWELL PARISH CHURCH AS RESTORED, 1867.
(From a Picture in the J. Ross Robertson Collection.)

Then, 'by the blessing of God,' must your 'mind be impressed with,' your heart 'made to taste of,' these great 'evangelical' truths; then, as a humbled, guilty, penitent sinner must you flee to Christ for refuge, and find forgiveness and acceptance through His atoning blood and perfect righteousness, and become 'a new creature' in Him, renewed, sanctified by the Spirit of life in Him. So our departed friend fled to Him, sought Him, was found of Him, and blessed with salvation by Him. And He is willing to be found of you and to bless you, if only you seek Him and come to Him with humble, believing, praying, submissive hearts. Hear His own gracious words (Matt. 11: 28), 'Come unto me, all ye that labour and are heavy laden, and I will give you rest; take my yoke upon you and learn of me, and ye shall find rest for your souls.' And again He says (John 6; 37), 'Him that cometh unto me I will in no wise cast out.' Oh, be persuaded, be encouraged to come to the Saviour while He thus invites you, while He yet 'waits to be gracious.' Oh, 'be wise, consider your

HER EVANGELICAL PRINCIPLES

latter end, and seek the Lord while He may be found,' that your latter end may be like hers whose death, you know, was full of peace, and whose resurrection will be full of glory.

"Let me remind you further that 'those evangelical principles which formed the happiness of her life' and 'of her death,' separated our friend from the vain pursuits, pleasures and amusements of the world. You know that she walked not in such ways; not because she had naturally no taste for such things, not because as a Christian she cut herself off from all pleasure, but because her principles raised her to higher and greater and better pleasures; her faith laid hold on nobler and loftier objects, and found delight in them. The toys of childhood delight the child; but the man, as the apostle expresses it, 'puts away childish things,' not because he has no pleasures, but because he has other and higher pleasures; so the toys of the world may delight 'the children of the world,' but the Christian, realizing in faith the great truths of the Gospel, leaves such things, because he finds delight in other and heavenly things; as St. Paul tells us (Rom. 8: 5), 'They that are after the flesh do mind the things of the flesh, but they that are after the Spirit the things of the Spirit.' Hear our Christian friend's testimony. Referring to the great truths of the Gospel, she says: 'If an individual really believed these things he could not pass so much of his time in the anxieties and disquietudes' (and doubtless she would have added, the vanities) 'of earthly things, and spend comparatively so little thought upon the things of eternity.' In faith her 'thoughts' dwelt much 'on the things of eternity,' not with feelings of doubt, disquietude and dread, but with an assured hope and expectation of a blessed inheritance there through that Saviour whose love she knew, and whom she loved, and that, be it remembered, not from any natural superiority or amiableness of disposition, but from the influence of the divine Spirit. Hear her again: 'Until a right spirit be implanted in us, which worketh by love, that we should love Him who died for us, we shall not delight in piety, but perform works of piety from duty rather than from pleasure; until we feel a love of Christ and communion with God through Him, what delight can we feel in the expectation of meeting our God?' This is an important and precious passage; it opens to us the source and substance of her especial pleasure and delight in 'piety and the works of piety, in communion with God, and in the expectation of meeting her God'; and that from 'a right spirit implanted'—not inborn, observe her language, but 'implanted,' produced by the power of the Holy Ghost in connection with the 'evangelical' truths before referred to. Now consider how blessed must have been her state of mind; and think not that religion—true, evangelical religion—would make you gloomy and melancholy, and cut you off from all enjoyment of pleasure; it would separate you from vain pleasures, but only to give you other pleasures, better, higher, purer, permanent, substantial, eternal. Oh, seek to have that right spirit implanted, sustained, strengthened, more and more in you, that you may 'delight yourself in the Lord' and in the ways of the Lord, and when called to 'meet God' you may 'rejoice and be glad in Him' as your God and Father in Christ Jesus.

"Nor were these the only effects of 'evangelical truth' in that 'blessed' disciple of whom I am now speaking; her faith was that 'which worketh by love,' and it showed its reality and power in a readiness 'to every good work.' Her good works need not be spoken of by me in this place, they are known to you all, felt and remembered by you all; you know that wherever among yourselves or your neighbours might be suffering or sorrow, want or woe, there was a kind friend (and, thanks to the Giver of all good, her mantle descends, her spirit rests on others who bear her honoured name), a friend whose heart was ever touched with compassion, whose hand was ever open to help and relieve. Nor were her labours of love confined to the neighbourhood; by various means, through private individuals and public societies, her bounty flowed forth to our country, our colonies, and to the heathen world, contributing to lessen the mass of human misery, and to bring Jews and Gentiles to the knowledge and love and service of her Saviour.

" Time would fail me to speak of the manifold fruits which clustered richly and beautifully on the faith of this devoted follower of Christ; but I would just advert to her great humility. Year after year she grew in grace, in holiness, in the enjoyment of the power and peace of true religion; and that was accompanied and widened by growing humility, a sure accompaniment of a real work of grace in the heart; there was not the ' stand by, for I am holier than thou,' nor ' my tower is so strong that I shall never be moved,' but a humbling remembrance of her own continual weakness, arising from an enlightened knowledge of her heart's deceitfulness and proneness to unbelief. As the divine light showed her more and more of her God, her Redeemer, and her Sanctifier, it showed her more and more her own sinfulness in the sight of God, her constant need of the Saviour's cleansing blood, and of the Holy Spirit's renewing and upholding power. And so it will be with the true Christian; as he advances in holiness, he will become more and more sensible of his own unholiness. You may have observed in a room that where a beam of sunlight shines with peculiar brightness little particles of dust, before invisible, are seen floating in the air; the light does not cause them to be there, but shows that they are where all before seemed pure. So, as the light of truth and holiness shines more and more brightly in the heart, evils will be discerned which were not perceived before; and, viewing and examining himself in that light, the Christian will be kept lowly on his knees at the foot of the Cross. So it was with our departed friend. Hear her words once more: ' Those who most thoroughly examine their own hearts best know the difficulty and extent of belief ' (the true working realizing faith in God's word), ' how prone man is to do otherwise (otherwise than act out Christian faith in all its various bearings and applications), ' how deceitful is our heart in this case.' And doubtless the following language expressed her own experience, for the great enemy would not have left such a servant of God untried: ' Satan uses every means to shake our faith in Christ, knowing it to be our only source of happiness here, and that the stronger our faith is the freer we are from his yoke and influence.' How true is this! The Christian's spiritual life, strength, holiness, happiness, depend on his ' faith in Christ.' And she adds: ' Let our daily prayer be—Lord, I believe; help Thou mine unbelief.' There spake her humility and her faith, looking in prayer to the Lord as able to help her unbelief and to keep her from falling. And observe where was her strength, her help, her defence, only ' in the Lord.' The corruption, deceitfulness, unbelief of her heart she knew, and who can tell the manifold struggles and conflicts of her protracted Christian warfare? But she knew with the Psalmist, ' Unto whom to lift up her eyes for help,' and with the Psalmist she found that ' the Lord Himself was her keeper, her helper, her defender.' She found that ' as the hills stood about Jerusalem, even so standeth the Lord round about His people for evermore.' But observe how she found this help from the Lord—in the faithful use of appointed means, seeking the blessing of the Lord in the ordinances of the Lord as they are observed and ministered in our branch of His Church. For with all her growing in grace and godliness (and well will it be for us if we grow up, in our measure, towards the fulness of her stature in Christ!), with all her spiritual growth, this eminent Christian never grew above the Church of England, as many seem in the imagination of their minds to suppose respecting themselves; a spirit of true piety kept her in a state of true humility, manifesting the feelings expressed by those words of the Psalmist which we have heard this morning, ' I was glad when they said unto me, let us go into the house of the Lord.' You know how regularly, constantly, devoutly she

378

used to come here 'into the house of the Lord,'—how, when her own strength failed, she used the help of others' strength to come 'into the house of the Lord,' the weakness of the body presenting an emblem of the humility of the soul leaning on the arm of the Lord Jesus, and 'resting on the arm of that Beloved One coming up more and more from the wilderness' of corrupt nature, and drawing nearer and nearer to the heavenly temple. And oh, that all partook of and manifested the same spirit of humble dependence on the Lord's help, diligently seeking the Lord's blessing in the ordinances of the Lord's house! But alas! how many neglect these things! How many, permitted to enjoy full bodily strength, pervert that strength to other purposes, and use it not in coming regularly 'to the house of the Lord,' while others make a measure of weakness which might be assisted an excuse for staying away from 'the house and the ordinances of the Lord!' No wonder if in such cases the soul be left unfed, unstrengthened, to sink, and languish and die. Beware, that it be not so with any of you; seek food, nourishment, strength for your souls where our devout friend sought and found it, in the ordinances of the Lord's house, and that not only from the sermon, but also from and through the prayers. The preaching of the word she highly valued, and so likewise the prayers; as a humble disciple not only, with Mary, 'sitting at Jesus' feet to hear His word,' but also, with the leper, 'kneeling before Him to supplicate His mercy, power and blessing, both in the holy sacrament of His Supper, and in the Sunday prayers with the congregation; and thus her lamp was fed and kept brightly burning with oil from the sanctuary. The prayers of our Church indeed she specially loved, not with a blind, bigoted attachment, but with an intelligent, enlightened regard, knowing them to be sound, scriptural, spiritual, suited to the soul's wants, and, when rightly used, profitable to the soul's welfare. In the use of them she found good for her soul, and a great stay to her sinking spirit midst the increasing infirmities of the flesh; and the testimony of one who was with her to the last is 'that amidst restlessness and pain and decay the Church prayers would arrest her attention and be fervently joined in'—those tried and well-known helps in the daytime of life, still ministering help at eventide when the night of death came on.

"And now she 'joins in prayer' no longer, such helps and stays she needs no more; upheld, sustained unto the end of her course, comforted with abundant peace, and finally strengthened unto complete and glorious victory, her happy spirit hath escaped from 'the burden of the flesh'—this prison-house of clay, gladly escaped 'like a bird from the fowler.' The fetters are all broken, and the emancipated spirit has taken its flight up to realms of bliss and blessedness beyond the reach of our present faculties, whither we can now only follow her in thought, in faith, in thanksgiving and praise. Human imagination cannot fully conceive, human tongue cannot describe, the blessedness 'of the spirits of the just made perfect'—to attempt doing so would be only to mar its glory and dim its splendour. Even the language of inspiration, with all its magnificent grandeur and sublimity, fails us here; even the beloved John, 'who lay in Jesus' bosom,' says, 'we know not what we shall be'; even the favoured Paul, who was 'caught up to the third heaven,' tells us that the words which he heard in paradise were 'unutterable words,' the very expresssion of the joys of the blessed spirits surpassing the power of human utterance! Yet it is good to think of that blessedness, though we are lost in utter inability to comprehend it; it is good in believing thought to muse upon it, to have the mind raised to the contemplation of it; good to know and remember that blessedness unspeakable, unalloyed, uninterrupted, unfailing, unending, eternal, only to be increased and perfected at the resurrection in the union of the glorified body with the glorified soul blessed with the entire fulness of blessedness in the presence of God for evermore; such is the blessedness in which our faith can contemplate, and rejoice to contemplate, our esteemed, revered, beloved and blessed friend! All, be it remembered, through Christ, the Saviour of sinners; all from the love, the free and undeserved love, of God in Christ Jesus. That love it was which, in its eternal counsels, gave the everlasting Son for this 'blessed' one's redemption; that love sought her in her natural state of alienation, awakened her to a sense of her sinfulness, led her to the knowledge of the Saviour, and enabled her in faith to lay hold on the hope set before her in Christ, and to find pardon and peace through His blood and righteousness, and strength and holiness in the spirit of life in Him; that love watched over her, guided, defended, sustained, upheld, comforted her in all her weakness, wants, difficulties, dangers, trials, tribulations, sufferings and sorrows; it 'led her all her journey through, safe to her journey's end,' and when she reached 'the verge of Jordan,' that love was there, like the ark with the Israelites of old, and its everlasting arms clave asunder the dark waters and bore her spirit through triumphant to join the company of the blessed gone before.

"And who will follow? who will follow? Oh, may I, may you, follow her as she followed the Saviour, follow her in 'faith and patience' here to 'the inheritance of the promises' hereafter; may we receive the truth in the love and the power of the truth as she received it, and live the truth in the humble and faithful practice of the truth as she lived 'in the Lord.' Oh, come, let us follow, in Christ, 'the way' towards the heavenly Canaan; if you have not yet entered on the heavenward path, oh, enter now; away with your carelessness, your worldliness, your ungodliness; whatever it be that is keeping you from the Saviour, cast it from you, and in humble penitence and prayer and faith come to Christ, and set your face heavenward, and follow on to know and serve the Lord; and if you have through grace entered on that 'narrow' but blessed way, press forward, be stimulated, cheered, encouraged to press forward with renewed vigour and watchfulness and hope; the 'blessed' friend who has gone before beckons and calls you on, she points to the love and power that were all-sufficient for her, as all-sufficient for you. Oh, brethren, come; the same divine, unfailing love invites, awaits, encourages us; the love of the Father bids us come, the love of the Saviour will receive us, the love of the Sanctifier, 'the Holy Ghost the Comforter,' will help us. Oh, then come; in faith and prayer and humble submission flee to this redeeming love, cleave to it, trust to it, follow its heavenward guidance, depend on its unfailing promises, and though difficulties and dangers, and tribulations and trials, and enemies from within and without stand in the way, 'who shall separate us from the love of Christ?' Oh, if we have anything of the apostle's faith, as our departed friend had, we may take up the apostle's triumphant language and say, 'I am persuaded that neither death, nor life, nor angels, nor principalities, nor powers, nor things present, nor things to come, nor height nor depth, nor any other creature, shall be able to separate us from the love of God which is in Christ Jesus our Lord.' And to Him, with our lips now and in our lives day by day, in our words and works, our faith and practice, let us humbly ascribe all honour and praise and power and glory for ever and ever."

CHAPTER XXV.

THE WILL OF MRS. SIMCOE.

Mrs. Simcoe's will was proved on the 19th of March, 1850. It was originally made in 1840, and her son, the Rev. H. A. Simcoe, and the Rev. John Clarke were appointed executors.

The first codicil is dated the 30th of March, 1841, and makes a new disposition of the land at Dunkeswell Abbey, in the parish of Dunkeswell.

The second codicil is dated the 9th of October, 1843, and adds the name of the late Honourable Sir J. T. Coleridge, afterwards Lord Coleridge, as an executor in conjunction with her son, Rev. H. A. Simcoe, and Rev. John Clarke.

The third codicil is dated the 7th of January, 1848, two years before her death. The Rev. John Clarke having died, she appointed Francis George Coleridge, son of Sir J. T. Coleridge, to act in conjunction with the Rev. H. A. Simcoe and Sir J. T. Coleridge as executors.

The copy of the will is extracted from the Principal Registry of the Probate, Divorce and Admiralty Division of the High Court of Justice in the Prerogative Court of Canterbury.

I, ELIZABETH POSTHUMA SIMCOE of Wolford Lodge in the county of Devon widow do make publish and declare this to be my last will and testament in writing in manner and form following that is to say in conformity to the wish of my late deceased husband John Graves Simcoe expressed in his will and pursuant to and in exercise and execution of the several powers and authorities to me given or in me vested either under all or any of the several Indentures of Settlement executed by us or by my late aunt Margaret Graves widow or under any other deed settlement will or writing whatsoever or me in any other manner thereto in anywise enabling I do by this my last will and testament in writing by me executed in the presence of and attested by the credible persons whose names are hereto subscribed as witnesses attesting my execution hereof give devise bequeath direct limit appoint and dispose of all and every sum and sums of money in whomsoever vested and whether invested or standing in any of the public stocks or funds or on mortgage or any other securities or whether arising or produced by or from the sale of any tenement lands or hereditaments in such settlement deed will or writing comprised or by any other means whereof I have any power of disposal unto and amongst my several daughters by my said husband in manner and in the parts and proportions following that is to say unto my daughters Eliza Charlotte Henrietta Maria Caroline and Sophia Jemima so much of the said trust monies

respectively as will amount unto and raise the sum of five thousand
pounds for each of them and to my two youngest daughters Katherine
and Ann (the latter of whom was born after the date and execution
of my said husband's Will) so much of the said trust monies respectively as will amount unto and raise the sum of six thousand pounds for
each of them and which said last mentioned sums I do appoint to them
my said two youngest daughters Katherine and Ann to the intent that
all my said daughters may be provided for in equal degree they my said
daughters Eliza Charlotte Henrietta Maria Caroline Sophia Jemima
having received legacies under the will of my late Aunt Margaret
Graves widow and being entitled to other legacies payable at my death
from my late Aunt Sophia Gwillim out of my Herefordshire property
but inasmuch as under my said husband's will the power hereinafter
mentioned of charging the estate with the payment of any provision
for any of my said daughters may be limited and restrained to the sum
of five thousand pounds for any one of them I do by this my said will
direct limit and appoint that my executors hereinafter named shall raise
and levy two several sums of one thousand pounds each in part of and
to make up the said sums of six thousand pounds for each of my said
youngest daughters by and out of the monies which at my death shall
be invested in the funds or on mortgage either in my name or in the
names of the trustees named in the said Indentures of Settlement and
shall pay and apply the same in discharge of so much of the said two
sums of six thousand pounds and I do by this my said will further
direct order limit and appoint that the several trustees in whose names
such several trust monies are or may be vested shall call in such parts
thereof as are in the public funds or are on mortgage and apply the
same agreeably to the intent of this my will in and towards discharge
of the legacies hereby by me given and in case such monies so in the
public funds or on mortgage or other security may not be adequate to
the making up of the whole of the said legacies and provision for my
said several daughters I do by this my said will executed and attested
as aforesaid pursuant to and in exercise of the power and authority
given for that purpose to me in and by the will of my said late husband
and of all and every other power and powers me hereunto in any wise
enabling subject and charge the residuary real estate by his said will
given and devised to and with the payment to my said several daughters
of such proportion of the respective sums of money hereby given or
appointed to them as such trust money shall fall short or be deficient
to make up for the portions or fortunes of my several daughters as
aforesaid and I do by this my said will appoint and charge that such
deficiency shall be made good to my said daughters respectively out
of such residuary real estate I give to my said daughter Eliza my prints
pictures plate books china linen wine horses cows carts carriages household goods and other furniture bank notes cash in Biddulph's Bank and
lastly in pursuance and in execution and exercise of all and every power
and powers either under my said husband's will or under or by virtue
of any settlement or settlements or in any other manner whatsoever
vested in me I do by this my said will by me executed and attested
as aforesaid give devise bequeath direct order limit appoint and dispose
of all and singular my messuages tenements farms buildings closes lands
hereditaments and all the rest residue and remainder of my real and
personal estate monies securities for money goods and effects whatsoever wheresoever not hereinbefore given and bequeathed and of which
I have any power of disposal subject to my debts and funeral expenses

and also subject to and charged and chargeable with the payment of
the said several portions or fortunes to my said several daughters hereinbefore given appointed or provided for them or intended so to be or
such part or parts thereof as the trust monies hereinbefore mentioned
shall fall short of paying and which I will and direct shall in every event
be fully paid and satisfied and also all and every sum and sums of
money trust estate and effects whatsoever in and by the said Indentures
of Settlement or either of them or by my said husband's Will or in any
other manner settled and not by me disposed of as aforesaid unto the
use of my son Henry Addington Simcoe his heirs executors administrators
and assigns to and for his and their own absolute use and benefit and
I do hereby make constitute and appoint my son the said Henry Addington
Simcoe and the Revd John Clarke to be joint EXECUTORS of this my
last will and testament hereby revoking all former and other wills by
me heretofore made and ratifying and confirming this to be my last.
IN WITNESS whereof I the said Elizabeth Posthuma Simcoe the testatrix have to this my last will and testament set my hand and seal this
eleventh day of September in the year of our Lord one thousand eight
hundred and forty — — ELIZABETH POSTHUMA SIMCOE (L S) — —
SIGNED and declared to be the last will and testament of the within
named Elizabeth Posthuma Simcoe in her presence and at her request
and in the presence of each other have subscribed our names witness
thereto — — JAMES TEMPLE MANSEL Clerk Curate of Dunkeswell
in the county of Devon — JOHN BURKE Clerk Vicar of Kilalgan Co
Galway Ireland.

I, ELIZABETH POSTHUMA SIMCOE do hereby publish and declare
this a CODICIL to my last will and testament dated the eleventh day
of September 1840 hereto annexed I give devise and bequeath all my
lands and estate whether freehold or leasehold situated at Dunkeswell
Abbey in the parish of Dunkeswell unto my daughters Eliza Simcoe and
Caroline Simcoe their heirs executors administrators and assigns as
joint tenants. And I do hereby revoke all and every devise and disposition of my said lands and estate contained in my said will IN WITNESS
whereof I have hereunto set my hand and seal this thirtieth day of
March in the year of our Lord one thousand eight hundred and forty-one
— E P SIMCOE (L S) — — SIGNED published and declared by the
said Elizabeth Posthuma Simcoe to be a codicil to her last will and
testament in our presence who in her presence and in the presence of
each other have subscribed our names as witnsses thereto — — PHILIP
KRULES — — JOSEPH BURROWS.

THIS IS A SECOND CODICIL to the last will and testament of
me ELIZABETH POSTHUMA SIMCOE of Wolford Lodge in the county
of Devon widow which will bears date the eleventh day of September in
the year one thousand eight hundred and forty. Whereas I am desirous
of naming the Honourable Sir John Taylor Coleridge Knight one of the
Justices of Her Majesty's Court of Queen's Bench an EXECUTOR of my
said will to act in the execution thereof in conjunction with my son
Henry Addington Simcoe and the Reverend John Clarke the executors
therein named I do therefore hereby appoint the said Sir John Taylor
Coleridge one of the EXECUTORS of my said will and I direct that my
said will shall be read and construed as if the name of the said Sir John
Taylor Coleridge had been originally inserted therein together with the
names of the said Henry Addington Simcoe and John Clarke and I
confirm my said will and the codicil thereunto annexed except as aforesaid IN WITNESS whereof I have hereunto set my hand this ninth

day of October one thousand eight hundred and forty three —— E P SIMCOE —— SIGNED by the said Elizabeth Posthuma Simcoe as and for a codicil to her last will and testament in the presence of us present at the same time who in her presence and at her request have hereunto subscribed our names as witnesses —— J D COLERIDGE Exeter College Oxford —— FRAS GEO COLERIDGE Ottery St Mary Solr —

THIS IS A THIRD CODICIL to the last will and testament of me ELIZABETH POSTHUMA SIMCOE of Wolford Lodge in the county of Devon widow which will bears date the eleventh day of September in the year one thousand eight hundred and forty Whereas the Reverend John Clarke one of the executors named in my said will hath lately departed this life I am desirous of appointing Francis George Coleridge of Ottery Saint Mary in the county of Devon Gentleman an EXECUTOR of my said will to act in the execution of the trusts thereof in conjunction with my son Henry Addington Simcoe and the Honourable Sir John Taylor Coleridge respectively named as executors of my said will in and by my said will and one of the codicils thereto I do therefore by this third codicil to my said will appoint the said Francis George Coleridge one of my EXECUTORS and direct that my said will and codicils shall be read and construed as if the name of the said Francis George Coleridge had been originally inserted therein together with the executors therein named In all other respects I ratify and confirm my said will and the several codicils thereto IN WITNESS whereof I have hereunto set my hand this seventh day of January one thousand eight hundred and forty-eight —— E P SIMCOE —— SIGNED by the said Elizabeth Posthuma Simcoe as and for a codicil to her last will and testament in the presence of us present at the same time who in her presence and at her request have hereunto subscribed our names as witnesses CHARLES E BAND —— JOSEPH BURROWS ——

Proved (with three Codicils)
19th March 1850
Fos 24
J J C
239

In order that the will of Mrs. Simcoe may be intelligible to the reader, the following synopsis has been made.

Testatrix in conformity to the wish of her husband, the late John Graves Simcoe, expressed in his will and pursuant to certain settlements executed by the testatrix and her husband or by her late aunt, Margaret Graves, or under any other deed, settlement, will or writing, devises and bequeathes: "All and every sum and sums of money in whomsoever vested and whether invested or standing in any of the public stocks or funds or on mortgage or any other securities or whether arising or produced by or from the sale of any tenement, land or hereditaments in such settlement, deed, will or writing comprised or by any other means whereof I have any power of disposal to the following daughters:

A SYNOPSIS OF THE WILL

Eliza
Charlotte
Henrietta Maria
Caroline
Sophia Jemima
} So much of said trust moneys as will amount to and raise £5,000 for each.

to the two youngest daughters:

Katherine.
Ann (the latter born after date and execution of will of John Graves Simcoe).
} So much of the trust moneys as will amount to and raise £6,000 for each.

The testatrix explains her reason for giving the additional £1,000 to her two youngest daughters is by reason of the fact that the six eldest daughters have received legacies under the will of the testatrix's late aunt, Margaret Graves, and will also be entitled to other legacies payable at the death of the testatrix from her late aunt, Sophia Gwillim, out of the testatrix's Herefordshire property.

Under the will of John Graves Simcoe it is provided that Mrs. Simcoe was only to charge the residuary real estate of her husband with payment to her children of such sums as she might think proper; no sum exceeding £5,000 shall be payable to any one child.

The testatrix directs her executors to raise the two several sums of £1,000 required to make up the said sums of £6,000 for each of the said two youngest daughters out of moneys which at the death of the testatrix shall be invested in funds or on mortgage either in her name or in the names of trustees named "in the said indenture of settlement."

In case such moneys in public funds or on mortgage or other security are not adequate to make up the whole of the said legacies the testatrix charges her residuary real estate with the payment to her several daughters of such proportion of the respective sums given to them as shall fall short or be deficient to make up the full amount of the legacies bequeathed to her several daughters.

The testatrix further directs that such deficiency shall be made good to her daughters respectively out of her residuary real estate.

The testatrix gives to her daughter Eliza the following: "My prints, pictures, plate, books, china, linen, wine, horses, cows, carts, carriages, household goods and other furniture, bank notes, cash in Biddulph's Bank."

The testatrix bequeathes all and singular her messuages, tenements, farms, buildings, closes, hereditaments and all the rest and residue of her real and personal estate, subject to the payment of her debts and funeral expenses and subject to the payment of the legacies to her several daughters above mentioned, unto her son, Henry Addington Simcoe.

25
385

The testatrix appoints her son, Henry Addington Simcoe, and the Rev. John Clarke joint executors of her will.

By her first codicil the testatrix devises and bequeathes all her lands and real estate, whether freehold or leasehold, of Dunkeswell Abbey in the Parish of Dunkeswell to her daughters Eliza Simcoe and Caroline Simcoe as joint tenants.

By a second codicil the testatrix appoints Sir John Taylor Coleridge, one of the Justices of her Majesty's Court of Queen's Bench, executor in conjunction with her son, Henry Addington Simcoe, and Rev. John Clarke.

By a third codicil the testatrix appoints Francis George Coleridge of Ottery St. Mary in the County of Devon to be one of her executors to take the place of Reverend John Clarke, who has departed this life, and to act in conjunction with her son, Henry Addington Simcoe and Sir John Taylor Coleridge.

Mr. Walcot, a cousin of Mrs. Simcoe's, died in 1830. He resided in Oundle, Northamptonshire. At his death he bequeathed to Eliza, Charlotte, Henrietta, Caroline, Sophia, Katherine and Ann Simcoe £2,000 each and to Mrs. Simcoe £100 and all his lands and houses in the counties of Norfolk, Huntingdon and Northampton. These "lands and houses" to be sold and divided "share and share" alike to the seven daughters of John Graves Simcoe. Mr. Walcot left his estate of Tichmarsh in Northampton to the Rev. Henry Addington Simcoe, the only surviving son of General Simcoe.

CHAPTER XXVI.

GENERAL SIMCOE'S ESTATE IN CANADA.

There was no large accumulation of wealth in the Simcoe family. The ancestors of the General were not men endowed with much more than respectable competences. They were plain living, godly people, content with their lot, doing their duty in their respective spheres of life as Christian men and women.

None of the Simcoes in Cheshire had estates, although some few of them were small land-holders. Those who lived in Northumberland and Durham were better off, for as rectors and vicars they were in the possession of "livings" that placed them in comfortable circumstances.

Captain John Simcoe, the son of a Northumberland vicar, had, through the thrift and saving of some of his ancestors, inherited enough money to enable him to wed; and this, with some thousands that his wife was endowed with and his naval pay, kept his home in Cotterstock in comparative comfort.

So that after the death of Captain Simcoe his widow was in circumstances that permitted her to leave Cotterstock and take up house in Exeter, bring up and educate her two surviving sons, Percy, who was unfortunately drowned at the age of fourteen, and John Graves, the future Governor of Upper Canada.

There is no trace of the disposition of the estate of Mrs. John Simcoe. Certain it is that it all came to General Simcoe, so that when he started life he had a few thousand pounds to his credit and the advantage of a good education.

During the American campaign he drew liberally upon his own funds and was thus enabled to secure many necessaries essential to his comfort which would have been denied him had he to depend upon his army pay.

His personal expenditure while in command of the Queen's Rangers was considerable, for he not only outfitted his men but, as the announcement in Rivington's N. Y. *Gazette* shows, he paid a premium for every recruit obtained in New York.

Of course, after his marriage in 1782, he was in better circumstances. His wife was an heiress in her own right, inheriting the wealth of the Gwillims, and it was her money that purchased Wolford in Devon.

The welfare of the estate was an ambition with Mrs. Simcoe and large sums were disbursed by her in improvements. The dwelling was practically rebuilt, in fact what was left of the original building, built by Peter Geneste, is now in the centre of the ground floor of the present mansion.

DIARY OF MRS. SIMCOE

Many thousands of pounds were expended by Mrs. Simcoe on the estate between the years 1782 and 1806; and the General also contributed a goodly share towards its upkeep.

But there were many personal calls upon the General's income. In connection with the military commands in the Western District his private purse was liberally drawn upon.

The Simcoe correspondence shows that he was anxious that his family should be provided for after his death. The urgent appeals he made to the Government of the day to grant him what was his due and his continued reference to this matter in his personal correspondence, justify the belief that he should have been recouped large amounts expended by him which could fairly be charged to Government account.

When he accepted the post of Lieutenant-Governor of Upper Canada he had no idea that his private purse would have to be drawn upon to enable him to keep up his position in Canada as was befitting the representative of his sovereign.

True, the income as Lieutenant-Governor was £2,000 per annum, with half fees on sales of lands and from the privilege and application of the Great Seal to divers private and public instruments, but while he received his pay and part of the fees, there was a large arrearage at the time of his death.

When Simcoe left the Province all of his accounts were not adjusted and he had to leave the collection of the arrearage to his agent, Captain John McGill, who was the Commissary of Stores in his government.

The General had also 4,770 acres of land in the Township of Yonge, the Johnstown District, and in other parts of the Province, including the Castle Frank property of 200 acres adjoining York. This latter property was registered in the name of his son Francis Gwillim Simcoe, who in April of 1812 fell at the siege of Badajoz.

At intervals he received remittances on account and down to 1802 it amounted to £1,760. John McGill in writing to the General said in reference to a payment of £873 made before 1800, he was instructed by Mr. Peter Russell to say that "it was not his fault that the sum was not more and that if the Attorney-General (Mr. White) had done his duty the sum for grants ought to have been from £1,000 to £2,000 annually, but why he was not made do his duty remains a mystery."

A subsequent return made as late as March, 1806, shows that an amount of £255 was paid to the General, making in all £2,015.

Mrs. Simcoe made repeated efforts to collect the arrearage, but records show that she did not receive many further payments. The lands owned by General Simcoe were sold in later years before Mrs. Simcoe's death and the amount received was duly transmitted to her. It is understood that this land brought about $2 an acre.

ABOUT YORK NINETY YEARS AGO

Mrs. Simcoe was always interested in hearing of the progress of York, for she had many friends residing there, the friends of her younger days in 1792-6, when she lived at Niagara and York.

In a letter dated April 1, 1819, Mr. McGill writes of York: "This place has increased greatly, both as to buildings and population since the war. You will hardly believe when I state that two acres and two-thirds (2 2-3), divided into fourteen house lots, was sold at auction a few days ago for eighteen hundred and fifty-five pounds, currency (Dollar, five shillings)."

This was a great surprise, no doubt, to Mrs. Simcoe and is a greater surprise to the people of Toronto at the present time. There is no proof of the location of these lots, but they are said to have been near the corner of King and Yonge streets. If so, the market price to-day would be about $2,500,000; for land in that vicinity in 1910, one hundred feet in depth, sold for nearly $10,000 per foot frontage.

Mr. Samuel Smith, who was the Administrator of the Government in Upper Canada in 1817 and in 1820, writes to Mrs. Simcoe on October 29, 1824, stating that: "The Town of York is increasing fast, the principal street (King) is about a mile long and the houses for most of the way tolerably compact. The roads likewise are getting good so that stages, four-wheel carriages, go from Kingston to Montreal and occasionally from York to Niagara. There are several steamboats on the lake that ply in different directions, which makes travelling by water very expeditious," and Mr. Smith adds: "The Falls of Niagara has become a fashionable resort, as many as some hundreds of people are seen there at a time in the summer season."

Mrs. Simcoe kept up her correspondence with Canadian friends until within a short period of her death. For the late Rev. Dr. Henry Scadding she had a profound regard; his father had been the manager of Wolford and settled in Upper Canada during her husband's term as Lieutenant-Governor.

CHAPTER XXVII.

JOHN BAILEY'S MEMOIRS.

Seldom, very seldom, do we have narratives written under the conditions in which John Bailey wrote these memoirs. As a rule servants and retainers, whether employed in the upper or lower duties of household work—either within or without the walls of the family home, prefer to perform their allotted duties faithfully, without indulging in any ambitions of a literary character. So that with the manifold duties that make up the daily routine of a household work it is a pleasant surprise to find a narrative from the pen of a man whose opportunities for education were probably limited to the mastering of the crude training presented by a primitive parish school in a Devon village.

The writing may not be of a character or interest that would secure for it a place on library shelves. But, nevertheless, it displays an ability worthy of those who claim a wider range of intelligence. Great opportunities were not, and could not, be within the reach of John Bailey, the writer of the unique story entitled "A few remarks on the lives of General and Mrs. Simcoe from 1802 to 1850."

During a visit to Wolford in the summer of 1904 I walked to the village of Dunkeswell, two miles distant from Wolford, and had an interview with the son of John Bailey, whose story is here presented. The son, named William, lived in one of the cottages of the village, belonging to the estate, and received a pension from Mrs. Simcoe. He had a fairly good recollection of Mrs. Simcoe, the widow of the General; for not only as a lad did he know her on the estate but he entered service at Wolford in 1850 some months prior to her decease. Of the Misses Simcoe, her daughters, his memory was excellent, and in his esteem they were all that women should be—"good, kind ladies who looked after the welfare of everyone, man and woman, young and old, in Dunkeswell"—so said William Bailey, who died in 1908, aged eighty-seven.

Another cottager, John Corrick, who for nearly sixty years had been in the employ of the family on the home farm and as under gardener, also added his meed of praise to the many virtues of Mrs. Simcoe, the widow of the General. As for "the young ladies at Wolford" he was unstinted in good words for all that they had done to promote the prosperity and happiness not only of those employed on the estate, but also of the tenants of the various farms.

He remembered Mrs. Simcoe and her daughters, for he saw them daily for many years, and added in an earnest tone that while all were "so good and charitable to everyone" yet Miss Anne was "terribly kind," an expression common in some parts of Devonshire, and used to illustrate perfection of character and the acme of charity. Corrick died in July, 1904, in his 78th year. Mrs. John Kennaway Simcoe, "The Lady of the Manor," and friends at Wolford attended the old man's funeral. As one of the family said, "He was a saint if ever there was one—a dear old man, respected and loved by all, so good-natured, no one ever spoke a hard word of him."

John Bailey was born in Awliscombe, four miles from Dunkeswell and two from Wolford, and as a lad of twelve he entered the service of the Simcoe family in 1802, as an attendant on the butler for one year, then he worked as a groom in the stable for four years, after which he was promoted to the position of footman and finally as coachman.

He was a good-looking, bright lad of average height—his son said about five feet, eight inches—of a cheerful and obliging disposition, always ready for the call of his butler, by whose grace he had received his position. He always had a most profound respect and reverence for the General, who on one occasion had declared that he was "a good lad."

After the death of the General in 1806, Bailey continued in Mrs. Simcoe's service for two years and in 1808 left Wolford. He concluded that a sea-faring life was better suited for him than household duties; but he tired of roaming over the ocean and in 1816 returned to his native heath and was again engaged by Mrs. Simcoe as footman, a position he held for twenty years—and then he stepped into the coachman's seat and held the reins for another twelve years—in all thirty-seven years of service.

He lived during the last years of his service and his life, at the Percy Cottages at the foot of Percy Hill, which leads down from Wolford into Dunkeswell. These dwellings are still inhabited.

Bailey married a tidy Devon maiden and had several children. All are now dead.

Some years before Mrs. Simcoe's death John Bailey was somewhat broken in health, and she bestowed a pension on him, which continued to be paid until the day of his death, 1st August, 1855.

If ever a man was faithful to his trust it was John Bailey. His goodness of character seems to have been exceptional, and his loving attention to his employers and their interests add to the story he has written—a diary in a general way—of the life in the happy home at Wolford. Bailey's memoirs—for so they may be justly called—are worthy of men who occupied a higher sphere in the social scale.

Bailey had received a fair education, was an excellent pupil at the village school, and so secured a large amount of general knowledge that served him in good stead after he had grown to manhood. It is most refreshing to read this man's manuscript, and in reading to remember that his heart and soul were full of more than the average of kindly thought for those who employed him.

Not only was John Bailey faithful in his work as between master and servant, but he possessed many attributes that commended him to

391

the Simcoe family. He was evidently an earnest Christian—
he knew the Good Book from cover to cover. He had a sincere
admiration for his mistress, whom he regarded as a model among
womankind. His whole narrative abounds in admiration for her;
and his devotion to the family seems to be that of one who endeavored
not only to serve them in the duties assigned to him, but to lead the
Christian life that was the distinguishing characteristic of those who
lived at Wolford.

I have given the narrative just as it came from the pen of its
author, adding an occasional note in parenthesis, in the body of the
text, explanatory of the location of the places mentioned. The MSS.
is entitled and inscribed as "A Few Remarks on the lives of General
and Mrs. Simcoe, by John Bailey, from 1802 to 1850." This title
is followed by a "preface" explaining in a way the nature of the
text of the narrative. Bailey writes of the "first and second editions."
The narrative is really in two parts. The first part includes the
period from 1802-8, and is devoted to "Remarks on the life of Mrs.
Simcoe by John Bailey." The second part embraces the period
from 1818-50 and this covers "the life of General and Mrs. Simcoe."
The hiatus from 1809-17 is explained by the fact that Bailey was
away at sea during that period.

This preface, moreover, does not foreshadow, as a preface generally
does, the interesting "remarks" concerning those whom he has undertaken to write about. It reads:—

Now in my first and second editions of the lives of General and
Mrs. Simcoe, I have not altogether dwelt on their lives, but some other
people also, and some other things, some things about religious things,
and some things about myself and other people; but my chief subject
is on the lives of General and Mrs. Simcoe. But all the particulars
of the lives of General and Mrs. Simcoe, this is far beyond my knowledge,
but I saw enough of them in my 37 years' service at Wolford Lodge to
make out a small history of them, particularly of Mrs. Simcoe's life, as
I have been so many years with her, and travelled so many thousands
of miles with her.

JOHN BAILEY.

CHAPTER XXVIII.

BAILEY'S OPINION OF THE SIMCOE FAMILY.

Now to speak of Mrs. Simcoe. In her lifetime very few have seen more of her ways than I myself, living in her service nearly forty years—twelve years as coachman, twenty years as footman and five years when a boy. Now in Mrs. Simcoe's lifetime I may very well say she was as good a mistress as ever ruled a house; her works told that she followed the example of good old Joshua, who said, "As for me and my house, we will serve the Lord." Now we can firmly say that at Wolford Lodge not a family in England was kept more regular at family worship; there was family prayer morning and evening, and some part of the Holy Scriptures read and explained to us. The Sabbath Day was kept holy, and it was Mrs. Simcoe's rule for all in her house who were able to go to church. She always showed the example herself; nothing scarcely would keep her from church—no, not even sickness, for I have known when she has been very unwell that she would endeavour to go to church. She would not lose the opportunity, if possible; she was like Mary, she had chosen that good part which shall not be taken from her, and it was seldom either wind or weather would keep her from church, nor the ladies (the daughters of Mrs. Simcoe), for I have known when the snow has been up level with the hedges and no horse or carriage able to go, the ladies and servants all set off, the men in front one after another to tread down the snow, then the ladies and maid-servants in our tracks. We had no cause to think that the deepness of the snow would prevent Mr. Clarke (the Rector of Clayhidon and Vicar of Dunkeswell) from coming to church, as I never remember him, not once, for the cause of bad weather to miss coming.

Now there was once something very remarkable at the time of the service in Dunkeswell Church. The service was at one o'clock; the first lesson was 1 Kings xviii., and just as Mr. Clarke was reading the words in the 44th and 45th verses, "And it came to pass at the seventh time, that he said, Behold there ariseth a little cloud out of the sea, like a man's hand." Now it seems this cloud which ariseth out of the sea is the same thing which I have seen and been very near to, what we call a waterspout; if a ship runs into it it will sink her, it will break the spout and down the water will come. "And he said, Go up, say unto Ahab, Prepare thy chariot and get thee down, that the rain stop thee not. And it came to pass in the meanwhile that the heaven was black with clouds and wind, and there was a great rain." And just at that time it became so dark that we could scarcely see

393

a word in our books, and soon the rain came down in torrents; it was such heavy rain that when we returned to Wolford the house was overflowed with water, the gratings and gutters choked, the stable yard like a river, the water running in at the back door and down the passage to the front hall and drawing-room, which was covered with water; the two maids that were at home quite frightened, going about without stockings or shoes. It was a very remarkable thing, the first lesson giving us notice of the rain. We soon put away the carriage and horses, and ran into the house and got off the water.

There is one thing more I shall just mention. I went with Mrs. Simcoe and Miss Caroline to attend a missionary meeting at Wellington (a market town in Somersetshire, at the foot of the Blackdown Hills). On our way home it came on to rain very much so that there was a flood. When we came to Millhayes (a farm in Hemyock—pronounced Hem-y-ock—in Devon, five miles from Wellington) the water was very deep. Mr. Manley, the tenant of the farm, said it was not safe to go through, as the main stream ran close to the road, and if I should chance to drive one foot out of the way we might get into it, and it was more than ten feet deep. Mrs. Simcoe asked me what was to be done. I told her we could first see the deepness of the water; so Mr. Manley sent someone through on one of his horses. The water was up to the horse's side, so I told Mrs. Simcoe I would quite trust to our horses. I thought "Venture makes the merchant." Old William Selway, the coachman, was with us, so we jumped on the dickey and started off, but just as we got about halfway through poor old Selway was quite frightened; he said the wheels were quite under the water, he could not see them. I told him not to say anything and not to be frightened, so I just gave the horses a flick with the whip. They gave a plunge or two in the water, and we were soon out of danger and got safe to land, and soon arrived home without any hurt.

Mrs. Simcoe used often to go on a visit to her son, the Rev. Henry Addington Simcoe, at Penheale, in Cornwall, five miles from Launceston. I was there with her a great many times; she often took the favourite old black pony for the purpose of taking her morning and evening rides, which she very much enjoyed, particularly when the little children rode with her, one before and one behind; the pony would go so carefully with them. The poor old pony would take Mrs. Simcoe so carefully over plank bridges, and would go over rocks with her like a goat, so that she could venture and feel quite safe going over the rough rocks at Bude, on the north coast of Cornwall, and other places near Penheale.

Mrs. Simcoe generally took two trips from home in a year, one to Penheale, and one up the country to different places, but her favourite places were North Wales, Godstone (in Surrey, nineteen miles from London), Herefordshire and Cheltenham. We often had to cross the old Passage near Bristol (the ferry across the Avon between Somersetshire and Gloucestershire), so as to go from Somersetshire to Here-

MRS. SIMCOE VISITS HER BIRTHPLACE

fordshire; and once when we came to Clifton (a suburb of Bristol) the news came that the vessel, in crossing the "old passage," was sunk full of passengers, and that all on board perished. I informed Miss Ann, as I thought Mrs. Simcoe would not go on; but Miss Ann told me not to say anything about it to Mrs. Simcoe, as it was not likely to be the steamer that was lost, as it does not cross the Passage on Sundays, so it must be a sailing vessel.

Off we started for the "Old Passage," and there we were informed of all the particulars of the misfortune. As the steamer did not cross on Sundays, and a great many people were wanting to cross that day, as Monday was the 1st of September, and there were shooting parties wanting to cross the Passage on Sunday to be in readiness for Monday morning, and Monday being also Bristol Fair, there were a great many jobbers wanting to cross to purchase cattle at the Fair, so they all hired a sailing vessel to cross. Just as the vessel had started, four or five more jobbers came in great haste and begged the captain to take them, but he told them he could not take them, but would return as quickly as possible and cross again. These men seemed very sorry to have been one minute too late; they were watching the vessel crossing, and just as she was about half-way across she gave a lee lurch, filled with water and went down, and everyone on board perished. There was one gentleman who had his carriage and horses and servants on board with him; this gentleman was found, about eight days afterwards, on part of his own estate, a great many miles distant from the place where the vessel sank.

They say there were many thousands of pounds went down in the vessel, which the dealers had with them to purchase stock at Bristol Fair. What a dreadful thing for so many of our fellow-creatures to be taken off so suddenly, and, worst of all, everyone on board was breaking God's Commandment on the Sabbath Day.

We arrived at Whitchurch, which is a large village in Herefordshire, on the River Wye. Mrs. Simcoe and the ladies stayed at Old Court, the former residence of Col. Gwillim and birthplace of Mrs. Simcoe, and I at the Crown Inn. I was speaking of the sad misfortune that had happened at the Old Passage (the ferry across the Avon between Somersetshire and Gloucestershire). The master of the inn was one of those that came to the Passage to cross, but was one minute too late. They told me he was then in bed, and he seemed to be quite a changed man, and he considered he was like a brand plucked out of the burning. There was a sermon preached at the Forest Church (in the Forest of Dean, an ancient royal forest between the estuary of the rivers Severn and Wye, in Gloucestershire) by Mr. Gurnsey, the minister, on the melancholy occasion.

Mrs. Simcoe stayed at Whitchurch some time; it had been her former home, and where most of her friends lay. Old Court is now a farmhouse, but formerly a grand place as the residence of Col. Gwillim. The house is something like Penheale. Whitchurch is a very beautiful place with a handsome little church quite close to the beautiful River Wye. I think I can venture to say that the River Wye is as fine a river as any in England.

From Chepstow, the market town in Monmouthshire, to the town of Ross, in Herefordshire, is very fine. The beautiful Forest of Dean; the ruins of Chepstow Castle, built in the eleventh century; the picturesque ruins of Tintern Abbey, built in the eleventh century and rebuilt in the thirteenth; Goodrich Castle, Goodrich Court, and many other grand places are close by the River Wye. This river is more than a hundred and thirty miles in length, and is very fine and beautiful all the way. I have been with Mrs. and Miss Ann Simcoe on by the river to the mountain (of Plynlymmon, in North Wales) where it springs. It is seldom that Mrs. Simcoe stays in Herefordshire long, only just to pay a short visit to her tenants at Old Court, on her late father's estate; then we returned home, and seldom go from home in the winter.

It is a most extraordinary and providential thing that so many thousand of miles as I have travelled with Mrs. Simcoe, not one misfortune or accident ever happened. Nor can we find out for what reason this great blessing was on us that we should always go out and come in with safety. I should say the reason was that on Mrs. Simcoe's leaving home on a journey, at family prayers the protection was put into the hands of the Almighty; and what can be safer than that? The 121st Psalm was also read before departure, trusting entirely to the Lord for protection on the journey. Mrs. Simcoe every day read, or had read to her, some part of the Holy Scripture, and in it she could plainly see the protection the Lord grants to His people, and there we can see it if we like to look at it. In the 13th chapter of Exodus, the 20th, 21st and 22nd verses, we can see the protection the Lord granted to them in their journey; and again, in the 2nd chapter of St. Matthew's gospel, in the 8th and 9th verses, what a prosperous journey to find what so many generations have been looking for so long. It was one of the first discoveries that ever was made, far greater than the discovery of all the gold mines of Peru or Mexico. They found the Saviour of the world. Look at the 24th chapter of St. Luke, verses 15, 30 and 31; then look at the 24th chapter of Genesis, verses 10 and 36, and there are many other places where we can see that the Lord has prospered His people in their journeys; and so He prospers Mrs. Simcoe in all her journeys, so that she always went out and came in without any misfortune or accident happening. We know that when Mrs. Simcoe is going on a journey she does not rush into the carriage as a horse rushes into the battle, without thinking of the danger it is running into. No, she looks before she leaps, and says, "Lord, hold Thou me up and I shall be safe."

Mrs. Simcoe certainly had a very great talent given her, and she greatly improved it; she certainly was of a good understanding and of good judgment, very quick and very clever. She was a very early riser, seldom in bed after five or six o'clock. In the summer she and her youngest daughter, Miss Ann, always take a ride at six o'clock in the morning before breakfast, and go four or five miles on the Black Down Hills, a rising ground on the borders of Devonshire and Somerset. Mrs. Simcoe was very fond of early riding. When she was young she has ridden from Wolford Lodge to Clovelly, a village on the North Devon coast between Bideford and Bude, on horseback, a distance of forty miles; and when she was on a journey she always started at six o'clock, and went fifteen or twenty miles before breakfast. Once she went to a watering-place, and a lady of the place asked one of the bathing women whether Mrs. Simcoe had arrived or not. She said she had not heard, but she had seen a lady at the other end of the beach that morning drawing at six o'clock, and if it was not Mrs. Simcoe she could not think who else it could be at that early hour.

General Simcoe, when living, followed the same plan of early rising. He would very often be either out riding or walking at five or six o'clock in the morning with Mr. Scadding, planning about planting the Plantations; and often General and Mrs. Simcoe would be out in the Canadian snow slides (sleighs) when the snow was deep. These snow slides do not go heavy and dead as anyone might suppose, but slip along on the snow, so that a pony could draw it, and General and Mrs. Simcoe often drove out so, and I formerly went with them. General Simcoe used to drive these snow slides himself; he brought them from Canada; the bottom is quite plain and flat, so they do not sink down into the snow, but slip along very easy. Now as General and Mrs. Simcoe were both so fond of being out early in the morning, it seems that Mr. H. A. Simcoe followed their example. I have many times, when he was visiting at Wolford, been with his hot water to call him at six o'clock, but when I came to his room he was up and gone walking, perhaps three or four miles.

There is another thing in which Mr. Simcoe seems to follow the example of his father. We see the great improvement General Simcoe made in the parish of Dunkeswell, so there was the very same done by Mr. Simcoe in the parish of Egloskerry, in Cornwall. Very soon after Mr. Simcoe was at Penheale, I went there on a visit with Mrs. Simcoe. I may very well say that the road from Egloskerry to Penheale was not fit for a cart to go over, and I had to go over it every day in the carriage, and had trouble enough to keep out of the deep ruts, and as Penheale was at that time a farmhouse there were no spare bedrooms, so I had to go five miles with Mrs. Simcoe to Launceston every night. The hill at Launceston was at that time as steep as the side of a house, but our horses were strong and staunch. We stayed at Penheale by day and Launceston by night.

Mrs. Simcoe is going to make great alterations at Penheale, and also at Egloskerry (five miles from Launceston). I was at Penheale with Mrs. Simcoe nine different times, and each time found it greatly improved, as Mr. Simcoe soon had all the house. The rooms at Penheale are certainly very beautiful, the fine wood-carved work I never saw the equal, the beautiful cornices and fine ceilings. The roads are now very good, and there is a nice lodge at the entrance of the house. The village of Egloskerry is very much improved by many new houses, and also a nice, large schoolroom, and there is a great improvement in the church. It certainly looks very nice, particularly when lighted up, for it is something remarkable to see a country church lighted up for evening service, and quite crowded.

Once I was with Mrs. Simcoe on a visit near Egloskerry; she was riding the black pony, and on our way back to Penheale, it being dark, we saw a very bright light on a hill. She asked me what light I should think it was. I told her it was Tremaine Church (six miles from Launceston and three miles from Egloskerry), lighted up for Wednesday evening service. Although we were a long distance from the church we could see the people in the church, and Mr. Simcoe in the pulpit, moving to and fro, as we supposed, preaching. (The parishes of Egloskerry and Tremaine are united.)

Now to turn again to Mrs. Simcoe's travels. Her favourite place was North Wales; the scenery there is most beautiful; the inhabitants are very civil people; the lofty mountains, fine lakes and waterfalls present a most delightful appearance.

There were two places in particular which Mrs. Simcoe very much admired. One was Snowdon, the other the Devil's Bridge (near a village in Cardiganshire, ten miles from Aberystwith), and the mountain Snowdon is certainly very grand from its great height, and the Devil's Bridge from its great depth. The Devil's Bridge is a very curious place. There is a very nice inn near it, and many people stay there to see the bridge and the waterfall. There are two bridges, one built over the other, and from the top bridge to the water measures 110 feet. (The bridge spans the narrow gorge of the river Mynoch.) I went down to the water's edge with Miss Harriet and Miss Ann Simcoe, for the purpose of taking a sketch of the bridges; it certainly is a very frightful place to behold when down by the water.

We had a guide with us, and he told me that he had been down many a time with gentlemen, and that before they had got half-way down they would return, afraid to venture any further. I asked the guide what made them call the bridge by such a curious name. He told me it was supposed that this name of the Devil's Bridge, or " The Bridge of the Evil One," was given it because no one could remember when it was built, neither could they imagine for what purpose the under bridge was built, and some fancy it was never built by the hands of man, because they never could find any account or history of its erection. I fancy myself that it could be plainly seen that the top bridge was built for the purpose of bringing the road more to a level, and to make it more convenient for the passengers, for the under bridge was very low, and I daresay they did not think it worth while to destroy it, as it did not cause the least inconvenience. Mrs. Simcoe very much admired this bridge and the waterfall; so she also very much admired Snowdon. I was on the top of it with Miss Harriet and Miss Ann Simcoe, but unfortunately there was a fog. There is a pillar erected on the top built of large, rough stones, and on it there is fixed a high staff. With great difficulty I climbed up the staff, merely for curiosity. The pillar is for a sea-mark. When clear, some parts of Ireland are visible from it.

Beddgelert was another place Mrs. Simcoe was very fond of. Whilst Mrs. Simcoe was there, Miss Harriet wished to go to Bala (in Merionethshire, Wales), and I was to go with her; so a fly was ordered, and we went to Capel Curig, fourteen miles, then to Cerniogge, both in Carnarvonshire, fifteen miles; then to Bala (in Merionethshire), thirteen miles, where we stopped two hours for the horses to rest; all these are in North Wales. Miss Harriet Simcoe remained there. Miss Simcoe then went to Aberhirnaut, a beautiful spot a few miles from Bala, where Mr. H. Richardson and his wife, who was a Miss Shuldham, of Deerpark, near Honiton, were residing. I was to return with the fly to Cerniogge, and to take the first coach to Beddgelert (at the foot of Snowdon, on the borders of Carnarvonshire and Merionethshire), but there was no coach going there until the next day at twelve o'clock, and as I thought Mrs. Simcoe would want me, I started off on foot. It was then eleven o'clock at night. I had to pass by a forest which seemed to be very lonesome and dismal, but I was very much amused by the nightingales and night crows singing so beautifully, and it sounded so remarkably well in the middle of the night, and I had also the grand sound of the waterfalls, which were a great way off; they could be heard ten or fifteen miles distant roaring down from the mountains. The road that I was travelling on was one of the largest and finest in England—from London to Holyhead and Dublin; although so many travel upon it, I did not meet or see man or woman except the Holyhead mail, which passed at two o'clock, although the stage is fifteen miles. I arrived at Capel Curig, and stopped to rest a little while; then off I started again another stage, fourteen miles.

About four or five miles this side of Beddgelert, the village near Snowdon, there is a fine view of Snowdon and other mountains, which I thought Mrs. Simcoe would like to see, to take a sketch of them. Beddgelert is a large village, in a green basin shut in by mountains and high precipices. It gets its name from the story of Llewellyn, who came here during the hunting season with his child and his greyhound, Gelert. The child, left unprotected in a hut, was attacked by a wolf. On Llewellyn's return he met Gelert wagging his tail, but covered with blood. Alarmed, and thinking that the dog had injured the child, the impetuous prince slew the hound. He entered the hut, to find the dead body of a wolf lying near his sleeping child, disclosing to him his fatal mistake and the fidelity of Gelert. In grief for his dog the prince erected a tomb and called the spot Beddgelert, from Bedd, the grave, and Gelert, the dog.

Although I had walked twenty-nine miles during the night I did not feel tired, so I informed Mrs. Simcoe of the fine scenery that I had passed through. She said she should like to go to see it, but I was to rest myself for a little while. I did not tell Mrs. Simcoe that I had been travelling all night, as I thought it might disappoint her of the ride, as she might think it too much for me; so I got two ponies, one for Mrs. Simcoe and one for Miss Ann Simcoe, and after I had rested a little while I informed Mrs. Simcoe that they were ready. So off we started and got to the place. Mrs. Simcoe was quite delighted with the scenery, and stopped there a long time drawing and taking the sketch of it. Then we returned, very much pleased, and although my walk was forty miles I did not feel tired, but quite delighted.

Close to Beddgelert there is a fine mountain called Moel Hebog, which Miss Ann Simcoe had a wish to go to the top of, and wished me to go with her. So off we started; we had four or five miles to get to the top by winding round it. There was a fog, but it made it look a great deal finer, as the fog would clear off, then suddenly the whole bottom would look beautiful. The village and church of Beddgelert looked remarkably fine. There is a very deep precipice—I should think eight or nine hundred feet deep—which looked rather frightful. Miss Ann Simcoe seemed to be very much pleased with her walk, so we went down the mountain and informed Mrs. Simcoe what a pleasant walk we had 'had. We left the delightful village of Beddgelert for Capel Curig Inn, and stopped there a few days.

There is a mountain near the inn, which Miss Ann Simcoe wished very much to go to the top of, so Mrs. Simcoe consented for her to go and me to go with her. This mountain very much reminded me of the mountain of Trincutte, one of the Nicobar Islands, off the Malay Peninsula in the Indian Ocean, which the officers of our ship went up. The distance straight to the top of it was about two miles, but they had to go thirty to get to the top, which took them two days. So Miss Ann Simcoe and I had to go many miles to get to the top of this mountain. It is most beautiful on the top, and it was a fine clear day, so that we could see a great distance. We could see the Sugar Loaf mountain, near Abergavenny, in Monmouthshire, quite plainly, although sixty miles off, and thirteen lakes—Bala Lake, twenty-five miles distant, quite plain.

After stopping on the mountain for some time viewing the fine sights, we returned to the inn, and then made our departure from North Wales for Herefordshire, going through Oswestry (a market town in Shropshire, fifteen miles from Shrewsbury), the town of Shropshire, Ludlow (a town twenty-five miles from Shrewsbury), Leominster and Hereford (the capital of Herefordshire), where we attended the cathedral services. Then on to Whitchurch, where we stayed a fortnight. The cholera was raging very bad in Devonshire, and also at Bristol, and in all England, but there was not a single case in North Wales.

Mrs. Simcoe enjoyed herself very much at Old Court, riding on a pony nearly every day, viewing the fine scenery. Then we left Whitchurch for home, went as far as the town of Ross and stopped the night. Mrs. Simcoe wished for me to go by the first coach to get home as quickly as I possibly could, as she had not sent any letter to say she was coming home; so I started by the first coach, and arrived at Taunton, in Somersetshire, about nine at night. There was no coach for Honiton, so I walked off for Wolford, then ten o'clock at night. My journey seemed to me rather dismal. I had not got the beautiful singing nightingales to amuse me as I had in North Wales. I cannot say I saw no one on my way from Taunton to Wolford Lodge, for I fell in with company which I did not very much like— a party of poachers by the Blackdown Plantation, between Wolford and Taunton, and about ten miles from Honiton; but they made off, and I got to Wolford quite safe, and arrived about three o'clock in the morning, after a walk of fourteen miles and a ride of one hundred.

Next day Mrs. and Miss Ann Simcoe arrived, and I never recollect Mrs. Simcoe having been so much pleased with a journey before as this to North Wales; the fine sights and those high mountains, which she used to say she had a great deal sooner go to see than any of the fine buildings or places in London—one was the work of man that can be destroyed by man again, the same as Jerusalem and the fine temple; this was built by man, and again all destroyed by man; but the fine mountains of North Wales cannot be destroyed by man. They are like the hills round Jerusalem, that stand fast forever.

Mrs. Simcoe generally went to Cheltenham (a watering-place in Gloucestershire, on the Chelten arm of the Severn) once a year in the season. It is wonderful to see the great improvements there are in Cheltenham. The first time I went there with Mrs. Simcoe was in 1824. At that time there was only one church, but in 1841, the last time I was there with Mrs. and Miss Simcoe and Miss Ann Simcoe, there were five large, beautiful churches, and the old church greatly enlarged, with a large new gallery erected all round the church, and also greatly improved; and it was delightful to see the fine, large congregations that attend there, and more delightful to see so many attend the Sacrament. They came at eight o'clock; sometimes there would be six or eight hundred attend, and again as many at the forenoon service. It was wonderful to see how many attended the evening service at six o'clock—every seat and aisle and gallery quite full. A large congregation is the proof of a good preacher, which was the case at the old church, as Mr. Close is supposed to be as good a preacher as there is in England. He was called Dean Close, and was a great friend of Mrs. Simcoe, and lived at Cheltenham. At the other churches in Cheltenham there are very good preachers.

It is wonderful to see the great improvements that have been made in Cheltenham since the first time I was there with Mrs. Simcoe in 1824—so many fine new streets, squares and terraces having been built, and also two very beautiful spas and bath houses, and very fine hotels and inns. It was formerly the saying that Leamington (on the river Leam, in Warwickshire) was the place for the remedy of the body, and Cheltenham for the remedy of the soul, but I think that Cheltenham is the place where we may get a remedy for our souls and bodies; as the bread and wine so often administered to us in the Sacrament, which is the sure remedy for the soul, so the Cheltenham waters are a remedy for the body; but so many thousands of people get so much benefit by drinking the waters. I think Cheltenham is as fine a place as any in England, both for spiritual and temporal things. It is, as we may say, a heaven on earth, for what can be more like heaven than being in a heavenly place. By such places as this England receives all its blessing, as the Lord saith, "Him that honoureth me, will I honour." Every time that I was at Cheltenham with Mrs. Simcoe, which was many times, it was quite a blessing to be there, to see the large congregations that attend on the Sabbath Day at all the churches to praise and glorify the God that made the heavens and the earth and all that in them is.

Mrs. Simcoe generally stayed at Cheltenham five or six weeks, and then returned home, generally a great deal better, both in temporal and spiritual things.

CHAPTER XXIX.

THE PASSING OF MRS. SIMCOE.

As Mrs. Simcoe advanced in years, as we might expect, her strength failed, and at the latter end of her life she did not go far from home. Sidmouth was the furthest place, and she would only stay a short time. At home she generally took a small drive every day when it was fine, and sometimes she went out in the wheel chair, which she very much enjoyed. The last time she was ever out she took two drives in one day, but she was very unwell; she then took to her bed. She was often visited by Mr. Muller, vicar of Dunkeswell, and also by Mr. H. A. Simcoe, her son; they both gave a very good account of the state of her soul. She was pressing towards the mark for the prize of the high calling of God in Christ Jesus, nothing doubting but that He who had begun a good work in her would perform it until the day of Jesus Christ. God is faithful that hath promised, and therefore she rests assured that He will remember her work of faith and labour of love, and patience of hope in our Lord Jesus Christ. O happy time for those blessed souls who have fought the good fight and kept the faith. We feel assured that Mrs. Simcoe is one of this number; although the lamp of life is nearly extinguished, yet another life is sprung up—the light of God's Holy Spirit, and that will be a light even when walking through the valley of the shadow of death. It will not be death to the believer, only the shadow of it, so she need fear no evil, but may say with the Psalmist, " For thou art with me, thy rod and thy staff they comfort me." What could she fear, whose soul is anchored upon the Rock of Ages, who has the God of Jacob for her help, whose hope is in the Lord her God? She knows that she is in the hands of a most gracious and merciful God, and now that her days are almost at an end I think that I can firmly say that Mrs. Simcoe, now at her last hour, can look back upon a life well spent, and can say with Hezekiah, " Remember now, O Lord, I beseech thee, how I have walked before thee in truth, and with a perfect heart, and have done that which is good in thy sight." What a happy death. What comfort it must be, not only to the dying person, but to the living friends and relations present; and now she may say, as good old Joshua said, " Behold, this day I am going the way of all the earth."

So her last day came, and she died in a good old age, full of days, riches and honour. Mrs. Simcoe departed this life at Wolford Lodge, January 17th, 1850, after forty-four years of widowhood. Her death will be lamented by many, and she will be missed by many, both at home and abroad, by the poor and the afflicted, and by the heathen in different countries abroad. She promoted the societies for sending to them Bibles, and missionaries to instruct them.

Now at Mrs. Simcoe's funeral all her six children attended, and all the clergy of the neighbourhood, and the tenantry, household servants and workmen. A beautiful escutcheon was placed over the front door, done by Mr. Ward, of Honiton. The body was taken from the front door, and the whole funeral procession went off from the front door, and went slowly round the front of the house and up the garden walks. I thought to myself how many journeys and to how many different places I had been with Mrs. Simcoe, and now going one more for the last—to her grave; what a hard stroke! The funeral service was read by Mr. Muller in the chapel. The body was then taken to the grave close to General Simcoe's. When it was let down into the grave I thought what a wonderful thing it was that I should have been present at General Simcoe's funeral, then only a boy of fifteen years of age, and now an old man of sixty to be present at Mrs. Simcoe's funeral forty-four years afterwards. She was the mother of eleven children—nine living when General Simcoe died. What a striking thing, what a charge to be left with such a family, and she at that time only little more than forty years of age! One would scarcely think it to be true, but such was the case.

General Simcoe's funeral was one of the largest that was ever known in Devonshire, he then being Commander-in-Chief of all the Western District. So by reason of that a very large body of troops attended the funeral, Infantry, Cavalry and Artillery, many thousands. As the procession left Exeter, a long train of carriages followed and the streets were lined with troops with arms reversed, so the procession left the city of Exeter for Wolford Lodge. Artillery were stationed with their guns at Straightway Head (near Escot, in Devon, owned by Sir John Kennaway), and Fenny Bridges (a hamlet belonging to the parish of Feniton, four miles from Honiton), and fired as the procession passed on. The East Devon Yeomanry Cavalry were stationed at the battery on St. Cyres Hill, close to Wolford. This regiment was raised by General Simcoe. The second troop was the Dunkeswell troop, chiefly General Simcoe's tenants. As the funeral procession passed through Honiton the shops were closed and the streets were lined with troops with arms reversed. Part of the 3rd Regiment of Dragoon Guards was in advance of the procession, and one thing looked very striking, one of the Dragoons led General Simcoe's charger, a favourite horse, with the General's arms on it. So the procession arrived at Wolford Lodge Chapel attended by thousands of people. The church field was crowded. The Luppitt Company of Artillery (Volunteers raised in Luppitt village by General Simcoe to oppose the expected invasion by Napoleon) was there with the guns, which were fired when the body was put in the grave, which shook the very house of Wolford.

But what a difference it will be when this body shall rise again at the resurrection. What a difference there will be between the sound of the great guns and the sound of the mighty trumpet, when the powers of Heaven shall be shaken; and what a difference there will be between the tribe of people that was in the church field (although that was a great number) and the tribe it will be when all the people that ever were born into this world, from Adam to this time, shall be assembled, when all who are in their graves shall rise again. And what another great difference there will be to those who have served the Lord, and to those who have served Him not. And what a difference there will be to those on the right hand, and to those on the left. And what a difference there will be in the places to which they are to go. To those on the right hand it will be said, " Come, ye blessed of my Father, inherit the kingdom prepared for you from the foundation of the World," but to those who have not served the Lord it will be said, " Depart, ye cursed." All of us now living have the choice, and if we wish to be like those on the right hand, we must follow the advice of good old Joshua, who said, " As for me and my house, we will serve the Lord."

Mrs. Simcoe was one who followed that advice in her house. See what a blessing it was to her to have such a happy death as she seems to have had, how she met her death without fear or amazement. She is gone, I hope, to a happy place, where the wicked cease from troubling, and where the weary are at rest. She is gone, and her works do follow her. The talent that she had given her was improved.

General Simcoe, like his wife, had talent and improved it. He was a very useful man in the world; by that he got to such high rank. How soon he reached the rank of General. See what good he did in Canada. When he went there as Governor there were no provisions but what were sent to them from England. But what a great change there was soon after; instead of our sending provisions to them they sent them to us, and he made great improvements there while Governor, and see, again, how much he did here in England. What danger the country was then in. The French were then preparing a very large expedition to invade England, and Devonshire was the place where it was the intention of Bonaparte to land, very likely at Tor Bay. The whole of the west of England was put under the care of General Simcoe; he was Commander-in-Chief. He raised a very large body of troops, and every man who was able in the West of England had something to do or perform if the enemy should land. All the carpenters were ready with their saws and axes to cut down the trees and lay them across the roads to prevent the enemy from passing; furze ricks put on the hills to set fire to them if the enemy did land, to alarm the country. There were camps at different places. It was supposed that Tor Bay, on the east coast of Devonshire, would certainly be Bonaparte's landing place, and to London his route, so that the great road from Exeter to London was General Simcoe's chief care, to prevent the enemy from passing that way; he had a large camp on Woodbury Common, six miles from Exeter, of many thousand troops, and also a very strong battery on St. Cyres's Hill, where there was plenty of room to work 200 great guns. I should think it impossible for an army to pass the bottom through Honiton, as the guns on that battery would very well carry balls as far as Fenny Bridges.

So great were the preparations made by General Simcoe in this part of the country that he left not a stone unturned, all the soldiers that were under his command in the four counties of Dorsetshire, Devonshire, Somersetshire and Cornwall were well trained, as the General often had sham fights. There was one very grand one; there were four thousand soldiers present, and, I should think, ten thousand lookers-on. The battle began at Fenny Bridges; the Militia and Regulars were the French, and the Volunteers, Yeomanry Cavalry and Volunteer Artillery with their cannon were to be the English. So the French retreated to Hembury Fort, owned by Admiral Graves, and on the lawns there was a very sharp attack. It was so sharp that there was great fear the soldiers would get in earnest, so orders were given for the Regulars to retreat to Hembury Fort Hill, the site of an ancient Roman camp and fort, the property of Admiral Graves, where the battle ended, and the English gained a complete victory. Hembury Fort, three miles from Wolford, was like a large fair with stands. The "French" encamped on Hembury Fort Hill for the night; the tents looked very grand on the hill. After they were pitched, the evening gun was fired at nine o'clock for all the soldiers to be in their tents. I was present and witnessed the whole of it. A few incidents happened. One young lad was very near being killed; he was close to the muzzle of a cannon when it was fired and the charge (but it was only powder) went to his head and face, so he was blinded. Great praise was due to the officers and soldiers for their soldierlike manner in the sham fight.

General Simcoe had another very large sham fight soon after this at Totnes (in Devonshire, eight miles from Torquay). He generally had some regular regiments at the sham fights to instruct the Volunteers and Militia, so by this means General Simcoe trained the Volunteers to become good soldiers, and fit for an army to meet the French when they landed. At Wolford Lodge, General Simcoe was just about the middle of the Western District, so when there he was at his post, and despatches were sent to him every day from the headquarters at Plymouth. There were three dragoons at the half-way house, stationed there to bring the despatches which came from Exeter and Plymouth. One of the dragoons came over to Wolford with despatches at 12 o'clock at night. He came by Buckerall, four miles from Honiton, and up the Grange road, a private road from Wolford to Awliscombe, but made a mistake and came through the Chase and under Sand Walk. Formerly there was a Canadian wooden bridge for foot passengers only; the bridge crossed over a deep gully. The dragoon thought to get his horse over it, so he led it, but in crossing the horse slipped and fell into the gully from the bridge to the bottom, so the poor man came to the house and rang the door bell. He said he had brought despatches for General Simcoe, but his horse was gone down. So some men with lights were sent out to see what had become of the poor horse, and to their great surprise they found the horse in the gully standing under the bridge where it fell down, although from the bridge to the bottom was nearly 20 feet, and also rough stones to fall on, and yet the horse was not hurt at all. They had to take it down a long way before they could get it up from the gully, and the horse was able to return to the half-way house again, after resting and feeding; but it was thought a most wonderful thing that the horse was not killed on the spot from so great a fall.

The training of the Volunteers was General Simcoe's great care; he had raised such very large bodies, not a parish in the West of England wherein there were not Volunteers. At every town eight or ten companies of them would meet for six or eight days' training and exercise; there was nearly a thousand of them met at Honiton for eight days' training; and those men were from the neighborhood of Honiton.

There were nearly fifty thousand Volunteers in Devonshire, and General Simcoe reviewed them all, so the Volunteers were nearly as good soldiers as there were in the regular regiments. General Simcoe sometimes had the Honiton Volunteers first and second companies at Wolford Lodge to exercise and fire, and then would treat them with a nice dinner, have tables fixed through the avenue for two hundred of them, the band at the front of the house playing some lively tunes. Sometimes the Volunteers would meet at the Battery on St. Cyres's Hill and the Luppitt Company of Volunteer Artillery commanded by Captain Pierce, of Greenway (a house in Luppitt parish, three miles from Wolford). On any particular day, such as the fourth of June, the King's birthday, a royal salute was fired by the Artillery, the Ensign was hoisted at the flag-staff. This flag-staff General Simcoe had fixed there when the battery was built, it was very high, the ensign was very large—the St. George's flag—it is at Wolford Lodge at this present time.

Now to proceed with Bonaparte's invading England, which we know for certain it was his intention to do, as the preparations for conveying the armies to England were prepared. It was arranged to convey the armies from France to England in large, flat-bottomed boats, many hundreds of which were built for the purpose; some of these boats would carry three or four hundred men, so that five hundred of these boats would bring over to England at least a hundred and fifty thousand men. It was Bonaparte's plan to come over by night, and land his troops so as to take England by surprise; but as General Simcoe was making such great preparations it was likely that Bonaparte was aware of it, as there were supposed to be many French spies in England spying out the country, but if Bonaparte does come he will come suddenly, like a thief in the night. We may say now that General Simcoe is ready, let it be what day or what hour;

if it be at evening, or at midnight, or at the cock-crowing or in the morning, he will be watching and ready to meet them.

General Simcoe has been so very busy in preparing for the French and to be ready to give them a meeting, so now he looks at home at his own parish, Dunkeswell; what great improvements he has been making there. If anyone could have seen it when he came there first, and see it now, they would think it was not the same place. Just look at Blackdown Hills, the high ridge from Luppitt Hill, up a very steep hill to Broadhembury Hill, near Wolford, not a hedge or tree was to be seen; no road, only wheel tracks. No road from Wolford to Dunkeswell, nothing but wheel ruts and not fit for a cart to pass on it. As for waggons, there was not one in the parish of Dunkeswell. General Simcoe had the first waggon that was in the parish.

CHAPTER XXX.

THE VILLAGE OF DUNKESWELL.

Now to view the village of Dunkeswell; when I came to service at Wolford Lodge in 1802 there were six old houses in the village, and the Church, which was so small that only about forty people could sit down in it, and it was the only place of worship in the parish. But just see it now in 1850! Instead of one little church there are three fine handsome churches (Luppitt, Dunkeswell and Dunkeswell Abbey churches), with sittings for nearly a thousand people in them, and instead of six houses in the village, there are thirty. Again, just view the Blackdown Hills in 1850, formerly no road, hedge or tree to be seen, but now many fine plantations, with many thousands of trees in them, and many thousands have been cut down. All these plantations were planned by General Simcoe and Mr. John Scadding. What great good these plantations have been to the neighbourhood from the timber, and the number of labourers employed about them, and also the great profit they bring in. And think what great improvements General Simcoe made in the house at Wolford, how many thousands of pounds it cost in building, and fifty men employed daily.

As General Simcoe was a military man he wished all that came there to come in a military way. All the tradespeople assembled at the end of the Avenue and fell in there two deep according to their trades, those of the highest rank in trade going first. When all were mustered they were marched off to the house with a drum and fife played before them, then all received their orders and were dismissed. When they left work all fell in again, and were marched off with drum and fife.

So much building at Wolford was a great expense, as all the timber was bought, there not being a tree on the Wolford estate fit for building, but if there had been, General Simcoe would not have had a tree cut down by any means; even the fire-wood for the use of the house was all bought, not a stick was to be cut down. The only timber at Wolford was the Long Copse, or plantation, so General Simcoe employed a great many people planting. So very much labour was going on at Wolford that if anyone wanted work if they went there they were sure to get it, there were so many new roads, new hedges, and so much planting of trees. One excellent thing General Simcoe was going to do, which was to make a new carriage road through the under sand walk and chase; the stones were drawn to build a bridge across the gully. This road was meant for an Exeter road through Buckerall to Fenny Bridges, and would make it near four miles shorter than going through Honiton, and also save two turnpikes and many long hills; and it was General Simcoe's plan to make this the road from Wolford to Honiton, instead of going through Combe Raleigh, so as to avoid the very steep hills, for the road from Honiton to Grange farm is very good and level; the only hill would be from Grange to the Chase gate, which is but little, and that little could have been made better. General Simcoe was going to have another new road instead of the Dunkeswell road, coming down the Limers Lane. When coming from Honiton he meant it to go on the old Taunton road for a little, then to branch off straight to Dunkeswell; and it was also General Simcoe's plan for Limers Lane, the road from Wolford Cross to Wolford, to be made a private carriage drive to Wolford, and to be the grand entrance to the house.

If it had pleased the Lord that General Simcoe had lived a few years longer, a very great improvement would have been made at Wolford, and also in the neighbourhood, for we see how much has been already done, for he very much liked Wolford, and it certainly is a very pleasant situation and has a very nice view from the front of the house, a fine rich vale for twenty miles, the little river Otter taking its course by Fenny Ridges to Ottery, five miles from Honiton, then on to Budleigh Salterton, a seaside place on the south Devon coast; the beautiful valley from Wolford Lodge to Budleigh Salterton, which is twenty miles, can all be seen from Wolford Lodge. This rich tract of land, as rich as any in England, also the beautiful hills that are in sight from the front of the house, the East and West Hills, Woodbury Hill, Haldon Hill, ten miles from Exeter; Gittesham, three miles from Honiton; Buckerall Knap ("knap" is a local term for a small hill or rising ground); some parts of Dartmoor, Bury Head, Beacon Hill, near Exmouth, all can be seen from Wolford Lodge, and also a very fine view of the sea. One can see the ships very plainly passing up and down the English Channel and going in and coming out of Tor Bay, Exmouth and Teignmouth Harbours, which all look very pleasant in fine weather.

There was one very great blessing at Wolford Lodge; it is a very healthy place, very little sickness ever was there. Although it was such a large establishment, particularly when General Simcoe was living, yet not one death took place from the year 1802 until 1846, when Miss Henrietta Simcoe died, and in 1850 Mrs. Simcoe died; for although we may live in a healthy place, death will surely come, "for since by man came death, by man came also the resurrection of the dead; for as in Adam all die even so in Christ shall all be made alive." We see God is all in all, and in him we live and move and have our being.

Although General Simcoe so much enjoyed being at Wolford Lodge, his services were very much required elsewhere. He had such a large body of troops under his command, particularly volunteers who wanted so much training and reviewing, and he had to watch the movements of Bonaparte's great expedition, and it was not known whether he would come or not, all had to be in readiness, for General Simcoe knew well that Bonaparte was a very covetous man, wanting all the world; and also, like the unjust judge who feared not God neither regarded man. If he had feared God he would not have done what he did when he took Spain, making the churches into stables for his horses; and again, when he took the large city of Warsaw (Moscow) he drove out the inhabitants to perish and die with cold, whilst he and his army lived in it. But Providence would not permit that he and his army should dwell in the city, for the Russians set fire to it and burnt it to ashes, and a great part of the French army perished from the cold; the remainder returned to France. Very likely if he had been permitted to land in England he would have been just as bad to us, but it was supposed if he had landed in Devonshire that he and all his great army would have been taken, as General Simcoe had thousands of troops all well trained and fit for battle; but Devonshire was the strongest part of the kingdom. It is supposed if Bonaparte had landed at Tor Bay that he would never have got as far as Exeter. But now came the glorious news of a great naval victory gained by Lord Nelson at Trafalgar. This glorious news came to Wolford in the evening; then General Simcoe sent to Captain Pierce to take the Luppitt Artillery, with their cannon, to the end of St. Cyres Hill, and there to fire a salute; it was then eight o'clock in the evening. The people of Honiton were rather alarmed at hearing the cannon so very near them; the guns were heard very plainly at Axminster and many parts of Devonshire.

General Simcoe gave a very grand dinner party; all the chief gentry of the neighbourhood were present; the great new room (the saloon on the south-west side of the house) was fitted up beautifully—more than five hundred lamps were lighted up in the room. The crown and " G.R." were formed with lamps, as well as many other devices. The dinner table was sixty feet long. The great room looked remarkably grand, and a grand party was there; nearly fifty carriages were in the front park. The front of the house looked very grand. The windows were all illuminated, a light in every square of glass. The cannons were fired in the front park, and fireworks let off. There was a large bonfire at the Cleve Farm (the plantation above Wolford), another at Ben Point (the plantation to the right of Wolford), and one on Buckerall Knap, which were all lighted after dinner was over. A grand ball took place in the evening, and all passed off with great joy. After this the party took their leave. The next morning all were very busy clearing up and preparing for another ball, which was to be the young ladies' party, and to take place very soon. The beautiful green at the front of the house was like a ploughed field from the carriages going over it to turn at the front door. The ladies' ball took place very soon after this, and was very grand. The house was again illuminated, fireworks let off, the cannon fired in the front park and bonfires as before.

Soon after this second ball General Simcoe had another very amusing thing done in the great new room. It was a fair. There were all sorts of things going on, some crying out " Moore's Almanacks,"

" Sheet Almanack," some crying " nuts," and crying " crack away, toss or buy." All these things General Simcoe had done by way of rejoicing for Lord Nelson's great victory at the battle of Trafalgar.

Soon after this General Simcoe was appointed Commander-in Chief of the British Forces in India, and had it pleased God that he should go very likely I should have been one of the party to go with him to the East Indies, for I was told by Mr. Morgan, the butler, that if I should like to go I was to ask my parents if they were willing to let me, and all were agreeable. Great preparations were going on at Wolford Lodge for the voyage, and large boxes made; but we see what man appointeth God disappointeth. If General Simcoe had lived and gone to India, and if it had pleased the Lord for him to have returned home again safe, he would have been a very great person in the world. But before his departure to India he was directed by Government to go to Lisbon, for the purpose of render- ing all the assistance he could against the French in that country; but on the voyage to Lisbon General Simcoe was taken alarmingly ill, and on his arrival there he was advised to return to England again, which he did, and put into Tor Bay, and then sent to Topsham. I have heard that the sudden illness of General Simcoe was supposed to have been caused by the ship he was on board having been newly painted. I remember one of the servants who went with General Simcoe said that the paint was the cause of his illness, the ship having been newly painted; and we know paint is slow poison, and we might almost as well eat it as be always smelling it. Mrs. Simcoe was as much afraid of paint as she was of a plague.

General Simcoe was taken to Archdeacon Moore's house in the Cathedral Close of Exeter, where he soon breathed his last. The news soon reached Wolford, and I remember very well that I was sent very early in the morning, long before daylight, to Mrs. Elliot's at Egland, with a letter for Mrs. Elliot, as Miss Harriet and Miss Caroline Simcoe were staying there. When I arrived Miss Harriet came to her bedroom window and asked me if I had come from Wol- ford, and if I had heard how General Simcoe was. I told her I was in hopes he was a great deal better. Great preparations were made at Wolford for the funeral.

NOTE.—Bailey then refers to the mural monument by Flaxman, erected in the Cathedral, Exeter, England, to the memory of General Simcoe and his son Francis Gwillim, who was killed at Badajoz and buried on the field of battle. Then he gives the inscriptions on the six niches of one of the outer walls of the private chapel at Wolford, where General Simcoe, his widow and children, except Francis and the first Katherine, are buried. Those who died and are buried away from Wolford are remembered in these inscriptions. He then resumes his narrative:

Now look and see what is inscribed on those six headstones. Just look at General Simcoe's, what we see on it. " As for me and my

BAILEY ON THE SIMCOE CHILDREN

house we will serve the Lord." What a blessing it is for those who dwell in such a house as this—to serve the Lord. It is quite different to those who dwell in such a house as that of which we read in Proverbs iii., 33 : "The curse of the Lord is in the house of the wicked." And again, just see the words on Mrs. Simcoe's headstone: "The heart of her husband doth safely trust in her; her children arise up and call her blessed," Proverbs xxi., 11, 28. What a blessing for a husband to get such a wife, and what a blessing for children to have such a mother. From the tenth to the thirty-first verses of that chapter there is not one but is suitable to Mrs. Simcoe.

The next, Mr. Francis Simcoe. What is there more that is required in a soldier than what we see on his headstone—good courage in battle. We know that is the chief work of a soldier in fighting.

Now the next, Miss Henrietta Simcoe. "My peace I give unto you." The peace of God, you know, passeth all understanding. We make our peace with God through Jesus Christ. There is no peace to the wicked; it is only for the righteous.

Now next to the infant children, Miss Katherine and Mr. John Simcoe. Those infants, we may feel assured, are in heaven, for Christ sayeth in St. Mark x., 14: "For of such is the Kingdom of God." All their troubles were at an end soon after they began. The Lord gave them, and the Lord took them again to Himself.

Now next, Miss Charlotte Simcoe, what we see on her headstone: "Be ye steadfast." Like the church which is built on the rock, the gates of hell shall not prevail against it. And I do believe that Miss Charlotte Simcoe was a steadfast member of this church, so we may feel assured that all her labours were not in vain in the Lord. We know that all those who were hired in the Lord's vineyard received what was due to them.

After the death of General Simcoe the establishment at Wolford was very much lessened. Only seven servants remained. I was one of the seven, and was to be in the stables as usual, and I had the care of General Simcoe's charger, a favourite horse, and four beautiful ponies which Mr. Francis and Mr. Henry A. Simcoe often rode, and I went with them. They were beautiful ponies, two of them black and two of them grey; they went like the wind.

I went to service to General Simcoe at the latter end of 1802, and remained with him until his death. Then I remained with Mrs. Simcoe two years; then I left, and was away nine years, and in that time I was in the four quarters of the world. I was in the Baltic Sea, Gulf of Finland, West Indies, South America, East Indies, China, Philippine Islands, Cape of Good Hope and the Mediterranean. I returned in 1816, and went again into Mrs. Simcoe's service, and remained with her until her death, thirty-two years afterwards; then I left.

Now during the last thirty-two years of my service with Mrs. Simcoe I never once knew her to go to any place of amusement, such as balls, plays or any such things; but very often to missionary meet-

413

ings, Bible meetings, Jews' meetings or such places as these, where good is to be done. She was always ready in a good cause with hand and heart ready to support it, ready to relieve the poor and distressed, a soldier or sailor.

It was General Simcoe's intention for his two sons, Mr. Francis Simcoe and Mr. Henry A. Simcoe, both to be in His Majesty's service—Mr. F. Simcoe to be in the army, and Mr. H. A. Simcoe to be in the navy; but as Mr. Francis Simcoe was killed in the trench at the siege of Badajoz in 1812, in the twenty-first year of his age, he being the heir and just of age and a large property coming to him, so by his death the heirship fell to the next son, Mr. H. A. Simcoe. As Mr. F. G. Simcoe was killed in battle, Mrs. Simcoe would not consent to Mr. H. A. Simcoe, the only son and heir, going into the navy, so he became a minister of the Gospel. Mrs. Simcoe lived to that wonderful age that she saw her children's children, even four generations, which very few are permitted to do.

CHAPTER XXXI.

INCIDENT AND COMMENT.

As has been stated, John Bailey divided his paper on the Simcoe family into two parts, covering the period 1802-50. The first part he devoted mainly to the family life at Wolford from 1802 until 1808. The second part, which is full of incident and comment down to the passing of Mrs. Simcoe in 1850, he calls " The Second Edition of the Life of General and Mrs. Simcoe."

Now to proceed with the lives of General and Mrs. Simcoe. By the help of the Lord I hope to do it, for without the Lord we can do nothing, and with Him we can do all things.

Now to speak of the greatness and usefulness of General Simcoe is far beyond my power. I can only mention what I saw in my three years' service with him. Now of Mrs. Simcoe's life I can give more particulars. First, I shall mention what I have seen done by General and Mrs. Simcoe in the parish of Dunkeswell, by planting and building. Just view all the trees round Wolford, the number of plantations; there is the Beach Plantation, the Roughborough, the Oak. This last was sown with acorns in my remembrance, and now at this time has come to fine timber. See the Blackdown and Roughgrey Plantations near Wolford, the higher and lower sand walks. All these were planned and planted by General Simcoe and Mr. John Scadding. The Chase, a plantation on the east side of the house at Wolford, was also sown with acorns, and is at this time very fine timber. There are also the Cleeve and St. Cyres Plantations. How many thousands of trees have been lately cut down. Look at the last sale paper, how many trees were advertised for sale in it. Ask Mr. Burrows, the estate bailiff, how many thousands of trees he has sold in the sixteen years that he has been at Wolford, and also the great quantity of wood. All these trees were planted by General Simcoe. And again, how much building there has been, how many houses have been built in the parish of Dunkeswell by General and Mrs. Simcoe. I will mention them—Grange Farms, barns, linhays (a Devonshire name for outhouses) and stables were all destroyed by fire and rebuilt by General Simcoe; Wolford itself greatly altered and enlarged, and a chapel built; Wolford Cottage; the Battery on St. Cyres Hill; the south aisle of Dunkeswell Church built and seated by Mrs. Simcoe; West Hill Farm, barns and stables; East Hill Farm, barns and stables also built by Mrs. Simcoe; Ball Nap Cottage, built by Miss Ann Simcoe; Southay Farm, barns and stables, built by Mrs. Simcoe; Blackdown House, coach house and stables, built by Mrs. and the Misses Simcoe; W. Selway's, John Tuck's, William Dimond's cottages,

415

built by Mrs. Simcoe; Parish Clerk Selway's, John Gosling's houses, built by General Simcoe; William Row's, William Carter's and James Cole's cottages, formerly a farmhouse, made into three cottages by Mrs. Simcoe; the parish house, built by General Simcoe and given by him for the poor, but now bought from the parish and made into three cottages by Mrs. Simcoe; Roughgrey Farmhouse, barn and stables, built by General Simcoe; John Hitchcock's house and homestead, built by Mrs. Simcoe; Dunkeswell Abbey School and school house, built by Miss Caroline Simcoe; Southay Farmhouse, barns and stables destroyed by fire and rebuilt by Mrs. Simcoe; Blackdown House, destroyed by fire and rebuilt by Mrs. Simcoe; Richard Marshall's cottage, leasehold to Mrs. Simcoe; Levi Richard's cottage, leasehold to Mrs. Simcoe; Henry Somerset's and John Russell's cottages and blacksmith's shop, leasehold to Mrs. Simcoe; Sarah Cox's cottage, leasehold to Mrs. Simcoe; and besides all the buildings and planting, think of the new roads and hedges. Most likely, if General Simcoe had not come into the parish, none of this would have been done. How thankful we should be to the Lord for permitting such a person to come amongst us. Was it by chance? No, there is no chance work with the Lord; it is with Him yea and amen. When the man was going to Jericho and fell among thieves which wounded him and left him half dead, it is said by chance there came down a certain priest that way, and when he saw him he passed by on the other side. What a thing for a priest to pass! You would think he would have been the first to help the poor, suffering man. No, he was by chance. He was not ordained to assist him. It was the good Samaritan the Lord ordained. It was not by chance. Most likely this poor, suffering man was a good man; so the Lord sends a good man to help him. Most likely he was a chosen man to the Lord. Like Moses, we know he was chosen. See how wonderfully he was nursed by Pharaoh's daughter; if she had not come down to the river to wash herself she would not have seen the child; but it does not say she came down by chance. There was no chance work, it was by the power of God. Again, in the 21st chapter of Genesis, from the 12th to the 21st verse, we see no chance work in the deliverance of Joseph from his brethren. Read the last thirteen chapters of Genesis and see if there is a word about chance. With God all things are done by word and power. God said, "Let there be light," and there was light. By the word of the Lord the heavens and the earth were made; not one thing came by chance.

And was it by chance that General and Mrs. Simcoe came into the parish of Dunkeswell? No, the Lord ordained it to be so. How many parts of the Scripture have been fulfilled by their coming. See by the Abbey how the Scripture was fulfilled—Isaiah lxi.: 3, 4, and many other places in the Bible. Again, how many Scriptures are fulfilled by Wolford?—Isaiah xli.: 19, 20, where it is said, "I will plant in the wilderness the cedar, the shittah tree, and the myrtle, and the oil tree. I will set in the desert the fir tree, and the pine, and the box tree together. That they may see and know and consider and understand together that the hand of the Lord hath done this, and the Holy One of Israel hath created it." And again, in the 55th chapter of Isaiah, verses 12, 13, " For ye shall go out with joy and be led forth with peace; the mountains and the hills shall break forth before you into singing, and all the trees of the field shall clap their hands. Instead of the thorn shall come up the fir tree, and it shall be to the Lord for a name, for an everlasting sign that shall not be cut off?" What can be plainer of the Scriptures being fulfilled? And also how plainly the Scriptures were fulfilled in the Abbey. Of how many different places we see the Lord said, " They shall build the old wastes, they shall raise up the former desolations, and they shall repair the waste cities, the desolations of many generations." We know that the Abbey was formerly a very large place, and who can tell if it will not become a large place again? We cannot tell what the Lord may do; the same hand that fed 5,000 people with five barley loaves and two small fishes can make Dunkeswell Abbey become a very large place. We can see that it was so formerly by the old buildings, and why not become so again? How did Chelten-ham become a large place? It was only by guidance of pigeons; those birds were often seen to come to a spring of water. Pigeons are very fond of salt, so for that reason they flocked there. The water was examined and found to be very good mineral water, so people came from all parts to drink it, and found much benefit; so Cheltenham is now become one of the grandest and most fashionable places in Eng-land. And who can tell if the pigeons may not come and find one of these springs of water at Dunkeswell Abbey? There is a very good beginning made at the Abbey, a handsome church and schoolroom built. We know it was not General Simcoe who built them, but he made the first beginning. He purchased the Abbey. The temple at Jerusalem was not built by King David, but he made the preparations for the work, but his son was to build it. Now it is very likely that if General Simcoe had not come into the parish of Dunkeswell there would not have been any more church room than there was before he came; but as there were so many houses built by General and Mrs. Simcoe, the church was greatly enlarged, and a new tower built. Before the church was enlarged the establishment at Wolford Lodge when General Simcoe was living there took nearly half the room in the church; but the family was very often away, particularly in the summer.

At this time I had a great deal of riding about; very often I had to go to Honiton two or three times in a day, but there were four fine little ponies that would go like the wind, and when the family was at Budleigh Salterton (on the south Devon coast, nine miles from Wolford), which was generally for two or three months during the summer, then I was frequently sent there, sometimes two or three times in a week. I often set off from Wolford at three o'clock in the morning, and was down there before anyone was up in the house;

27 417

and I generally had a great many things to take there. General Simcoe would ask me how I could be there so early from such a long distance. I was generally back at Wolford by three o'clock in the afternoon, a 40-mile ride.

Soon after this I took a journey with M. de Luc, a French gentleman who was a visitor at Wolford. But before I say anything about M. de Luc I will endeavour to give a short account of my first going out to service. My father was informed that there was a boy wanted at General Simcoe's, of Wolford Lodge, to clean knives and forks. I was the youngest son, and about twelve years of age. I had a brother then at home who was about fourteen years of age, so my father took us both to Wolford Lodge, to offer one of us to fill the situation, thinking if one did not do the other might. When we came to Wolford we had to appear before Mr. Morgan, the butler, for him to take his choice of us; so after my father and Mr. Morgan had held a little conversation he decided upon me, and I was to come soon; so in a few days I went. The establishment at Wolford Lodge was at that time very large—twenty-one servants. My father promised me that if I was a good boy and kept my place he would give me a new suit of clothes, and he soon had the pleasure of hearing that I was going on very well, so he sent a tailor of the name of Ham, from Ulverstone, a small place comprising some cottages and farms near Awliscombe below Pen Point, to take my measure, and he was to ask me what sort of clothes I would like to have; which he did, and I, seeing the other servants cutting about in their gay livery, fancied I should like to have mine the same—it was blue turned up with white. I ordered the tailor to make mine exactly like it, and off he went to Honiton for the cloth, and in a few days he came with my new livery, and I, being anxious to see how I looked in it, started upstairs and put it on instantly. Now it can be well supposed that I was not a little proud of it, and wishing to display it as much as I could, down I went to the servants' hall to show myself. They, of course, were all struck with surprise on seeing me in livery and said, " Dear me, you are looking smart enough." " What, Jack, are you put in livery ?" Now this soon reached Mr. Morgan's ears, and down he came to the hall looking rather smiling, and said to me, " Oh, Jack, who ordered you to put on livery ?" He desired me to take it off immediately and let the tailor have it to take off all the trimmings. I was very much disappointed that I was not permitted to wear it. Shortly after this a boy was wanted in the stable under John Gosling, the groom. So Mr. Morgan sent me to my father telling him of it, and asked whether he had another son he could send him; so my father sent my other brother, and it was settled for him to come; but he being the elder, Mr. Morgan thought it would be better for him to be in the house under the butler, and for me to be in the stable, which was done.

I will now return to my journey with M. de Luc, a French gentleman, but I must say that the time I was with him was not very long, neither was the distance very great. M. de Luc was on a visit to Mrs. Burgess, at Ashfield, and was wanting to go to the north coast of Somerset. He moreover wished to take his journey on horseback, so General Simcoe lent him a horse for the purpose, and I was to go with him, and also Henry Rowe, the gardener at Ashfield. He was to keep us both as long as he liked. So we started off together by Wolford, through Dunkeswell and Hemyock, in the Culme Valley, four miles from Dunkeswell, and went as far as Wellington, in Somersetshire, the first day. This journey took us a long time, as M. de Luc wished to see a little of the country, and there was one place in particular where he was engaged for a considerable time. It was Simonsborough; it lies between Hemyock and Wellington, and at this place there was a large heap of stones, supposed to be many thousand waggon loads, and it appeared as if they had been there many hundred years, for no one could give any account how they came there, or for what purpose they were put there. M. de Luc was very much interested in viewing these stones, for it was wonderful how they could have been placed to such a great height, and where they could all have been brought from. We then made the best of our way to Wellington, where we arrived safe that night. The next morning our route was to Sir John Trevelyan's at Nettlecombe, near Watchet (in Somersetshire). I have before stated that M. de Luc had liberty to keep me as long as he liked, and the horses also; yet the horse he rode was the one which General Simcoe always rode himself, but the General respected M. de Luc very much, as did also all the head gentry round there, so he wished to oblige him in any way he could. I was told that M. de Luc had often visited the royal family, King George the 3rd and Queen Charlotte, but notwithstanding his being of such high rank he would stop and talk with a poor man working on the road, just the same as he would with a nobleman. Before leaving Wellington, M. de Luc considered that he did not need two persons to go with him, so he sent Henry Rowe back to Ashfield, and we proceeded on our journey to Nettlecombe, passing through Milverton (a small town in a dell seven miles from Taunton) and Wivelscombe (pronounced Wilscombe, near Milverton). Near the latter place there was a large limestone quarry, and many men at work there. We rode up to it, and stayed there some time. M. de Luc asked the men all particulars about the stone, and also about the country round. M. de Luc not being able to speak very plain English, the men were rather afraid that he was a French spy; there was very hot war between England and France at this time, and it was reported that there were many French spies about England, so they thought he was one of them, and many of them came and asked me what country my master was from, and whether he was a Frenchman or not. I told them that I was not his servant. They then asked me where he came from. I told them that I was General Simcoe's servant and lived near Honiton, and that the horses belonged to General Simcoe, and that we were going to Sir John Trevelyan's, at Nettlecombe. They said they thought he was asking a good many questions, which they did not like very well, but I assured them that he was a very nice gentleman and no spy, so then they became a little more reconciled.

After M. de Luc had looked about the place as long as he liked we proceeded on our journey, and arrived at Nettlecombe the same night. This was a very beautiful place, the house very large and very ancient. The parish church was close to the house, and it appeared by the very great resemblance of the building that they were built at the same time. The village of Nettlecombe is some distance from the church.

Sir John Trevelyan's park was very beautiful, with many hundred deer in it, and as Sir John took M. de Luc to the village of Watchet the next day in his carriage, I had the opportunity of taking a walk round the park, and also of seeing a little of Nettlecombe. The following day they went to Dunster (in Somersetshire) and other places, and the next day we left Nettlecombe and went to Bridgewater (Somersetshire). We found the road very pleasant; we had in our view the Bristol Channel, and also the south of Wales. We went through Nether Stowey (Somersetshire), where we stopped and fed the horses, and then proceeded on again, and arrived at Bridgewater the same night.

The next day M. de Luc sent for me, and told me that he was not going on horseback any further, and that I could return to Wolford with the horses. He seemed very much satisfied with all I had done for him, and I then took my departure and returned to Wolford quite safe.

Now there was another journey which I had—a very quick trip on horseback to Bath. An express came for Miss Charlotte Simcoe to go to Bath. Accordingly the carriage was ordered to take her, and I was to go on horseback to Taunton (Somersetshire) and order a post chaise, and a saddle horse for myself, which were to be ready by the time the carriage reached Taunton, which I did. The horse I rode was to stay there until I returned again. When the carriage arrived I was ordered to gallop on to Burrow Bridge and order another post chaise and another saddle horse. These were also to be ready by the time the former one reached, and from this I was to gallop on to Street Inn, and do the same, and then to Old Down Inn, and there Mrs. Graves', widow of the late Admiral Graves, carriage was intended to be waiting to take on Miss Charlotte Simcoe, but when we arrived it had not come. If it had been there I was to have returned by the first coach, but as such was not the case Miss Charlotte Simcoe asked if it would be too much for me to ride on to Bath. I told her it would not, and I moreover said I could go on directly. She seemed very much disappointed at not finding Mrs. Graves' carriage there, but I was quite overjoyed with thinking I was to see Bath; so another post chaise was ordered and another saddle horse, and we set off again, and soon arrived at 15 Lansdowne Crescent, Bath. This was 63 miles from Wolford Lodge in little more than seven hours. I stayed in Bath that night and the next day, and saw some of the principal places in Bath. Mr. Smith, Mrs. Graves' coachman, was kind enough to show me round the place. We went to the Abbey, the Pump Room and many other places. The next morning I started by coach at six o'clock for Taunton, arrived safe at the White Hart, found my horse quite well, and returned to Wolford, and here I end this journey.

There is one thing I will mention which happened after General Simcoe's death. Mrs. Simcoe went on a morning visit to Ashfield; she went on horseback, and I went with her. Before starting she ordered the pony carriage to be brought to the end of the long avenue plantation leading to St. Cyres and to wait until we returned. But when we came back it was not there. I told her it certainly had been there, for the wheel marks were quite plain where it had turned; so we went on, and when we came to the first gate we found it burst open and part of the carriage there. When we came to the large white gate leading to the Sand Walk there lay more of it, and when we came to the park gate there was some more of the carriage, and on reaching Wolford we were told that the horse came galloping by the front of the house and up the stable yard with part of the carriage. It appears that the cause of the horse running away was a gun being fired near, which frightened it. One of the wheels was knocked off at the entrance of the park, and was found long afterwards a great distance off, it having been knocked off with such force that it had run a long way.

CHAPTER XXXII.

MANY JOURNEYS WITH MRS. SIMCOE.

Now I hope to give an account of all the counties, cities and towns I have seen, and particularly those I have visited with Mrs. Simcoe and the Misses Simcoe:

1. Devonshire.—Exeter, Axminster, Shute House (the seat of Sir W. E. Pole, built in 1787-8).
   (Some of the MSS. missing.)
7. Warwickshire.—Warwick, Coventry, Stratford, Alcester, Southam, Atherstone, Leamington.
8. Worcestershire.—Evesham.
9. Oxfordshire.—Oxford, Witney.
10. Northamptonshire.—Brackley.
11. Buckinghamshire.—Beaconsfield, Stoney Stratford, Stowe (the seat of the Duke of Buckingham), Colnbrook.
12. Surrey.—Guildford, Dorking, Croydon, Reigate, Kingston, Farnham, Godstone.
13. Kent.—Bromley.
14. Berkshire.—Reading, Windsor, Maidenhead, Hungerford.
15. Wiltshire.—Swindon, Chippenham, Wootton Bassett, Cricklade.
16. Hampshire.—Winchester, Southampton, Lymington, Romsey, Ringwood, Christchurch.
17. Middlesex.—London, Hounslow, Staines.
18. Shropshire.—Shrewsbury, Ludlow, Oswestry.
19. Herefordshire.—Hereford, Ross, Leominster, Whitchurch, Goodrich Court and Castle, North and South Wales.
20. Brecknockshire.—Brecon, Crickhowel.
21. Radnorshire.—Radnor.
22. Montgomeryshire.—Machynlleth.
23. Cardiganshire.—Aberystwyth, Devil's Bridge.
24. Merionethshire.—Bala, Dolgelley.
25. Denbighshire.—Llangollen.
26. Carnarvonshire.—Beddgelert, Capel Curig, Snowdon.

Places we were at in the Isle of Wight:

Newport, Cowes, Ventnor, Ryde, Godshill, Yarmouth.

The names of the railroads I was on with Miss Simcoe:—

1st. The London and Birmingham. The only railroad at this time in England, and was just then opened in November, 1839.

We went from Coventry by Rugby, Crick, Weedon, Roade, Brandon, Ellsworth, Wolverton; the Duke of Buckingham's carriage was there waiting to take us on to Stowe. This is a most splendid and magnificent place, and very large. I was shown over the house, and was in the bedroom where the King and Queen slept.

The names of the stations I was at with Miss Simcoe on the Great Western Railway.—Taunton, Bridgewater, Highbridge, Weston-super-Mere, Clevedon, Nailsee, Bristol, Keynsham, Saltford, Tiverton, Bath, Box, Evesham, Chippenham, Swindon, Minety, Cirencester.

Now I have already mentioned all the places, and to think of going through most of them so many times with Mrs. and the Misses Simcoe for so many years, and to think what the Lord has done for us, that in all those journeys not one misfortune or accident ever happened. "The Lord himself is thy keeper, the Lord is thy defence upon thy right hand. The Lord shall preserve thee from all evil. The Lord shall preserve thy going out and thy coming in, from this time forth for evermore."—Psalm cxxi., 5, 7, 8. "They that put their trust in the Lord shall be even as the Mount Zion: which may not be removed, but standeth fast forever. The hills stand about Jerusalem: even so standeth the Lord round about his people, from this time forth for evermore."—Psalm cxxv., 1, 2.

In how many places in the Bible we see the Lord's guidance of His people, and the Lord is willing to help any of us if we pray to Him. Whatever we ask of the Father in Christ's name He will give it to us. The Holy Spirit is willing to direct and assist us when we read our Bibles, so that we may understand what we read. We may as well not read the Bible at all if we do not pray for the Holy Spirit to help us. As we see by the man of Ethiopia, in the 8th chapter of the Acts, the 30th and 31st verses: "And Philip ran thither to him, and heard him read the prophet Esaias, and said, Understandest thou what thou readest? And he said, How can I, except some man should guide me? and he desired Philip that he would come up and sit with him."

Pity but what we could humble ourselves as the Ethiopian did, to ask of those who understand the Bible better than we do. We know that there are many parts of the Bible very hard to understand, but there is a meaning or it would not be in the Bible. There is not a verse but what is useful, neither is there a word but what is profitable. I remember hearing a sermon preached at Dunkeswell Church, and the text was only one word. Some people say there is a great deal in the Bible which is of no use. If we look at the works of a clock or a watch, how many wheels there are, we might think one-half of them are not wanted, but if one of those wheels were taken out of the clock or watch, they would stop going immediately.

Also, if we look at a ship, and if we had never seen one before, we should be quite surprised at so many ropes, and we might think that one-half cannot be of any good; but there is not one rope but what has its use. What use is the anchor without a cable, or what use is a mast without the rigging?

There are the stays and tackles, traces, lanyards, clews, bowlines, halyards, and many other ropes, and not one of all those ropes but what is useful, and without them the ship would not be properly rigged. It is the same thing with the Bible; if any of the chapters

423

or verses were left out it would not be complete. We cannot be too thankful for being permitted to read our Bibles; how thankful we should be that we have not got the Pope to prevent our doing so. What should we be without our Bibles? We should be as ignorant as the heathens are, worshipping all kinds of graven images, which we see in our Bibles is spoken against, especially in the second Commandment. It would be almost as well for a ship to take a long voyage without chart or compass as for us to be without our Bibles. We know that the chart, the compass, the quadrant are the ship's guides. I remember our voyage to Madras, in the East Indies; it was very long, we were five months making the passage, yet when land in sight was reported from the masthead, there was the city of Madras straight before us. If we had seen the place before our eyes all the way from England we could not have come straighter. Now our Bible, if we go by its directions, will take us safe to the heavenly Canaan, but we must go entirely by its guidance. We must not be one point out of the course. If we break one of the Commandments we are guilty of all. Now in the matter of our ship going to Madras. If the master of the ship had not been particular about the latitude and longitude, most likely we should not have had Madras so straight ahead when land was reported in sight. And it is just the same in reading our Bible, if we read it without the assistance of the Holy Spirit to direct and guide us through the wilderness of this world, in the same way as the charts, compass and quadrants guide the ship to the places where she is bound. The quadrant is the chief thing to go by, but the quadrant is no good to us unless the sun shines; and it is the same in reading our Bibles, if we do not look up to God and pray to Him to grant us His Holy Spirit to shine on us and direct us when we read, that we may understand. We must pray to God, through His Son Jesus Christ; we must not leave out Christ in our prayers; the quadrant is no good without the sun, and our prayers are no good if Christ is left out. "Whatsoever ye ask of the Father in My name ye shall receive it." "Without me ye can do nothing." The wedding garment was no good to the man in the parable because he did not put it on when it was offered him. If a servant, waiting at table at a party, had not put on his livery—either from thinking his own clothes looked the best, or from being too proud to wear livery—do we not think his master would be angry, and would say, "How came you hither, not having on your livery?" If we wish to be Christ's disciples we must follow His steps and do His commandments. We know there was no pride in Christ. When He was going into Jerusalem He chose a poor donkey to ride on. I remember when Mrs. Simcoe always rode on a donkey, although she had plenty of beautiful ponies. Pride has been the ruin of thousands of people, so let us humble ourselves and follow the steps of our Saviour, who went about doing good. To trust in Christ is a great blessing. I never read in the Bible of Christ refusing any request that was asked according to His will, even when the Levites, tempting Him, asked if it was lawful to give tribute to Cæsar

GENERAL SIMCOE AND A WORKMAN.

or not, they had the answer, " Render unto Cæsar the things which are Cæsar's, and unto God the things which are God's." How much better had they asked, " What must we do to be saved?" or say as the publican, " God be merciful to me, a sinner." What a thing it is to have so many invitations and not to accept them. The door of mercy will soon be closed; as the tree falls so it must lie; time rolls away. It seems but a little while ago since I came to live at Wolford Lodge, and yet how many changes there have been in that time. I first went in 1802; what a difference between that time and now. At that time there were nearly forty persons belonging to the house, and now only thirteen, and also nearly forty workmen. General Simcoe was not pleased unless there was plenty of work going on, and it was his delight to go out and see the workmen, and have a little talk with them about their work. I remember once he was talking to one of the men. The man took off his hat and held it in his hand. The General told him to put it on his head, but the man did not like to do so whilst he was talking to him. The General told him if he did not put it on he must take off his, too, so they stood talking a long time both with their hats in their hands.

General Simcoe was a very liberal gentleman. When work pleased him the men were sure to have something given them. I remember once a poor man coming to Wolford with a petition; his donkey had died. The General asked him how much the donkey was worth. He said thirty shillings. The General gave the man the thirty shillings, and told him he need not go any further with the petition but go and buy himself another donkey.

General Simcoe was generous to the rich and liberal to the poor as long as he lived. General Simcoe never let the work stand still, but was always busy; something or other planned out every day—new roads, new bridges. General Simcoe was very fond of the Canadian bridges. One was made to cross the gully leading to the under Sand Walk at Wolford.

CHAPTER XXXIII.

TRIBUTE BY BAILEY.

When General and Mrs. Simcoe returned from Canada they brought with them a great many curious things, such as bows and arrows, swords, spears and many other things such as the Indians use; there were also a great many dresses made of sheet iron, caps, jackets, breeches and leggings, about a hundred dresses. They wear them in battle, so that a sword or a spear cannot hurt them. The only part they have to guard is the face.

The General also brought home three beautiful brass cannon—field pieces (from San Domingo). They are now at Wolford. There was also a very beautiful canoe, with paddles; it was very long. It was made from the bark of a tree, and sewn together with bark cord. There was not a nail used in it. I remember its coming very well. A waggon was sent to Topsham, where it was landed. It was a great deal longer than the waggon. I think it was nearly thirty feet long. The General told Mr. Scadding to put it in some safe place where it could not be hurt; so Mr. Scadding made a place for it in the stable yard under a bank, but very unfortunately it had not been there long when the bank rushed down on it and smashed it all to pieces after coming safe so many thousand miles.

There were also the Canadian snow slides (sleighs), which were kept in the coach house. All these many different things were quite a curiosity and amusement to the gentry who visited Wolford. The visitors at that time were a great many; there were often ten or fifteen carriages there in a day, as all the head gentry in Devonshire visited Wolford, and so many officers came on duty for orders I have known three or four lords staying at Wolford at one time. I believe there was not a great person in Devonshire who did not very much respect General Simcoe. But Lord Rolle and General Simcoe were not very friendly. There was strife between them, I suppose, as to which of them should be the greater. The contention was so sharp between them that there was a duel challenge; Lord Rolle offered to fight with his fists, but General Simcoe would not consent unless it was said what the quarrel was about. Lord Rolle wanted to have a camp near Bicton, ten miles from Exeter and his place of residence. His lordship was commander of two regiments, which were both at a camp near Bicton. General Simcoe ordered him to take his regiments to Plymouth, but Lord Rolle refused to do so, and wrote to the Duke of York for leave to have his camp near Bicton. The Duke of York told him he was to ask leave of General Simcoe, the Commander-in-Chief of the Western District. This rather nettled Lord Rolle. He then petitioned to remove his regiment from the district. The petition was granted, and the regiment was sent to Liverpool. Soon after this there was a situation appointed far greater than that of being Commander-in-Chief of the Western District. The Government appointed General Simcoe to be Commander-in-Chief of all the British forces in India.

Bonaparte had quite given up all his plans of invading England, but he was still bent on mischief, and his plan was to go against Spain and Portugal; and it was wonderful the mischief he did. Spain formerly was the richest kingdom in the world, and now the poorest. How thankful England should be that he was not permitted to land on our shores. How thankful we should be to those who strongly fortified the country. But what I said in my first edition—if Bonaparte had landed at Tor Bay, which was certainly his intention, he never would have got as far as Exeter. He was not aware of the preparations made. He did not know of the large body of Volunteers raised in such quick time, more than fifty thousand in Devonshire alone. Before going to India, General Simcoe was directed to go to Lisbon, and to render any assistance against the French in that country. Now it was certain that before General Simcoe went to India he would be knighted or made a lord, as the Commander-in-Chief in India has always those titles before taking the command. General Simcoe made such great improvements whilst he was Governor of Canada, so most likely he would have done the same in India, as improving was his chief study. We ourselves have seen it at Wolford Lodge and Dunkeswell.

The General and Mr. John Scadding used to be out so early in the morning. Mr. Scadding was with General Simcoe in Canada so long that their plans suited, and what one said the other approved. Mr. Scadding was a very good, kind person, and much liked by all classes of people. He was estate manager at Wolford for many years.

The two brothers, Mr. John and Mr. Thomas Scadding, married two sisters, the Misses Triges. Mr. John Scadding's wedding was very grand. I remember it very well. General Simcoe's carriage took them from Wolford to Dunkeswell Church. General Simcoe was brideman and gave away the bride, and a grand dinner was given at Wolford to the party. Mr. John Scadding took Wolford Farm and rented it for many years, but was still manager at Wolford. He remained at the farm until April, 1818; then there was a sale, all the stock and goods were sold.

Mr. John Scadding went again to Canada, and Mrs. Scadding returned to Wolford. The two elder sons of Mr. Scadding went to school at Sittingbourne (in Kent), and the youngest, Henry (late Rev. Dr. Henry Scadding, of Toronto), a little boy, came with his mother to Wolford.

After a few years Mr. Scadding came home, and then took his wife and the two elder boys, John and Charles, back with him to Canada. Henry was with Mr. Simcoe at Penheale for some time, and then went to college and became a minister of the church, and is now at Toronto, where he has a church. It must be such a great comfort to him to be in the same place as his aged mother, and also his brother Charles.

Now to turn again to the lives of General and Mrs. Simcoe. Most particulars I have given in my first edition, but there cannot be too much said about both of them. It did not please the Lord that General Simcoe should live to a great age; if such had been the case, no doubt he would have been a very great person in the world. You know when great people go to India they generally return much greater, have a higher title, often get from a lord to an earl or marquis. India is the place for riches and honour. It is not often that people get honour in their own country; did Lord Nelson or Lord Wellington? And what brought General Simcoe so soon to the rank of general was his going abroad. So very likely, if it had pleased the Lord that he should go to India and return home again, he would have been greatly promoted; but he had finished his work.

We know the great things he did in England, even enough to frighten Bonaparte, for he was afraid to come with his great expedition, although his army was all ready to come over, and would very likely have come had there not been such a large body of Volunteers raised, and the country put in such a fortified state, particularly Devonshire, where it was Bonaparte's intention to land. What a confusion all England was in at that time. I remember it very well, many people hiding away their treasures and property; and what was General Simcoe doing? He was busy enough with sham fights, reviewing Volunteers, military and cavalry, and warning them all to hold themselves in readiness to meet the enemy. Such was General Simcoe's employment and study. It was the same in those days as it was in the days of old, as we see by Joshua, Hezekiah, David and all those great warlike people. Only read the history of those noble men, see in all their plans, what did they do? Before they made war they first enquired of the Lord, and He directed them. We do not see this in Pharaoh, nor in Nebuchadnezzar, the one who said of the three Jews who were cast into the burning fiery furnace, "And who is that God that shall deliver you out of my hands?" And in Exodus, v. 2, "And Pharaoh said, Who is the Lord, that I should obey his voice to let Israel go? I know not the Lord, neither will I let Israel go." See what a difference there is between those who serve the Lord and those who serve Him not. We do not hear such holy men as Joshua, Samuel and David say, "Who is that God that shall deliver you out of my hands?" or say, "I know not the Lord, neither will I let Israel go." No, it is not so with those holy men; they say, "It is the Lord, let him do what seemeth him good." David said, "Lord, thou hast searched me and known me. Thou knowest my down-sitting and mine uprising; thou understandeth my thoughts afar off. Thou compasseth my path and my lying down, and art acquainted with all my ways. For there is not a word in my tongue, but lo, O Lord, thou knowest it altogether." Psalm cxxxix., 1, 2, 3. And again, in another psalm, "My soul truly waiteth still upon God, for of him cometh my salvation. He verily is my strength and my salvation; he is my defence, so that I shall not greatly fear." And that "thou, Lord, art merciful; for thou rewardest every man according to his work." Psalm lxii., 1, 2, 12.

And again we sing:

"My lot is fall'n in that blest land
Where God is truly known;
He fills my cup with lib'ral hand,
'Tis He supports my throne.

"Thou shalt the paths of life display,
That to Thy presence lead,
Where pleasures dwell without allay,
And joys that never fade."

NOTE.—These lines are from Tate and Brady's paraphrase version of the 16th Psalm, 5th and 11th verses. This paraphrase version of the Psalms was sanctioned and recommended by the Bishop of London in 1698.

Now in the book of Psalms we do not find one place in which David does not give all the glory to God, from the first verse of the 1st Psalm to the last verse of the 150th Psalm. In the first verse of the 1st Psalm we read, "Blessed is the man that walketh not in the counsel of the ungodly, nor stood in the way of sinners, and hath not sat in the seat of the scornful." And in the last verse of the 150th Psalm it is said, "Let everything that hath breath praise the Lord." In all the history of David we only find two occasions in which he sinned, and what did he do then? He did not do as Adam and Eve did, laying the fault on each other. No, he directly confessed "I have sinned," adding, "but these sheep, what have they done?" We see he wished to have all the blame himself. He knew that he had sinned, and he knew that the Lord is gracious, His mercy is everlasting, and his truth endureth from generation to generation. I do wish myself and all the rest of us could have this faith to pray to God for pardon of our sins. We know that we have the same privileges as David had. "Ask and ye shall receive, seek and ye shall find, knock and it shall be opened unto you." Our beautiful church service begins, "I acknowledge my transgressions, and my sin is ever before me. Hide thy face from my sins and blot out all mine iniquities." Psalm li., 3, 9. "The sacrifices of God are a broken spirit; a broken and a contrite heart, O God, thou wilt not despise." Psalm li., 17. "O Lord, correct me, but with judgment; not in thine anger, lest thou bring me to nothing." Jer. x., 24. "Enter not into judgment with thy servant, for in thy sight shall no man living be justified." Psalm cxliii., 2. And then we hear those beautiful words, "Dearly beloved brethren, the Scripture moveth us in sundry places to acknowledge and confess our manifold sins and wickedness; and that we should not dissemble nor cloke them before the face of Almighty God our heavenly Father, but confess them."

We see plainly these promises are to us, as much as they were to David. David was a man after God's own heart, and so should we be if we were to follow David's steps, and, like him, to give the Lord the honour due unto His name, all honour and glory and might and power. All this David gave to the Lord, and all the holy men of old did the same. And if we did so too, we should be like David and be people after God's own heart; and also like good old Joshua, who said "As for me and my house, we will serve the Lord." I hope there are now many who do so. It was General and Mrs. Simcoe's rule, and for that purpose the chapel at Wolford was built, and by so doing our children will arise up and call us blessed. In so doing we know what enemies we have to overcome—the world, the flesh and the devil, all to be conquered, and what do we require to do it? "Be of good courage, and let us behave ourselves valiantly for our people, and let the Lord do that which is good in his sight." But this is not all that we have to do. We are to be steadfast, unmovable, always abounding in the work of the Lord, forasmuch as ye know that your labour is not in vain in the Lord. In whatever our crosses or losses may consist, either in our substance or in the loss of friends or children—for we may expect these things to happen—let us remember that the Lord gave, and the Lord taketh away, and say, "Blessed be the name of the Lord." Again, we must expect wars and commotions, but the Lord says, " My peace I give unto you."

INDEX

INDEX

INDEX

INDEX

pleases Mrs. Simcoe, 81; scenery in vicinity of, 83; Simcoes leave for Upper Canada, 89; a great fire and a narrow escape for, 352-3.

Queen Charlotte, her birthday celebrated in Quebec, 74; a salute fired in honor of anniversary, 213.

Queen's Rangers, in Revolutionary War, 17; raising a corps for service in Canada, 20; encamped at Kingston, 110; at Niagara, 125; of Niagara history, 132-5; encamped at Queenstown, 132; first regiment stationed at Toronto, 179.

R.

Randolph, John, U. S. Indian Commissioner, at Niagara, 164; an American orator, 165.

Rattlesnakes numerous in Upper Canada, 196, 298.

Recollet Church, Quebec, 1791, Protestants allowed to hold service therein, 55; present site, 55; description of, by Mrs. Simcoe, 67-8; burned, 352.

Reeve staff, of Saxon origin, 38.

Regiments—Royal Fusiliers, formation of and where staioned, 54; band of, 55; as actors, 77, 80; in ballroom, 79, 81; 60th or King's Royal Rifle Corps, a coincidence in connection with, 248; rifles first issued to a battalion of, 310.

Richardson, Dr., of the Queen's Rangers, 176.

Richardson, Mrs., 176, 290, 301.

Rogers' Rangers, original corps of Queen's Rangers, its strength, 132; the command of, 132.

Rolle, The Misses, 40.

Rosskilly, Rev. Thomas, performs marriage ceremony of Colonel Simcoe, 30.

Rousseau, St. Jean Baptiste, 179.

Russell, Hon. Peter, arrival in Canada, 85; administrator, 86; his house at Two Mile Creek, 226; his residence at York, 311.

Russell, Miss (Elizabeth), sister of Hon. Peter Russell, 85; an admirable woman, 311.

Ryland, Herman Witsius, dinner and ball on occasion of his marriage, 262; civil secretary to Lord Dorchester, 263; his descendants in Canada, 263.

S.

Sable Island, 47-8.

Samos, afterwards Woodfield, owners of the estate of, 56; description of original house, 56; final disposition of site, 56.

Sans Bruit, an amusing incident in connection with name, 58.

Sassafras trees near Navy Hall, 290.

Scadding, John, Sr., manager at Wolford, 32, 215; in Canada, 215; his descendants, 215.

Scadding, Rev. Dr. Henry, a personal friend of Mrs. Simcoe, 215.

Servos, Colonel Peter, 230; ancestors of, 233.

Servos House at the Four Mile Creek, 230; oldest house in district, 230.

Servos Mill, 294.

Severn River, 196; McDonald's Rapids on, 196; Big Chute, 199; Gloucester Pool, an enlargement of, 200.

Shank, Captain David, arrives from York with detachment for the Miamis, 241; his life in Canada, 241.

Shaw, Captain Æneas, member of Executive Council, 21, 79; travels from New Brunswick, 79; brings his family to Niagara, 161.

Sheaffe, Lieutenant (General) Roger, visits Navy Hall, 241; arbitrator about American settlements on south shore of lake, 241-2; commands at York in 1813, 242; his conduct criticised, 242.

Sheehan, Walter Butler, of Indian Department, 315; married Miss Andrews, daughter of Captain Andrews, 315; his descendants, 315.

Sillery, near Quebec, immortalized by "Emily Montague," 85; originally a mission, 352.

Simcoe, Anne, her birth, 361; writes about her mother, 368.

Simcoe, Caroline, birth of 32.

Simcoe, Charlotte, birth of, 32.

Simcoe, Eliza, birth of, 32; leaves £30,000 for upkeep of Wolford, 369.

Simcoe, Francis Gwillim, birth of, 32; friendly with Indians, 210; in honor of his third birthday a salute of 21 guns is fired from a two-inch cannon, 228; has severe illness, 262, 263, 265; gives a birthday dinner, 276; his picture made by Mr. Pilkington on his fifth birthday, 315; anxious to be a sailor, 357; most important for his age, for he had "talked to the Indians," 360; a lieutenant in the army, 363; killed at Badajoz, 363.

Simcoe, Henrietta, birth of, 32.

Simcoe, Rev. Henry Addington, his birth, 361; purchases Manor of Penheale in Cornwall, 363; his wife and family, 364; a printer, 364; visits Wolford, 367; his mother's affection for him, 367; his loving disposition, 367; inherits Wolford, 368; never resided there, 368; his death, 368.

Simcoe, Captain John, R.N., father of Governor Simcoe, 8; in command of "Prince Edward," 8; naval career, 14; author "Maxims of Conduct," 14; his children, 14; arms of, 14-5; his ancestors, 387.

Simcoe, John Cornwall, his birth, 361.

Simcoe, John Graves, marriage of, 8; his ancestors, 12-3; education of, 16; enters army, 16; sails for America, 16; at Boston, 16; Major Commander Queen's Rangers, 17; receives rank of lieutenant-colonel, 17; colonel in the army, 17; opinion regarding freedom to administer affairs of Upper Canada, 19; hampered at outset, 20; journeys to Kingston, 21; takes oaths of office, 21, 115; visits western parts of the province, 25; humiliated by Dorchester, 25; later military appointments, 26-7; return to England after Revolutionary War, 29;

INDEX

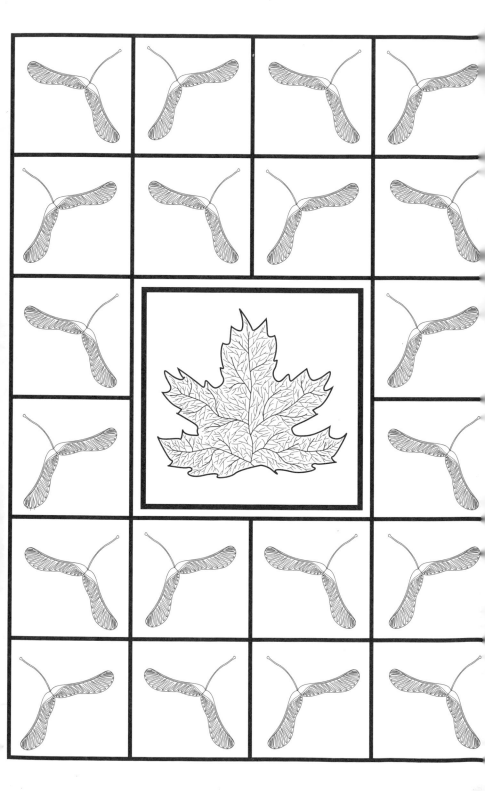